C000077965

The Genesis of the New England Churches
by Leonard Bacon

Address:
HardPress
8345 NW 66TH ST #2561
MIAMI FL 33166-2626
USA
Email: info@hardpress.net

The genesis of the New England churches

Leonard Bacon

THE GENESIS

OF

THE NEW ENGLAND

CHURCHES.

By LEONARD BACON.

WITH ILLUSTRATIONS.

NEW YORK:
HARPER & BROTHERS, PUBLISHERS,
FRANKLIN SQUARE.
1874.

8.74
A

1880. June 24,

Y.e Author.

TO ALL WHO HONOR THE MEMORY OF

THE PILGRIM FATHERS,

AND ESPECIALLY TO THE

FIRST CHURCH OF CHRIST IN NEW HAVEN,

WHICH I SERVED IN THE PASTORAL OFFICE THROUGH MORE THAN FORTY
YEARS, THIS ENDEAVOR TO "BRING FORTH FRUIT IN
OLD AGE" IS RESPECTFULLY OFFERED.

PREFACE.

A FEW words will sufficiently explain to the reader of this book the design of the author.

The history of Protestant Christianity in the United States of America is the history, not of a national church, but of voluntary churches. I have attempted to show how it began, and to trace the origin and development of the idea which generated the churches of New England.

It is hardly necessary to say that the Baptist churches —a name which, in the United States, comprehends more churches than any other save one—are constituted on the same platform of polity with the church which came in the *Mayflower*. I have had no occasion to speak of them or of their influence in giving character to our American civilization; inasmuch as the history of churches bearing that name, on this side of the Atlantic, begins later than the latest date in the volume now submitted to the public. It has been claimed for those churches that, from the age of the Reformation onward, they have been always foremost and always consistent in maintaining the doctrine of religious liberty. Let me not be understood as calling in question their right to so great an honor.

My life has been too busy for researches among the remotest sources of history. The story in this volume is derived chiefly from works which may be found in all good libraries. Instead of going to the British Museum that I might inspect the *editio princeps* of some Separatist book

for which the author was hanged, I have made use of the
abstracts and extracts in Hanbury's " Historical Memorials." The documents which were collected, arranged, and
published by the late Dr. Alexander Young, with his careful annotations, in those two volumes, the " Chronicles of
the Pilgrims " and the " Chronicles of Massachusetts," were
worth more to me for my purpose than the originals from
which he copied them could have been. Inasmuch as I had
before me Bradford's " History of Plymouth Plantation,"
transcribed and published at the expense of the Massachusetts Historical Society, with annotations by its learned
secretary, Mr. Deane, there was no need of my crossing the
ocean to consult the venerable autograph which, having
been stolen from the Prince Library when the Old South
Meeting-house was occupied by British soldiers, was found
after many years in the library of Fulham Palace. I have
been as well provided for the work which I have attempted as I could have been if the Bishop of London and the
Queen of Great Britain had not said their " *Non possu-
mus*," or if the omnipotent Parliament had authorized the
rendition of the precious relic to its rightful proprietor.

The Prince Library can not be named without honorable mention of its founder, Thomas Prince, the earliest
American bibliographer, whose " Annals of New England "—though less important as an authority since the recovery of Bradford's History than it was when Dr. Young
incorporated much of it into his " Chronicles "—is so helpful a guide in the study of our history, whether of church
or state. The title of his work shows that he did not forget
how different is the task of the annalist, collecting facts
and arranging them in strictly chronological order as in a
table of dates, from that of the historian, who, dealing with
the same facts, describes them in their significance and
their natural connections. Whatever disappointment may

be experienced by a reader who opens Felt's "Ecclesiastical History of New England" with the expectation of finding on its pages a continuous and lively narrative, the reason of that disappointment will be that, while all the facts of the story are there, the book, instead of being really history, is little else than a chronological arrangement of events, set down with exemplary carefulness and diligence, but almost as dry as a volume of statistics. I take pleasure in acknowledging my indebtedness to the annalists and to the collectors and editors of historical documents—to Felt, Young, Prince, and Hanbury, as well as to the Anglican Strype. I do not profess to have gone behind them for the facts which they give me; but, on the other hand, I do not regard my work as bearing any resemblance to theirs. I have only attempted to construct a story out of the materials which they, and others like them, have provided.

This book, then, is offered to readers as a history digested from materials which others have prepared for me. It makes no profession of bringing to light new facts from documents heretofore inedited, or from black-letter books heretofore overlooked. It simply tells an old story, giving perhaps here and there a new interpretation or a new emphasis to some undisputed fact. My purpose has been to tell the story clearly and fairly, not for the instruction or delight of antiquarians, nor merely for those with whom church history is a professional study, but for all sorts of intelligent and thoughtful readers. He who writes only for scholars, or for the men of some learned profession, can say, " Fit audience let me find, though few ;" but my labor has been thrown away if the story which I have written is not so told as to invite the attention and to stir the sympathies of the many. Those who read the story will understand, I trust—what many are ignorant of, and what some historians have not sufficiently explained—the difference between " our Pilgrim Fathers " and " our Puritan Fathers." In the old world on the other side of the ocean, the Puritan was a Nationalist, believing that a Christian nation is a Christian church, and demanding that the Church of England should be thoroughly reformed ; while the Pilgrim was a Separatist, not only from the Anglican Prayer-book and Queen Elizabeth's episcopacy, but from all national churches. Between them there was sharp contention—a controversy quite as earnest and almost as bitter as that which they both had with the ecclesiastico-political power that oppressed them both, fining and imprisoning the Puritan, and visiting upon the Separatist the added penalties of exile and the gallows. The Pilgrim wanted liberty for himself and his wife and little ones, and for his brethren, to walk with God in a Christian life as the rules and motives of such a life were revealed to him from God's Word. For that he went into exile ; for that he crossed the ocean ; for that he made his home in a wilderness. The Puritan's idea was not liberty, but right government in church and state—such government as should not only permit him, but also compel other men to walk in the right way. Of all this the ingenuous reader will find, I think, some illustration in the history before him.

The words, written or spoken, of the actors in the story are often introduced for the sake of bringing the reader into closer connection with the men whom I describe and with their times ; but, in so doing, I have not always deemed it necessary to transcribe with scrupulous exactness every pleonasm or tautology, and every careless mislocation of words in the structure of a sentence. If in any instance I have misrepresented the meaning of a quotation, let me receive such censure as the unfairness may seem to deserve. Though I am not aware that I have used a larger liberty in this respect than is conceded to writers of history, I may say that, if I have erred, the error was because of my desire to make the meaning of every sentence clear, at the first glance, to an ordinarily intelligent reader.

The history of the colonization of New England has been admirably written by Dr. Palfrey ; and it would have been folly in me to attempt a repetition of what he has done so well. Mine is a very different undertaking. The story which I tell is the story of an idea slowly making its way against prejudices, interests, and passions—a story of faith and martyrdom, of heroic endeavor and heroic constancy. It includes only so much of secular history as is involved in the history of the idea, and of the men whom it possessed, and who labored and suffered to make it a reality in the world of fact. I have attempted nothing more than a humble contribution to our ecclesiastical history—only a book of Genesis, which, had I written it earlier, might have been followed by a Puritan Exodus. Mr. Punchard's "History of Congregationalism," and Dr. Waddington's most elaborate "Congregational History" (of which a second volume has been lately published), cover a much wider field than I have ventured to traverse.

I take the liberty of expressing here my thanks to Professor Fisher of Yale College, who has kindly assisted in revising the proof-sheets of this volume, and whose suggestions have contributed to its accuracy especially in the earlier chapters. In the later and most important chapters, beginning with Chapter X., I have had also the benefit of corrections and suggestions from the Rev. Dr. Henry M. Dexter, who is better acquainted, I suppose, than any other man with every foot-print of the Pilgrim Fathers, at Scrooby, at Amsterdam, at Leyden, or in New England. Yet I must not represent him as responsible for every thing on those pages; for, being less imbued than he with the antiquarian spirit, I have sometimes ventured not to follow where he seemed to lead me. For example, when he tells me that the first governor of Salem, under the Massachusetts corporation, wrote himself John Endecott, I can not doubt the fact, yet I leave the name in the form in which it has passed into history and poetry—John Endicott. In regard to any more important matter of fact, I should not dare to reject the advice of a friend so learned and so accurate.

L. B.

New Haven, *July* 1, 1874.

CONTENTS.

ILLUSTRATIONS.

O God ! beneath Thy guiding hand,
  Our exiled fathers crossed the sea ;
And when they trod the wintry strand,
  With prayer and psalm they worshiped Thee.

Thou heard'st, well pleased, the song, the prayer—
  Thy blessing came ; and still its power
Shall onward to all ages bear
  The memory of that holy hour.

What change ! through pathless wilds no more
  The fierce and naked savage roams ;
Sweet praise, along the cultured shore,
  Breaks from ten thousand happy homes.

Laws, freedom, truth, and faith in God
  Came with those exiles o'er the waves ;
And where their pilgrim feet have trod,
  The God they trusted guards their graves.

And here Thy name, O God of love,
  Their children's children shall adore,
Till these eternal hills remove,
  And spring adorns the earth no more.

THE GENESIS

OF THE

NEW ENGLAND CHURCHES.

CHAPTER I.

WHAT WAS IN THE BEGINNING.

In the beginning, Christianity was simply Gospel. Ecclesiastical organization was not the cause, but the effect of life. Churches were constituted by the spontaneous association of believers. Individuals and families, drawn toward each other by their common trust in Jesus the Christ, and their common interest in the good news concerning the kingdom of God, became a community united, not by external bonds, but by the vital force of distinctive ideas and principles. New affections became the bond of a new brotherhood, and the new brotherhood, with its mutual duties and united responsibilities, became an organized society. The ecclesiastical polity of the apostles was simple—a living growth, not an artificial construction.

How was it at Jerusalem? A few persons—about one hundred and twenty in all—after the ascension of their Lord, were in the practice of assembling in an upper room, which seems to have been the head-quarters of the eleven who had been nearest to him, and whom the others recognized as leaders. These persons were Jews, whose distinction from their countrymen was that, having been followers of Jesus

B

before his ignominious death, they had not lost their confidence in him ; but, in the face of an immense and triumphant majority, believed that though he had been rejected by the priests and rulers of the nation, and crucified by the Roman power, he was the Messiah risen from the dead, and invested with all authority on earth and in heaven. Waiting for some new manifestation of his glory, they " continued with one accord in prayer and supplication "—not those of the sterner sex only, as if they were planning a revolutionary movement in the state, or were setting up a new school in philosophy, but the men " with the women, and Mary, the mother of Jesus, and with his brethren." Thus they were unconsciously forming that new commonwealth of men and women, and of households, united by personal attachment to Jesus, and living in the atmosphere of worship—that commonwealth of faith and love which was to realize in its future all the promise of a new earth encircled by new heavens.

At first the few disciples seem not to have thought much about how their society should be organized and its affairs administered, their minds being otherwise occupied. The earliest appearance of any thing like organization among them is when it seemed necessary that one of them should be designated and recognized as an apostle in the place that had been made vacant by the defection and death of Judas. On that occasion the whole proceeding, though essentially theocratic in its spirit, was democratic in its form. It seems to have been doubtful which of the two brethren toward whom the minds of the assembly had been turned was best qualified for the work of an apostle. An expedient was resorted to, which, had the assembly been unanimous concerning the superior fitness of either candidate, would have been preposterous. The question whether Barsabas or Matthias should be " numbered with the eleven apostles " was decided by lot, religiously, and with prayer that thus God's will might be manifested. The religious use of the lot for the decision of doubtful questions was customary among the

Jews from the earliest period of their history, but no other instance of it appears in the New Testament.

On the fiftieth day after that Passover at which Christ was crucified, the new dispensation which had been prepared in his life and death, and completed in his resurrection and ascension, was publicly introduced by the manifestation of a special divine presence, the promised Holy Spirit illuminating and guiding the apostles. Suddenly the one hundred and twenty became three thousand. Of this growing multitude it is said that " they continued in the apostles' doctrine and fellowship, and in breaking of bread and in prayers." In other words, the " three thousand souls " were bound together by their constant attendance on the apostles' teaching, and their sympathy of thought and feeling with the movement which those witnesses for Christ were leading ; they had a certain distinctive practice of breaking bread together, as if they were all one family, and they continually prayed together. Their new ideas and new sympathies and hopes were a bond of union ; and though not yet separated from the Jewish people, nor anticipating such a separation, they were beginning to be a distinct community with a life of their own—a community almost unorganized, so far as the record shows, and yet distinct in the midst of the Jewish nation, like that nation in the midst of the Roman Empire. A new and unique commonwealth had begun to live, and must needs grow into some organized form according to its nature.

How, then, shall the new community be organized ? What officers and functionaries shall it have ? How shall it be governed ? The silence of the record seems to show that the apostles, busy with their work of teaching, daily repeating to the thousands of new disciples the remembered words of their Master, telling as eye-witnesses the story of Jesus from his baptism to his ascension, and preaching the good news of the kingdom, gave themselves little concern beforehand about the organization of the community which was coming into existence as the result of their testimony concerning the resurrection and glory of the crucified Christ. Yet something of organization was inevitable, and could not be long deferred.   To sustain so large a community—so suddenly constituted, and including multitudes who had come to Jerusalem only as pilgrims, many of them from distant regions—large contributions were necessary, and were made by those who had any thing to give.   In the emergency, all that they had was thrown, as it were, into a common stock; for such as had convertible property of any kind sold it, and made generous distribution of the proceeds to all that were in want.   When this liberality is first mentioned [Acts ii., 44, 45], it is as if the distribution were made by the donors themselves, or by their personal friends, without any formal arrangement.   Afterward [iv., 34, 35], when the work had become more arduous, and when those of the disciples who had " lands or houses," in Jerusalem or near it, sold them for the benefit of the common cause, the distribution seems to have been in a more systematic way under the direction of the apostles.   But after a while the number included in the new community had been so multiplied, and the amounts to be received and distributed had become so great, that these methods were found unsatisfactory.   Then it was—and apparently not till then—that special officers or commissioners were appointed to that service.

The procedure in making the appointment was full of a religious spirit, and at the same time democratic.   It may be compared with a parallel passage in the history of the Wesleyan polity.   After Wesleyanism, with its exquisitely adjusted organization, had become powerful in England, and while John Wesley was still holding the reins of power, he undertook to tell, at one of the conferences of his helpers, what his power was, and how he came by it.   He told how a few persons came to him, first in London, and then in other places, desiring that he would advise them and pray with them.   "The desire," said he, "was on their part, not on mine"—"but I did not see how I could refuse them my help and be guiltless before God.   Here commenced my power—namely, a power to appoint when, where, and how they should meet, and to remove those whose life showed that they had no desire to flee from the wrath to come.   And this power remained the same whether the people meeting together were twelve, twelve hundred, or twelve thousand."   After a time, the people who had thus come under his care and direction proposed a subscription of quarterly payments for certain common interests—such as rent and repair of the building in which they held their meetings—and he permitted them to subscribe.   "Then I asked," so he continued the story, "'Who will take the trouble of receiving this money and paying it where it is needful?'   One said, 'I will do it, and keep the account for you;' so here was the first steward.   Afterward I desired one or two more to help me as stewards, and in process of time a greater number.   Let it be remembered it was I myself, and not the people, who chose the stewards, and appointed to each the distinct work wherein he was to help me as long as I chose."   He gave a similar account of his power over the preachers, whether as individuals or as assembled in conference.   Without raising any question as to the wisdom or the rightfulness of the autocracy which Wesley asserted over the voluntary association by which he was hoping to revive religion in the Church of England, we can not but observe the contrast between his account of what he did in the appointment of receiving and disbursing officers in the community which he was founding, and Luke's account of what the apostles did in the appointment of similar officers for the community under their teaching at Jerusalem.

The apostles seem to have been proceeding on Wesley's plan, which was natural and reasonable in the circumstances. Offerings for the support of the community had been brought to them, and the distribution seems to have been made by them personally, or by others acting for them.   A complaint had arisen that the distribution was not perfectly equitable.

In dealing with that complaint the apostles convoked not a conference of preachers only, whom they had taken under their direction and control as their "helpers" in the work, but "the multitude of the disciples." Instead of explaining how it was that the power of appointing stewards fell into their hands, and how reasonable it was that they should retain the power, they refused to have any burden of that kind laid upon them. The financial affairs of the growing community were not to be managed by them nor by their agents. "It is not meet," said they, "that we should leave the word of God and serve tables." Their proposal was that special officers for this trust should be designated by popular election. "Brethren," said they, "look ye out among you seven men of honest report, full of the Holy Ghost and of wisdom, whom we may appoint over this business. But we"—your teachers and the commissioned witnesses for Christ—we, instead of burdening ourselves with your affairs—"will give ourselves continually to prayer and to the ministry of the word."[1]

In this record of an office instituted by the vote of a church meeting, and of officers designated by "the whole multitude of disciples" acting as electors, we have an explanation of passages that might otherwise be doubtful touching the organization and polity of the apostolic churches as described or implied in the New Testament. Having seen that the process of organization in the mother church at Jerusalem was essentially democratic while under the immediate guidance of the apostles, we need positive information to convince us that in other places the process by which believers in Christ became an organized body was materially

---

[1] The original shows that when the apostles say, "It is not meet that *we* leave the Word of God," and "*We* will give ourselves to prayer," etc., the pronoun is emphatic; but when they say, "Whom we may appoint," etc., the pronoun, being merely implied in the form of the verb, can have no special emphasis, but must be understood as including the multitude of disciples with the apostles. See the entire story, Acts vi.

different. But there is no such information. On the contrary, there are indications that in every place the society of believers in Christ was a little republic.

We get glimpses of the church at Antioch, which soon became, not less than that at Jerusalem, a metropolitan centre of Christian ideas and enterprises. Even in its origin, it startled the Pharisaic portion of the Jerusalem Church by receiving into fellowship unproselyted Gentiles. It was a community by virtue of the new faith which the members of it had received, and which bound them to each other. Some of its members were prophets and teachers, but all were brethren. It undertook for itself, at a divine suggestion, the first formal mission for the propagation of the Gospel through the Gentile world. When invaded by men from Judea, teaching, in the name of the original apostles, that the Gospel of Christ was to impose the ceremonial and national law of Moses on all Gentile believers every where, it resisted them with strenuous disputation, and instead of waiting for a rescript or a bull from Jerusalem, it sent its own message thither, not only to learn what the facts were there, but also to tell what the facts were at Antioch, and to show that God's blessing had attested the genuineness of a Gospel without Judaism. Thus it obtained from the apostles and elders at Jerusalem, and from "the whole church there," a conclusive declaration in behalf of a Christianity free for all nations.[1]

We get more than glimpses of the church at Corinth. We see its parties and disputes; its disorderly and almost turbulent assemblies; its gross offender, whose sin was a reproach to the whole body while he remained uncensured, and on whom the heaviest censure must therefore be inflicted by the many in a full assembly; its faults and excesses, incidental to an ecclesiastical democracy; the strange diversity and multiplicity of gifts among its members; and, at the

---

[1] Acts xi., 19–30; xiii., 1–3; xiv., 26–28; xv., 1–35; Gal. ii., 1–14.

same time, its ready submission to rebuke and advice from Paul its founder. All that we see of it in the two epistles addressed to it, or in the historic record, shows us an intense vitality working in discordant elements to bring them into unity—an organizing force striving against tendencies to anarchy, but the organization not yet complete—a fermenting chaos, as it were, of Greek, Jewish, and Roman materials; seething with enthusiasms, speculations, infirmities, and errors; yet hallowed by the formative Spirit brooding over it, and the light of divine truth and love shining into it.[1]

Every reader of the New Testament books may gather up for himself the hints which they give, incidentally, about the churches of Galatia, or the saints at Philippi "with the bishops and deacons," or "the Church of the Thessalonians," or "the seven churches of Asia," or the seemingly unorganized fraternity of believers at Rome. He may observe the traces and rudiments of organization among "the holy and faithful brethren in Christ" at Colosse, or among those whom Peter and James and the author of the Epistle to the Hebrews addressed in their writings. He may scrutinize the pastoral epistles to ascertain how far the development of ecclesiastical institutions had advanced in the latest years of the apostle Paul. For the purposes of this history, it will be enough to give some results of such an inquiry without repeating the process.

I. The churches instituted by the apostles were local institutions only. Nothing like a national church, distinct and individual among co-ordinate national churches—nothing like a provincial church, having jurisdiction over many congregations within certain geographical boundaries, natural or political—appears in the writings or acts of the apostles. A church, as mentioned in those venerable documents, is always local or parochial, the church of some town or municipality, like Ephesus or Thyatira, Corinth or Cenchrea, Thessalonica

---

[1] Acts xviii., 1–18.   Epistles to the Corinthians, *passim*.

or Philippi.   To say that the church of a given place was always congregational, in the sense of never meeting for worship in two places at once, or of not being divided into two or more assemblies, with one body of "elders" or of "bishops and deacons," would be to say what can hardly be proved. But that the organized church, in the primitive age of Christianity, was always a local institution—never national, never provincial or diocesan—is a proposition which few will deny.

II. Each local church was complete in itself, and was held responsible to Christ for its own character, and the character of those whom it retained in its fellowship.   The apostles, indeed, had a certain authority in all the churches, as they have now in all churches built on their foundation, for they were Christ's commissioned witnesses to testify what he had taught, as well as the facts of his life and of his resurrection and ascension.   If a question arose involving a doubt as to the nature and extent of the new kingdom of heaven—for example, the question whether all converts to Christ must be naturalized in the Hebrew commonwealth, and so brought under the restrictions and obligations of the national law; or the question whether, in the fellowship of Christ's disciples, there should be a *caste* distinction between converted Jews and converted Greeks or Romans—there might be " no small dissension and disputation," as happened at Antioch and in many other places; but if the question could not be settled in that way—if the disputants could not, by arguments from the prophetic Scriptures and from the story of the Gospel as they had received it, bring each other and the church to agree in a common conclusion—the apostles were of course appealed to as most likely to know the principles of the Gospel and their application, or, in other words, as most likely to know the mind of Christ.

The reference from Antioch to Jerusalem[1] was a reference

---

[1] Acts xv.

to the apostles for information concerning the nature and genius of that Gospel which they were commissioned to publish, and which, at that time, had not been put upon record in any authoritative Scripture. If we permit the story to speak for itself, we see that the reference was not made because the church at Jerusalem was supposed to have a metropolitan jurisdiction over the church in the capital of Syria, but because some ill-informed and narrow-minded men from Judea had alleged that the practice at Jerusalem under the teaching of the original apostles was opposite to the practice at Antioch and in the churches founded by Paul and Barnabas, whose authority as apostles was itself in question. What the brethren at Antioch wanted was information, full and conclusive, on a question of fact, and that information could be obtained at Jerusalem, if they would send competent messengers to get it. The question of fact was: Did the original apostles, in the holy city of the Jews, preach another Gospel than that which was preached by the new apostle to the Gentiles? Had they contradicted that catholic doctrine of justification by faith without the deeds of the law, on which the church at Antioch was founded, and which had been proclaimed so widely by the missionaries from that new centre of evangelization? The party which Paul afterward stigmatized as "the concision"—the narrow, ultra-conservative, anti-evangelical party of the apostolic age —had begun to show itself; and it must be encountered and put down at Jerusalem as well as at Antioch. So far as the two churches were concerned, the procedure was not an appeal from an inferior court to a higher, but only the sending of a committee from the one to confer with the other, so that there should be no misunderstanding between them on a question of great interest to both.

III. Particular churches, in that age, were related to each other as constituent portions of the Universal Church. Their unity was their one faith and hope. It was the unity of common ideas and principles distinguishing them from all the world besides—of common interests and efforts, of common trials and perils, and of mutual affection.   It was manifested not in their subjection to a common jurisdiction, nor in dogmatic formularies, nor in identity of liturgical forms, but in their common willingness to labor and suffer for Christ, and to do good in his name.   When in that conference at Jerusalem it had come to be clearly understood that the Gospel in Palestine and the Gospel in Syria and Cilicia, and the regions beyond, were one Gospel, and when James, Cephas, and John "gave the right hands of fellowship to Paul and Barnabas," one permanent manifestation of the unity thus ascertained and professed was stipulated for.   Paul tells us what the stipulation was—"Only that we should remember the poor, the same which I also was forward to do."[1] The "contribution for the poor saints at Jerusalem," which Paul had been concerned in at Antioch, from the beginning of his labors there,[2] and which he was zealous for wherever he went,[3] answered the purpose, which is more imperfectly answered by doctrinal standards and books of common prayer, by ruling priesthoods and ruling preacherhoods, or by representative assemblies receiving appeals and complaints from all points of the compass, and exercising jurisdiction co-extensive with the boundaries of nations.   One word [κοινωνία—koinonia], in its twofold meaning, was at once the "contribution" for impoverished and suffering brethren and the "communion" of the saints.   As the unity of the three thousand, after the day of Pentecost, and then of the five thousand, was manifested in their generous and loving koinonia—when none of them said that aught of the things which he possessed was his own, but they had "all things common;" so afterward, when "it pleased them of Macedonia and Achaia" to do the same sort of thing for suffering brethren whom they had never seen, that contribution of theirs was the recognition and manifestation of unity.   The

---

[1] Gal. ii., 9, 10.   [2] Acts xi., 27–30.   [3] I Cor. xvi., 1 ; 2 Cor., viii., ix.

communion " in things carnal," expressed and testified the communion in "things spiritual."[1]   More significant than any other symbol could have been, such transactions were a demonstration of the fact that all the particular churches, however separated by distance, or diversified in forms and circumstances, were the one Catholic Church of Christ.   In this way it became palpable that believers in Christ, wherever dispersed, were members of one holy commonwealth, and that there was " one body and one spirit, even as they were called in one hope of their calling."[2]

IV. In all the churches there was one rule to be observed in dealing with offenders.   Christ had given an explicit law : "If thy brother shall trespass against thee, go and tell him his fault between thee and him alone ; if he shall hear thee, thou hast gained thy brother.   But if he will not hear thee, then take with thee one or two more, that in the mouth of two or three witnesses every word may be established.   And if he shall neglect to hear them, tell it to the church : but if he neglect to hear the church, let him be unto thee as a heathen man and a publican."[3]   It would be preposterous to suppose that when the apostles gathered their converts in one place and another into societies for spiritual communion and fraternal helpfulness, they were forgetful of that rule, or that in any arrangements which they made for the working of such societies that rule was superseded.

V. The earliest stated assemblies of Christian worshipers were formed on the model of the synagogue, with its simple arrangements for orderly worship and for instruction out of the Scriptures, rather than of the Temple with its priesthood and its ritual.   Centuries before the coming of Christ, there grew up in Palestine, and afterward among the Jews of the dispersion, a religious institution which has outlived the Temple, the sacrifices, and the altar of ancient Judaism—the simple institution of local assemblies on the Sabbath-day for

---

[1] Rom. xv., 27.   [2] Eph. iv., 4.   [3] Matt. xviii., 15–17.

prayer, and for the public reading and explanation of the holy books. In the synagogue, as may be seen now wherever there are Jews enough for a meeting, there was the worship of God without priest or altar—an intelligent worship, impressive in its simplicity. The Sabbath created for itself the synagogue, and thus became a day of public worship every where, instead of being only a day of religious abstinence from labor and of home enjoyment. The earliest Christians, whether in Palestine or in any other country, were Jews, or "devout" Gentiles, who found in the Gospel, not a new religion, but the fulfillment of God's ancient promises; and on all sides they were regarded as a Jewish sect, like the Pharisees or the Sadducees, though more obnoxious because of the newness and the revolutionary tendency of their opinions. In whatever place they were excluded from the assemblies of the Old-school Jews, or withdrew of their own choice, they became a Christian synagogue. Perhaps in some instances the synagogue itself became Christian. In the Septuagint translation of the Old Testament, two words—εκκλησία [ecclesia], and συναγωγή [synagoge]—are used interchangeably for the word which in the English Bible is "congregation." Once in the New Testament the latter word is used to denote a Christian assembly;[1] but it seems to have come to pass, in the gradual separation of Christian from Jewish congregations, that the name *ecclesia* was given distinctively to the worshiping society of believers in Christ.

Such were the churches at the date of the New Testament Scriptures. It is not difficult to understand the process of their origin and organization if we recollect distinctly what Christianity was at the beginning, before it was developed into what is now called doctrine, and what change it wrought in the consciousness and relations of those who received it.

---

[1] James ii., 2 : " If there come into your *synagogue*," etc.

1. The Gospel, as the apostles preached it, was essentially a story and a hope—the story the warrant of the hope. Even now we talk about "the story of the Gospel," though preachers, as well as theologians, ordinarily find it more natural to talk about "the doctrines of the Gospel." We still speak of the four books which record the life, death, and resurrection of Jesus as "the four Gospels." But to the apostles and their hearers the story was all—the story about Jesus of Nazareth. All doctrine was involved in that story, all duty was related to it. All the inspiration which made the believer "a new creature" was in the story, and in the hope which it warranted. Those who received the story, and into whose consciousness its inspiration entered, were related to each other as brethren. The religious element in human nature is pre-eminently social, and the new religious consciousness which believers had in common made them members of a new society. At Philippi, for example, Lydia and the other converts were in a new relation to each other from the hour of their conversion.[1] By virtue of their new faith and hope, they became at once, independently of any conventional arrangement, the church of Christ in Philippi.

2. Wherever the Gospel found reception, the converts must needs have their meetings for prayer, for mutual encouragement and help, and for such instruction as the best informed and most gifted among them could impart, if no other teaching was at hand. A convenient time for such meetings—a season redolent of sacred memories—was the first day of the week, beginning with the sunset of the Sabbath, and this they called "the Lord's day."[2]

3. The first converts, who were the earliest members of such a meeting, had made profession of their faith in Jesus the Christ, and of their joining themselves to the new kingdom of God, by a simple ceremony of washing, significant of the divine cleansing which was their entrance into a new

---

[1] Acts xvi., 12–15, 40.   [2] Acts xx., 7 ; 1 Cor. xvi., 2 ; Rev. i., 10.

and holy life. Of course, any who afterward came into their fellowship were in like manner baptized.

4. As at Jerusalem, so in all other places, the believers, assembled for mutual help and the mutual expression of their fellowship in the Gospel, had a certain "breaking of bread" together in remembrance of him whom they gratefully acknowledged as Christ the Lord. Their eating and drinking as at their Lord's table, and their initiatory washing, seem to have been all that was distinctive in their formal observances, unless we add their habit of meeting on the first day of the week.

5. The name which they gave to their religion, as distinguished from the story by which it was inspired—the name of that new life which they had begun to live—was "godliness," or the right worship [ευσηβεια]; and the name by which they spoke of themselves as a community, or of each other, was "saints," or "holy brethren." Having such thoughts and aspirations, they were under a necessity of sympathizing with each other in any trouble, and of helping each other in any distress. That necessity was not imposed upon them merely by rule or stipulation—it was an instinct of their new life.

6. At first, such a society may have been without formal organization. The most capable, by a certain law of human nature, would lead the rest. Each member, prompted by his new ideas and sympathies, would use, for the common cause and the edification of his brethren, whatever gifts he had, and of whatever kind.[1] But soon organization, in a more definite way, would become necessary. There must be a recognized distribution of duties: one must do this work, another must do that. Somebody must preside in their meetings, and take the lead in worship and conference or in more formal teaching. Somebody (and naturally somebody else) must receive contributions and expend them. If we would know

---

[1] Rom. xii., 4–8.

how the organization was completed by the appointment of officers to perform these various functions, we must forget for the moment all modern systems of ecclesiastical polity, and let the apostolic documents teach us.   Paul and Barnabas revisited carefully the places where they had, in the first visit, made disciples.   They went, "confirming the souls of the disciples," or, in another phrase, "confirming the churches;" and one thing in that work of confirming or consolidating the believers in the fellowship into which they had been introduced was the leading of them to a formal choice of officers in each society as "the seven" were chosen at Jerusalem.[1]   It was to that work of "confirming the churches" that Timothy and Titus were afterward designated, when they were commissioned to set in order the things that had not been completed, and to constitute "elders in every city."   When a missionary, the modern evangelist, in some unevangelized country, gathers his converts into churches, leads them in the choice of the officers necessary to the completeness of their organization, trains them to habits of self-support and self-government, and at last leaves them to the protection of God's providence and the guiding influence of God's word and Spirit, the difference between him and those whom he ordains in every city is surely intelligible.   Such was the difference between those primitive evangelists, the apostles, with their fellow-laborers, and the presbyter-bishops in every city.

Such was the simplicity of organization in the primitive churches.   There was no complex constitution, no studied distribution of powers, no sharp distinction of ranks.   Each congregation—like a patriarchal tribe, like a Hebrew village, like a synagogue—had its "elders."[2]   Some were to preside in the assembly, leading and feeding the flock; others to serve in the communion of the saints, almoners for the church to the needy, comforters to the afflicted.   Bishops or dea-

---

[1] Acts xiv., 21–23 ; xv., 36–41.   [2] Stanley, "Jewish Church," 181, 182.

cons, they were servants of the community, not lords over it.   In a brotherhood where all were "kings and priests to God," no elder was king over his brethren, or stood as priest between them and the Father of their Lord Jesus Christ.

[The reader who would examine more in detail the subject of the foregoing chapter may be referred to the following works accessible in the English language :

Neander, "Planting and Training of the Christian Church by the Apostles."   Books I.–III.

Schaff, "History of the Apostolic Church."   Books II.–IV.

Mosheim, "Historical Commentaries."   Century I., Sections 37–48.

Milman, "History of Christianity."   Book II., Ch. iv.

Jacob, "Ecclesiastical Polity of the New Testament."

Whately, "Kingdom of Christ."]

C

CHAPTER II.

FROM THE PRIMITIVE TO THE PAPAL.

WHEN Christianity, by the conversion of Constantine (A.D. 312), became the dominant religion in the Roman Empire, the church polity then existing was in some respects widely different from that of the primitive churches. Less than three hundred years after the beginning at Jerusalem, the government of churches had become essentially episcopal, though the bishops every where were elected by the Christian people. Often, if not always, the authority of the bishop, instead of being simply parochial, extended over many congregations, the mother church, in which the bishop had his throne, or *sedes* [see], being surrounded with dependent congregations, all under one government. The bishop had under him a body of presbyters, who were his council and helpers, and to whom he assigned their duties. Not unfrequently the bishops of a district or province were assembled in synods or councils to deliberate on affairs of general interest, such as disputed points of doctrine, and questions about uniformity in worship and discipline. There was a firmly established distinction between clergy and laity, the clergy consisting of three orders or gradations, bishops, presbyters, and deacons.

It has been sometimes assumed that what was in the fourth century must have been from the beginning. The fact, so conspicuous in the survey of that age, that the then existing church polity was substantially what is now called episcopal, has been thought to prove that the churches never were organized and governed in any other way; especially as there are no traces of any revolutionary conflict by which one polity was substituted for another, and no exact line can be drawn to mark the beginning of the distinction between presbyters and bishops, or the transfer of power from self-governing Christian assemblies to a hierarchy.   Constantine did not institute the episcopal form of government over the churches—he found it already existing, with its roots in the past; and in adopting Christianity as the religion of the empire, he adopted that ecclesiastical polity.   What, then, had become of the polity which we find in the New Testament? At what date was it superseded?   Who introduced another constitution in the place of it?   Such is the outline of an argument which often seems conclusive.

The fallacy lies in the assumption that church government, once instituted, will perpetuate itself, and can be changed only by a revolutionary agitation.   It is easy to assume that from what existed in the early part of the fourth century we may safely infer what existed in the early part of the third or of the second; and that from what existed when Christianity, early in the second century, emerges as an organized force into secular history, we may infer with certainty what existed in that formative and rudimentary period of which we have no record but in the New Testament.   We know that the church polity which Constantine found in full shape and action was modified under his influence, and that the history of the church through all the ages from Constantine to Luther is full of changes in the polity of what was called the Catholic Church.   We know, too, that in the earlier period, from the days of Ignatius and Polycarp onward, the constitution of the Christian commonwealth throughout the Roman Empire, the powers and functions of its officers, and the relations of local churches to each other, had been gradually changed.   Need we marvel then if, in the early years of the second century, we find a difference between such bishops as Ignatius of Antioch or even Polycarp of Smyrna and those whom Paul exhorted at Miletus, or those to whom he addressed the epistle which he wrote for the church at Philippi, or those whom he described in his Pastoral Epistles?

As the New Testament gives us no system of definite and

formulated dogmas in theology, so it gives us no completed system of church government. Ecclesiastical polity grew, age after age, just as theology grew. What there was of organization in the primitive churches was more like the organization of a seed than like the organization of the tree in its maturity. The period between the day of Pentecost and the middle of the second century—or the narrower period between the date of the Pastoral Epistles and the beginning of that century—could not but be a period of rapid development in the Christian commonwealth. Nor did the growth of ecclesiastical polity terminate then. It went on, imperceptibly but steadily, to the age of Constantine—as it went on afterward to the age of Luther—as it goes on now, even in communities most abhorrent of progress and most observant of traditions.

The circumstances of that early development determined, in many respects, its character and tendency. In that age the churches had no experience to guide them or to warn them. They knew nothing of what we know from the history of eighteen centuries. Why should they be jealous for their liberty? How should they be expected to detect and resist the beginning of lordship over God's heritage? We must remember, too, that in those times of inexperience the development of the Christian organization was a development under pressure. Christianity, often persecuted, always "an illicit religion," was making its way in the presence of powerful enemies. Its natural leaders, the "bishops and deacons," freely chosen in every church, were, of necessity, intrusted with large powers over the endangered flock, and, of course, power was accumulating in their hands. The churches were in cities; for it was in cities that the new doctrine and worship could obtain a foothold. Such churches, as they grew, were naturally distributed, rather than divided, into a plurality of assemblies governed by one venerable company of bishops or elders, and served by one corps of deacons. Equally natural was it for each mother church to

become still more extended by spreading itself out into the
suburbs and surrounding villages; all believers in the city
and its suburbs, or in the country round about, being recognized as constituting one *ecclesia* with one administration.

In the growth of such a community, as its affairs become
more complicated, one of the elders or overseers must needs
become the moderator or chairman of the board; and to him
the chief oversight must be intrusted.   At first that presiding elder is only a leader, foremost among brethren who are
equal in authority; but by degrees he becomes a superior
officer with distinctive powers.   A tendency to monarchy
begins to be developed in what was at first a simple republic.
The principle of equality and fraternity begins to be superseded by the spirit of authority and subordination.   This
may be noted as the first departure from the simplicity of
the primitive polity.

Primitive bishops—the elders whom the apostles ordained
in every city—were not necessarily preachers in an official
or professional way.   They were rather a board of managers,
not unlike to class-leaders in the system of Wesleyan Meth-
odism.   Some of them "labored in word and doctrine," and
"aptness to teach" was regarded as an important qualification for their office.   It was their duty to preside in the
worshiping assembly; to watch for the prosperity of the
church and for the welfare of individual souls, and, among
other things, to call out those who could fitly speak a word of
exhortation or of doctrine—as the rulers of the synagogue at
Antioch, in Pisidia, called out Paul and Barnabas.[1]   Preaching was by apostles, evangelists, prophets, or gifted brethren
[$\pi\nu\epsilon\nu\mu\alpha\tau\iota\kappa o i$], some of whom—if there were such in the church
—would be among the elders.   In the next generation, when
the apostles and their fellow-laborers in the first preaching
of the Gospel had passed away, the duty of feeding the people with knowledge, and of speaking to them the word of

---

[1] Acts xiii., 15.

God, came with additional weight upon the rulers of the Christian synagogue. Then the elder who is to preside over his brethren must be a preacher with gifts of knowledge and of utterance; and the elder who presides and preaches becomes *the* bishop. So there comes to be a distinction of rank and of functions between the bishop and his presbyters. Once he and they were co-presbyters, taking heed to the flock " over which the Holy Ghost had made them " jointly " overseers;" but the silent progress of change has made them his subordinates.

Such was the rudimentary beginning of episcopal power over the churches. At first it was simply a parish episcopacy. While the mother church in a city—the principal and central congregation—had its full staff of presbyters, the bishop's advisers and helpers, it naturally followed that the subordinate congregations which had grown up in the near vicinity were supplied with presbyters, or teachers and rulers, under the direction of the bishop, and responsible to him. As yet there was properly no diocese—only a large and growing parish, with dependent and outlying districts. But by imperceptible gradations the parochial bishop of the second century had begun to be, in the third century, a diocesan bishop, though of moderate pretensions. The ancient civilization, even more than the modern, made cities the seats of power; and it was most natural for the mother church of a city to become the mother church for all the region of which that city was the market town or the political centre. At an early period the churches of Greece, represented by their bishops, began to meet in occasional synods for consultation and agreement on questions of doctrine or of order; and gradually the theory was accepted of an œcumenical church under a common government, and of councils whose decrees, or " canons," enacted in the name of catholic unity, were to have the force of law in all particular churches. When Christianity became, under Constantine, the religion of the emperor, that sagacious statesman found already developed more than the rudiments of the ecclesiastical government which he proceeded to establish. He divided the territory of the empire into ecclesiastical patriarchates, provinces, and dioceses, corresponding with the divisions and subordinations of civil jurisdiction; and thus the system of diocesan epis- copacy, as it exists to-day in Roman Catholic Europe, in En- gland, in Russia, and in the old Christian communities of the Turkish Empire, was completed.

Meanwhile another change, departing more widely from the simple Christianity of the New Testament, had been in progress. The primitive elder, whether bishop or deacon, was only an officer in a local society where all were brethren. In the Christian assembly, as in the Jewish synagogue, there were rulers to preside and direct; there were "prophets and teachers;" there were servants of the congregation; there was the obvious distinction between brethren appointed to certain duties and brethren not in office; and, doubtless, those brethren who, though neither bishops nor deacons, had special gifts for the service of the Gospel, were in some way recognized and distinguished; but the distinction between clergy and laity, afterward so wide, had not then been made. As in the synagogue, so in the *ecclesia*, there was neither sacrifice nor altar. In the new kingdom of God on earth, all were "kings and priests unto God;" and the High-priest was none other than Jesus the Christ, who, having offered him- self once for all, had passed beyond the veil, and was making intercession for all his saints. The Christianity of that age knew nothing of a clergy superior to the brotherhood by virtue of some mysterious power conferred in ordination, or of a laity dependent on priestly mediation for access to God. But certain errors adverse to spiritual Christianity have their origin in human nature, ever prone to superstition. In the third and fourth centuries, the rulers of the Christian synagogue—the bishops and deacons appointed to certain duties in the local church—became, by gradual change, a Christian priesthood.

That change was inseparably connected with other changes adverse to the simply spiritual religion of the New Testament. It was not without significance that what had been only a teaching and guiding ministry in the churches began to be called by names and titles borrowed from the Jewish or the Gentile sacerdotal system. Superstition had already begun to misunderstand and pervert the symbolic observances instituted by Christ, and to regard them as having a supernatural efficacy if rightly performed. The elder who not only labors in word and doctrine, and helps to guide the flock, but also communicates supernatural grace by his manipulations, has become more than a ruler in the Christian synagogue—more than a minister of the Gospel. He is a priest, and is rightly designated by sacerdotal titles. Being a priest, he must magnify his priestly office. Baptism, instead of being only a symbolical washing, significant of the new life into which the believer in Christ is born, becomes itself a regenerative act, deriving its efficacy from the priest who administers it. The primitive elder having grown into a priest, "it is of necessity that this man have somewhat also to offer."[1] Thus the primitive eating and drinking in affectionate remembrance of Christ becomes a mysterious transaction, invalid without a ministering priest; and at last, when superstition has been formulated into dogma, the table of the Lord's Supper is displaced by the altar, the bread has become "the host" [*hostia*, victim], the sign is confounded with the thing signified, the simple memorials are transubstantiated into the actual body and blood and divinity of the Incarnate Son of God, and the officiating priest by a few muttered words of Latin creates the world's Creator.

In the earliest centuries, after the fall of Jerusalem, the church of Antioch, where "the disciples were first called Christians," and whence Paul and Barnabas with their associates were sent forth on their missionary journeys; the

---

[1] Heb. viii., 3.

churches of Ephesus and Smyrna, where there had long been a marvelous confluence of ideas and superstitions, as well as of commerce from the East and from the West; and the church of Alexandria, where the new religion began to claim for its service the world's philosophy and learning, were more important, more honored, and more authoritative than the church of the imperial city. Beginning at Jerusalem, Christianity was in those ages more of a power on the southern and eastern shores of the Mediterranean than in any European country, with the exception, perhaps, of Macedonia and Achaia. Even in Rome its language, as at Antioch and Alexandria, was Greek. But when Christianity had organized itself more widely through the empire, it began to be felt that the church in the greatest of all cities—the centre of the world's civilization, and the seat of almost universal empire—was in some sense the most important of all churches. Gradually, what had been a mere feeling, was becoming a claim on the one hand and a concession on the other, and something like a primacy among churches was recognized as a prerogative of the church in the imperial city. When the seat of empire was transferred to the New Rome on the Bosphorus by the Christian emperor Constantine, the consequent rivalry between the church of Rome and the church of Constantinople, and between their bishops, for the primacy, was the beginning of a division which ultimately separated the Greek Church from the Latin, the Christianity of the East from that of the West. The first great attempt to convert the invisible and spiritual unity of Christ's Universal Church—such unity as may co-exist with freedom and diversity—into the organic unity of a body politic, resulted in the first great schism.

Rome having ceased to be the chief city of the world, the claim of the Roman bishops to precedence must rest upon another foundation. Was there not a primacy among the apostles? Did not Christ give to Peter the keys of the kingdom of heaven? Was it not to Peter that he said,

"Feed my sheep?"   How could Peter govern the Universal Church as Christ's vicar, without making Rome the seat of his apostolic empire?   Where else could he so fitly die and leave his authority to his successors?   So came the pious fraud which made Rome the apostolic see, and its bishop the vicar of Christ.   This was a deep and sure foundation, not to be shaken by so trifling an 'event as the removal of the imperial court from the Tiber to the Bosphorus.   Resting on such a foundation, the claim of primacy among bishops became at last a claim of supremacy over all Christians. The continued absence of the imperial court, the increasing imbecility of the empire in the West, the irruption of barbarians even into Italy, and the gradual displacement of paganism by a modified Christianity, combined to invest the bishop of Rome with ever-growing authority.   That authority became, in the absence of an efficient secular government, a barrier against anarchy.   The bishop—"the holy father"—was the father of the people, and for his sake the Greek word *papa*, or pope—a familiar title applied to all priests in the Greek Church—was transferred into the Latin language.   In pagan Rome the priests were pontiffs, and from the days of Numa Pompilius, there was always a *Pontifex Maximus*, or supreme pontiff.   When the Emperor Augustus was completing the subversion of the republic, and gathering into his own hands all the elements of power, he was the Pontifex Maximus, and thenceforth that was an imperial title; for the emperor must needs be the highest functionary of the national religion.   But when the emperors were no longer pagan, they abdicated that old pagan priesthood.   Why then should not the chief priest of the new religion snatch from the ruin of the old, and claim as his inheritance, the title and the powers of Pontifex Maximus?

In the early centuries, the law of God revealed in the Scriptures was the rule of life for Christians, while the civil government, being unchristian, had another standard.   There was a higher law for Christians, and a lower law for those

who adhered to the old religion.   A striking instance of this
was the difference between Christians and unbelievers in the
law of marriage and in regard to offenses against chastity.
While the Roman law was not quite regardless of conjugal
rights and domestic sanctities, it permitted divorce almost
at the discretion of either party, and it had no censure for
any licentiousness save that which robbed a husband of his
wife not yet divorced.   But among Christians, marriage was
a religious contract, in which the parties were united under
the benediction of the church, and which was indissoluble
without a forfeiture of character and standing by at least
one of the parties.   A divorce might be lawful before Cæsar
and unlawful before God.   The church, therefore, applying
in its discipline the law of Christ, must take cognizance
of every divorce within its jurisdiction, and at its tribunal
the invalidity of a marriage or the rightfulness of a divorce
might be tried and decided.   In like manner other offenses,
whether against morals or against religion, if committed
by persons claiming the Christian name, came under the
cognizance of the church.   Moreover, the early Christians
had been taught by the apostles not to appear against
each other as litigants before heathen magistrates, but rather to settle their differences among. themselves by friendly
arbitration.   Thus in each church, wherever Christianity
grew into an organized institution, there must needs be
some judicial power both for the trial and censure of
public offenses and for the adjustment of private controversies among the faithful.   When the government of those
early churches had become episcopal, the judicial power
rested in the bishop and his subordinates.   As the nominally Christian population, in one city and another, became more numerous, age after age, the judicial and admin-
istrative functions of the clergy, presided over by the bishops, became continually more extensive and more arduous.
Less scrupulous than the apostles, the bishops did not refuse
to take upon themselves, in addition to the administration

of spiritual discipline and the trial of causes between Christian litigants, various duties pertaining to what we have
learned to call the secularities of the church.   Dependent
widows, friendless orphans, and all arrangements in the name
of the church to relieve the poor, were under their care.
Wills were referred to the bishop for approval, and the division of inheritances fell under his superintendence.   When
the hierarchical principle had been developed, and with it
the correlate principle of an œcumenical church, governed as
one body by its hierarchy ; and when councils, provincial
and œcumenical, had begun to legislate for the churches, and
their decrees or canons had begun to be recognized as law,
the idea of appeals from one tribunal to another, and finally
to the church at Rome, as the tribunal of ultimate resort,
was an easy consequence.   Constantine and his successors
in the empire, having removed from Christianity the stigma
of an illicit religion, proceeded to recognize and legalize the
power of the bishops over the communities under their care.
The distinction, now so familiar, between church government and civil government, had never been defined or discussed, and it was therefore natural for the ministers of a religion recognized and protected by the state to become in
some sort and to some extent functionaries of the imperial
power.   The decisions of bishops, in certain cases, were to
be enforced without question or appeal by civil officers.
Certain exemptions and immunities were gained for the
clergy, so that for many offenses, and at last for all offenses,
they were responsible only to the ecclesiastical authority,
and must be divested of their sacred character by the church
before the civil power could touch them.   Of all this, nothing was lost—indeed, the progress of ecclesiastical usurpation was greatly accelerated—when, at the downfall of the
empire in the West, its barbarian conquerors were themselves conquered by the church.

In the new world which slowly emerged, as from a deluge,
after the overthrow of the old civilization, and which became

the world of the Middle Ages, the church, converting the barbarians and humanizing their ferocity, was among the foremost powers. The Catholic Church, with its one ubiquitous priesthood, with its superstitions and imposing ritual, with its ever-growing splendor and grandeur, with its government centralized under the supreme Pontiff at the historic seat of universal empire, and with what still remained to it of intellectual culture and aspiration, and of the Christian spirit and doctrine, became the bond of union among nations of diverse races and dissonant languages. Its canon law was a distinct body of jurisprudence, supposed to be authoritative over all men, touching all human relations, and having force as law wherever the primacy of Rome was acknowledged—whether on the Tiber or on the Thames, whether in France or in Germany. Its tribunals were every where co-ordinate with the courts of secular justice, and every where the magistrate was bound to respect and obey their decisions.

But while the church was thus encroaching on the state, it came to pass that the state in its turn transcended its legitimate powers and invaded the province of the church. At every stage in the progress of the hierarchy and of the superstitions which made it powerful, there was a corresponding increase of the wealth devoted to religious uses and controlled by ecclesiastical functionaries. The election of bishops, after being transferred from the people to the clergy of the cathedral churches, had been virtually given to the pope, whose approval was considered necessary to the validity of an election. By similar methods the control of appointments to lucrative or honorable stations in the church, throughout all the countries subject to papal authority, was gradually centralized in the court of Rome. The power of the pope in these respects, together with the taxes which he levied under various names and pretenses, became burdensome. In one country and another, the drain on the national wealth gave rise to loud and frequent complaint. It was a

serious question whether the ever-growing wealth of the ecclesiastical power should bear its part, with the wealth of
laymen and of secular corporations, in the tribute which
wealth pays to government for protection.   When the ecclesiastical power had become so great and so formidable,
there could not but be resistance unless the state were content to be merged in a spiritual despotism.   Some limit
must be set to the power that was centred at Rome, or
there would soon be no other power.   If princely archbishops, with princely dignity and power, and bishops with the
wealth and state of barons, were appointed by the pope, and
were responsible only to him for the exercise of their most
formidable powers, the king—the secular and civil government, under whatever name—must have a voice in the appointment; and the ecclesiastical lord, no less than the lay
lord, must be invested with the lands and temporal possessions of his office by the sovereign to whom he owed allegiance.   The conflict about ecclesiastical investitures which
runs through the history of the Middle Ages was essentially
a conflict between the church and the state about the appointment of church officers.   No such conflict could have
arisen had the churches retained their original simplicity of
constitution.   But when the church had become a hierarchy
with immense possessions, and that hierarchy had become
complicated with all the machinery of government in the
state, the long conflict between the popes, on the one hand,
and emperors and kings on the other hand, was an inevitable
consequence.

The celibacy of the clergy was not a papal invention.   In
the early churches—as early, perhaps, as the latter part of the
second century—there was an ascetic sentiment which forgot
that "marriage is honorable in all," and ascribed superior
sanctity to a life of voluntary celibacy.   Before the schism
between the Greek Church and the Latin, before the excision
of the Oriental churches, that sentiment had acquired almost
the force of law.   Yet to this day, in the Greek Church, in

the Armenian Church, and in the Nestorian, celibacy is required only of bishops, who are therefore selected generally, not from among the parochial clergy, but from among the monks in convents. But in the Latin Church of the Middle Ages, an unmarried life became at last, after many conflicts, the indispensable rule for all orders of the hierarchy. The priests of that great organization which, in the name of Christ, aspired to universal dominion, were excluded from the most important and sacred of human relations, and were to be an isolated class incapable of the sympathies, so tender and so powerful, which live in the atmosphere of home and of household love and duty.

Yet the parochial clergy, dwelling in their own parishes, watching over their own flocks, serving their neighbors in the ministrations of religion, and responsible each to his own bishop, were thought to be not sufficiently cut off from human relations and sympathies. Though doomed to ignorance of parental and conjugal affections, though exempt from all ordinary duties in society and from responsibility to civil government, they were, after all, citizens in some sort, and capable of patriotic sympathies. As being in the world, they were called the secular clergy. The monastic orders, those great fraternities organized under vows of obedience as well as of celibacy, were the regular clergy—exempted from the jurisdiction of the bishops, withdrawn from the world, generally secluded in monasteries, governed by their own officers like a military organization—the standing army of the great High-Priest at Rome.

Into those bodies many of the best men, in those ages of ignorance and violence, were attracted, by whose withdrawal from their natural relations to society, the world, which might have been the better for their example and their direct beneficence, was really made worse. Doubtless the monasteries and the monastic orders were instituted, originally, with the best intentions. Doubtless they served some good purpose under that divine Providence which makes all things in some way subservient to itself. It may be that, without them, learning, in those ages of barbarism, would have perished. It may be that, without them, Christianity, finding no place of refuge, would have degenerated into a religion of ferocity, or into a superstition as besotted as that which exists in Abyssinia. But we know that human nature in those ages was just what human nature is to-day. We know that neither human passions nor human infirmities can be laid down at the gate of a monastery, and that the community within, which receives the neophyte into its bosom and subjects him to its ascetic rules, is only a community of men in a most unnatural and unmanly condition. We know, too, that a sentimental Christianity, shirking all natural duties, retreating from conflict with the world's temptations, and shutting itself up in a cell for communion with God, is Christianity misguided, morbid, and deformed, and that it can not recover its vigor or its divine beauty but by going forth to walk and to work in the sunshine. Nor can we forget that as the idea of monastic life had its origin partly in the exaggeration, but still more in the perversion of Christian sentiments, so the monastic orders, instead of having any tendency or fitness to restore the true ideal of the Christian life, were the foremost supporters of superstition and the most efficient instruments of spiritual despotism.

CHAPTER III.

WHAT THE REFORMATION IN THE SIXTEENTH CENTURY DID FOR CHURCH POLITY.

THE great Reformation in the sixteenth century was an attempt to recover the primitive Gospel. Its success, so far as it was successful, resulted from a concurrence of various forces adverse to that huge system, compacted of superstition, scholastic theology, and spiritual despotism, the growth of fourteen hundred years, which had usurped the name and place of Christianity. The revival of learning, the invention of printing, and the general movement toward a new stage of civilization, were among the influences which contributed to the result. What was, at first, the experience of individual souls struggling with the great question, "How shall man be just with God," driven back from tradition to the Scriptures, and finding rest in Christ the one mediator between God and men, became, at that juncture, a new announcement of the primitive Gospel. As in the first century, so in the sixteenth, the Gospel, "to wit, that God is in Christ reconciling the world to himself," was the power that took hold of human souls to bring them out of darkness into light, and out of bondage into the liberty of the sons of God. Agitation ensued, opposition, conflict, papal excommunication, and at last a permanent revolt of Protestant nations against the power enthroned at Rome.[1]

In what ecclesiastical forms did Protestantism organize itself? When we ask this question, we meet the fact that every where a political element was combined with the simply religious element in effecting the Reformation.

---

[1] See " History of the Reformation," by Prof. George P. Fisher.

D

The Roman Catholic religion, or, more properly, the church under the hierarchy centralized at Rome, was every where a political institution.   For ages the pope and the bishops under him were often, not to say habitually, in conflict with civil governments; for the church, professing to wield the power of Him to whom is given all power on earth and in heaven, was every where—whether in Spain or in England, in Sicily or in Sweden—one corporation, claiming its exemptions and its privileges, not under the law of the land, but under a superior law of which it was itself the sole expositor.   The ecclesiastical theory of those ages was not "a free church in a free state," but one œcumenical church dominant over subject states, and executing its decrees by the ministry of the secular power.   If there were to be a church reformation, the movement could not but be political as well as religious.   In the relations then existing between church and state, if the institution known as the church were to be reformed in its doctrines, worship, and polity, that reformation must take place either under the protection of the civil power, and in some sort of co-operation with it, or in the form of a political revolution.

Earlier attempts at reformation failed and were suppressed because they came to be regarded by the civil power, sooner or later, as dangerous and revolutionary.   But when Luther in Northern Germany, and Zwingli in German Switzerland, began simultaneously to recall men's minds from superstitious reliance on priestly intercessions and manipulations, and to exhibit the freeness of God's grace and the simplicity of the way to be saved, the political condition of Europe was such that they found protection and encouragement, and in some sense help, from secular powers.   Under the Providence that rules the world, the success of the Reformation, wherever it was permanently successful, was brought about by that combination of political with religious forces.   Luther would have been crushed but for the constant friendship of Frederick the Wise.   Zwingli was sustained by the free spirit of Switzerland.   The little republic of Geneva made itself illustrious by receiving Calvin as its religious leader.

It was an inevitable consequence of this combination that every where the political element of the Reformation predominated in determining the form of ecclesiastical institutions and arrangements.   Already, in each state or kingdom, the church was inseparably complicated with the state.   No reformation was possible but by asserting and maintaining liberty for the state or kingdom against the tyranny of Rome or of the ecclesiastico-political power.   Acquiescence, on the part of the Reformers, in such arrangements for public worship and for the religious instruction of the people as could be obtained by consultation and agreement with the political power that protected them, was inevitable in the circumstances of the conflict.   What they were contending for was the primitive Gospel rather than the primitive church polity.   The ecclesiastical polity, therefore — especially in relation to the forms of public worship, the selection and designation of ministers, and the provision for their support —was determined, in each reformed state or kingdom, not so much by a reference to the primitive model as by considerations of temporary and local convenience.

It was in this way that national churches, independent of each other as well as of Rome, came into being.   No doubt there had been long before some rudimentary notion of a national church; but in the Reformation, as wrought out by the co-operation of religious and political forces, that idea was developed, and became the basis of ecclesiastical organization.   It was assumed, as a first principle, that the people of a Christian state or kingdom, being all baptized, were all Christians and members of Christ's church in that state or kingdom.   It was also assumed that the Christian people were represented in their government, and that whatever rights and powers in matters ecclesiastical had originally belonged to the Christian laity, but had been usurped by the

pope or the clergy, were in the people as politically organized, or (wherever the Reformation came by a political revolution) in the Protestant as distinguished from the Roman-
ist people.   Arrangements were therefore made for the reforming of ecclesiastical institutions — such as public worship, the choice and induction of ministers, the administration of sacraments, and the infliction of censures—in conformity with the theory which it will be convenient to des-
ignate as *Nationalism.*   The underlying idea was that the
baptized people of an independent state, being a distinct
church, were as independent of Rome as Rome was of them,
while they were also a constituent part of the true church
catholic.   Before the Reformation there was no ecclesiastical independence any where in Western Christendom.   National churches, if any body thought of such a thing, were
only portions of one organized and governed church—the
Roman Catholic.

Where kings or sovereign princes led the Reformation,
and had the shaping of its institutions, the reconstructed
church government was, essentially if not in name, episcopal.
In proportion as the political element concurring with the
religious reformers was popular, the new church government
was essentially presbyterian, or classical and synodical, tending toward the independence and self-government of each
particular congregation, but guarding the official authority
as well as the parity of the clergy.   At Geneva, Calvin, not
to be out-voted by fellow-presbyters unfriendly to the Reformation, established a consistory in which representatives
of the laity, annually chosen, were consessors with the clergy.
That consistory at Geneva became a model of government
for the churches of the Reformation in France, in the Netherlands, in various German cities and principalities, and in
Scotland ; and the laymen whose voices and votes in the
consistory were to check the power of the ministers were
afterward called " lay-elders."

It would be folly to suppose that the Reformers, as dis-

tinguished from the secular powers that protected or be-
friended them, regarded themselves as having achieved their
own ideal of church organization.   On the contrary, they
seem to have regarded the various ecclesiastical systems resulting from the Reformation as obviously imperfect, and to
have accepted them as the best they could obtain in the circumstances.   Luther, Zwingli, Calvin, Cranmer, and Latimer
wanted something better, and hoped that in another age the
work begun by them would be completed.   The religious
tendency, in the reconstruction of ecclesiastical institutions,
was in the direction of a theory which was nowhere realized.[1]

Nine years after the beginning of the Reformation in Germany (1526), there was prepared for the churches of the great
principality of Hesse, or Hessia, a scheme of ecclesiastical order which was almost a purely Congregational platform, but
which never went into operation there.   Francis Lambert,
of Avignon, was the author of it.   A fugitive from France,
he had found in Philip, the Landgrave of Hesse, a protector
and a patron.   In an informal synod convened by Philip to
settle the Reformation in his principality, the exiled Frenchman had the opportunity of presenting certain *theses* on
church government which he had published not long before
under the title of " Paradoxes ;" and a plan of reformation
was adopted by the synod in conformity with the views
which he had gained from a careful and independent study
of the Scriptures.

The method which Lambert proposed, and which the informal synod seems to have heartily approved, provides, first,
for the organization of local churches.   It " contemplates the
formation of a pure congregation of true believers, in which
the right of ecclesiastical self-government should be exercised immediately by the congregation, not mediately through
representatives and delegates."   Reasons for the self-government of parochial churches were adduced from the Script-

---

[1] Gieseler, " Eccl. Hist." (translated by Prof. H. B. Smith), iv., 520–532.

ures. "The law of Christ, in Matt. xviii., requires it to be 'told to the church' when a brother will not hear admonition; but the church of God is nothing but the assembly of believers. The believers must therefore be assembled from time to time, otherwise it would not be possible for the contumacy of an offending brother to be reported to them. Furthermore, according to the word of Paul (1 Cor. v.), the believers must be gathered together for the public censure and excommunication of a scandalous person. There are other purposes, also, for which the believers must assemble —to pass judgment on the sentiments of their pastors; to elect, and, if necessary, to depose bishops and deacons (that is, parish ministers and their assistants), and officers for the care of the poor,[1] and to decide on any other matter that concerns the whole Church.

"Accordingly," said the author of the plan, "we ordain that in every parish, after the Word of God has been preached for a sufficient length of time, a meeting of believers shall be held, in which all men who are on Christ's side and are reckoned with the saints shall come together, in order that they may, in conjunction with the bishop"—that is, the bishop of that parish—"settle all the affairs of the church according to the word of God. Believing women may attend the meeting, but without the right of voting.

"But inasmuch as opposers of the faith ought not to be admitted to the assembly of the faithful, let a *separation* between true and false brethren be undertaken in the following way: After the word of God has been preached for a time, let the minister invite all believers to a meeting on the next Sunday, at which, however, only those are expected to be present who are willing to submit themselves to the word of God, and in particular to the rule that whosoever

---

[1] Another account of this platform describes it as providing for "two kinds of church officers"—the pastors (*episcopi*) and their helpers (*diaconi*, or *adjutores episcoporum*), on the one hand, and the almoners (*diaconi ecclesiarum*) on the other hand.

gives offense by evil-doing shall be put out of the church. After this has been repeatedly announced, and after the people have been individually exhorted to repentance and amendment of life, shall the meeting take place.   Those who are not willing to devote themselves to a life of Christian piety shall withdraw, and shall be considered not as brethren, but as heathen men and 'those that are without.'   Let prayer, however, be made for these as well as for the brethren.

"The power of excommunication and absolution by no means rests with the bishop alone, but only with him in conjunction with the church.   But those who wish to be numbered with the saints, and to put themselves under the Christian discipline, are to be enrolled in a register — not shrinking from this even when they are very few in number; let them be assured of this, that through the operation of God's word their number shall speedily increase, even though, at the outset, it be no more than twenty or thirty.

"In the congregations of brethren or saints that may be organized as the result of these preparatory steps, all church business is to be transacted—choice of ministers, excommunication, restoration ; the bishop, to whom it belongs to preside in the meeting, seeing to it that, in accordance with the word of God, every one shall have a patient hearing."

Such was the plan which Francis Lambert, in the early years of the Reformation, had deduced from the precedents and principles of the New Testament.   The church, as organized and governed, was to be a local or parochial institution, complete in every parish.   It was to be constituted, not by including all baptized inhabitants, but by a separation of its members from such as were not willing to submit themselves to the word of God, and by mutual agreement.   The church thus constituted was to be self-governed, having power over its members to admonish the erring, to excommunicate the stubborn offender, to restore the penitent.   It was to have power over its officers, both bishops and deacons —the power to elect, to judge, and, if necessary, to depose.

The bishop—each church having a bishop or bishops of its own—was to preside in the church-meeting, but was to have no power of exclusion from communion without the votes of the brethren. In every parish the brotherhood of believers was to be, simply and purely, a spiritual democracy under Christ.

Another part of the platform made provision for a yearly synod of the churches, which was to be "composed of the assembled pastors and of delegates chosen immediately before in the church-meetings." The functions and powers of the synod were defined in a remarkable accordance with the powers and functions of councils in the polity of the New England churches, the most important difference being that the synod was to meet annually at a fixed time and place, instead of being convened like a New England council on a definite occasion and at a special call. In the annual meeting there was to be an examination of the doings of congregations in the choice and removal of pastors, an inspection and superintendence of the three visitors annually appointed, and finally the decision of questions and difficulties laid before them by the churches. But it was declared in an intensely Congregational spirit, "that the word of God outweighs a majority;"[1] and that the decisions of the synod were to be set forth solely on the authority of substantial proofs from Scripture for the edification of all the churches, and were to be announced not as decrees or statutes, but only as "the answer of the Hessian Synod."

Yet—and this was the greatest defect—the church was not to be completely separated from the state, but was still to be in some sort under the superintendence of the secular government. The business occurring between one synod and the next was to be in the charge, partly, of a select synodal committee of thirteen, partly of three visitors, to be

---

[1] "*Major* enim est *Dei sermo* omni hominum *multitudine;* et melius est adherere *uni* habenti verbum Domini, quam multis proprium judicium sequentibus."

named for the first year by the landgrave and afterward by the synod, and partly of the church in the synodal city of Marburg. The same synodal committee was to superintend and manage the business of the synod when in session. In the selection of this committee, the prince, with the nobility, if present in the assembly, was to have the right of voting; and in its sessions the prince, with such persons as he should introduce, and the nobility favorable to the Gospel, might be present.

This Hessian platform almost extinguishes the idea of clerical power—an idea essential to all the national churches produced by the Reformation, to the Presbyterian no less than to the Episcopal. A Presbyterian system of church government may change the priest into a minister of the word of God, and may deny that there is any cleansing efficacy or sacrificial value in his manipulation of the sacraments; but if it make all preachers, by virtue of their ordination, and independently of their being called to office in a local church, rulers by divine right in the church at large, it simply changes the ruling priesthood into a ruling preacherhood. But there was as little of ruling preacherhood as of ruling priesthood in Francis Lambert's system. The platform which he deduced from the Scriptures recognizes no bishop at large, nor any bishop other than the simple pastor of a parish church. It knows nothing about what is called the "indelibility of ordination," but affirms that "each pastor and pastor's assistant is appointed for such time only as he shall preach God's word purely and simply, and shall walk worthily," a position which assumes and explains the duty of the assembled believers "to pass judgment on the sentiments of their pastors." It excludes the idea that only members of a clerical order can be chosen to the pastoral office; and, on the contrary, it maintains that "citizens and workingmen, whatever their business may be, if only they are devout, blameless, and instructed, are eligible to the pastorate." It even maintains that men may be preachers without being in any sense church officers. Where it prevails, there shall be no clerical body, not even a body of pastors, with an exclusive right to speak in the congregation; for it holds that "men without office in the church, being devout and strong in the Scriptures, are not to be forbidden to preach, inasmuch as there is an inward call from God."

Had this scheme been proposed to Luther as an ideal theory of church polity, or as a plan which might be adopted at a later stage of the Reformation, doubtless he would have most heartily approved it; for the ideal which it portrayed was substantially his own. But when the question of attempting such a polity in the churches of Hesse was submitted to him by Philip, early in the following year, he could not believe that the time had come for building the house of God according to the pattern given in the Scriptures. He advised the prince not to promulgate the plan immediately, but first to appoint capable men over the parish schools and churches; and when a number of these should have come practically and cordially into agreement, and others should be ready to follow them, to introduce the plan by a public ordinance. Thus a certain usage, being first settled, might be elevated into law. Evidently the great Reformer thought that the scheme was a devout imagination not to be realized in that age when so much depended on princely patronage; and that Lambert was only an amiable dreamer.

Luther's advice prevailed, and Lambert's platform of church discipline was set aside to wait for better times. Melanchthon, as well as Luther, thought that the age was not ripe for the emancipation of the churches and the coming in of a simply evangelical church polity. Accordingly, the ordering of ecclesiastical affairs remained in the hands of the reforming landgrave; and his "instructions" to the ecclesiastical visitors, issued after much deliberation, made no mention of local self-governed churches with their several bishops and their synods, but only of parish priests and superintendents. Two years later Lambert died, but not till he had renewed his testimony with unfailing aspiration. "When shall we have the joy of seeing our churches ordered strictly according to the law of Christ? Where is the power of excommunication, that most essential thing to any church, which so many, in opposition to the plain testimony of the Scriptures, are throwing away?"

Another year, and instead of provisional officers for the superintendence of the clergy and the parishes, superintendents for life were appointed. Then followed a second assembly at Homberg, by whose advice the duty of admonishing and of excommunicating unworthy parishioners was laid upon pastors only. At last, after thirteen years of such reformation by the secular power with the advice of reforming theologians, the lay-eldership was introduced into the Hessian churches; and the share of each local church (or rather of each parish) in its own government was that it might choose half of the lay-elders in its consistory, the other half being chosen by the magistrate to represent and maintain the dependence of the church on the civil government.

In this last arrangement, "the ideal plan of Lambert vanished away, leaving behind it no enduring fruit."[1]

---

[1] *Congregational Quarterly*, July, 1864, p. 276–280; Lechler, "Geschichte der Presbyterial- und Synodal-verfassung seit der Reformation" (Leyden, 1834), 14–21; "Leben und ansgewählte Schriften der Väter und Begründer der reformirten Kirche (Elberfeld, 1861), ix., 41–47. These writers refer to RICHTER, "Sammlung Evangelischer Kirchenordnungen," i., 58 sq., which contains the original document : " Reformatio Ecclesiarum Hassiæ juxta certissimam sermonum Dei regulam ordinata in venerabili synodo," etc.

CHAPTER IV.

THE ENGLISH REFORMATION AND THE PURITANS.

In England, the twofold character of the Reformation was more conspicuous than in any other country. Elsewhere, as we have seen, that great revolution was effected, under the providence of God, by a concurrence of political with religious forces. Princes and statesmen, or the leaders of petty republics, on the one hand, and reforming preachers and writers on the other hand, were fellow-workers. But in England, more than any where else, the Reformation resembled some great river formed by the confluence of two streams which, like the Missouri and the Mississippi, refuse to mingle though flowing in one channel. On one side, it was a religious movement among the people, an inquiry after truth and salvation, a revolt of earnest and devout souls against the superstition, the false doctrine, and the despotic priesthood that hindered their access to God. On the other side, it was a politico-ecclesiastical revolution, an attempt of king and Parliament to drive out of the kingdom the insolent intrusions and vexatious exactions of the court of Rome, a breaking of what had long been felt as a galling yoke on the neck of a proud people.

Considered as a religious movement, the Reformation in England began with Wycliffe, more than a hundred and fifty years before Luther. Fitly has the stout-hearted Englishman been called " the morning star" of the day which had its sunrise in the sixteenth century. Though protected for a while by some of the most powerful of the nobles, and encouraged by the sympathy of Parliament in his Luther-like attacks on the mendicant orders and the pope, he was not sustained by any adequate political power in his efforts to

evangelize the people.   His disciples, under the name of Lollards—a reproachful designation imported from the Continent
—carried on his work after his death; and though persecuted, and often giving their testimony in prison and at the
stake, they could not be suppressed.   The Protestant martyrology of England, long before the age of Luther, is rich in
records of their suffering heroism.   Their books, multiplied
by the slow process of transcribing, were widely, though secretly, distributed; were read with closed doors in many a
household and in many a private assembly ; and were hand-
ed down from sire to son as precious heir-looms.   Their itin-
erant preachers, passing quietly from place to place, and
eluding—though not always—the vigilance of their enemies,
kept alive the tradition of their doctrine, and strengthened
the scattered disciples by making them know each other's
faith and patience.   When the Reformation began on the
Continent, Wycliffism or Lollardism was soon lost, or rather
perpetuated, in Lutheranism or Protestantism, which found
in England a soil well prepared for it.

Considered in the other aspect, namely, as a political or
national movement, the English Reformation, at its beginning, had no visible connection with the religious movement
among the people.   The history of England through the
Middle Ages is largely the history of a chronic conflict between the state, as represented by the king and Parliament,
and the church, as governed by a foreign potentate, the
pope.   But that change in the ecclesiastical establishment
of the realm which is commonly called by English writers
"the reformation from popery," began when Henry VIII.,
who had written a book against Luther, and had been re-
warded by the pope with the title "Defender of the Faith"
—a title borne by all his successors—procured the consent of
Parliament to his declaring himself the Supreme Head (1534)
under Christ of the Church of England, and then constrained
the clergy in Convocation to acknowledge his supremacy.
Other changes followed.   First was the suppression of the

monasteries and the confiscation of their property in lands and treasures. That great wealth, instead of being reserved (as the religious reformers would have chosen) to be a fund for the education of the people, or for any public use, was lavishly—but, on the whole, perhaps not unwisely—distributed by the king among his nobles and courtiers. Thus the breach between England and Rome, politically considered, was not only widened but made irreparable. Every lord who held any of the rich domains once belonging to monastic corporations might be relied on for a steadfast opposition to all measures tending toward a restoration of the old order of things.

Such being the position of the government, it became important, in a political view, that the popular mind be turned against Rome. Accordingly, the Bible, translated into English by Tyndale a few years before, instead of being, as it had been, a prohibited book, smuggled in from the Continent, was permitted, after a few unimportant corrections, to be printed and published in England; and thus that great point —the right of the people to read the Scriptures—was indirectly conceded. But it was not till the following reign (that of the boy king, Edward VI., 1547) that the authorized doctrine and the devotional formularies of the Established Church were subjected to the hands of such reformers as Cranmer and Ridley; and then it was that the scattered and persecuted followers of Wycliffe, as well as the many who had caught the new opinions then spreading on the Continent and floating across the sea, found their cause victorious, as they supposed, in England. Thus, in that reign, and afterward at the commencement of the reign of Elizabeth (1558), there was a temporary union of the religious reformation, originating and spreading among the people, with the politico-ecclesiastical reformation conducted by the government. The ecclesiastical establishment was so modified, and the administration of it was so changed, that the remnant of Lollardism and the adherents of the Continental reformers regarded it as having virtually come over to them.   Accordingly they were no longer excluded from the Church of England, but were recognized as among the most zealous of its members.   By their enthusiasm, propagating itself among the people, the reformed establishment was strengthened against the common enemy, and the chances of a reconciliation with Rome, and of a consequent restitution of confiscated church property, were greatly diminished.

That politico-ecclesiastical reformation brought the Church of England, considered as an establishment, with its endowments and its clergy, into a complete dependence on the crown, and a closer alliance than before with the landed aristocracy.   In former ages, the Catholic Church in England, though connected with the state and to some extent influenced by the crown, had an independence which made it sometimes formidable to the secular power.   But the great change begun under Henry VIII., and made permanent by the necessities and the policy of his daughter Elizabeth, disturbed the balance of power by annexing to the crown all that dominion over the Church which had formerly belonged to the pope.   The ecclesiastical courts, with an extensive jurisdiction which in these days would be called civil, became virtually the king's courts, and there was no more appealing of causes to Rome.   By the removal of the " mitred abbots " from the House of Lords—where they with the bishops had always been a majority—and by the loss of the immense wealth which, at the dissolution of the monasteries, had passed into the hands of the king, and thence into the hands of the lay aristocracy, the separate importance of the clergy as one of the estates of the realm was almost destroyed.   At the same time, the great amount of church patronage—including the appointment of thousands of clergymen to their livings—which was transferred from the monastic corporations to the king and to lay lords, separated the church, as an establishment, more than ever from the interests and sympathies of the lower orders, and completed its connection, not merely with the state, but with the king and the nobility. To all this must be added that unlimited superintendence over ecclesiastical affairs and over the religion of the people which was considered as belonging to the king by virtue of his being Head of the Church.

Such was the political bondage of what is called the Church of England, as the government reformation left it: all the great ecclesiastical dignities, and thousands of the humbler benefices, at the disposal of the government; the people, except in here and there an anomalous instance, excluded from influence, direct or indirect, over the appointment of their own parochial ministers; no synods or conventions, general or diocesan, with a lay representation, to regulate matters of common interest; no convocation, even of the clergy, permitted to assemble save at the king's command, or, when assembled, permitted to engage in any business save by the king's particular warrant.

Another result of that revolution in the ecclesiastical institutions of England is conspicuous in the subsequent history. The National Church contained, thenceforward, the elements of internal strife. Two dissimilar movements, as we have seen, were united in the English Reformation, but, though united as it were mechanically, they were not blended. An irrepressible conflict was the consequence—a conflict which continues to this day. On one hand was the great body of the old clergy, with their opinions and their sympathies and prejudices mostly unchanged. Having been coerced into the acknowledgment of bluff King Harry as their Supreme Head on earth, they were led or driven from one change to another, till they found themselves using the English service-book instead of the old Latin Missal, and reading from their pulpits, as well as they could, the "Homily against Idolatry," in edifices despoiled of the relics and the images which once adorned them. These men were naturally a conservative party with reactionary tendencies. They had accepted the revolution, not spontaneously, nor

with a burning conviction that the old system was full of
great errors and abuses which must be reformed at all hazards, but passively, and under the force of a habit of subordination.   The law which compelled their celibacy having
been taken away, they had generally become married men;
and their lawful wives and children—lawful while the Reformation lasted—were hostages for their fidelity to the Protestant establishment.   At first, and for a long time, the parochial clergy were generally of this description, for how
could it be otherwise?   Their tendency as a body was to
keep the Reformation stationary by their dead weight, and
to perpetuate in the Reformed Church of England the religious ideas in which they had been educated before the change.
They were likely to feel that the Reformation had gone far
enough; and when they looked upon the churches no longer smoking and fragrant with incense, nor gorgeous with the
gold and gems of the altar; when they saw pictures and
statues, before which the faithful once kneeled in worship,
borne away, and the holiest relics cast out as unclean things;
still more, when they saw some old monastic building desolate and falling into ruin; most of all, when they looked upon
some stately pile where, in the good old times, grave abbots
had given alms to the poor, and had dispensed due hospitality to pilgrims and to princes, now possessed by some sacri-
legious lord, masque and revel and the noise of boisterous
banquets succeeding to the chanted prayers of men devoted
to religion — it would not be strange if they felt that the
Reformation had already been carried too far.

Here was one great party in the National Church, which,
having submitted to the new arrangements without much
of a revolutionary spirit, looked toward the past with a feeling akin to regret.   But on the other hand, the ecclesiastical
establishment had received into itself a very different sort
of men — wide-awake men, who were not merely reformed
by an order from the King in Council or by an act of Parliament, but were reformers in their own persons—men whose

E

ideas of reformation had come to them by tradition from
Wycliffe, or by communication and sympathy with reformers on the Continent—men whose quarrel with Rome was
not on the question of ecclesiastical supremacy merely, but
on the whole system of religion—men whose protest against
the pope, instead of being careful and measured, was uttered as in words of fire, and who were ready to die for
their testimony.   These were the movement party—the
radicals — the destructives — if any choose to call them
by such names.   With them, or with many of them, reformation, even to the destruction of every thing which they
regarded as idolatrous or popish, was a passion.   Their sympathies were with the people more than with the court; they
were fitted for influence with the people; and therefore, when
the government would thoroughly bring off the people from
the old ways, it called these men to its aid; and some of
them—such as the plain-dealing Latimer, Fox, the author of
the "Book of Martyrs," the sturdy and scrupulous Hooper,
and even (at one time) that intractable Scotchman, John
Knox—were placed in stations of honor and wide influence.
While the Reformation was going forward, men of this quality were in their element; but when its progress was arrested, and the government had resolved that it should go no
farther, they were disappointed and dissatisfied.   So long as
the permanency of the changes which the government had
undertaken to introduce was not yet sure, and fiery spirits
were needed to carry the work forward, these men were necessary to the government, and were therefore in favor; but
when the business of reforming was no longer in hand, and
the objects which sovereign and courtiers had in view were
felt to be well enough secured, such men were no longer in
alliance with the court.   Gradually they fell back to their
original position among the people as reformers on their own
account.

Then began that age-long conflict in the Church of England between the government Protestantism, on the one

hand, completed and immovable, and the demand, on the
other hand, for a more thorough reformation that should
carry the National Church and the national Christianity back
to the original purity portrayed in the Scriptures. On one
side were the court, and those who were called "the court
clergy." On the other side were the PURITANS, so named
from their demand for purity in the worship of God and in
the administration of Christ's ordinances. As in many a
similar conflict, the line of division was not very sharply
drawn between the parties. There were Puritans more or
less decided in their opinions, and more or less resolute in
word and deed; but, at first, there was no Puritan party acting in concert under acknowledged leaders.

Such was the origin of Puritanism in England, and such
was its position three hundred years ago, when Elizabeth
was queen. It was not, nor did it intend to be, a secession
or separation from the National Church. It must not be
thought that the Puritans were "Dissenters" in the modern
meaning of that word. They were not Congregationalists
in their theory of the church; nor, at first, were they even
Presbyterians. Certainly the great body of them, in the
earliest stages of the conflict, had not arrived at the conclusion that diocesan episcopacy must be got rid of. At first
the most advanced of them were only "Nonconformists,"
deviating from some of the prescribed regulations in the performance of public worship. As Christian Englishmen, they
were, according to the theory which I have called Nationalism, members of the Church of England; and what they desired was not liberty to withdraw from that National Church
and to organize what would now be called a distinct "de-
nomination;" nor was it merely liberty *in* the National Church
to worship according to their own idea of Christian simplicity and purity—though, doubtless, many of them would have
been contented with that. What they desired was reformation of the National Church itself by national authority.

While the conflict was in its earliest stage, the episcopal

element in the constitution of the ecclesiastical establishment seems not to have been seriously called in question.   On the contrary, it was conceded by those who desired more reformation that the king might lawfully appoint officers to superintend and govern the clergy, and those superintendents, though called bishops, were regarded as deriving their authority from the king.   Puritanism first appeared in the form of a protest against certain ceremonies and vestments which were required by law in the celebration of public worship.   The Act of Uniformity, in the first year of the reign of Elizabeth, established the Book of Common Prayer as the only form for the worship of God by any religious assembly; and every minister deviating from the directions printed in that book (called "rubrics," because originally printed with red ink) was liable to severe penalties.   Some of those directions required the use of certain ceremonies which were regarded by the more advanced Protestants as teaching or sanctioning an unchristian and pernicious superstition.   The sign of the cross in baptism, the use of a ring in marriage, and kneeling to partake of the Lord's Supper, were particularly objected to on that ground.   But, most of all, some of the vestments required to be worn by ministers in the prescribed worship were protested against.   Nobody found fault with the scholar's gown which the clergy wore in preaching. On all sides, that was admitted to be a becoming dress for those who served as teachers in the church, and something of the kind was universal in the Protestant churches of other countries.   But the priestly surplice, which the minister must wear when administering sacraments or performing "divine service," was associated in all minds with the superstitions which Protestants abhorred, and which the Reformation had undertaken to abolish.   It was a sign that the official who wore it was not merely a recognized minister of the Gospel, but a veritable priest with supernatural functions. Every body knew that the wearing of it was required out of deference to popular superstition.   To the ignorant people, who were disposed to hanker after the old ideas, it had as real a meaning as the "wearing of the green" has now to Irish Fenians. To earnest Protestants it had the same sort of meaning which the gray uniform of the "Confederates" in the late war had to the "boys in blue" who were fighting for the Union. The controversy about ceremonies and vestments, in the reign of Elizabeth, was essentially the same with the Ritualistic agitation in the reign of Victoria —an agitation which shakes the Church of England to-day, and is not wholly unfelt in the United States. After so many ages of philosophic sneering at the Puritans for their scrupulousness about such matters as the cut and color of a prescribed garment, all parties in the English establishment are now compelled to confess that questions about things indifferent in themselves—as, for example, whether the French flag shall be white or tricolor—may acquire a significance which shall make them worth dying for. That conflict three hundred years ago was the same in principle with the conflict now; for behind the sacerdotal millinery and frippery, behind the significant and pompous ceremonies, there stood then, as there stands now, a body of anti-evangelical and really antichristian doctrine—another Gospel, which is really no Gospel at all—another theory than that of Paul and of Jesus Christ concerning the way to be saved.

Conscience, in conscientious men, when it has been roused to declare itself, is an obstinate thing. The conscience of the Puritans, and especially of the Puritans among the clergy, did declare itself against the symbols of superstition; and so numerous were those who, in one point or another, refused to conform, and so eminent were they for fidelity and ability in their ministry and for learning, that for a while their nonconformity was connived at by the ecclesiastical authorities, and the more because many of the bishops were in sympathy with that party. But in a few years after the accession of Elizabeth (1565), when such ecclesiastical reformation had been made as she chose to tolerate, a royal proclamation was issued demanding a strict conformity. In the city of London, thirty-seven out of ninety-eight beneficed clergymen refused to make the promise which was required of them, and were immediately excluded from the performance of their ministry.[1] A company of Puritans who ventured to meet for worship in their own way (1567), found that there were penalties for the nonconforming laity as well as for nonconforming clergymen. Their meeting was broken up, and a large number of them were imprisoned to study in their confinement the principles of church order.[2] In all parts of England there were similar proceedings.

Not many years passed before the conflict entered on another stage of its progress, and new questions were opened between the Puritans and those who ruled the ecclesiastical establishment. The rigorous enforcement of the Act of Uniformity by bishops on laity as well as clergy, and the forcible suppression of the private assemblies in which nonconformists ventured to meet for social worship, had an effect which a little knowledge of human nature might have anticipated. Puritans, instead of being convinced by such arguments, began to consider whether the system of ecclesiastical government which was so conservative of superstitious vestments and ceremonies ought not to be more radically reformed. Thomas Cartwright, Lady Margaret Professor of Divinity in the University of Cambridge, a man of great celebrity for learning and eloquence, began (1570) to discuss in his lectures the theory of church government as given in the Scriptures; and he did not hesitate to say in what particulars the actual arrangements for the government of the Church of England were widely divergent from the most ancient examples, and especially from the authoritative precedents and principles of the New Testament. Still holding the vicious theory that an independent Christian nation is an independent Christian church, he aimed at nothing more

---

[1] Neal, i., 98, 99.   [2] *Ibid.*, p. 108, 109.

than a complete reformation by the government; but the
system which he would have the queen and Parliament establish in England was essentially that of Geneva and of
Scotland. Thenceforward the Puritans, as a party, looked
for something more than the removal of a few obnoxious
ceremonies, and the privilege of officiating in a black gown
instead of a white surplice. Thenceforward they would be
satisfied with nothing less than an entire revision and reconstruction of the ecclesiastical establishment. Under Cartwright's influence, English Puritanism became, essentially, in
its ideas and aspirations, Presbyterianism like that of Holland or of Scotland.

To describe the progress of that controversy in the Church
of England would be aside from our purpose. It was a long
and bitter controversy. On one side there was power, on
the other side there was the obstinacy of conscience. On
one side was the queen, with the splendor of her court and
government, with her inborn love of pomp as well as of
power, with her imperious will, and with her unbounded pop-
ularity as a princess whose right to the throne, and even the
legitimacy of her birth, were identified with Protestantism.
On the other side was the people's abhorrence of the pope
and all his works—the English " no-popery," which had been
long growing, especially among the middle-class people, and
which had gained both extension and intensity from the vividly remembered atrocities in the reign of Mary. On one
side were some good men and learned, conservative by nature and by training, who thankfully accepted as much of reformation as the queen would give them, and quietly waited
for more, with many other men, not so good nor so learned,
whose feeling was that the queen had already done quite
enough, and even more than enough, in the way of church
reformation. On the other side there was no less of learning, and much more of earnest religious feeling. On one
side was the fixed purpose of Elizabeth Tudor, and (after a
while) of the prelates who depended on her favor, to extin-

guish the nonconforming and reforming party by depriva-
tion and silencing, by exorbitant fines, by confinement in
loathsome and pestilential prisons.   On the other side there
was the invisible yet invincible might of those who suffer
for conscience' sake.

On both sides it was held that the bishop of Rome had
no rightful authority in England.   On both sides there was
a fatal error—fatal to liberty, and fatal in the end to godliness—the error of supposing that Christian England, being
an independent nation, was therefore an independent church
—the Church of England.   Both held a fatal error in assuming that there must be a national church, one and indivisi-
ble, and that the reformation of the church could be wrought
only by the legislative and executive sovereignty of the nation.

Something better than Puritanism was necessary to liberty,
and to the restoration of simple and primitive Christianity.

CHAPTER V.

REFORMATION WITHOUT TARRYING FOR ANY.

WHAT Puritanism demanded was an ecclesiastical reformation to be made by the national authority. Queen Elizabeth and the Parliament, as having full legislative power in England, were to revise the established forms of public worship and purge out all idolatrous symbols and superstitious ceremonies. The laws concerning uniformity were to be changed, not in the interest of liberty or of " broad-church " principles, but in the interest of primitive purity and simplicity. The entire constitution of ecclesiastical government, which had really undergone no change except by putting the queen into the pope's place, was to be taken down and reconstructed. The reforming party, in its study of the Scriptures, had learned that archbishops and archdeacons were not known to the apostles; that the bishops mentioned in the New Testament were officers of local churches only, and not rulers over many churches in one diocese; that the so-called ecclesiastical courts, with their fines and imprisonments [*pro salute animarum*] for the health of the souls of nonconformists and other offenders, bore no resemblance to the arrangements instituted by the apostles for the primitive churches. Therefore the Puritans demanded that all these things, and more of the same sort, should be set right by the national authority, inasmuch as the English nation itself, baptized and Protestant, was the Church of England. No withdrawal from the National Church was to be thought of, for that would be schism.

When Puritan clergymen officiated without the surplice, or baptized without the sign of the cross, or pronounced the nuptial benediction on bride and bridegroom who had been

married without a ring, or administered the Lord's Supper
to communicants who received it without kneeling, they
did not consider themselves as seceding from the National
Church, but only as disregarding, in deference to the supreme
authority of Christ, certain regulations which, being made in
derogation of his law, were without force in his church, and
ought to be disregarded at all hazards.   When, after being
silenced and deprived of their livings for their nonconformity, they met with their friends in private assemblies for
worship, they had no intention of organizing another church
outside of the Church of England, but, as members of the
National Church, they insisted on obeying God rather than
men.   So in these days, the Old-Catholic clergy and laity in
Germany do not regard themselves as seceding from the
Catholic, nor from the Roman Catholic Church.   It is as
Catholics and not Protestants that they reject the authority of the Vatican Council, and maintain that the sentences
of excommunication hurled against them by a not infallible
pope are invalid.

But under oppression men sometimes get new light.   As
the urging of conformity to an obnoxious ritual led Thomas
Cartwright and others to investigate the theory of church
government, and to demand a warrant from the Scriptures
for the system of diocesan episcopacy, so, under the discipline of impoverishing fines and tedious imprisonments,
some of the sufferers began to doubt whether the exception-
al institution called the Church of England—having Elizabeth Tudor as its supreme ruler on earth, to whom every
minister of God's word was responsible for his preaching
and for all his spiritual administrations—was really a church
of Christ in any legitimate meaning of that phrase.   The
more they studied the New Testament, the less they could
find bearing a resemblance to that or any other National
Church.   Questions were beginning to emerge which had
not yet been fairly considered.   Did the apostles institute
any national church?   Did Christ intend that his Catholic

Church should be made up of national churches mutually independent? Was it his plan that in every nation the Cæsar or other sovereign, if baptized, should be supreme over the church also? If not, what was his intention when he sent forth his disciples to convert all nations? Nonconformists were holding conventicles in private rooms, with the doors shut for fear of informers and persecutors; but in what capacity or character were they thus assembled? What was the relation of such assemblies, and what the relation of, the queen's National Church to the true church of Christ in England?

Such questionings among the Puritans gave origin to another party aiming at a more radical reformation. The men' of the new party, instead of remaining in the Church of England to reform it, boldly withdrew themselves from that ecclesiastico-political organization, denouncing that and all other so-called national churches as institutions unknown to the law and mind of Christ. The idea of separation, in some sort, from the State Church, in order to regain the simplicity of Christian institutions, must have occurred to many minds, before any attempt was made to propound a theory of separation and to embody it in organized churches. Every act of nonconforming worship by Lollards before the Reformation, or by Protestants in that bloody restoration of Romanism which filled up the five years between the death of Edward VI. and the accession of Elizabeth, was, practically, though not in theory, an assertion of religious liberty. On the part of the worshipers, every such act implied, logically if not consciously, a denial of any right in the civil power to prescribe by law what they should believe and profess concerning God, or in what forms they should worship. But ordinarily the protests against what remained of superstition in the National Church were not protests against the theory of Nationalism; and the private meetings of Nonconformists for the enjoyment of a purer worship were nothing more than a practical appeal to a higher law with which the lower law was in conflict, but which ought to be recognized and enforced by the legislative authority of England. Even when congregations were organized, as they seem to have been in some instances, to meet statedly for worship according to the Scriptures, using the Geneva Service-book instead of the Book of Common Prayer, it does not appear, save in one obscure instance, that they regarded themselves as any thing else than provisional congregations of oppressed Christians in the Church of England, separating not so much from the National Church as from its disorders and corruptions, till "the reliques of Antichrist" should be swept away by act of Parliament.

Documents, without date, not long ago discovered in the State Paper Office of the English government, show that, as early perhaps as the tenth year in the reign of Elizabeth (1567), there was a congregation calling itself "the Privye Church in London," and describing itself as "a poor congregation whom God hath separated from the churches of England and from the mingled and false worshiping therein used." It was a church professing that its members, "by the strength and working of the Almighty, our Lord Jesus Christ, have set their hands and hearts to the pure, unmingled, and sincere worshiping of God according to his blessed and glorious word . . . abolishing and abhorring all inventions and traditions of men." It held its Lord's-day and its week-day meetings. "So as God giveth strength," said they, "we do serve the Lord every Sabbath-day in houses, and on the fourth day in the week we come together weekly to use prayer and exercise discipline on them which do deserve it, by the strength and sure warrant of the Lord's good word." It was a persecuted church. "This secret and disguised Antichrist," said they, "to wit, this canon law with the branches and maintainers"—in other words, the ecclesiastical courts and the queen's High Commission—"have by long imprisonment pined and killed the Lord's servants, as our minister Richard Fitz, Thomas Rowland, deacon . . . and besides them a great multitude . . . whose good cause and faithful testimony—though we should cease to groan and cry unto our God to redress such wrongs and cruel handlings of his poor members—the very walls of the prisons about this city (as the Gate-house, Bridewell, the Counters, the King's Bench, the Marshalsea, the White Lion) would testify God's anger kindled against this land for such injustice."[1]

That "secret and disguised Antichrist" complained of by the sufferers was an important element in the ecclesiastical government of England, and was every where present to suppress both separation from the Established Church and nonconformity within the church.   What was it?

All persons within the realm of England were under the government of the Church of England, and were therefore subject to the judicial authority of the bishops in their several dioceses.   That authority was exercised in ecclesiastical or "spiritual" courts.   Lowest of these was the *Archdeacon's Court*, which was held, in the absence of the archdeacon, by a judge appointed as his substitute, and called his *official.*   Next was the *Consistory Court* of the diocese, held in the cathedral, the bishop's chancellor or commissary presiding as judge.   The *Court of Arches*, in London, was that to which appeals were brought from the consistory courts in the several dioceses in the province of Canterbury, there being a similar court for appeals in the province of York. The judge in each of these courts was supposed to represent the "spiritual" authority of the archbishop; and the final appeal was from these archiepiscopal courts to the supreme head of the ecclesiastical establishment, namely, to a *Court of Delegates*, or commissioners, appointed by the sovereign to represent that supremacy over the Church of England which had been wrested from the pope.   Other ecclesiastical courts there were—some of them mere shops for the sale of "dispensations, licenses, faculties, and other remnants of the

---

[1] Waddington, "Congregational History," p. 742-745.

papal extortions "—but no description of them is necessary here.

All these courts, except the last, were from ancient times, and were spared by the conservative genius of the English Reformation. But that Reformation itself had created another tribunal — higher, more powerful, and more terrible than all the rest. By the Act of Supremacy, which stands first among the statutes of the reign of Elizabeth, and which finally separated the ecclesiastical establishment of England from the see of Rome, the queen was empowered to establish what was afterward known as the "High Commission for Causes Ecclesiastical." Her commissioners, "being natural-born subjects," but otherwise appointed at her absolute discretion as "supreme governor" of the Church of England, were authorized "to use, occupy, and exercise, under her, all manner of jurisdiction, privileges, and pre-eminences touching any spiritual or ecclesiastical jurisdiction within the realms of England and Ireland." By that authority, they were "to visit, reform, redress, order, correct, and amend all errors, heresies, schisms, abuses, contempts, offenses, and enormities whatsoever." As reconstituted, with some unimportant changes, in the latter part of the reign of Elizabeth (1584), the High Commission consisted of forty-four commissioners. Twelve of these were bishops, several were members of the Privy Council, others were clergymen or laymen of lower degree. The commissioners—or any three of them, one being a bishop—were empowered to make inquiry concerning "all heretical opinions, seditious books, contempts, conspiracies, false rumors or talks, slanderous words and sayings;" to punish all persons willfully "absent from church or divine service established by law;" to "visit and reform all errors, heresies, and schisms," and to do many other like things. They were empowered "to call before them all persons suspected" of ecclesiastical offenses, to examine them on their oaths, though (or rather, in order that) in their answers they might criminate themselves, and to punish them, if refractory, by excommunication (a terrible penalty in English law), by fines at discretion, and by unlimited imprisonment. All "sheriffs, justices, and other officers," were to be at their command for the purpose of apprehending or causing to be apprehended any persons whom they might require to be brought before them. This terrible enginery for the enforcement of worship and of religious opinion was employed not in London only—the chief seat of the High Commission—but throughout the realm wherever one of the twelve bishops and two of the other commissioners might choose to hold a commission court.[1] Proceeding, like other ecclesiastical courts, against offenders and suspected persons according to the methods of the canon and civil law, the High Commission for Causes Ecclesiastical might well be called the English Inquisition.

That we may see clearly in what school the more advanced and uncompromising Puritans were studying, and what means were employed to give them right views of church polity, we must look at some instances of individual experience.

The old town of Bury St. Edmunds, in the county of Suffolk, is in the diocese of the Bishop of Norwich. Of that diocese, John Parkhurst, a Puritan Conformist, had been bishop from the time of the restoration of Protestantism by Elizabeth. His ideal of reformation was the ecclesiastical order which he saw at Zurich when he found refuge there from the persecution under Mary. Being himself a diligent preacher, he had been much more intent on having the Gospel intelligently preached in every parish than on persecuting those preachers who were more scrupulous than he about the ceremonies and the vestments. Consequently the diocese, at his death (1574), was greatly infested with Puritanism.[2] His successor, Edmund Freke, was of another sort, and was a

---

[1] The queen's patent appointing the High Commissioners, as the court was reconstituted, Jan. 7, 1583–4, may be read in Neal, i., 160, note.

[2] Neal, i., 92, 128, 133, 134.

bishop after the queen's own heart.   From the beginning of
his administration, the established method of dealing with
scrupulous consciences was perseveringly employed.   Ministers of the Gospel, beloved and honored for their work's sake
in their parishes, were vexed with prosecutions in the ecclesiastical courts, were suspended from their ministry, were
sentenced to imprisonment for six months, for a year, or for
life.   All this, instead of reconciling the Puritan clergy or
people to the system imposed upon them, made them more
obstinate in their scruples and more daring in their inquiries.
At Bury, especially, and in its vicinity, the growing dislike
to the imprisonment of godly men, as a method of church
discipline, seems to have prepared some advanced minds for
the revolutionary idea of churches mutually independent,
formed by the voluntary union of believing souls, and governing themselves by Christ's authority without asking leave
of prince or prelate.

Among the earliest who received and attempted to realize
that conception were John Copping, Elias Thacker, and Robert Browne, all clergymen of the Established Church.   The
first of these, with another clergyman, Tyler, was shut up in
the common jail of Bury for nonconformity (1576), only a
few months, at the latest, after the consecration of Freke as
Bishop of Norwich; and there he remained seven years, while
the bishop and his very zealous commissary, aided by the
High Commission, were using with desperate persistence all
the oppressive enginery with which the Act of Supremacy
and the Act of Uniformity had armed them to put down
Puritanism.   But Puritanism would not be put down.   When
earnest ministers of the Gospel were suspended, deprived of
their livings, silenced, and imprisoned for conscience' sake,
their sufferings and remonstrances (for it was not their wont
to suffer such things without remonstrance) stimulated the
growth of nonconformity in the parishes.   Something of the
English spirit of resistance to aggression, and of the old-time
conflict between the common law and the law administered

by ecclesiastical functionaries, entered into the growing excitement.   The bishop found himself in conflict with the secular authorities of Bury, and knowing that his policy was the queen's policy, he sent forward charges (1581) to the Lord Treasurer Burleigh against the justices who had used their influence, official and personal, in favor of the nonconforming clergy and against his proceedings.   Four of those magistrates, for themselves and their associates, replied to the bishop's complaint.   Professing their own loyalty, and affirming that they "countenanced none but such as are lovers of God's true religion and dutiful subjects to her majesty," they charged the bishop with sinister intentions in not removing Copping and Tyler from the common jail in Bury, where they had been so many years imprisoned, to his own prison in Norwich; and they boldly maintained that he, by his pertinacious attempts to introduce into the parishes of his diocese clergymen too ignorant to preach, had shown himself a patron of ignorance in the church and an enemy to the preaching of the Word of God.   The bishop's complaint against the justices appears to have been dismissed, but there was no relief for the prisoners, and — though Lord Burleigh himself interceded by writing to the bishop —no less rigor in the treatment of nonconforming clergymen.

Robert Browne was a young man of impetuous and reckless zeal, and eloquent in popular discourse, but of an imperious, passionate, and unstable disposition.   He was an active and daring agitator, not only in that diocese, but in other parts of England.   More than once he had been called to account for ecclesiastical irregularities; and once, at least, he had been imprisoned at Norwich by the High Commission Court.   But being a kinsman of the queen's most trusted and most powerful counselor, Lord Burleigh, he had a measure of impunity from which he seems to have taken courage.   Not long after his release, in compliance with Lord Burleigh's request to the bishop, from the prison

F

at Norwich, he was constrained to flee from England, as many had done already, and at Middleburg, in the Dutch republic, he gathered a church of English exiles, chiefly friends of his who had accompanied him (1582). At that place he printed two books or pamphlets, setting forth distinctly the new idea of church reformation, which was nothing else than to restore the purely voluntary Christianity of the New Testament. Such books could not have been printed in England but by stealth; yet they were printed for circulation and effect in England, as Tyndale's translation of the New Testament had been more than fifty years before that time.

The first of those books was entitled "A Book which showeth the Life and Manners of all true Christians, and how unlike they are unto Turks and Papists and Heathen Folk. Also, the Points and Parts of all Divinity—that is, of the Revealed Will and Word of God—are declared by their several Definitions and Divisions." Some of the statements and definitions in that book are worthy to be remembered, as indicating the depth and breadth of the new reformation which was contemplated, and the simplicity of its idea.

"The New Testament," said this radical reformer, "which is called the Gospel, or glad tidings, is a joyful and plain declaring and teaching, by a due message, of the remedy of our miseries through Christ our Redeemer, who is come in the flesh, a Saviour unto those which worthily receive this message, and hath fulfilled the old ceremonies." Christianity, in this rudimental definition of it, is a simple thing—not a hierarchy, not a ritual, not a system of dogmas—but the intelligible story of a remedy for human miseries through Christ our Redeemer, who by his coming has fulfilled, and by fulfilling has abolished, the old ritual prophetic of his redeeming work; and "all true Christians" are all those who worthily receive the story.

But is there, then, no church? Is Christianity nothing more than a story told and received? Is the church noth-

ing more than the unorganized and invisible unity of those
who receive the Gospel?   Yes.   "The church planted or
gathered [the organized institution] is a company or number
of Christians or believers, which, by a willing covenant made
with their God, are under the government of God and Christ,
and keep his laws in one holy communion, because Christ
hath redeemed them unto holiness and happiness forever,
from which they were fallen by the sin of Adam."   "The
church government is the Lordship of Christ in the communion of his offices; whereby his people obey his will, and
have mutual use of their graces and callings, to further their
godliness and welfare."

If the church is no more than this—if the government of
the church is only the free obedience of Christ's people to
his will in mutual helpfulness, in order to their godliness and
welfare—where and what is Christ's kingdom?   How can he
have a kingdom without ecclesiastical courts and canon law?
"The kingdom of Christ," in the programme of that new
reformation, "is his office of government, whereby he useth
the obedience of his people to keep his laws and commandments to their salvation and welfare."   "The kingdom of
Antichrist is his government confirmed by the civil magistrate, whereby he abuseth the obedience of the people to
keep his evil laws and customs to their own damnation."
The pope, then, may be dethroned; but if the civil magistrate
come into his place to confirm the "evil laws and customs"
which the apostasy brought in, the kingdom of Antichrist
remains.

What, then, of excommunication?   Are there to be neither
consistory courts nor presbyterial judicatures in the kingdom of Christ?   Are there to be no "spiritual" penalties of
fine and imprisonment inflicted in the name of the church—
no sentence of excommunication with consequent civil disabilities?   What is to be substituted for all this?   Simply
the voluntary action of the church freely separating itself
from offenders and the offenders from itself.   "Separation

of the open, willful, or grievous offenders is a dutifulness of the church in withholding from them the Christian communion and fellowship, by pronouncing and showing the covenant of Christian communion to be broken by their grievous wickedness, and that with mourning, fasting, and prayer for them, and denouncing God's judgment against them."

Is the church, then, an ungoverned and unorganized assembly? No; it is served and guided by officers of its own choice, each with appropriate and definite duties. "A *pastor* is a person having office and message of God, for exhorting and moving especially, and guiding accordingly; for the which he is tried to be meet, and thereto is duly chosen by the church which calleth him, or received by obedience where he planteth the church." "A *teacher* of doctrine is a person having office and message of God for teaching especially, and guiding accordingly, with less gift to exhort and apply; for the which he is tried to be meet, and thereto is duly chosen by the church which calleth him, or received by obedience where he planteth the church." "An *elder*, or more forward in gift, is a person having office and message of God for oversight and counsel, and redressing things amiss;" and he, too, is in like manner tried and chosen by the church. "The *reliever* is a person having office of God, to provide, gather, and bestow the gifts and liberality of the church as there is need; to the which office he is tried and received as meet." "The *widow* is a person having office of God to pray for the church, and to visit and minister to those which are afflicted and distressed in the church; for the which she is tried and received as meet."

But what service does this utopian church render to the queen? What obedience does it pay to those who rule by her commission and under her supreme authority? The answer is not wanting. "Civil magistrates are persons authorized of God, and received by the consent or choice of the people, whether officers or subjects, or by birth and succession also, to make and execute laws by public agreement, to rule the commonwealth in all outward justice, and to maintain the right welfare and honor thereof, with outward power, bodily punishments, and civil forcing of men." This was written, or at least printed, under the protection of a republic; the reference to "the consent or choice of the people" was therefore natural. But the book was to have its circulation and effect in England, and therefore it recognized "birth and succession also" as a method in which "persons" might be "authorized of God and received" to rule the commonwealth, and to maintain its rights, welfare, and honor in peace or war, not bearing the sword in vain.[1]

Of the other book printed under Browne's direction at Middleburg and sent into England, we know little more than its title, which was strikingly significant of the contents. It announced itself as a treatise "Of Reformation without tarrying for any; and of the wickedness of those preachers who will not reform themselves and their charge, because they will tarry till the magistrate command and compel them." The very title was a declaration of war against Puritanism, waiting and agitating for Reformation of the National Church by act of Parliament. It implied that those who would follow Christ in the regeneration of England must begin by withdrawing from the queen's ecclesiastical establishment, and gathering believers into voluntary churches just as the first believers were gathered into churches by the apostles and their helpers.

These two books, printed out of the reach of English laws and English officers, were sent into England; for in Holland they could be read only by a few exiles. At that time Copping had been five years a prisoner "for his disobedience to the ecclesiastical laws of the realm, whereunto he would not yet conform himself, although he had been sundry times exhorted thereto by many godly and learned preachers re-

---

[1] Hanbury, "Historical Memorials," i., 19–22.

pairing publicly to him to bring him to conformity." A child had been born to him there in Bury, and had remained month after month unbaptized, because he had insisted that no mere priest—none but a preacher of the Gospel—should baptize a child of his, and that no godfathers and godmothers should have part in the baptism. It is also reported concerning him that he held many fantastical opinions, whereby he did very much hurt there in Bury," so that "learned preachers," as well as Puritan magistrates, "wished him to be removed out of the prison for preventing the doing of more hurt." On the morning of the feast of All Saints, when the chaplain, as required by the regulations, had "said morning prayer to the prisoners," Copping, embracing so good an opportunity for disputation, called him a "dumb dog," and said that the keeping of saints' days was idolatry. He even said something to the effect that a coronation oath to set forth God's glory directly in conformity with the Scriptures, if taken and not performed, was perjury; and if he did not infer, others made the inference for him, that the queen was therefore perjured. The infectiousness of his "fantastical opinions" is implied in the anxiety of Puritan preachers and magistrates for his removal, and the removal of those who for the same cause were his fellow-prisoners, to the ecclesiastical jail at Norwich; and it may have been the reason why the bishop would not consent to the desired removal. Norwich itself was full of Puritanism, and there, no less than at Bury, imprisoned Nonconformists, if Copping were among them, might take the infection of his opinions as naturally as they might take the jail fever.

When those ominous books made their appearance in England, the diocese of Norwich, especially the county of Suffolk, had already become a field prepared for the reception of such seed; and from the jail at Bury the seed seems to have been dispersed. Elias Thacker, of whom little else is known than what is now to be related, was a fellow-prisoner with Copping, and took part with him and others in the arrangements for putting the books into circulation.   It is not unreasonable to suppose—though positive evidence is wanting — that the relation of these men, and of others whose names have not come down to us, to Browne's attempt, was more than that of accessories after the fact; in other words, that the books were written and printed in conformity with a plan agreed upon before Browne's departure from England, and were the result of consultation among thoughtful and resolute men who had already accepted the theory of separation.   Be that as it may, the agitation thus inaugurated was regarded as a high crime against the government; and for their co-operation in "spreading certain books seditiously penned by Robert Browne against the Book of Common Prayer," Copping and Thacker, having been thus far in the hands of the bishop and the High Commission, were transferred to the secular power, and tried under a charge of sedition (1583, June).   The alleged sedition was that, in the books distributed by them, the queen's supremacy over the church was denied. That they incited the queen's subjects to any rebellion or tumult, or to any breach of the peace; that they denied in anywise her civil supremacy over all persons and all estates within the realm—was not pretended.   But only for holding the church polity of the New Testament, namely, the inalienable right and duty of Christian men to associate, voluntarily, for worship and communion, in separate and self-governed churches — only for putting into circulation certain tracts for the times, in which that theory was set forth and vindicated—those two clergymen were found guilty of sedition, under the ruling of the Lord Chief Justice of England.

One of the archbishop's chaplains, as in duty bound, labored with his two brethren thus condemned to die; but he could not bring them to the desired repentance.   Nor is it likely that the success of his spiritual counsel would have been greater had the time been extended.   It was only a "short shrift."   Thacker on the 4th of June, and Copping on the 6th, died, not indeed as heretics, amid "the glories of the burning stake," like the martyrs in Queen Mary's reign, but only as felons, their sole felony being that they held and published what is now called Congregationalism.   In England, under Queen Elizabeth, Congregationalism was punished as sedition.[1]

The queen and her counselors judged rightly that the principles of the two books were dangerous to the notion of the royal supremacy in matters of religion, and to the system built upon that notion ; for, instead of proposing to amend the system here and there, in the Puritan fashion, and to bring the ecclesiastical establishment of the realm into a better shape, those new principles struck at the root of the tree.   If such principles were to prevail—if a church were nothing else than a society of Christian disciples, separated from the world, and voluntarily agreeing to govern themselves by the law of Christ as given in the Holy Scriptures —if churches were to be instituted at Bury St. Edmund's, at Norwich, and at London, by the same right by which churches were first instituted at Antioch, at Corinth, and at Rome— if England, with its hierarchy, were not a church at all, but only a kingdom in which Elizabeth was queen—the entire fabric of the National Church was in peril.   For that reason it was that John Copping and Elias Thacker were so sternly dealt with.   The purpose was to make an example which should deter all men from any thought of independent churches.

Robert Browne was not a martyr.   He was not of the stuff that martyrs are made of.   The passion that impelled him was the love of agitation.   When that passion had partly spent itself, he did what mere agitators often do as they grow older—he turned conservative, and betrayed the cause for which he had contended.   After about two years in Hol-

[1] Strype, " Annals of the Reformation," iii., pt. i., 15–17, 186, 187 ; Bradford, in Young's "Chronicles of the Pilgrims," p. 427; Neal, i., 149–154; Hopkins, "Puritans and Queen Elizabeth," ii., 280–320. Neal calls these two martyrs "ministers of the Brownist persuasion ;" but neither Strype nor Bradford speaks of them as ministers.

land, he passed over into Scotland (1584), his flock at Middleburg having been broken up, as might have been expected in view of his imperious and impulsive temper. A pastor of such a temper may be a much better man than Browne was, and yet bring ruin upon a much stronger church than that little society of English exiles could have been. In Scotland, the agitator was as obnoxious to the Presbyterian establishment as he had been to Bishop Freke in his native country. The next year (1585) we find him in England again, presuming on the comparative immunity which he had by virtue of his high connection, and soon renewing his work of agitation. Five years after the martyrdom of Copping and Thacker he was vanquished by the civil disabilities consequent on a sentence of excommunication which had been pronounced against him in a bishop's court for the contempt of not appearing in answer to a citation. Thereupon he "submitted himself to the order and government established" in the Church of England, and was restored to good standing, not only in the church, but in its priesthood. By the influence of his friends at court he obtained "means and help for some ecclesiastical preferment," and in a short time after his submission he received a benefice (1591). This does not imply that he recanted his opinions, or made any profession of repentance for what he had done—it was enough that he submitted. He had not even the desperate self-respect which prompted Judas to hang himself; but, like Benedict Arnold, he took care not to lose the poor reward of his baseness. He was the rector of a parish, and received his tithes; but never preached. By his idle and dissolute life he disgraced his ministry; but, inasmuch as he could not be charged with nonconformity, he retained his living. The quarrelsome temper which had broken up his little church at Middleburg vented itself upon his wife in acts of cruelty, and they could not live together. In a quarrel with the constable of the parish, he took the responsibility of beating that officer. Arraigned before a justice for the unclerical offense, he used such violence of speech that he was sent to prison for contempt, and there he died at the age of eighty, a miserable and despised old man, but a beneficed minister of the Church of England, and in regular standing.[1]   He died in the year 1630, when the Separation which he deserted, and for which Thacker and Copping suffered an ignominious death, had founded a Christian commonwealth in New England.   They died in their early manhood; he lived on, and " the days of his years, by reason of strength, were fourscore years ;" yet how much better and more blessed was it to die as they died, than to live as he lived !

---

[1] Fuller, "Church History," v., 63–70.

CHAPTER VI.

SEPARATISM BEFORE THE HIGH COMMISSIONERS.

It was not so easy as Elizabeth and her prelates had supposed to suppress the new theory of freedom in the church. The idea of "Reformation without tarrying for any," as it survived the hanging of its first confessors, survived also the treachery of their unworthy associate.   Only ten years after that hanging there was a bill in Parliament (1593) for a new law against "the Brownists," so called though Browne was no longer one of them; for some new securities were thought necessary against a party that was growing formidable.   On that occasion, Sir Walter Raleigh, arguing against the bill —not that he cared for the Brownists, whom he pronounced "worthy to be rooted out of the commonwealth," but because he valued those principles of English liberty which the bill proposed to sacrifice—made a significant statement: "I am afraid," said he, "there are near twenty thousand of them in England."   Twenty thousand of them in England, only ten years after that hanging at Bury St. Edmund's!

Already the Separation was beginning to be spoken of among the people by another name than Browne's.   Henry Barrowe, "a gentleman of a good house" in Norfolk, and a graduate of the University of Cambridge, became, after leaving the university, a member of the legal profession in London, and "was sometime a frequenter of the court" of Queen Elizabeth.   Governor Bradford has given us that account of him which was current fifty years later among the Separatist founders of Plymouth, some of whom had been "well acquainted with those that knew him familiarly both before and after his conversion," and one of whom had received information from a servant of his who "tended upon

him both before and sometime after" the great change in
his life.

"He was a gentleman of good worth, and a flourishing
courtier in his time."   "Walking in London one Lord's day
with one of his companions, he heard a preacher at his sermon, very loud, as they passed by the church.   'Let us go in,'
said he, 'and hear what this man saith that is thus earnest.'
Moved by the sudden impulse, in he went and sat down.
And the minister was vehement in reproving sin, and sharply applied the judgments of God against the same ; and, it
should seem, touched him to the quick in such things as he
was guilty of, so as God set it home to his soul, and began
to work for his repentance and conviction thereby.   For he
was so stricken as he could not be quiet, until by conference
with godly men, and further hearing of the word, with diligent reading and meditation, God brought peace to his soul
and conscience after much humiliation of heart and reformation of life."   In this process of reformation " he left the
court and retired himself to a private life, sometime in the
country and sometime in the city, giving himself to study
and reading of the Scriptures and other good works very diligently ; and being missed at court by his consorts and acquaintance, it was quickly bruited abroad that Barrowe was
turned Puritan."[1]   Another account of his conversion, given
by one who may have known him as a young man at court,
is that he "made a leap from a vain and dissolute youth to
a preciseness in the highest degree, the strangeness of which
alteration made him very much spoken of."[2]

Long afterward, the life which he lived in his youth was
unkindly referred to as a disgrace to his memory.   Enemies
of the Separation reported that he " was a great gamester
and a dicer when he lived in court ; and, getting much in
play, would boast of loose spending it "—as if there were no

---

[1] Bradford's "Dialogue," in "Chronicles of the Pilgrims," p. 433, 434.
[2] Lord Bacon's Works (Philadelphia, 1842), ii., 249.

such thing as the true conversion of a sinner, or as if the conversion of Augustine from a wayward and vicious life to eminence among the saints were less marvelous or more miraculous than the conversion of that young man in the court of Queen Elizabeth. "That he was tainted with vices at the court before his conversion is not very strange," said Bradford; "and if he had lived and died in that condition, it is like he might have gone out of the world without any public brand on his name, and have passed for a tolerable Christian and member of the church." From the "vain and dissolute" life of a courtier, he was strangely converted to a life of serious godliness. The fact was notorious at the time, as we know from indubitable testimony.

"Barrowe is turned Puritan" was the story among the lawyers at Gray's Inn, and among gay courtiers. Any man who seemed in earnest to do the will of God, taking the Bible for his guide, was in those days called a Puritan. But, as to the question of church reformation, this young man, no longer "vain and dissolute," did not rest in mere Puritanism. His inquiries soon brought him to the more advanced position of separation from all national churches. His connections and the notoriety of his conversion, as well as his talents and his zeal, made him conspicuous among the Separatists; and soon the name "Barrowist" began to be used instead of "Brownist."

The name of Henry Barrowe is inseparably associated in history with that of his friend and fellow-sufferer, John Greenwood. Of Greenwood we know that he had taken a degree at Cambridge, had received ordination from episcopal hands, had served as chaplain in the family of a Puritan nobleman (Lord Rich, of Rochford, in Essex), but had renounced all connection with the so-called Church of England, and, in co-operation with Barrowe, had made himself obnoxious to the ruling powers by his conspicuous activity among the Separatists. He was a young man—probably not thirty years of age — a husband, and the father of a young son, when we find him a prisoner in the Clink prison in Southwark.   The date of his arrest and confinement does not appear.

On a Lord's day in November (Nov. 19, 1586), six years and a half after Copping and Thacker had been put to death for maintaining that Christians in England ought to unite in separate and voluntary churches, according to the New Testament, Henry Barrowe, having heard that his friend Greenwood was in prison, made haste to visit him.   The keeper of the prison took the opportunity of detaining Barrowe without a warrant, and hurried to Archbishop Whitgift, at Lambeth, with the news of the capture.   On his return with two of the archbishop's officers, the captive was conveyed by water to the Lambeth Palace, and underwent an examination before Whitgift and two others of the High Commission; for the business, being ecclesiastical, was not thought inappropriate to the Lord's day.

The examination was far from satisfactory to the examiners, as will appear from some passages which show strikingly what the man was, and what were his principles.

At the beginning, Barrowe found opportunity to allege that his imprisonment by the keeper of the prison, without warrant, was contrary to the law of the land.   He was asked, "Know you the law of the land?"   "Very little," he replied; "yet I was of Gray's Inn some years."   When the archbishop and the two doctors derided his unskillfulness in the law (it being to them ludicrous that an English subject should complain of being shut up in prison without a warrant from a magistrate), he added, "I look for little help by law against you."

The archbishop, proposing that, according to the usage of the High Commission, he should be sworn to answer whatever questions might be put to him, asked him, "Will you swear?"   He answered, "I hold it lawful to swear, if it be done with due order and circumstances."   "Reach a book," said the archbishop, "and hold it him."   With a provoking simplicity, the prisoner asked, "What shall I do with it?"

"Lay your hand upon it, man," said Whitgift. "For what purpose," said Barrowe, asking as if he did not know. "To swear," said Whitgift. "I use to swear by no books," was the grave and resolute reply. Whitgift explained: "You shall not swear by the book, but by God only." "So I purpose when I swear," was the answer. One of the two doctors, Cosins, interposed to inform the prisoner that, if he were a witness in a cause before a secular court, and should refuse to lay his hand on a book and swear, his testimony would not be taken; and thereupon the archbishop added, "Why, man, the book is no part of the oath: it is but a ceremony." "A needless and wicked ceremony," said the fearless respondent. Being reminded that the book in question was the Bible, the firm Separatist answered, "I will swear by no Bible." Cosins cried out, "Schismatics are always clamorous." "True," said Whitgift; "such were the Donatists of old; and such art thou, and all other schismatics such as thou art." Unabashed by their vituperation, Barrowe replied, "Say your pleasure. God forgive you. I am neither schismatic nor clamorous. I only answer your demands. If you will, I will be silent." Then followed more altercation about the book-oath, he maintaining that he would "join no creatures to the name of God in an oath;" and that if it were, as they alleged, "only a custom commanded by law," "the law ought not to command a wicked custom." At last, "the archbishop commanded Dr. Cosins to record 'that Mr. Barrowe refused to swear upon a book.'"

Finding that they could not induce him to take the oath, the commissioners proceeded to interrogate him without that formality; but his answers, though prompt and peremptory, were little else than a continued refusal to become his own accuser—although the archbishop threatened him with the deadly peril of a trial for heresy, which, if he were found guilty, would consign him to the fire. When they proposed to him that he should find security for his good behavior, he professed his readiness to do so in any amount they might require ; but when the explanation was given that he would be bound to frequent the churches of the establishment, he replied, "Now that I know your mind, I will enter into no such bond." The end was that he was sent to the Gate-house prison.

On Monday of the following week (Nov. 27), he was brought again before the High Commission at Lambeth Palace, the Bishop of London (Aylmer) and the Dean of St. Paul's being present with the archbishop. Again he refused the oath. He would not be sworn to answer questions designed to make him give testimony against himself. An informal paper was read containing certain things which he was reported to have said concerning the Church of England ; but he persisted in his refusal. "There is much more cause," said he, "to swear mine accuser ; I will not swear." "Where," cried the angry archbishop, "is his keeper ? You shall not prattle here. Away with him. Clap him up *close*, *close*. Let no man come to him. I will make him tell another tale, ere I have done with him."

Of course Barrowe was immediately conveyed back to his prison. There he remained, "clapped up close," to meditate on the liberty of an Englishman and the theory of the Church of Christ. After four months (1587, March 24), he was brought up for a new examination before a more imposing array of the High Commission. There were present, not only the archbishop and the Bishops of London and Winchester, but also "the two lord chief justices, the lord chief baron, and many others." Again there was the difficulty about the oath. The prisoner would not swear by any books or Bibles, but only by "the Eternal God himself." He would not swear to be his own accuser. He would take no oath but with "great regard and reverence," and "for confirmation" of his testimony if it were contradicted by some false witness. "By God's grace," said he, "I will answer nothing but the truth." At last the archbishop, remembering that "a Christian man's word ought to be as true as his oath," gave up the conflict, and proceeded to interrogate the Christian man before him.   The questions proposed to the prisoner were designed to draw out from him the opinions of which he was suspected, and which were, in the judgment of the inquisitors, dangerous to the church and realm of England.   His direct and fearless answers to the several "articles of inquiry," show clearly enough what the controversy was between him and the church of Queen Elizabeth, and what the crimes were of which Barrowe and the so-called Barrowists were guilty.

1. " In my opinion, the Lord's Prayer is rather a summary than an enjoined form, and, not finding it used by the apostles, I think it may not be constantly used."

2. " In the word of God, I find no authority given to any man to impose liturgies or forms of prayer upon the church; and it is therefore high presumption to impose them."

3. " In my opinion, the Common Prayer "—the form of worship actually imposed in England—" is idolatrous, superstitious, and popish."

4. " The sacraments of the Church of England, as they are publicly administered, are not true sacraments."

5. " As the decrees and canons of the church are so numerous, I can not judge of all; but many of them, and the ecclesiastical courts and governors, are unlawful and antichristian."

6. " Such as have been baptized in the Church of England are not baptized according to the institution of Christ; yet they may not need to be baptized again."

7. " The Church of England, as it is now formed, is not the true church of Christ; yet there are many excellent Christians in it."

8. " The queen is supreme governor of the whole land, and over the church, bodies and goods; but may not make any other laws for the church of Christ than He hath left in his word."

9. " I can not see it lawful for any one to alter the least

G

part of the judicial law of Moses without doing injury to the moral law, and opposing the will of God."

10. The question being, whether a private person may reform the church if the prince neglect it: "No private persons may reform the state; but they ought to abstain from all unlawful things commanded by the prince."

11. "The government of the church of Christ belongeth not to the ungodly, but every particular church ought to have an eldership."

Nothing was more evident to Whitgift and his fellow-inquisitors than that such opinions ought not to be tolerated under a Christian government, and that there would be danger to the realm of England if a man conscientious and courageous enough to confess that he held them should be permitted to go at large. So Barrowe was clapped up again— "close, close"—none being allowed to visit him; and "though he earnestly requested a copy of his answers, the favor could not be obtained."

After another period of almost three months, he was again brought before the High Commission (June 18, 1587); present, the Archbishop of Canterbury, the Lord Chancellor Hatton, the Lord Treasurer Burleigh, Lord Buckhurst, the Bishop of London, Justice Young, Dr. Some, and others. Burleigh began the examination; and, after the first question and answer, it proceeded in this fashion: "Why will you not come to church?" "My whole desire is to come to the church of God." "I see thou art a fantastical fellow; but why not come to our churches?" "My lord, the causes are great and many: as, *first*, because all the wicked in the land are received unto the communion; *secondly*, you have a false and an antichristian ministry set over your church; *thirdly*, you do not worship God aright, but in an idolatrous and superstitious manner; and, *fourthly*, your church is not governed by the Testament of Christ, but by the Romish courts and canons." "Here is matter enough, indeed. I perceive thou takest delight to be an author of this new religion."

Matter enough—no doubt! Hatton, the lord chancellor, was moved to betray his ignorance of religious questions and his contemptuous indifference: " I never heard such stuff in all my life."

Bishop Aylmer, at that exclamation, thought it was time for him to give a helping hand. He interposed with questions about the Book of Common Prayer; and, being unwary enough to reply as well as to ask questions, he denied that his church gave any part of God's worship to any creature. Barrowe's answer was, " Yes, you celebrate a day and sanctify an eve, and call them by the names of saints; and thus you make a feast, and devise a worship unto them."

Martinmas, then, and Michaelmas, and all the rest of the saints' days, must be wiped out of the calendar. Burleigh resumed his questioning. " Why may we not call the days by their names? . Is not this in our liberty?" " No, my lord." " How do you prove that?" " In the beginning of the Bible it is written that God himself named all the days, the first, the second, etc." " Then we may not call them Sunday, Monday, etc.?" " We are otherwise taught to call them in the word of God." " Why, thou thyself callest Sunday the Lord's day." " And so the Holy Ghost calleth it in the first of Revelation."

The grave lord treasurer paused, and Aylmer, eager to defend the church, which had done so much for him, resumed. "We have nothing in our saints' days but what is taken forth of the Scriptures." " In that you say true; for you find no saints' days *in* the Scriptures." " We find their histories and deeds in the Scripture." " But not their days and festivals."

" He is a proud spirit," said Lord Buckhurst. " He has a hot brain," said Lord Burleigh, and proceeded to draw forth from that hot brain more objections to the mode of worship established by law and imposed inexorably on all Englishmen. The stream of talk flowed on till Buckhurst cried out again, " He is out of his wits!"

Barrowe, who probably remembered, better than his lordship, what Festus on a similar occasion said to Paul, replied, "No, my lord, I speak the words of truth and soberness, as I could make appear, if I might be suffered."

Without seeming to notice the interruption, Lord Burleigh went on in his serious way, and drew from the prisoner a frank acknowledgment that we ought to pray that our lives may be such as the lives of the saints were. The acknowledgment was followed up and explained by a protest against being "tied to days and times," and against being "restrained or stinted in our prayers, as to time, place, manner, kneeling, standing, etc.;" at which Lord Buckhurst exclaimed, "This fellow delighteth to hear himself talk." Whereupon Whitgift, silent thus far, began to show his mind and temper. "He is a sower of errors," said the archbishop; "and therefore I committed him."

The undaunted Separatist replied to the Primate of all England, "You, indeed, committed me half a year close prisoner in the Gate-house, and I never until now understood the cause; neither do I yet know what errors they are. Show them, therefore, I pray you."

"He has a presumptuous spirit," said Buckhurst. "My lord," said Barrowe, "all spirits must be tried and judged by the word of God. But if I err, it is meet I should be shown wherein." Doubtless they all felt that in regard to the matters of controversy between the queen's church and the Separatists, it would not be easy to shew that man, so that he should see, wherein he had erred. After, perhaps, a moment's pause, the Lord Chancellor Hatton said, "There must be stricter laws made for such fellows."

At the suggestion of "stricter laws for such fellows," the spirit that can mount the scaffold or march to the stake rather than deny a persecuted truth, uttered itself in the words, "Would God there were, my lord! Our journey would then be the shorter."

Things were taking a very serious aspect. We may suppose that even the frivolous Hatton was touched by that last answer, and was beginning to have some vague feeling of how much deeper than his thoughts about religion had ever gone, must that conviction be which would not be surrendered even if "stricter laws" were made against it. Law had made him a Protestant, and if it should change, it might make him a Papist again, or a Presbyterian, or a Pagan. What sort of a man, then, was this prisoner whose journey would only be the shorter if a little more stringency in the laws should require him, under penalty of death, to surrender his convictions concerning the church of Christ and the worship of God.

Burleigh resumed the examination, and, like a man accustomed to deal with concrete and practical questions, he said to the prisoner, "You complained to us of injustice. Wherein have you suffered wrong?" "By being imprisoned, my lord, without trial," was the answer. How can this be? was Burleigh's instant thought. "You said [at the beginning of your examination] you were condemned upon the statute [against recusants]." Yet Barrowe had not contradicted himself; he had been examined and imprisoned by the archbishop, but not tried; and they all so understood him when, without any explanation, he replied, "Unjustly, my lord. That statute was not made for us." He was right, and they knew it. The Parliament that enacted that law—unjust and unwise—against Roman Catholics, did not intend that it should be an engine of persecution against any true Protestant.

Then said Burleigh, "There must be stricter laws made for you." "Oh, my lord!" was the reply, "speak more comfortably. We have sorrows enough." In his response to Hatton's threat of "stricter laws," the prisoner, without breach of courtesy, had answered a fool according to his folly; but in giving this reply to a similar intimation from Burleigh, he was appealing to a man of larger and more generous nature.

After a few words more about the injustice complained of, his lordship asked, "Have you not had a conference?" Thereupon Bishop Aylmer, without waiting for the prisoner to answer that question, said, "Several have been with them, whom they mocked." Barrowe, having small respect for bishops, contradicted him. "We have mocked no man. Miserable physicians are you all. We desired a public conference, that all might know our opinions and wherein we err."

A public conference! As if it were not the chief end of the High Commission to suppress all public discussion of such themes as these! Whitgift was roused by the suggestion. "You shall have no such conference. You have published too much already; and therefore I committed you to prison." "But contrary to law," insisted the prisoner. The lord treasurer interposed again, "On such occasions it may be done by law. Have you any learning?" Obviously, the question referred to Barrowe's professional studies; and he replied, modestly, "The Lord knoweth I am ignorant. I have no learning to boast of. But"—turning to the archbishop— "this I know, that you are void of all true learning and godliness."[1] "See the spirit of this man," cried Buckhurst. Whitgift, out of temper with a prisoner who had charged him to his face with lack of true learning and godliness, renewed the threat with which he had attempted to terrify the same man seven months before: "I have matter to call you before me as a heretic." That threat meant more than continued imprisonment, more than fines, however exorbitant, more than the gallows: it meant the stake, the iron chain, the heap of fagots, and the fire. Again the stubborn Separatist replied, "That you shall never do. You know my former judgment in that matter. Err I may; but heretic, by the grace of God, I will never be." Such a reply was, in reality, almost a challenge—as if he had said, Prove me a heretic if you can.

Burleigh turned the conversation to another topic. "Do

---

[1] The last sentence of this answer is inconsistent with the respectful tone of all that the prisoner said to Burleigh and to the other lay lords in that examination; but it is entirely consistent with the style of his replies to the two prelates.

you not hold that it is unlawful to enact a law for ministers to live by tithes, and that the people be required to pay them?" The answers to that and other questions propounded an extremely radical doctrine—the identical doctrine with which Wickliffe had terrified the clergy so long ago. Ministers of the Gospel—in Barrowe's theory of the relations between church and state—should be supported not by tithes, nor by any other assessments on the people at large, but wholly by the voluntary contributions of those to whom they minister. The text was quoted, "Let him that is taught in the word communicate unto him that teacheth in all good things"—a rule very different from the law of tithes. "Wouldst thou, then," said Burleigh, "have the minister to have *all* my goods?" "No, my lord; but I would not have you withhold your goods from helping him: neither rich nor poor are exempted from this duty."

The lord treasurer's religion was not much infected with sacerdotalism. For some reason, he threw out a remark more Protestant than the theory which the bishops were upholding in the Church of England: "Ministers are not now called priests." "If they receive tithes, they are priests," was the prompt reply; "they"—who receive tithes—"are called priests in the law." Pedantic Aylmer, not relishing the intimation that Christian ministers are not priests, and fearing what might come of it, thought that the argument for tithes might be helped by suggesting the etymology and origin of the English word priest. "What is a presbyter, I pray thee?" "An elder." "What, in age only?" "No: Timothy was a young man." "Presbyter," said the Bishop of London—who had been tutor to Lady Jane Grey, and had made her famously learned in Latin and Greek— "Presbyter is Latin for priest." "It is no Latin word," said the prisoner, "but is derived from the Greek, and signifieth the same as the Greek word, which is elder." As if impelled to expose more completely the weakness of the argument which he was trying to suggest, the bishop asked one question more: "What, then, dost thou make a priest?" The answer was obvious. "One that offereth sacrifices; for so it is always used in the law."

The High Commissioners present in that court could not but observe the courtesy which characterized the prisoner's answers, bold as they were, to the lord treasurer, the lord chancellor, and the queen's kinsman, Lord Buckhurst; nor could they help seeing that all customary terms of reverence toward the highest dignitaries of the Church were wanting when he addressed the Bishop of London or the Archbishop of Canterbury. As if he were a precursor of George Fox, he had not once said "My Lord" to Aylmer, nor "Your Grace" to Whitgift. Hatton, who was almost a Roman Catholic, but whose frivolous nature was incapable of any religious earnestness, had evidently been impressed with such a defect of courtliness on the part of one who was formerly a courtier. Either in the simplicity of his ignorance, or because he was willing to tease those prelates and to see them worried out of all self-command, he pointed at the bishop and archbishop, and said to the prisoner, "Do you not know these two men?" "Yes, my lord," was the answer; "I have cause to know them." The lord chancellor asked again, "Is not this the Bishop of London?" "I know him for no bishop, my lord." This was Barrowe's explanation. He could honor the nobles of England and the queen's officers representing her supremacy in the state; but he would acknowledge no bishop who was not a bishop according to the New Testament. Hatton, not yet satisfied, persisted in his question, "What is he, then?" The answer came at last: "His name is Aylmer, my lord. The Lord pardon my fault that I did not lay him open as a wolf, a bloody persecutor, and an apostate." So much for my lord of London; next for Whitgift, toward whom the merciless chancellor's finger was directed. "What is that man?" In other words, What is the title which designates his rank and office? Thus challenged to declare his judgment concerning the functionary known as archbishop in an ecclesiastical establishment which was half Roman, and less than half Protestant, the fearless Separatist replied, " He is a monster, a miserable compound; I know not what to make of him. He is neither ecclesiastical nor civil. He is that second beast spoken of in the Revelation"—which "exerciseth all the power of the first beast before him, and causeth the earth and them which dwell therein to worship the first beast, whose deadly wound was healed."

Mischievously or earnestly, Burleigh seemed to be interested in that matter. The question whether the prelacy in the English establishment was of God or only of men — whether bishop and archbishop derived their power from the "King of kings and Lord of lords " by apostolic succession, or from Queen Elizabeth under the laws of England—had already been urged on his attention; and the manner in which that power was used by Whitgift had been the subject of a disagreeable correspondence, and almost of altercation, between the primate and the premier. The statesmanship which was working with consummate skill to govern England, and which found nothing in its great task more difficult than to manage the queen and those obsequious creatures of her will, the bishops, had reasons of its own for saying of a functionary so composite and anomalous as an archbishop, " I know not what to make of him;" and Burleigh, with all his gravity, could not but smile inwardly at the alleged resemblance between that officer and " the second beast spoken of in Revelation." " Where is the place ?" said he; " show it."

My lord's Grace of Canterbury could endure this no longer. While the prisoner was turning the leaves to find the thirteenth chapter of the Apocalypse, Whitgift rose from his seat, and, " gnashing his teeth," exclaimed, " Will you suffer him, my lords?" Thus the examination ended. " Then by the wardens Mr. Barrowe was immediately plucked from off his knees and carried away."

Greenwood underwent a similar examination, and gave a similar testimony. He refused to be sworn by or upon any book, though not refusing to swear by the name of God, "if there be any need." When the commissioners proceeded to interrogate him without an oath (for it seems to have been their opinion that an oath was of no account without a book), they found him not reluctant to tell what he believed, though protesting against the attempt "to bring him within the compass of their law by making him accuse himself." In reply to the question, "Are you a minister?" he said, "I was one, according to your orders," or ordination. Had he been degraded from the clerical order by due course of canon law? No; but, said he, "I degraded myself, through God's mercy, by repentance." They interrogated him on the lawfulness of using "any stinted forms of prayer in public or in private;" on the Book of Common Prayer—whether it was contrary to the Scriptures, and whether it was "popish, superstitious, and idolatrous;" on marriage—whether he had married "one Boman and his wife" in the Fleet prison; on the Church of England, whether it was "a true established church of God"—whether, as governed by bishops, it was antichristian—whether the sacraments therein administered were true sacraments—whether the parish were the church— whether the church ought to be governed by a presbytery, and what the presbytery ought to be. They also touched the more radical topic of voluntary church reformation without tarrying for the prince, and whether the prince might be excommunicated by a voluntary church. Some of his answers may be given here, as showing not only the spirit of the man, but also the character of the movement in which he was a leader, and for which he was a witness.

On the general question of "stinted forms of prayer," or liturgies prescribed and imposed by authority, his testimony was, "It does not appear lawful to use stinted prayers, invented by men, either publicly or privately, from any thing I can see in the Scriptures."

Respecting the Book of Common Prayer (after being assured by the lord chief justice, one of the commissioners, that he should have liberty to call back whatever statement he might afterward desire to revoke), he said, "I hold it is full of errors, and the form of it disagreeable to the Scriptures."

In opposition to the notion which makes marriage a sacrament, and some priestly intervention essential to its sacredness, he denied that marriage is "any part of the minister's office." He held that the contract between the parties to be thenceforward husband and wife made them one under the law of God, and that their mutual consent, expressed before faithful witnesses—though in the case referred to he had offered prayer—needed no priest or minister to make it an indissoluble bond.

When he was asked whether the Church of England—the institution represented before him at that moment by the High Commission Court—was "a true established church of God," he answered, "The whole commonwealth is not a church." When urged with the question in another form: "Do you know any true established church in the land?" he answered, "If I did, I would not accuse it unto you." As governed by bishops, and by the laws then enforced, it was "contrary to Christ's word."

Of the sacraments in the national establishment, he said, "They are not rightly administered, according to the institution of Christ; nor have they the promise of grace:" "If you have no true church, you can have no true sacraments." Yet he held that there was no need of baptizing again those who had received baptism in the establishment. While he was "no Anabaptist," "differing from them as far as truth is from error," his own boy, a year and a half old, had received the name Abel without its being given to him in baptism; "because," said the father, "I have been in prison, and can not tell where to go to a reformed church, where I might have him baptized according to God's ordinance."

To the question, "Do you not hold a parish to be the church?" he answered, "If all the people were faithful, hav-

ing God's law and ordinances practiced among them, I do."
A church would then be constituted by "the profession which
the people make;" and, as for its government, "every congregation of Christ ought to be governed by that presbytery which Christ hath appointed." To him the presbytery
which Christ hath appointed was not the Genevan or classical presbytery which the Puritans would introduce in place
of the existing establishment, but a congregational presbytery—the "pastor, teacher, and elder" in each congregation
of Christ. The church thus constituted, "people and presbytery," would be Christ's church, and ought to practice God's
laws, and "correct vice by the censure of the word." But
"what if the prince *forbid* them?" Then "they must, nevertheless, do that which God *commandeth*."

That phrase, "the censure of the word," pointed toward excommunication. Queen Elizabeth had been excommunicated
by the pope; might not this church government according
to the New Testament do the same thing? In reference to
the presbyterial government which the Puritans were endeavoring to establish, this was a very grave question; for,
under that system, the queen, instead of being by virtue of
her own crown and her baptism the supreme governor of
the Church of England, would be a simple member of the
church, on the same level with every other baptized English-
woman. The crucifix in her private chapel might be complained of to the session or consistory of the parish. As a
woman, she could sustain no ecclesiastical office, not even
that of lay elder. She might be excommunicated by the consistory, and her appeals to presbytery, synod, and general
assembly might be in vain. "If the prince offend," said the
examiners to Greenwood, "may the presbytery excommunicate him?" His answer was, "The whole church—not the
elders—may excommunicate *any member of that church*, if
the party continue obstinate in open transgression." Even
if the prince should have become, by free consent and mutual
covenant, a member of that church, "there is no exception of

persons." If our queen should become a voluntary member of that voluntary church, "I doubt not her majesty would be ruled by the word."[1]

The queen's supremacy in ecclesiastical matters would vanish, and no place be found for it. Each congregation of worshipers freely consenting to be ruled by the word of God would be self-governed under Christ; for "the Scripture hath set down sufficient laws for the worship of God and the government of the church, so that no man may add unto it nor diminish from it." The queen "is supreme magistrate over all persons, to punish the evil and defend the good;" but "Christ is the only head of his church, and his laws may no man alter."

Having given this testimony, the confessor was sent back to the prison.

---

[1] Brook, "Lives of the Puritans," ii., 24—28. The story of Barrowe and Greenwood before the High Commissioners is told briefly by Neal, i., 201, 202, and more at length by Hopkins, iii., 460—469.

CHAPTER VII.

CONTROVERSY UNDER DIFFICULTIES.—NATIONALISM, CONFORM-
IST AND PURITAN, AGAINST SEPARATISM.

HAD not John Bunyan been shut up to dream in Bedford
jail, he would never have found time to write the "Pilgrim's
Progress." His influence would have been limited and tran-
sient in comparison with what it has been for two hundred
years, and will be for centuries of years to come. Witnesses
for liberty and truth may be imprisoned; but ideas that
have life in them find wings and fly abroad. The word of
God is not bound.

It does not appear that Barrowe or Greenwood had written any thing for publication before Archbishop Whitgift
took them under his tutelage, and set them to study in prison
the argument for a National Church, governed by the queen
through her bishops and her High Commission. In due time
the fruit of those studies began to appear. While the years
of their imprisonment were passing, and while the published
account of their bold answers at their several examinations
was provoking inquiry and discussion in various places, Barrowe—though often he could not "keep one sheet by him
while writing another"—found means and opportunity for
the writing of a book, sheet by sheet, which, notwithstanding
the restrictions on the press, was printed in Holland, and began to be circulated in England (1590). It was entitled
"A Brief Discovery of the False Church," and was subscribed
"by the Lord's most unworthy servant and witness, in bonds,
Henry Barrowe." To intimate the relation between the
new establishment and the old, it bore upon its title-page
the motto (from Ezekiel xvi., 44): "As the mother, such the

daughter is."[1] While it exposed in the most unsparing fashion whatever Puritanism had found fault with in the established government and imposed liturgy of the National Church, it went farther and deeper; and—more explicitly, perhaps, than ever Robert Browne had done—it assailed the foundation-principle of every national church, however conformed to the Puritan ideal.

The author of that book was aware of the peril to which he was exposing himself. "The shipmasters," said he, " the mariners, merchantmen, and all the people that reign, row, and are carried in this false church, will never endure to see fire cast into her—they will never endure to suffer loss of their dainty and precious merchandize; but, rather, will raise up no small tumults and stirs against the servants of God, seeking their blood by all subtle and violent means, as we read in the Scriptures their predecessors have always done—accusing them of treason, of troubling the state, schism, heresy, and what not. But unto all the power, learning, deceit, rage of the false church, we oppose that little book of God's word, which, as the light, shall reveal her — as the fire, consume her—as a heavy millstone, shall press her and all her children, lovers, partakers, and abettors, down to hell; which book we willingly receive as the judge of all our controversies, knowing that all men shall one day, and that ere long, be judged by the same."

Professing small respect for what Roman Catholic and Anglo-Catholic theologians call " the notes of the church,"[2] he proposes a more excellent way. " Let us, for the appeasing

It was printed in quarto, pp. 268. See Hanbury, i., 39–47.

[2] "'The time is short' to run the race of Christianity, even when we have entered on it : how necessary, then, is it that we should endeavor to find speedily, as well as certainly, the arena in which it is to be run. It is with such views that theologians in various ages have endeavored to lay down rules for the discrimination of Christ's church by a comparatively short and intelligible process, and these rules are styled *notes* or *signs* of the church."— Palmer, " Treatise on the Church" (New York, 1841), i., 45.

and assurance of our consciences, give heed to the word of
God, and by that golden reed measure our temple, our altar,
and our worshipers; even by these rules whereby the apostles—those excellent, perfect workmen—planted and built
the first churches."

The issue between the theory of the ecclesiastical establishment and that of the Separation, or between Nationalism
and Congregationalism, was clearly stated. Nationalism rests
on "this doctrine,' That a Christian prince which publisheth
and maintaineth the Gospel, doth forthwith make all that
realm (which with open force resisteth not his proceedings)
to be held a church, to whom a holy ministry and sacraments
belong, without further and more particular and personal
trial, examination, and confession.' " In other words, if the
sovereign be Christian, the nation is a church, and all subjects not in arms against the Christian sovereign are church
members. "This doctrine," said the author, "we find, by the
word of God, to be most false, corrupt, unclean, dangerous,
and pernicious doctrine; contrary to the whole cause, practice, and laws, both of the Old and New Testament; breaking at once all Christian order, corrupting and poisoning all
Christian communion and fellowship, and sacrilegiously pro-
faning the holy things of God." Such being the fundamental assumption on which a national church is constituted
and governed by national authority, there are good reasons
for a vehement rejection of it. "First, we know that no
prince, or mortal man, can make any a member of the church.
Princes may, by their godly government, greatly help and
further the church, greatly comfort the faithful, and advance
the Gospel; but to choose or refuse, to call or harden, that
the Eternal and Almighty Ruler of heaven and earth keepeth in his own hands, and giveth not this power unto any
other. This also we know, that whom the Lord hath before
all worlds chosen, them he will, in his due time and means,
call by his word; and whom he calleth, them he sealeth with
his seal to depart from iniquity, to believe and lay hold of

Christ Jesus as their alone Saviour—to honor and obey him as their anointed king, priest, and prophet—to submit themselves unto him in all things — to be reformed, corrected, governed, and directed by his most holy word, vowing their faithful obedience unto the same as it shall be revealed unto them.   By this faith, confession, and profession, every member of Christ, from the greatest unto the least, without respect of persons, entereth into and standeth in the church. In this faith have all the faithful congregations in the world, and true members of the same body, fellowship each with other; and out of this faith have the true servants of God no fellowship, no communion with any congregation or member, how flourishing titles or fair shows soever they make here in the flesh."

What theologians have called the doctrine of particular election—in other words, the doctrine that God, in saving men through Christ, deals not with generic human nature only, nor with nations only, but with the individual souls, one by one, whom he chooses, whom he calls, whom he sanctifies—was incorporated into the conception of the true church in Barrowe's "Discovery of the False Church." The individuality of human souls in the presence of God is their individual responsibility. Responsible each for others by reason of those mutual relations and reciprocal duties and influences which constitute society, all human souls are individually responsible to God. "Now, then, seeing every member hath interest in the public actions of the church, and [all] together shall bear blame for the defaults of the same; and seeing all our communion must be in the truth, and that we are not to be drawn by any into any willing or known transgressions of God's law, who can deny but every particular member hath power, yea, and ought to examine the manner of administering the sacraments, as also the estate, disorder, or transgressions of the whole church; yea, and not to join in any known transgression with them, but rather to call them all to repentance," and even "to leave their fellowship rather than to partake in

H

their wickedness." It seems to have been a saying in those days, by way of apology for not separating from an ecclesiastical establishment that would not be reformed, "Every man eateth to his own salvation or damnation; therefore the open sins of minister or people do neither hurt the sacraments there administered nor the godly conscience of the receivers." The Separatist's answer was, "What sense or sequel is in these reasons? What can be devised more false or foolish? Because every one is to look to his own private estate, *therefore* no man may meddle with another man's, or with the public estate! Were he not as foolish that could be led or carried with these reasons, as they that made them?"

Some description of the true church was necessary to any full exposure of the false church. Is the spiritual commonwealth of Christ's disciples a hierarchy? What offices of dignity and power does its constitution provide for or require? Barrowe's positive doctrine on that point is very simple: "The ministry appointed unto the government and service of the church of Christ we find to be of two sorts, elders and deacons—the elders, some of them to give attendance unto the public ministry of the word and sacraments, as the pastor and teacher; the other elders, together with them, to give attendance to the public order and government of the church —the deacons to attend the gathering and distributing the goods of the church."

The Book of Common Prayer, imposed on all Englishmen with its ceremonial uniformity, as the only mode of worship, was the first occasion of Protestant opposition to the ecclesiastical establishment, and of a demand for more thorough reformation. The more rigorously the vestments and ceremonies supposed to be "popish" were enforced upon scrupulous consciences, the more numerous and the more obstinate were the scruples of Nonconformists. Yet the Puritans, generally, demanded only a reformation of the prescribed forms of worship. Some of them might have been satisfied with a few changes,

others would have accepted no liturgy less Protestant in form
or spirit than that which Calvin introduced in Geneva, and
which had been adopted with only slight changes in the Reformed churches of Scotland and of the Continent. But the
Separatists, as the examinations of Barrowe and Greenwood
have shown us, had taken a more advanced position in the
controversy about the Book of Common Prayer. So radical
was their doctrine, that to them any possible form of prayer,
prescribed by whatever authority, and imposed upon Christ's
churches as a substitute for free and spiritual worship, was
like the interposition of a visible image between the worshiper and God. The discoverer of the false church had no
lack of objections against particular things in the queen's
prayer-book, nor was he careful to measure the language in
which he stated his objections. In some passages the coarse-
ness of his vituperation, though less offensive to English ears
in the reign of Elizabeth than it would be if used in the reign
of Victoria, is such as can not be justified, even if it should
be paralleled with quotations from Luther, who was sometimes more vehement than any Hebrew prophet. But the
stress of his argument against the English liturgy was not
so much against the contents of it—" abstracted out of the
pope's blasphemous mass-book "—" old rotten stuff," reeking
with odors of decay—as against the principle of prescribed
and imposed forms of worship.

"This book," said he, " in that it standeth a public prescript
continued liturgy "—" if it were the best that ever was devised by mortal man, yet, in this place and use (being brought
into the church, yea, or into any private house), becometh a
detestable idol, standing for that it is not in the church of
God and consciences of men, namely, for holy, spiritual, and
faithful prayer." Nay, being not prayer, but a form substituted for the spirit of prayer, it is " an abominable and
loathsome sacrifice in the sight of God, even as a dead dog.
Now, under the law . . . every sacrifice must be brought quick
and new unto the altar, and there be slain morning and even-

ing : how much more in this spiritual temple of God, where the offerings are spiritual, and God hath made all his servants kings and priests to offer up acceptable sacrifices unto him through Jesus Christ, who hath thereunto given them his Holy Spirit into their hearts, to help their infirmities and teach them to say, Abba, Father! How much more hath he who ascended given graces unto those his servants whom he useth in such high places to the repairing of the saints, the work of the ministry, and the edification of the church ! God useth them as his mouth unto the church; the church again, on the other side, useth them as their mouth unto the Lord. Shall we think that God hath any time left these his servants so singly furnished and destitute of his grace that they can not find words according to their necessities and faith to express their wants and desires, but need thus be taught line unto line, as children new weaned from the breasts, what and when to say, how much to say, and when to make an end ?"

"Prayer I take to be a confident demanding, which faith maketh through the Holy Ghost, according to the will of God, for their present wants and estate. How can any prescript stinted liturgy which was penned many years or days before be called a pouring forth of the heart unto the Lord, or those faithful requests which are stirred up in them by the Holy Ghost according to their present wants and the present estate of their hearts or church ?" "Is not this"— this imposing of prescribed forms of prayer upon the churches —"presumptuously to undertake to teach the Spirit of God, and to take away his office, who, as hath been said, instructeth all the children of God to pray, even with inward sighs and groans inexpressible, and giveth both words and utterance ?" "Is not this, if they will have their written stuff to be held and used as prayer, to bind the Holy Ghost to the froth and leaven of their lips as it were to the holy word of God ? Is it not utterly to quench and extinguish the Spirit of God both in the ministry and people, while they tie both them and God to their stinted, numbered prayers ?"

All this is significant as to the divergence of Separatism from Puritanism.   But much more significant are the passages in which the author exposed the attempt of certain Puritan clergymen to institute and carry on a presbyterial government in the National Church.   Such an attempt, having been commenced many years before, was still in progress. Several presbyteries or classes had been organized, meeting secretly, and vainly endeavoring to administer a reformed discipline, which, till a reforming sovereign, or at least a reforming Parliament, should arise, might in some degree supply the lack of really evangelical discipline in the ecclesiastical establishment of the kingdom.   The severity of language with which Barrowe described that scheme and its authors is worthy of notice :

"Let me, in a word or two, give you warning of the other sort of enemies of Christ's kingdom—the Pharisees of these times.   I mean your great learned preachers, your good men that sigh and groan for ' reformation,' but their hands, with the sluggard, deny to work.   These counterfeits would raise up a second error, even as a second ' beast,'[1] by so much more dangerous, by how much it hath more show of the truth.   These men, instead of this gross antichristian government which is now manifest and odious unto all men, would bring in a new adulterate forged government in show (or rather in despite) of Christ's government."   "They, in their pride, rashness, ignorance, and sensuality of their fleshly hearts, most miserably innovate and corrupt" Christ's government over his churches.

---

[1] See *ante*, p. 105.   The figure of that "second beast," which, though "he had two horns like a lamb," nevertheless "spake as a dragon," which "exerciseth all the power of the first beast," which "deceiveth them that dwell on the earth," and "causeth all, both small and great, rich and poor, free and bond, to receive a mark," so that "no man might buy or sell save he that had the mark"—seems to have been, with Barrowe, a favorite illustration of what a state church, pretending to maintain a church government over all the subjects of the realm, must needs be.

"The thing itself they innovate and corrupt, in that they add new devices of their own—as, their pastoral suspension from their sacraments, their set continued synods, their select classis of ministers, their settled supreme council."   As yet their scheme of discipline existed only in the germ, for the only power which a Puritan minister in a Church of England parish had of inflicting any thing like a church censure was the power of privately admonishing and repelling from the Lord's table any gross offender.   Out of this germ of " pastoral suspension from their sacraments" they hoped the whole scheme of a presbyterial church government over the nation might, in due time, be developed.   Barrowe and the Separatists, as they compared that scheme with the model which they found in the New Testament, were of the opinion which Milton, himself a Separatist, afterward expressed—

"New 'presbyter' is but old 'priest' writ large."

No man who had dared to withdraw from the National Church, and to denounce the idea of it as essentially antichristian, could be expected to speak very respectfully of the timid and stealthy manner in which those non-separating reformers were proceeding.   Barrowe did not disguise his contempt of " the weak and fearful practice of some of their forward men, who, that they might make a fair show among their rude, ignorant parishioners, set up, instead of Christ's government, their counterfeit 'discipline' in and over all the parish, making the popish churchwardens and perjured questmen elders.   And for Mr. Parson himself, he takes unto him the instrument of that 'foolish shepherd' [Zech. xi., 15], his pastoral staff or wooden dagger of 'suspension,' wherewith he keepeth such a flourishing as the flies can have no rest ; yea, by your leave, if any poor man in any parish offend him, he may, peradventure, go without his bread and wine that day."

It did not escape the notice of Barrowe that the Puritan scheme proposed an ecclesiastical government *of* the people,

but not *by* the people.   "Their permanent synods and councils," he said, "which they would erect—not here to speak
of their new Dutch classis, for therein is a secret—should
only consist of priests—or ministers, as they term them.   People of the churches [must] be shut out, and neither be made
acquainted with the matters debated there, nor have free voice
in those synods and councils, but must receive and obey,
without contradiction, whatever those learned priests shall
decree.   These synods' and councils' decrees ... are most holy,
without controlment, unless it be by the prince or the high
court of Parliament."   "The ' ancient ways' of the Lord are
the only true ways; whatever is second, or diverse, is new and
false.   This I say, because both these factions (of our pontifical and reforming priests) have sought rather to the broken
pits and dry cisterns of men's inventions, for their direction
and groundwork, than unto the pure fountain of God's word."

"You see how the one side—the Pontificals, I mean—
... reject all claim the people can make, refuting them by
Machiavel's considerations and Aristotle's politics instead of
the New Testament ; alleging, I wot not how many, inconveniences in way of bar.   The other sect, or faction rather—these
Reformists—howsoever, for fashion's sake, they give the people a little liberty, to sweeten their mouths and make them
believe that they should choose their own ministers; yet,
even in this pretended choice, they do cozen and beguile
them also, leaving them nothing but the smoky, windy title
of election only, enjoining them to choose some university
clerk, one of these college-birds of their own brood, or else
comes a synod in the neck of them, and annihilates the election whatsoever it be.   They have also a trick to stop it, before it come so far ; namely, in the ordination, which must,
forsooth, be done by other priests, for the church that chooseth
him hath no power to ordain him.   And this makes the
mother church of Geneva, and the Dutch classis—I dare not
say the secret classis in England—to make ministers for us
in England."

The Reverend George Giffard, who wrote himself "Minister of God's holy word in Maldon" (Essex), "was a great and diligent preacher, and much esteemed by many of good rank in the town, and had brought that place to more sobriety and knowledge of true religion." He had suffered as a Puritan, "there being some things in the Book of Common Prayer which he was not persuaded of to be agreeable to the word of God." For this and other alleged offenses, he had been suspended from his ministry, brought before the High Commission, and imprisoned ; but, for want of evidence to sustain the charges against him, he had been released and permitted to resume his work. Persisting in his opinions and practices, he came again under the censure of Bishop Aylmer, more than two years before the imprisonment of Barrowe and Greenwood, and was a second time suspended from his functions. On both occasions his friends—among whom were some of the aldermen and other official persons in that town—made their earnest petition to the bishop in his behalf, and in both instances he was released and restored—probably because the influence of Lord Burleigh, to whom they represented the case, and whom they persuaded to intercede for them with Archbishop Whitgift, was too powerful to be resisted. What Giffard's position was among the Puritan clergymen of Essex appears from a supplication which twenty-seven of them made, about that time, to the Lords of the Council, and in which, after protesting their loyalty as subjects and their fidelity as preachers of the Gospel, they said, "We are in great heaviness, and some of us already put to silence, and the rest living in fear, . . . because we refuse to subscribe ' that there is nothing contained in the Book of Common Prayer contrary to the word of God.' " Of the names subscribed to that petition, George Giffard is the first. So it came to pass that, notwithstanding the vigilance of Aylmer and Whitgift, that "minister of God's holy word" was still at his post in Maldon, carrying on "the reformation he had made in that market-town by his preaching," and steadily puritanizing the whole parish, when Barrowe sent forth, from his prison, the "Discovery of the False Church."[1]

It was only among Puritans, and in parishes where there were ministers·who felt themselves to be not priests, but "ministers of God's word," that such a book was likely to find readers.   We may presume that in the market-town of Maldon, and in other parishes of Essex under the twenty-seven Puritan ministers, there were some whose Puritanism was almost ready to lapse into Separatism, and to whom the arguments and invectives of that book, or even the bold and incisive answers which the Separatist confessors had given before the High Commission, would be as fire to fuel prepared for burning.   The Maldon preacher found himself called to refute the opinions of Barrowe and his fellow-confessor; and, very promptly, he published " A Short Treatise against the Donatists of England, whom we call Brownists, wherein, by answers unto certain writings of theirs, divers of their heresies are noted, with sundry fantastical opinions." Very convenient was that word "Donatist."   It was a name taken from ecclesiastical history; few of the laity would know the meaning of it, and most readers would assume that it meant something very bad, and that even a godly man was in danger of lapsing into Donatism if he had fellowship with the Brownists.   "There is risen up among us," said Giffard, " a blind sect, opposite to these [the Papists], which is so furious that it cometh like a raging tempest from a contrary coast, so that our ship is tossed between contrary waves.   For these cry aloud that our assemblies be Romish, idolatrous, and antichristian synagogues; that we worship the beast, receive his mark, and stand under his yoke; and, finally, that we have no ministry, no word of God, nor sacraments."   Briefly, the embarrassing question for the Puritans who maintained their connection with the National

---

[1] Brook, ii., 273–278. Strype, "Aylmer," 71–73 ; " Whitgift," i., 152, 153.

Church in the hope of reforming it, was this, If the Church of England is a true church, why is not the Church of Rome a true church? The question which Giffard, by the very title of his book, committed himself to answer was, How is it that those who separate from the Church of England for the sake of a purer worship and a strictly evangelical discipline deserve to be stigmatized with the name of an ancient and maligned schism, unless the Church of England itself have become Donatist by separating from the self-styled Catholic Church under the pretense of reformation and for the sake of throwing off an unwarranted government and superstitious worship? Doubtless his solution of that difficulty was satisfactory to himself, but it did not satisfy those whom he called the Donatists of England.

Another champion of the National Church was already in the field. Even before the " Discovery of the False Church " had been printed, Dr. Robert Some had assailed Barrowe and Greenwood in a book which he dated " from my Lord's Grace of Canterbury his house in Lambeth," and which he entitled " A Godly Treatise, wherein are examined and confuted many execrable fancies, given out and holden, partly by Henry Barrowe and John Greenwood, and partly by other of the Anabaptistical order." Dr. Some had already attempted to defend the National Church against Puritan reformers, and his earlier " Godly Treatise," five times larger than this, will be mentioned in the progress of our story. He had now found that another movement, more revolutionary in its remoter tendencies than Puritanism, was stirring the thoughts of some earnest Englishmen; and as the Reformist preacher in Maldon called those men Donatists whose plans of reformation were more radical than his own, so to this Conformist writer in Lambeth Palace it seemed equally convenient and more efficient to call them by a name which was not only more reproachful theologically, but more alarming to the secular power. He called them Anabaptists. Dedicating his pamphlet to Lord Chancellor Hatton and

Lord Treasurer Burleigh, he complained that "the Anabaptistical sort" were growing bold. "Henry Barrowe and John Greenwood," said he, "are the masters of that college; men as yet "—after so many years of imprisonment—"very willful and ignorant. The way to cure them, if God will, is to teach and punish them."

The two prisoners, notwithstanding the difficulties under which they labored, were prompt in sustaining their part of the controversy. In the same year with the publication of Giffard's treatise (1590), there came forth, printed, doubtless, at some foreign press, Greenwood's "Answer to George Giffard's pretended Defense of Read Prayers and Devised Liturgies." It was a vehement attack on the Puritan party, not only exposing the erroneous principles of those reformers who retained their connection with the ecclesiastical establishment, and recognized it as the church of Christ in England, but even assailing their persons with most uncharitable vituperation. "Railing accusations," however inexcusable, are a natural weapon in such a conflict as that which the Separatists were waging. Overwhelmed with opprobrium from the Prelatists, on one side, and the Puritans on the other, they did not always follow the example of Him "who when he was reviled, reviled not again." That we may fairly appreciate the controversy between Puritanism and Separation, we must see with what invectives each assailed the other.

Giffard's position in the National Church was only that of a lecturer or "stipendiary preacher." A special sermon on a week-day, or in the afternoon of the Lord's day, was called a lecture, and could be preached by ministers whose nonconformity made them unable to serve in the care of a parish. The Puritan clergy were zealous preachers; their chief work in their own estimation was the holding forth of God's word rather than the reading of prayers or the administration of sacraments. The Puritan laity were diligent hearers of sermons, and earnest to have their neighbors hear with

them.   It was natural, therefore, for the sermon-loving inhabitants of a parish, especially in a market-town, to establish a lecture, providing a stipend for the lecturer either by a
temporary subscription or by a settled endowment.   Under
such an arrangement George Giffard was a "minister of God's
holy word in Maldon."   Against him holding such a place,
and yielding only that partial and compromising conformity
to the usurpations of the ecclesiastical establishment, the uncompromising Greenwood gave indignant testimony.

   "He writeth himself 'minister of God's holy word in Maldon.' . . . He hath not in Maldon the credit or room of so
much as a curate, the pastor there supplying his own office;
but he is brought in by such of the parish as, having 'itch-
ing ears,' get unto themselves a heap of new-fangled teachers, after their own lusts, disliking and watching the ministry that is set over them, to which, notwithstanding, in hypocrisy and for fear of the world, they join in prayer and
sacraments, and pay tithes and maintenance as to the proper
minister.   To such people, being rich and able to pay them
well, these sectary precise 'preachers' run for their hire and
wages, but chiefly for vain glory and worldly ostentation.
And there they teach and preach . . . for the most part under some dumb and plurified pastor, from whom, as from insufficient and blind guides, they withdraw not the people. . . .
Yet, for their own estimation, advantage, and entertainment,
they will by all subtle means, underhand, seek to alienate
the hearts and minds of this forward and best-inclined people from these their pastors, and slily to draw them unto
themselves.

   "Long it were to relate their arts and engines whereby
they hunt and entangle poor souls; their counterfeit shows
of holiness . . . austereness of manners, preciseness in trifles,
large conscience in matters of greatest weight—especially of
any danger; straining at a gnat and swallowing a camel;
hatred and thundering against some sin; tolerating, yea, col-
oring some other in some special persons . . . holding and with-

holding the known truth of God in respect of times, places, and persons . . . under the color of peace, Christian policy, and wisdom.

" Hence arise these schisms and sects in the Church of England ; some holding with these ' preachers,' who make a show as though they sought a sincere reformation of all things according to the Gospel of Christ, and yet both execute a false ministry themselves, and . . . stand under that throne of Antichrist (the bishops, their courts and accomplices, and all those detestable enormities) which they should have utterly removed, and not reformed. And these are, hereupon, called Precisians, or ' Puritans,' and now lately ' Martinists.'   The other side are the ' Pontificals,' that in all things hold and jump with the time, and are ready to justify whatever is or shall be by public authority established ; and with these hold all the rabble of atheists, dissembling papists, cold and lukewarm Protestants, libertines, dissolute, and facinorous persons, and such as have no knowledge or fear of God."   These opposite parties are like " that ancient sect of the Pharisees and Sadducees—the one in preciseness, outward show of holiness, hypocrisy, vain glory, covetousness, resembling, or rather exceeding the Pharisees ; the other, in their whole religion and dissolute conversation, like unto the Sadducees, looking for no resurrection, judgment, or life to come—confessing God with their lips, and serving him after their careless manner, but denying him in their heart, yea, openly in their deeds, as their whole life and all their works declare."

Such vehemence of vituperation was, doubtless, too generally characteristic of those earliest Separatists.   To conceal this, or to overlook it, would be inconsistent with the truth of history.   Greenwood, and others like him, used the same violence of speech concerning their adversaries—whom they held to be adversaries of truth—which their adversaries used toward them, and which Luther and the Reformers used concerning the pope and the upholders of his power.   When a

Separatist confessor, testifying and suffering for the universal priesthood of Christ's redeemed ones, and for their right to associate in free and self-governed churches, cries out of his prison against Puritan lecturers in the Church of England, and calls them "these Pharisee-sectary-teachers," "these stipendiary, roving predicants, that have no certain office or place assigned them in their church, but, like wandering stars, remove from place to place for their greatest advantage and best entertainment," we seem to hear in these harsh tones a voice like that of Knox or of Wycliffe.

The great offense of those whom Giffard insisted on calling "Brownists," in spite of their disclaimer, was that they disowned the National Church, and withdrew from it.   Giffard had said of them, "They can not, but with heresies and most heinous injury and inordinate dealing, condemn a church as quite divorced and separate from Christ, for such corruptions and imperfections in God's worship as be not fundamental nor destroy the substance."   Greenwood replied, "We never condemned any true church for any fault whatsoever, knowing that where true faith is, there is repentance, and where true faith and repentance are, there is remission of all sins."   But "for their idolatry, confusion, sacrilege, false and antichristian ministry and government, obstinacy in all these sins, hatred of the truth, and persecution of Christ's servants, we have proved the Church of England not to be the true, but the malignant church. . . . We but discover their sins and show their estate by the word of God, refraining from and witnessing against their abominations, as we are commanded by that voice from heaven, 'Go out of her, my people, that ye communicate not in her sins, and that ye receive not of her plagues.' . . . Let her shipmasters, then, her mariners, merchantmen, enchanters, and false prophets, utter and retail her wares—deck and adorn her with the scarlet, purple, gold, silver, jewels, and ornaments of the true tabernacle; let them, in her, offer up their sacrifices, their beasts, sheep, meal, wine, oil, their odors, ointments, and frankincense ; let them daub and undershore her, build and reform her — until the storm of the Lord's wrath break forth, the morning whereof all these divines shall not foresee . . . until the wall and the daubers be no more. But let the wise, that are warned and see the evil, fear and depart from the same; so shall they preserve their own souls as a prey, and the Lord shall bring them among his redeemed to Zion 'with praise,' and 'everlasting joy' shall be upon their heads; 'they shall obtain joy and gladness, and sorrow and sighing shall flee away.'"

Another reply to Giffard was prepared by the two prisoners, and was printed (1591) at Middleburg, in Zealand. Barrowe's part of it purported to be, "A Plain Refutation of Mr. Giffard's Book, intitled 'A Short Treatise against the Donatists of England:' Wherein is discovered the Forgery of the whole Ministry, the Confusion, False Worship, and Antichristian Disorder of these Parish Assemblies called 'The Church of England.' Here also is prefixed, A Sum of the Causes of our Separation, and of our Purposes in Practice." Greenwood's contribution to the volume was, " A Brief Refutation of Mr. Giffard's supposed consimilitude betwixt the Donatists and us : Wherein is showed how his arguments have been and may be, by the Papists, more justly retorted against himself and the present estate of their church." The "Epistle Dedicatory to the Right Honorable Peer and grave Counselor," Lord Burleigh, was subscribed, "Henry Barrowe and John Greenwood, for the testimony of the Gospel, in close prison." In that dedication of their work to perhaps the only member of the queen's government whom they could reasonably regard as a possible friend and protector, they complained of the hardships they had suffered, and apologized for the " bold presumption " of defending themselves and the truth, for which they were God's witnesses. "Our malignant adversaries have had full scope against us, with the law in their own hands." "They have made no spare or conscience to accuse, blaspheme, condemn, and punish us."

"Openly in their pulpits and in their printed books—to the ears and eyes of all men—they have pronounced and published us as 'damnable heretics, schismatics, sectaries, seditious, disobedient to princes, deniers and abridgers of their sacred power.'" "No trial has been granted us: either civil, that we might know for what cause and by what law we thus suffer (which yet is not denied the most horrible malefactors and offenders), or ecclesiastical, by the word of God, where place of freedom might be given us to declare and plead our own cause in sobriety and order." "They have shut us up, now more than three years, in miserable and close prisons, from the air, and from all means so much as to write, ink and paper being taken and kept from us." "We have been rifled from time to time of all our papers and writings they could find." "While we were thus straitly kept and watched from speaking or writing, they suborned, among sundry others, two special instruments—Mr. Some and Mr. Giffard—to accuse and blaspheme us publicly to the view of the world, the one laboring to prove us 'Anabaptists,' the other 'Donatists.'" "Wherefore we addressed ourselves, by such means as the Lord administered, and as the incommodities of the place, and the infirmities of our decayed bodies and memories would permit, to our defense; or, rather, to the defense of that truth whereof God hath made and set us his unworthy witnesses."

At the time when these partners in testimony and in suffering had overcome "the incommodities of the place," and notwithstanding the vigilance of their enemies had their book ready in some sort for the printer, and when their manuscripts were smuggled "beyond seas" to be printed, Francis Johnson was ministering as chaplain to the English merchants at Middleburg, being supported by them with a commendable liberality. Like most of the English clergymen who found employment of that sort in foreign ports, he was an advanced Puritan, zealous not only against superstitious vestments and ceremonies, but against the government established in the Church of England. At the University of Cambridge, two years before, he had given offense to the ruling powers by a sermon, after the manner of Cartwright, maintaining that the church ought to be governed by teaching and ruling elders, and implying that any other government in the church is unauthorized. For that sermon he was summoned before the vice-chancellor and the heads of the colleges, and was by their authority committed to prison. Being required to make a public recantation, and refusing to make it in the terms prescribed, he was expelled from the university. He appealed against that sentence, and was then imprisoned again because he would not go away till his case had been decided. The result was that, after a twelvemonth of academic agitation between the Conformist and Reformist factions, he withdrew from Cambridge, and we next find him "preacher to the Company of English of the Staple at Middleburg, in Zealand." The fact came to his knowledge that a book by two Separatists so notorious and so obnoxious as Barrowe and Greenwood was in the hands of printers there; and, as a loyal though Puritan member and minister of the Church of England, he was alarmed at the thought of how much harm might be done by the circulation of that book in England. He communicated the alarming information to the English embassador, and was employed to "intercept" the publication, and to take care that the edition should be destroyed. He waited till the last sheets had gone through the press; and then he executed his commission so thoroughly that he permitted only two copies to escape the fire—"one to keep in his own study that he might see their errors, and the other to bestow on a special friend for the like use." So the great labor of the two prisoners, amid "continual tossings and turmoils, searches and riflings, and with no peace or means given them to write or revise what they had written," seemed to have been in vain.

Yet it was not entirely labor lost. It took effect in an unexpected way, first on the overzealous Puritan who had "in-

I

tercepted " and destroyed the edition. " When he had done this work, he went home, and being set down in his study, he began to turn over some pages of this book, and superficially to read some things here and there as his fancy led him. At length he met with something that began to work upon his spirit, which so wrought with him as drew him to this resolution, seriously to read over the whole book; the which he did once and again. In the end he was so taken, and his conscience was troubled so, as he could have no rest in himself until he crossed the seas and came to London to confer with the authors, who were then in prison."

Fourteen years later, the "intercepted" book was reprinted at Amsterdam. Francis Johnson, banished from England as a Separatist, had become the pastor of a banished church which had found a refuge in that city; and there " he caused the same books which he had been an instrument to burn, to be new printed and set out at his own charge." [1]

---

[1] Hanbury, i., 39–70 ; Bradford, in "Chronicles of the Pilgrims." 424. 425 ; Strype, "Annals," iii., pt. ii., 589–592 ; App., 267–269 ; Book ii., 89–96.

CHAPTER VIII.

THE MARTYR CHURCH: THE JAILS AND THE GALLOWS.

WHEN Francis Johnson returned to England that he might confer with Barrowe and Greenwood in prison, he committed himself to the cause of the Separatists in London, and shared thenceforth in their testimony and in their sufferings. They could not but be encouraged by the accession of a clergyman who had lately been a fellow in one of the colleges at Cambridge, who as a Puritan had suffered imprisonment and loss for conscience' sake, and who, having been as zealous as Giffard against Separation, had given up safety and a comfortable support from an English congregation in the Netherlands for the sake of helping the cause he had opposed. Soon after his coming among them, they proceeded to institute, under his leadership, a formal organization.

Before that time they had held their "secret conventicles" or prayer-meetings, such as we may suppose the Lollards to have held in the foregoing ages. By the government they were held to be a "wicked sect" with "wicked opinions," and, to detect their wickedness, they were watched as if they were a gang of thieves. Some of them were subjected to examination; and from their "confessions," together with certain pamphlets of the time, a statement was drawn up, by the queen's attorney-general, to show how dangerous a sect they were, and how detestable were their opinions. The grave annalist of the Church of England, writing while the facts were less significant than they now are, and when passion had not yet cooled, deemed that paper so important that he inserted it in his history; and so it has come down to us.[1]   It is in some points a vivid picture of the people whom the government of Queen Elizabeth thought worthy of persecution as criminals dangerous to society.[2]   These were some of their nefarious practices:

"In the summer-time they meet together in the fields, a mile or more [from London].   There they sit down upon a bank, and divers of them expound out of the Bible as long as they are there assembled.

"In the winter-time they assemble themselves by five of the clock in the morning to the house where they make their conventicle for the Sabbath-day, men and women together. There they continue in their kind of prayers and exposition of Scriptures all the day.   They dine together.   After dinner [they] make collections to pay for their diet.   And what money is left, some one of them carrieth to the prisons where any of their sort be committed.

"In their prayers one speaketh, and the rest do groan and sob and sigh, as if they would wring out tears, but say not after him that prayeth.   Their prayer is *extemporal*.

"In their conventicles they use not the Lord's Prayer, nor any form of set prayer.   For the Lord's Prayer, one who hath been a daily resorter to their conventicles this year and a half on the Sabbath-days, confesseth that he never heard it said among them.   And this is the doctrine of the use of it in their pamphlets: To that which is alleged that we ought to say the Lord's Prayer because our Saviour Christ saith: 'When you pray, do you say thus,' we answer he did not say, 'Read thus,' or 'Pray these words;' for that place is to be otherwise understood, namely, all our petitions must be directed by this general doctrine."

"For the use of set or stinted prayers, as they term it, this they teach: That all stinted prayers, or said service, is

---

[1] Strype, "Annals," iii., pt. ii., 579–581.

[2] The reader can hardly fail to remember Pliny's famous letter to Trajan concerning the persecuted Christians in Bithynia, at the commencement of the second century.

but babbling in the Lord's sight, and hath neither promise
of blessing nor edification, for that they are but cushions for
such idle priests and atheists as have not the Spirit of God.
And therefore to offer up prayers by reading or by writ
unto God is plain idolatry.

" In all their meetings they teach that there is no head or
supreme governor of the church of God but Christ; and that
the queen hath no authority to appoint ministers in the
church, nor to set down any government for the church,
which is not directly commanded in God's word.

"To confirm their private conventicles and expounding
there, they teach that a private man, being a brother, may
preach to beget faith; and, now that the office of the apostles
is ceased, there needeth not public ministers, but every man
in his own calling was to preach the Gospel.

"To come to our churches in England, to any public prayer
or preaching of whomsoever, they condemn it as a thing unlawful, for that they say, as the Church of England standeth, they be all false teachers and false prophets that be in
it.   Their reason is, for that our preachers, as they say, do
teach us that the state of the realm of England is the true
church, which they deny.   And therefore they say that all
preachers of [the Church of] England be false preachers sent
in the Lord's anger to deceive his people with lies, and not
true preachers to bring the glad tidings of the Gospel.   And
all that come to our churches to public prayers or sermons,
they account damnable souls.

"Concerning the authority of magistracy, they say that
our preachers teach we must not cast our pollutions out of
the church until the magistrate hath disannulled the same;
which they say is contrary to the doctrine of the apostles,
who did not tarry for the authority of the magistrate."
"And therefore our preachers, they say, be false prophets,
for that we ought to reform without the magistrate if he
be slow, for that, they say, the primitive church, whose example ought to be our warrant, sued not to the courts and

parliaments, nor waited upon princes for their reformation. When the stones were ready, they went presently forward with their building."

Other things were set down against them. They abhorred the Book of Common Prayer as " full of errors and abominations." They " condemned as apostates " those who, having been of their brotherhood, had fallen away from them. They even inflicted in such cases a solemn censure of excommunication. They would not have their children baptized in the Church of England, " but rather chose to let them go unbaptized." It " could not be learned where they received the sacrament of the Lord's Supper," and " one who never missed their meeting-place a year and a half confesseth that he never saw any ministration of the sacrament, nor knoweth where it is done." Nor did they marry and give in marriage according to the ritual of the Church of England—" if any of their church marry together, some of their own brotherhood must marry them."[1]

At the time when that statement was drawn up, the London Separatists had not quite completed their organization as a church. The facts that they had among them no celebration of the Lord's Supper, and that they chose to let their children go unbaptized rather than to have them baptized by a parish priest, are thus explained. But encouraged by the accession of Francis Johnson, and confident in his ability to lead them, they determined to become a completely organized church according to the rules and precedents of the New Testament. Cartwright, the great Puritan, had said not long before to his sister-in-law, who was one of them, and who had argued that the Church of England was not the church of Christ, inasmuch as it had no free election of ministers, " If for this want we be not of the church of Christ, how much more are you not of that church who have no ministers at all, and no election at all?" He added, " There

---

[1] Compare what Greenwood said in his examination, p. 107.

is not so much as one among you that is fit for the function of the ministry by those necessary gifts which are required in the ministry of the word."[1]   This reproach on the London Separatists was taken away when a Puritan clergyman so well known as Francis Johnson joined himself to them.   They had been a church, and had so regarded themselves, for we know not how long a time, each member at his admission entering into a sacred covenant "that he would walk with the rest of the congregation, so long as they did walk in the way of the Lord, and as far as might be warranted by the word of God;" but as yet they had elected none to any office.   It was evidently their belief that the church makes the officer, and not the officer the church.   They had been acting on the principle afterward defined by the fathers of New England—"There may be the essence and being of a church without any officers;" and now they were ready to act on the co-ordinate principle (September, 1592), "Though officers be not absolutely necessary to the simple being of a church, yet ordinarily to their calling they are, and to their well-being."[2]   Francis Johnson, of whom Bradford afterward testified, "A very grave man he was, and an able teacher, and was the most solemn in all his administrations that we have seen,"[3] was chosen pastor; John Greenwood, teacher; Daniel Studley and George Kniston, ruling elders; and Christopher Bowman and Nicholas Lee, deacons. With what formalities those brethren, when elected, were inducted into their offices, does not appear from any document that has come down to us.   But we may be sure of this: They held that "ordination is not to go before, but to follow election," and is only "the solemn putting a man into his place and office whereunto he had right before by election, being like the installing of a magistrate in the common-

---

[1] Waddington, "John Penry," p. 85, 86.
[2] "Cambridge Platform," ch. vi., § 1, 2.
[3] Bradford's "Dialogue," in Young's "Chronicles of the Pilgrims," p. 445.

wealth."[1] Nor could they have been so forgetful of their
own principles as to dream for a moment that the imposition
of prelatical hands, by which Johnson and Greenwood had
formerly been introduced into the national priesthood, was
a reason for not ordaining them to their offices of pastor and
teacher.   Doubtless there was solemn prayer, devoting and
commending them to God.   Probably they were " set apart "
by " the laying on of the hands "[2] [ἐπίθεσις τῶν χειρῶν] of
brethren deputed by the church to perform that service.
Yet it may be that the lifting up of the hands of the church[3]
[χειροτονήσαντες] was deemed a sufficient ordination.   The
persecuted church had its four " bishops " and its two " deacons."

Then, for the first time in that church, there was the administration of baptism.   Seven children, " being of several
years of age," were presented, " but they had neither godfathers nor godmothers."   The pastor " took water and washed the faces of them that were baptized," " saying only . . .
' I do baptize thee in the name of the Father, of the Son,
and of the Holy Ghost,' without using any other ceremony."
Then, too, having their own official ministers of the word,
they could orderly celebrate the Lord's Supper.   It was
with strict adherence to the precedents recorded in the New
Testament, and therefore with the utmost simplicity of ceremonial, that they " broke bread " in remembrance of Christ.
" Five white loaves, or more, were set upon the table.   The
pastor did break the bread, and then delivered it to some
of them, and the deacons delivered to the rest, some of the
congregation sitting and some standing about the table.
The pastor delivered the cup unto one, and he to another,

---

[1] "Cambridge Platform." ch. ix., § 2.

[2] 1 Tim. iv., 13; 2 Tim. i., 6; Heb. vi., 2.

[3] Acts xiv., 23; 2 Cor. viii., 19.   Some churches in England (if I am
rightly informed) ordain their ministers only by "the lifting up of hands."
So eminent a minister as Robert Hall, whose name is among the treasures
of the universal church of Christ, received no other ordination.

till they all had drunken." At the delivery of the bread
and the cup he used the words of Christ set down by the
apostle Paul, "Take, eat; this is my body which is broken
for you: this do in remembrance of me;" and, "This cup is
the new testament in my blood: this do ye, as oft as ye
drink it, in remembrance of me." Nor could he fail to add,
"As often as ye eat this bread and drink this cup, ye do
show the Lord's death till he come."[1] In no English cathedral was our Lord's memorial supper celebrated more fitly,
or more impressively, than in that humble conventicle, "when
the doors were shut, where the disciples were assembled, for
fear of the" High Commission.

How it happened that Greenwood, the prisoner, was present when the church completed its organization—if, indeed,
he were present—does not appear. It may be that he was
there by the connivance of the jailer who was responsible
for his safe-keeping.[2] It may be that, though absent and in
prison, he was chosen teacher in the hope that he would soon
be at liberty. Or it may be that the church, in choosing its
pastor and teacher, remembered them that were in bonds, as
bound with them, and that for that reason Greenwood,
though a prisoner, was chosen to be one of the ministers.
The number of Separatists in the prisons of London was so
considerable, that not far from that time they made a formal
petition to Lord Burleigh, beseeching him to procure for
them a "speedy trial together, or some free Christian conference;" or that they might be "bailed according to law;" or,
if such favors could not be granted to them, that they might
be collected into one prison, "where they might be together
for mutual help and comfort." That petition was subscribed
by fifty-nine prisoners (including Barrowe and Greenwood),
and the names of ten more who had already died in prison

[1] 1 Cor. xii., 24–26.
[2] Some instances of such kindness on the part of jailers toward ministers
imprisoned for the Gospel's sake are well authenticated. Waddington's
"Penry," p. 126, 254.

were appended.[1]   If the survivors could have been brought together in one prison, Greenwood being one of them, there would have been an obvious division of labor between the pastor and the teacher—one ministering to the imprisoned portion of the church, the other laboring in word and doctrine among those who had not yet been cast into prison.

The proceedings which have just been described seem to have been followed by a more vigorous persecution of the Separatists.   In the estimation of those who then governed England, such proceedings—the voluntary association of believers in a church, their election of bishops and deacons according to precedents in the apostolic age, and their administration of Christian sacraments, all in disregard of the queen's ecclesiastical supremacy and of the Act of Uniformity—were atrocious, and not to be borne.   The petition to the lord high treasurer brought no relief to the prisoners; or, if it had any effect, its effect was an increase of their sufferings.   Another memorial, not long afterward, was addressed to the "lords of the council," and was a more elaborate and ample statement of their case.   That paper, entitled "The humble supplication of the faithful servants of the church of Christ, in the behalf of their ministers and preachers imprisoned," may be taken as a formal manifesto from the church, setting forth, officially, the issue between the persecuted and the persecutors.

After courteous expressions of respect, the petitioners, in the first and comprehensive statement of their grievance, took occasion to affirm their innocence and their loyalty to the queen.   "We are," said they, "her majesty's poor, oppressed subjects," "whose entire faith unto God, loyalty to our sovereign, obedience to our governors, reverence to our superiors, innocency in all good conversation toward all men, can not avail us for the safety of our lives, liberty, or goods— not even by her highness's royal laws, and the public char-

---

[1] Strype, iv., 91-93.

ter of this land—from the violence and invasion of our adversaries, her majesty's subjects."

They proceeded by referring to the fact that the queen, as
a Protestant sovereign, had not only permitted the publication of the Bible, but had "exhorted all her subjects to the
diligent reading and sincere obedience thereof." By such
use of the Scriptures, "we," said they, "upon due examination and assured proof, find the whole public ministry, ministration, worship, government, ordinances, and proceedings ecclesiastical of this land, to be strange and quite dissenting
from the rule of Christ's Testament; not to belong unto, or
to have any place or use, or so much as mention in his church;
but rather to belong unto, and to be derived from, the malignant synagogue of Antichrist, being the selfsame that the
pope used and left in this land;" wherefore "we dare not by
any means defile or subject ourselves in any outward subjection or inward consent thereunto." Their withdrawal
from all communion with the ecclesiastical establishment was
to them a conscientious necessity.

But they had not simply withdrawn from the parish churches. They had done what the primate and the High Commission regarded as a much greater sin. "We," said they,
"by the Holy Scriptures, find God's absolute commandment
that all which hear and believe the Gospel of our Lord Jesus
Christ should forthwith thereupon forsake their evil walk,
and from thenceforth walk in Christ's holy faith and order,
together with his faithful servants, subjecting themselves to
the ministry, and those holy laws and ordinances which the
Lord Jesus hath appointed, and whereby only he is present
and reigneth in his church. Wherefore, both for the enjoying of that inestimable comfort of his joyful presence and
protection, and to show our obedience to God's holy commandment, we have, in his reverent fear and love, joined ourselves together in that Christian faith, order, and communion
prescribed in his word, and [have] subjected our souls and
bodies to those holy laws and ordinances which the Son of

God hath instituted, and whereby he is present and ruleth his church here beneath; and [we] have chosen to ourselves such a ministry of pastor, teacher, elders, deacons, as Christ hath given to his church here on earth to the world's end." In this organized fellowship, "notwithstanding any prohibition of men, or what by men can be done unto us," we expect "the promised assistance of God's grace," which will enable us "to worship him aright, and to frame all our proceedings according to the prescript of his word, and to lead our lives in holiness and righteousness before him, in all dutiful obedience and humble subjection to our magistrates and governors set over us by the Lord."

They professed themselves ready to prove against all men that their proceedings were "warrantable by the word of God, allowable by her majesty's laws, noways prejudicial to her sovereign power, or offensive to the public peace of the state." At the same time, they affirmed that the only adversaries against whom they had any special complaint were the clergy—"the officers of Antichrist's kingdom—namely, the Romish prelacy and priesthood left in the land." The persecution which they suffered was carried on in the name, not of the state, but of the church, and the particulars of their complaint to "the lords of the council," against that "residuary Romish prelacy and priesthood," were such as these:

"Their dealing with us is, and hath been a long time, most injurious, outrageous, and unlawful, by the great power and high authority they have gotten in their hands, and usurped above all the public courts, judges, laws, and charters of this land; persecuting, imprisoning, detaining at their pleasures our poor bodies, without any trial, release, or bail permitted yet; and, hitherto, without any cause either for error or crime directly objected." "Some of us they have now more than five years in prison (1587–92); yea, four of these five years in close prison, with miserable usage, as Henry Barrowe and John Greenwood, at this present in the Fleet. Others they have cast into their limbo of Newgate, laden with as many irons as they could bear; others into the dangerous and loathsome jail, among the most facinorous and vile persons—where it is lamentable to relate how many of these innocents have perished within these five years, and of these, some aged widows, aged men, and young maidens—and where so many as the infection[1] hath spared shall lie in woeful distress, like to follow their fellows if speedy redress be not had.   Others of us have been grievously beaten with cudgels in the prison, as at Bridewell, and cast into a place called 'Little-ease' there, for refusing to come to their chapel service there; in which prison they, and others of us not long after, ended their lives.   Upon none of us thus committed by them, dying in their prison, is any search or inquest suffered to pass, as by law in like case is provided."[2]

The "humble supplication" had other details for her majesty's council.   "Their manner of pursuing and apprehending us," said the petitioners, "is with no less violence and outrage.   Their pursuivants, with assistants, break into our houses at all hours of the night. . . . There they break up, ransack, rifle, and make havoc at their pleasure, under pretense of searching for seditious and unlawful books.   The

---

[1] The "jail fever," so common at that time, and long afterward, in the English prisons. See Hopkins, iii., 487–490.

[2] The significance of this fact should be remembered. English law required, in cases of that kind, a coroner's inquest. But a jury, inquiring into the death of an "aged widow," or an "aged man," or a "young maiden," dead in Bridewell, might give a censorious verdict, and might express and stimulate the indignation which pitying souls could not but feel at such cruelties. The traditional jealousy of the people against punishments inflicted by church courts might break out, and the verdict of a coroner's jury might bring on a conflict between the ecclesiastical jurisdiction and the courts of common law. The genius and methods of the English common law are more favorable to individual liberty than the genius and methods of the canon or of the civil law. The Separatists believed that the common law, fairly applied and executed, would protect them. It was natural, therefore, for them, whenever one of their number perished in prison, to desire a coroner's inquest; and it is easy to see why they could not have it.

husbands, in the deep of the night, they have plucked out of bed from their wives and haled them unjustly to prison." " About a month since their pursuivants, late in the night, entered, in the queen's name, into an honest citizen's house on Ludgate Hill, where, after they had at their pleasure searched and ransacked . . . the house, they apprehended two of our ministers—Francis Johnson, without any warrant at all, and John Greenwood[1]—both whom, between one and two of the clock after midnight, they, with bills and staves, led to" prison, "taking assurance of Edward Boys, the owner of this house, to be true prisoner in his own house until the next day," "at which time the archbishop, with certain doctors, his associates, committed them all three to close prison, two unto the Clink, the third again to the Fleet, where they remain in great distress."

Some additional instances of arrest, still more recent, having been mentioned, the petitioners proceeded to complain of the "secret drifts and open practices whereby" their adversaries, the bishops, were seeking to draw them "into danger and hatred." Especially were they aggrieved by the polemic trick of "defaming and divulging" them "as Anabaptists"—"as Donatists and schismatics"—as "seditious"—and "as abridgers and encroachers upon the royal power of the queen." Against the calumny that they were disloyal to their sovereign, they made their protest: "We from our hearts acknowledge her sovereign power, under God, over all persons, causes, and actions, civil or ecclesiastical. . . . We gladly obey, and never willingly break any of her godly laws.

---

[1] The mention of Johnson, as taken by the pursuivants (the "familiars" of the English Inquisition) "without any warrant at all," implies a distinction in that respect between his case and Greenwood's, whom the petitioners had just mentioned as having been "four years in close prison." It may be supposed that at the time, "about a month since," when the two ministers were "apprehended," and "with bills and staves led to prison," Greenwood had been permitted, by the connivance of a friendly jailer, to go abroad for an evening, under the watch, perhaps, of a responsible attendant.

. . . We never attempted, either secretly or openly, of ourselves, to suppress or innovate any thing, how enormous soever, by public authority established; patiently suffering whatsoever the arm of injustice shall do unto us for the same; doing such things as Christ hath commanded us in his holy worship; but always leaving the reformation of the state to those that God hath set to govern the state."

The simplicity of their confidence in the truth for which they were in prison, and in their ability to make the truth appear if they could be heard, is even pathetic. "We can but, in all humble manner, beseech, offer, and commit our cause and whole proceedings to be tried by the Scriptures of God, with any that is of contrary judgment, before your honorable presence." "We confidently undertake both to disprove their public ministry, ministration, worship, government, and proceedings ecclesiastical, established (as they vaunt) in this land, and also to approve our own present course and practice by such evidence of Scripture as our adversaries shall not be able to withstand; protesting, if we fail herein, not only willingly to sustain such deserved punishment as shall be inflicted upon us for our disorder and temerity, but also to become conformable to their line and proceedings if we overthrow not them—we will not say, if they overcome us." To that offer or challenge they appended a modest suggestion of the serious responsibility which the "lords of the council" would incur by denying or any longer deferring "this Christian and peaceable course."

In the mean time—till their cause should be decided after such a hearing—they made petition, in the name of God and of the queen, that "for the present safety of their lives" they might have "the benefit and help of her majesty's laws and of the public charter of the land—namely" (in their own words), "that we may be received unto bail, until we be by order of law convict of some crime deserving bands. . . . It standeth not with your honorable estimation and justice to suffer us to be thus oppressed and punished—yea, thus to perish—before trial and judgment, especially imploring and crying out to you for the same. . . . However, we here take the Lord of heaven and earth, and his angels, together with your own consciences, and all present in all ages to whom this our supplication may come, to witness that we have here truly advertised your honors of our case and usage, and have in all humility offered our cause to Christian trial."[1]

This was not the first memorial, nor the last, addressed to her majesty's council by "the persecuted church and servants of Christ called Brownists." An earlier "supplication," more vehement in its tone, alleged that those "sworn and most treacherous enemies of God," "the prelates of this land and their complices," were then "detaining in their hands within the prisons about London—not to speak of other jails throughout the land—about threescore and twelve persons, men and women, young and old, lying in cold, in hunger, in dungeons, in irons," for no other offense than that of going beyond other English Protestants "in the detestation of all popery, that most fearful antichristian religion," and "drawing nearer in some points of practice unto Christ's holy order and institution." "Of which number they have taken, the Lord's day last past, . . . some fifty-six persons, hearing the word of God truly taught, praying, and praising God for all his favors showed unto us, and unto her majesty, your honors, and the whole land, and desiring our God to be merciful unto us, and to our gracious princess and country." The persons taken were "employed in these holy actions, and no other, as the parties who disturbed us can testify." It is mentioned as a significant circumstance that "they were taken in the very same place where the persecuted church and martyrs were enforced to use the like exercise in Queen

---

[1] Strype, "Annals," iv., 94–98. This supplication, as given by Strype. is without date; but it is believed to have been written in January, 1593. Dr. Waddington ("Penry," p. 105) mentions December 5, 1592, as the time when Johnson and Greenwood were apprehended at the house of Edward Boys, which, the petitioners say, was "about a month since."

Mary's days;" and the petitioners affirm for themselves, "We have as good a warrant to reject the ordinances of Antichrist, and labor for the recovery of Christ's holy ordinances, as our fathers in Queen Mary's days," only a little more than thirty years ago. They complain that the prelates have committed those "threescore and twelve persons" into close confinement, "purposing, belike, to imprison them unto death, as they have done seventeen or eighteen others, in the same noisome jails, within these six years." "Bishop Bonner, Story, Weston"—the persecutors under Mary—"dealt not after this sort; for those whom they committed close, they brought them, in short space, openly into Smithfield, to end their misery and to begin their never-ending joy; whereas Bishop Aylmer, Dr. Stanhope, and Mr. Justice Young, with the rest of that persecuting and blood-thirsty faculty, will do neither of these."

In the conclusion of their supplication, they said: "We crave for all of us but liberty either to die openly, or to live openly, in the land of our nativity. If we deserve death, it beseemeth the magistrates of justice not to see us closely murdered; if we be guiltless, we crave but the benefit of our innocency, that we may have peace to serve God and our prince in the place and sepulchres of our fathers. Thus protesting our innocency, complaining of violence and wrong, and crying for justice on the behalf and in the name of that righteous Judge, the God of equity and justice, we continue our prayers unto him for her majesty and your honors."[1]

There was also a later memorial, written by another hand, less vehement in style than either of its predecessors, but stating the case of the persecuted church with a more convincing clearness. It began with "a brief declaration of our faith and loyalty to her majesty," in ten particulars; and nothing more explicit in the way of profession could be rea-

---

[1] Hanbury, i., 88–90. The date of this document is incidentally indicated by a reference in it to "the Lord's day last past, being the third of the fourth month [June], 1592."

K

sonably demanded. It made "short answers unto two rumors given out against us:" first, "the rumor that we differ from all the land in some opinions, gainsaying not only the bishops and whole clergy, but the magistrates and all the whole land;" and, secondly, "the rumor that we are heretic, schismatic, holding most ungodly opinions." As for the first of those rumors, while they profess "reverence in thought and deed" for the magistrates, they say frankly, "Indeed, we dissent from all our nation in some doctrines concerning the true worship, offices, and government of God in his church;" but they protested against the conclusion that "therefore no prison is too vile, nor any punishment too grievous" for them. "Seeing we have thus laid open our faith and loyalty to God, our queen, and our country, is there no more favor and credit due to us than to languish away in prisons without bail or trial?" To the second, they answered, "Right honorable, this rumor is false. In error it may be that we are, . . . but heretic or schismatic none can prove us." In this memorial, as in the others, their petition was that they might have a speedy trial according to law, or "be bailed out of those noisome prisons" upon adequate security for their appearance to answer whatever charges might be preferred against them.

These petitions seem reasonable to us in the nineteenth century. But there was one comprehensive and (as the lords of the council thought) all-sufficient reason for disregarding them. In the judgment of Burleigh, as well as of Whitgift, the petitioners were obstinate men, who might at any time obtain their liberty by promising conformity and submission to the ecclesiastical laws, and renouncing their pretended right of instituting voluntary churches according to apostolical principles and precedents. It seemed altogether reasonable that such men should lie perishing in prison, and that all the civil rights of English subjects, guaranteed by the great charter, should be broken down for the sake of keeping them there; for there was danger that others might be infected with the same preposterous notions of religious liberty overtopping the queen's supremacy in all affairs of religion. How unreasonable was it in these men that they would not be contented and quiet, but were importuning the council with their petitions!

It was evident that the Separatists were not to be subdued without some greater severity. Men who had shown that, when imprisoned for their opinions, they could not be hindered by their keepers from writing and in some way publishing books against the deepest foundation of the queen's ecclesiastical establishment — men who would pray and preach even in the jails in which they were confined for that identical offense of praying and preaching—were dangerous to the entire system of church government which Elizabeth had set up in England, and was determined to maintain. Neither the High Commission nor the Privy Council, neither the primate nor the queen, could tell whereunto this would grow. The spirit of John Wycliffe was abroad again. The Lollards and Gospelers, whom centuries of persecution under the papacy had not been able to exterminate, and who had fallen in for a while with the general movement of the nation revolting against Rome, were reappearing under a new name, with more advanced ideas, and were resuming their old relations to the government, because the Reformation, as managed by the government, had not been what they expected. Either the principle must be surrendered by which the Church of England had been reformed from a dependence on the pope to a dependence on the queen—the great principle that all Englishmen were to believe and worship according to the dictation of Elizabeth Tudor—or some effective measures must be taken to check the progress of the Separation.

It should be remembered that all the persecution which these men—Barrowe, Greenwood, and their brethren—had been suffering, was purely ecclesiastical. The secular government of England, *as secular*, had taken no part in it. Whatever penalties were inflicted for violations of the Act

of Uniformity were inflicted in the administration of church
government.   There was, indeed, an Act of Parliament recognizing the queen's supremacy in the church and incorporating that idea into the laws of England; but the High Commission Courts authorized by that act were courts in which
the queen's "commissioners for causes ecclesiastical" made
inquisition by ecclesiastical methods.   It was by the ministry of those commissioners that the supreme ruler of the
Church of England exercised "the full power, authority,
jurisdiction, and supremacy in church causes which heretofore the popes usurped and took to themselves."[1]

All that the Separatists were suffering was nothing but
church government by church officers; and therefore they
demanded so importunately that the law of the state, and
the justice meted out by secular courts, should protect them
against the tyranny of what was called the church.

There was a limit to the power of ecclesiastical courts, not
excepting those of the High Commission.   They could punish
by fines and forfeitures—could deprive clergymen of their
benefices—could arrest and imprison on suspicion—could interrogate their prisoner under oath to make him testify
against himself—could hold him in a pestilential jail till he
died, and could then cast out his body to be buried without
a coroner's inquest; but they could not mutilate the bodies
of their victims, nor put them to death by the hangman.   It
was resolved, therefore, that some of those importunate Separatists should be hanged by sentence of a secular court.
The method of suppression which had been employed ten
years before at Bury St. Edmund's was to be tried again.

Accordingly Henry Barrowe and John Greenwood, after
their six years of imprisonment, were indicted, with three
others less conspicuous, "for publishing and dispensing seditious books," an offense which by an Act of Parliament
more than ten years before had been made a felony, and was

---

[1] Strype, "Whitgift," p. 260.

therefore punishable with death.   The statute, like many others of that reign, was aimed against the really seditious rumors and publications which the enemies of the Reformation and of the queen were at the time dispersing through England, in the interest of the Roman Catholic pretender, Mary Queen of Scots.   It was a perversion of the statute to a purpose which the enacting Parliament did not dream of when Copping and Thacker were indicted under it for dispersing Robert Browne's pamphlets in behalf of voluntary churches.   By a similar perversion, the five men above mentioned were indicted for their share in the publication of books against the ecclesiastical establishment of England. The trial was not a protracted one.   Only two days after the indictment they were found guilty, and sentenced to be put to death on the morrow.

From a report made on the same day by the attorney-general (Egerton) to the lord-keeper (Hatton), it appears that one of the five prisoners, " with tears, affirmed himself to be sorry that he had been misled."   He was consequently pardoned.   "The others," said the attorney-general, "pretend loyalty and obedience to her majesty, and endeavor to draw all that they have most maliciously written and published against her majesty's government, to the bishops and ministers of the church only, and not as meant against her highness; which being most evident against them, and so found by the jury, yet not one of them made any countenance of submission, but rather persisted in that they be convicted of."   So found by the jury!   How could it be otherwise? The prisoners had frankly acknowledged their part in the writing and publication of the books; and the jury had been instructed from the bench that whatever was written and published in derogation of the queen's supremacy over all religious questions and affairs—or maintaining that Christian believers in London, under Elizabeth, had the same right of instituting voluntary churches which Christian believers in Rome had under Nero—was " most maliciously written and published against her majesty's government." Nothing was more obvious to all concerned than that those prisoners were heartily loyal to the queen's person and to her authority as a secular sovereign.

The two less conspicuous confessors were permitted to live; but "Henry Barrowe, Gentleman," and "John Greenwood, Clerk," were to die. Barrowe, in the time between his condemnation and execution, wrote a letter, giving an account of the trial and what followed, "to an honorable lady and countess of his kindred," probably the Countess of Warwick. In the hope that his friend might effectively represent his case to the queen, he appealed to her Christian sympathy. There is no evidence that she received the letter, or that, if she had received it, she could have had timely access to the sovereign for the purpose of making the desired representation. But the letter, or a copy of it, was retained among the members of the persecuted church; and, eleven years afterward, it was published in Holland, giving almost all the information now attainable concerning the particulars of the trial and the singular experience of the prisoners after their condemnation to death.[1]

Writing to that noble "lady and countess of his kindred," Barrowe said: "Though it be no new or strange doctrine unto you, right honorable lady, who have been so educated and exercised in the faith and fear of God, that the cross should be joined to the Gospel—tribulation and persecution to the faith and profession of Christ; yet this may seem strange unto you, and almost incredible, that in a land professing Christ such cruelty should be offered unto the servants of Christ, for the truth and Gospel's sake, and that by the chief ministers of the church, as they pretend."

In making the statement of his case, he said: "For books

[1] Hanbury, i., 48, 49; Waddington, "Penry," p. 117, 118; "Cong. Hist.," ii., 79. Hanbury's quotations are from a copy published by Henry Ainsworth at Amsterdam, 1604, in an "Apology or Defense of such True Christians as are commonly, but unjustly, called Brownists."

written more than three years since — after well-nigh six years' imprisonment sustained at their hands — have these prelates, by their vehement suggestions and accusations, caused us to be indicted, arraigned, condemned for writing and publishing 'seditious' books, upon the statute made the twenty-third year of her majesty's reign." Proceeding through all the particulars of the indictment, he showed that there was nothing "seditious" in the books, "the matters being merely ecclesiastical, controverted betwixt this clergy and us;" and then he said, "But these answers, or whatever else I could say or allege, prevailed nothing—no doubt, through the prelate's former instigations and malicious accusations. So that I with my four other brethren were . . . condemned, and adjudged to suffer death as felons."

He proceeded with a narrative of what had taken place since their condemnation; and then, with the urgency of one who prays that if it be possible the cup may pass from him, he appealed to the countess: "Let not any worldly and politic impediments or unlikelihoods, no fleshly fears, diffidence, or delays, stop or hinder you from speaking to her majesty on our behalf before she go out of this city; lest we, by your default herein, perish in her absence;" for we "have no assured stay or respite of our lives, and our malignant adversaries [are] ready to watch any occasion for the shedding of our blood, as we by those two near and miraculous escapes have found."

Two "near and miraculous escapes"—what were they? "Early in the morning" of the day after the trial ("direction having been given for execution to-morrow as in case of like quality," and the night having come and gone with no intimation of "her majesty's pleasure to have execution deferred") preparation was made for the execution of the condemned. They were brought out of the dungeon, their "irons smitten off," and they were "ready to be bound to the cart"—tasting the very bitterness of death—when a reprieve came. After that "the bishops," thinking, perhaps, that their courage might have failed, "sent certain doctors and deans" to exhort them and confer with them. "But," said Barrowe, "we showed them how they had neglected the time. We had been well-nigh six years in their prisons; never refused, but always humbly desired of them Christian conference . . . but never could obtain it; that our time now was short in this world." Another week in the dungeon; and again, "early," the daylight struggling with the fog, Barrowe and Greenwood—the two less conspicuous offenders being left behind—are brought forth to die; again they undergo those grim preparations: they are bound to the cart, and "secretly," along the streets not yet astir with traffic, they are "conveyed to the place of execution"—"tied by the necks to the tree," and permitted to speak a few last words. Let Barrowe himself tell us how they speak: "Craving pardon of all men whom we had any way offended, and freely forgiving the whole world, we used prayer for her majesty, the magistrates,[1] people, and even for our adversaries." Then, at the last moment, when they have tasted again the bitterness of death, there comes another reprieve, and they go back to the dungeon. "Having almost finished our last words," says Barrowe, "behold! one was, even at that instant, come with a reprieve for our lives from her majesty; which was not only thankfully received of us, but with exceeding rejoicing and applause of all the people, both at the place of execution and on the ways, streets, and houses as we returned."

There was another month of waiting in prison, with "no assured stay or respite." Could the prisoners have been subdued by the twice-encountered terrors of death—could they have been brought, by any method of persuasion, to renounce the truth which it was their mission to maintain— could they have been induced, as Robert Browne had been,

---

[1] 1 Tim. ii., 1, 2: "First of all . . . for kings, and all that are in authority."

to dishonor their own testimony by a promise simply of submission to the Church of England—there was no room to doubt that the reprieve would have been made a pardon. But the labor of " doctors and deans," with the gallows in the background of every exhortation and every syllogism, was unsuccessful.   Those prisoners had seen the gallows, and had felt the cord around their necks; but they had also seen a truth which the " doctors and deans " could not see, and for that truth they were willing to die.

An explanation of those successive reprieves has been suggested, which is not improbable.   It rests on the authority of a contemporaneous document—a letter from a person apparently well-informed to a friend.   The first reprieve may have come in consequence of the suggestion in the attorney-general's report of the case to the lord-keeper, and its being kept back till the prisoners were " ready to be bound to the cart " may have been accidental—as, on the other hand, it may have been intended and arranged for effect.   The second is referred to the influence of the Lord Treasurer Burleigh, who conferred with the archbishop, and finding him " very peremptory," " gave him and the Bishop of Worcester some round taxing words, and used some speech with the queen, but was not seconded by any."   Yet his personal influence was such that the prisoners, ' as they were ready to be trussed up, were reprieved." [1]

A certain bill, designed to make the law more effective against the Separatists, had passed the House of Lords, which might have been called in those days the H use of Bishops; but in the House of Commons, where Puritanism was powerful, it had encountered opposition, and had been subjected to amendment.   It was about a month since the last reprieve of Barrowe and Greenwood, and they were still lying in jail and in irons, with " no assured stay or respite," when these

[1] Letter of Thomas Phelipps to William Sterrell.   In the British State-Paper Office, transcribed by Dr. Waddington, and printed by Mr. Hopkins in " Puritans and Queen Elizabeth," iii., 516, 517.

proceedings, so distasteful to Elizabeth and her prelates, were had in the House of Commons. The next day, "early in the morning," the twice-reprieved prisoners were brought out once more; their irons were once more smitten off; once more they were bound to the cart, and hastily driven to Tyburn. Again, under the gallows, with the ropes about their necks, they prayed for the queen and for England, spoke their last words to the people gathered around the scaffold; but there came no reprieve, and so they were hanged.[1]

---

[1] Phelipps, in the letter above cited, adds: "It is plainly said that their execution proceeding [proceeded] of the malice of the bishops to spite the nether house, which hath procured them much hatred among the common people affected that way."

CHAPTER IX.

JOHN PENRY, THE MARTYR FOR EVANGELISM.

EIGHT months before the martyrdom of Barrowe and Greenwood (September, 1592), there came to London, from the north country, a young man of eminent gifts and eminent zeal, who, though he had been hunted out of England into Scotland for his efforts in behalf of reformation, had not yet become a Separatist. Being thrown into association with members of the little persecuted church, he was attracted to them by his sympathy with their afflictions, and soon adopted their distinctive principle of "reformation without tarrying for any." This was John Penry; and the story of his life illustrates the relation between the spirit of evangelism and the principle of voluntary church reformation.

John Penry, or ApHenry, was a Welshman, born in the year of Elizabeth's accession to the throne (1555). At the age of nineteen, he became a student in the University of Cambridge. There his strong religious sensibilities, which at first had been fascinated by the Roman ritualism, were roused and enlightened by the Puritan influences which lingered in that seat of learning. Embracing with his whole heart the Gospel of personal salvation from sin by personal faith in Christ the Redeemer, he seems to have been, from the beginning of his new life, much more intent on a religious reformation, and especially on the evangelization of his benighted countrymen in Wales, than on any questions about vestments and ceremonies or about Church polity. Could he have had the religious liberty which was yet to be achieved for all the subjects of the British crown by ages of conflict, he would have been such a reformer as Whitefield and the Wesleys were in their day—an evangelist flaming with the

ST. ALBAN'S HALL OXFORD (PENRY'S COLLEGE).

love of souls and preaching with a tongue of fire.   Little did he care for questions about prelacy and parity in the clerical body — still less for questions about clerical costumes and the other trumperies of the queen's ritual.   His soul groaned over the ignorance and the sins of his Welsh countrymen, and his longing was that to the poor the Gospel might be preached.   After taking his first degree in arts at Cambridge, he removed to St. Alban's Hall, in Oxford, where there happened to be, just then, more favor for men of Puritan sympathies; and there he proceeded, and became Master of Arts when twenty-five years of age (1586).   He declined the offer of ordination " without a call to the ministry by some certain church," and contented himself with such a license to preach as the university could give.

His earliest publication was printed at Oxford in the course of the next year.   It was, as he described it in his title-page, " A Treatise containing the Equity of an Humble Supplication, which is to be exhibited to her Gracious Majesty and the High Court of Parliament, in the behalf of the country of Wales, that some order may be taken for the preaching of the Gospel among those people: Wherein is also set down as much of the estate of our people as without offense could be made known, to the end (if it please God) we may be pitied by those who are not of this assembly, and so they may be drawn to labor in our behalf."

In an introductory address " to all that mourn in Zion until they see Jerusalem in perfect beauty, and, namely, to my fathers and brethren of the Church of England," he expressed himself with unaffected humility, yet with the unconscious dignity of one who, bringing a message from God, thinks only of the message.   " It hath been the just complaint, beloved in the Lord, of the godly in all ages, that God's eternal and blessed verity, unto whom the very heavens should stoop and give obeisance, hath been of that small reckoning and account in the eyes of the most part of our great men, as they valued it to be but a mere loss of time to yield any at-

ST. ALBAN'S HALL OXFORD (PENRY'S COLLEGE).

tendance thereupon. Hence it cometh to pass that the truth being at any time to be countenanced, none, very often, are found in the train thereof but the most contemptible and refuse of men; and because these also, being guilty unto themselves of great infirmities (and foul sins many times), and not ignorant that affliction is the sequel of earnest and sincere profession, do pull their necks from the yoke, and their shoulders from the burden, the Lord is constrained very severely to deal with them before they can be gotten to go on his message. And (which is far more lamentable) inasmuch as the drowsy and careless security, the cold and frozen affections of the godly themselves, in most weighty affairs, is never wanting—the Lord suffereth his own cause to contract some spot from their sinful hands. These considerations, beloved — but especially the latter — kept me back a great while from this action, which I have now, by the goodness of God, brought to this pass you see. It would be a grievous wound unto me, all my life long, if the dignity of a cause worthy to have the shoulders of all princes under the cope of heaven for its footstool, should be any whit diminished by my foul hands—which, notwithstanding, I profess to have washed, so far as their stains would permit."

With such feelings did Penry enter on his life-work, protesting that God had thrust him upon that work almost against his will, yet comforted by the thought that "the honor of Jesus Christ" was involved in it. "My silence—though speech be to the danger of my life—shall not betray his honor. Is he not a God? Will he not be religiously worshiped? Will he not have their religion framed according to his own mind? Hath he not regard whether his true service be yielded him or not? If he have, woe be unto that conscience that knoweth this and keepeth it secret, or is slack in the promoting thereof."

The one aim of the "Treatise" is announced on its descriptive title-page. The author described the moral and religious condition of his countrymen in Wales, "whose state," said he, "is so miserable at this day, that I think it were great indiscreetness for me to spare any speech that were likely to prevail. Nay, I would to God my life could win them the preaching of the Gospel." He challenged the pity of all the godly for the "scars of spiritual misery" which his book described. He protested that "a conscience must be wrought in the people;" and that, in order to this, the Gospel must be preached to them in their mother tongue by men whose experience had taught them what the Gospel is. He presented the details of a plan for the evangelization of Wales. To the coast, and to the border towns, where English was spoken, preachers should be sent from the universities. Three hundred, he thought, might be found for that service, who would be competent after a little practice. Of these, perhaps a dozen would be Welshmen, capable of preaching in districts where the Welsh was the only spoken language. Besides these, he would have all Welsh ministers who were serving in England sent home to preach in their native tongue. He thought the effect in Wales would be that "a number of the idle drones," the non-preaching incumbents of livings, would learn to preach. But his scheme of evangelism was still more comprehensive. It included something of lay agency, and something even of what is now known as the voluntary principle. "There be many worthy men in the Church of England that now exercise not their public ministry; these would be provided for among us. I hope they will not be unwilling to come and gain souls unto Jesus Christ. Private men, that never were of university, have well profited in divinity. These no doubt would prove more 'upright in heart' than many learned men. As for their maintenance, they whose hearts the Lord hath touched would thresh to get their living, rather than the people should want preaching. Our gentlemen and people, if they knew the good that ensueth preaching, would soon be brought to contribute."

Such was the scheme for preaching the Gospel to his

brethren, the Cambrian Britons, which Penry proposed to bring before the queen and Parliament in a "humble supplication." His petition was in due time presented to the House of Commons by a member who affirmed that its representations concerning the condition of Wales were true. No objection was made to it, and nothing came of it in Parliament. But the book in which the bold scheme of evangelization had been laid before the public was, to Archbishop Whitgift, an inexpiable offense. "Orders were issued, immediately, for the seizure of the book and the apprehension of its author. Penry was thrown into prison, and the strictest injunction given to the jailer to keep him safely. For a month he remained in doubt of the charge that was to be preferred against him "—just as Barrowe was put into prison, and kept there, without any definite charge on which he was to be tried, and against which he might prepare to defend himself. At the end of the month he was brought before the High Commission for an examination like those to which Barrowe and Greenwood were subjected.[1] In other words, he was brought into the presence of Whitgift and other dignitaries to be questioned and scolded like a schoolboy. His scheme was denounced by the archbishop as "intolerable." The underlying idea of the obnoxious book was, "How shall they believe in Him of whom they have not heard, and how shall they hear without a preacher?" Having this conception of the way to save men, the author had intimated that the non-preaching clergy were not really ministers; and that idea, the primate said, was "heresy." Penry's answer was, "I thank God that I ever knew such a heresy, as I will, by the grace of God, sooner die than leave it." Cooper, Bishop of Winchester, interposed : "I tell thee it is a heresy, and thou shalt recant it as a heresy." "Never," said the prisoner, "God willing, so long as I live." After some further imprisonment, he was, for that time, set at

---

[1] *Ante*, p. 94–108.

L

liberty.[1] Evidently enough, such a man was likely to appear again before the queen's High Commissioners for causes ecclesiastical.

We can not but observe a sort of audacity, and almost defiance, in the answers of Separatists when a charge of heresy against any of their opinions was intimated by a bishop of the High Commission. England, under the preceding reign, had seen enough of burnings for heresy; and it would hardly be safe for Queen Elizabeth's bishops to follow too closely the example of Queen Mary's. One instance of that punishment there had been since the restoration of Protestantism. About twelve years before this examination, Smithfield had been illuminated with the burning of two Dutch Anabaptists, whom a sentence from the Consistory Court of the Bishop of London had delivered for that purpose to the secular power, and it may be supposed that the effect on the sensibilities of the people had not been such as to encourage a repetition of the atrocity. When Whitgift attempted to terrify Barrowe by a suggestion of fire and fagots,[2] and when he made the same experiment on Penry, the tone of their answers was as if they had said, " Hang us, if you will—burn us, if you dare."

Certainly that first attempt in authorship had not been successful. The edition of five hundred copies had been seized, and the author imprisoned. What printer would dare to be concerned in the publication of another such book? Under that discouragement, Penry consulted with other advanced Puritans in and about Northampton, where he was then residing with the wife whom he had lately married. Their consultations brought them to the determination that, so far as their cause was concerned, the art of printing should not exist in vain, and that, if they could not have a free press, they would have a secret press. Arrangements were therefore made for that purpose; though on so small a scale

---

[1] Strype, " Annals," iii., pt. ii., 573, 574.   [2] *Ante*, p. 102.

that the entire establishment, when hunted out of one place, could be readily and safely transported to another. Penry's second publication seems to have been the first product of that secret press. It was entitled " A View of some Part of such Public Wants and Disorders as are in the Service of God within her Majesty's Country of Wales; together with an Humble Petition unto the High Court of Parliament for their speedy redress." In its spirit and aim, as well as in its subject, it was like its predecessor. The author had lost nothing of his ardor, and he uttered his mind not less freely than before, ending his petition with these words:

"Thus I have performed a duty toward the Lord, his church, my country, and you of this High Court, which I would do, if it were to be done again, though I were assured to endanger my life thereby. And be it known that, in this cause, I am not afraid of earth. If I perish—I perish. My comfort is that I know whither to go; and in that day wherein the secrets of all hearts shall be manifested, the sincerity of my cause shall appear. It is enough for me, howsoever I be miserable in regard to my sins, that yet unto Christ I both live and die; and I purpose by his grace, if my life should be prolonged, to live hereafter not unto myself, but unto him and his church otherwise than hitherto I have done. The Lord is able to raise up those that are of purer hands and lips than I am, to write and speak in the cause of his honor in Wales. And the Lord make them, whosoever they shall be, never to be wanting in so good a cause; the which, because it may be the Lord's pleasure that I shall leave them behind me in the world, I earnestly and vehemently commend unto them as by this last will and testament. And have you, right honorable and worshipful of this Parliament, poor Wales in remembrance, that the blessing of many a saved soul may follow her majesty, your honors and worships, overtake you, light upon you, and stick unto you forever. The eternal God give her majesty and you the honor of building his church in Wales; multiply

the days of her peace over us; bless her and you so in this
life that in the life to come the inheritance of the kingdom
of heaven may be her and your portion forever.   So be it,
good Lord!"

The one thought ever present to John Penry was the
preaching of the Gospel in his native mountains.   His next
pamphlet, issued from the same press, was an "Exhortation
unto the Governors and People of her Majesty's Country of
Wales, to labor earnestly to have the preaching of the Gospel planted among them."   Perhaps, as he advanced, his vehement zeal grew more unsparing in its censures on the existing order of things, and on those who were responsible for
it.   Yet he protested, "Let no man do me the injustice to
report that I deny any members of Christ to be in Wales.   I
protest I have no such meaning, and would die upon the persuasion that the Lord hath his chosen in my dear country;
and I trust the number of them will be daily increased."
Yet he insisted on his principle, denounced by prelates as a
heresy, that the non-preaching incumbents of livings were
not ministers of Christ.   "The outward calling," said he,
"of these dumb ministers, by all the presbyteries in the
world, is but a seal pressed upon water which will receive
no impression."   In advising his countrymen how to apply
and carry out the principle, he almost reached, unconsciously,
the position of the Separatists.   "The word preached, you
see, you must have.   Live according to it you must.   Serve
the Lord as he will, in every point, you must, or so be forever in your confusion.   Difficulties in this case must not be
alleged, for if you seek the Lord with a sure purpose to serve
him, he hath made a promise to be found of you.   Away,
then, with these speeches: 'How can we be provided with
preaching?' 'Our livings are impropriated—possessed by non-
residents.'   Is there no way to remove these dumb ministers
but by supplication to her majesty, and to plant better in
their stead?   Be it you can not remove them.   Can you bestow no more to be instructed in the way of life than that

which the law hath already alienated from your possession? You never made of your tithes as of your own. For shame! Bestow *something that is yours*, to have salvation made known unto you." So near did he come to the idea, which he had not yet accepted, of " reformation without tarrying for any."

It was not in a frenzied thoughtlessness of consequences that he made this appeal to his countrymen. But the thought of personal danger, though manifestly present in his mind, was overborne by higher considerations. He told the story of that ancient city which, being at war with the Athenians, "made a law that whosoever would motion a peace to be concluded with the enemy should die the death;" and how, when the city was pressed by the besiegers, and the people were beginning to perish with sword and famine, "a citizen, pitying the estate of his country, took a halter about his neck, came into the judgment-place, and spake : 'My masters, deal with me as you will—but, in any case, make peace with the Athenians, that my country may be saved by my death.'" Aware that the enemies of his cause had power to hang him, he said : "My case is like this man's. I know not my danger in these things. I see you, my dear and native country, perish; it pitieth me. I come with the rope about my neck to save you. Howsoever it goeth with me, I labor that you may have the Gospel preached among you. Though it cost my life, I think it well bestowed."

These publications were the more obnoxious to the High Commission because the secret press from which they proceeded was at the same time employed in printing a series of satirical pamphlets bearing the name of " Martin Marprelate." The memory of John Penry has suffered under the imputation of sharing in the authorship of those pasquinades. Doubtless he had much to do with the secret press; but nothing could be more unlike him than any participation in the authorship of the Marprelate tracts, or any sympathy with their characteristic spirit, and there is no evidence that he was in any way responsible for them.   His work was of another sort.   The weapons of his warfare were of another temper.   All the authentic indications of his character show us an intense earnestness, a most unaffected seriousness, a singular frankness and fearlessness, and a most transparent simplicity.   It would be unreasonable to believe, without the most conclusive proofs, that he had any connection with the anonymous " Martinists," other than that his pamphlets and theirs were printed at the same press.   He said that he would not "feed the humors of the busybodies who, increasing themselves still more unto ungodliness, think nothing so well spoken or written as that which is satirical and bitingly done against the lord-bishops."   Dr. Some, who wrote against Barrowe and Greenwood while they were in prison, and called them Anabaptists, had previously assailed Penry in a style of insolence which would have justified a severe reply.   But Penry, instead of answering the scorner according to his folly, defended his own positions with a modesty and meekness most unusual in the controversies of those times.   "Unless you alter your judgment," said he, "I can never agree with you in these points, because I am assured you swerve from the truth.   Yet this disagreement shall be so far from making a breach of that love wherewith, in the Lord Jesus, I am tied to you, that I doubt not but we shall be one in that day when all of us shall be at unity in him that remaineth one and the self-same forever.   Pardon me, I pray you.   I deal as reverently as I may with you, retaining the majesty of the cause I defend."   "I would be loth to let that syllable escape me that might give any the least occasion to think that I carry any other heart toward you than I ought to bear toward a reverend, learned man, fearing God."

There was little need of imputing to Penry the authorship of the Marprelate tracts in order to find matter of accusation against him before the High Commission.   In successive publications, to which his own name was always subscribed, he had denounced the established hierarchy, not—as other Puritans were denouncing it—because its methods of government and its forms of worship were inconsistent with Christian simplicity, but for the deeper reason that it hindered and opposed the preaching of the Gospel to the people.   " The least part," said he, " of the sin of our bishops hath been in the maintenance of unprofitable, superstitious, and corrupt ceremonies.   If they would but yield free passage unto the truth, and her authority unto the church, in other matters, they should not be greatly molested for these things.   Our controversies arise, because they are not permitted, with the consent of the servants of God, to smother, persecute, deprave, and corrupt the truth of that religion which in name they profess, and to undermine and lead captive the church of God in this land."   Such an adversary, continually imputing to the ecclesiastical establishment and its rulers the notorious " famine of the word of God," was pre-eminently obnoxious.   The emissaries of the High Commission were on the scent of the secret press which was so dangerous a machine, and he was suspected of connection with it.   His study, at Northampton, was searched in his absence (Jan. 29 O. S. = Feb. 7 N. S., 1589) by an officer of that arbitrary court, who took away with him all such printed books and papers " as he himself thought good;" and then, at his departure, charged the mayor of the town to apprehend Penry as a traitor, giving out that he had found in that search " printed books and also writings which contained treason."

Standing for those traditions of English liberty which were imperiled in his person, Penry immediately published another tract, " The Appellation of John Penry unto the High Court of Parliament, from the vile and injurious dealing of the Archbishop of Canterbury, and others, his colleagues in the High Commission, wherein the Complainant, submitting himself and his cause unto the determination of this honorable assembly, craveth nothing else but either release from trouble and persecution or just trial."   Admitting, frankly, that he had labored to destroy " the wicked hierarchy with whatsoever corruption dependeth thereon," he denied that he had used or sought to use any other force than truth. He made a most earnest profession of his loyalty. "I have been," said he, "all the days of my life at my studies. I never, as yet, dealt in any cause, more or less, in any thing that any way concerneth civil estate and government; and as for attempting any thing against her majesty's person, I know that Satan himself dares not be so shameless as to intend any accusation against me on that point." "The cause is the cause of God: it is the cause of the church, and so the cause of many thousands of the most trusty, most sure, most loving subjects that her majesty hath; whose hearts, by the repelling of this my suit, must be utterly discouraged and thrown down. My only suit and petition is, that either I may have assurance of quietness and safety; or that, the causes of my trouble being laid open by mine adversaries, I may receive the punishment of my offenses. I crave no immunity; let me have justice—that is all I crave."

A few days after that search and seizure, a royal proclamation was issued (Feb. 13 = 23) against seditious and schismatical books. The books aimed at were described as "tending to bring in a monstrous and dangerous innovation of all manner of ecclesiastical government now in use, and, with a rash and malicious purpose, to dissolve the state of the prelacy, being one of the three ancient estates of the realm under her highness, whereof her majesty mindeth to have a reverent regard." Of course, detectives were immediately put upon a search for such books, and for their authors and publishers. The time had come when Penry must find a refuge not only for himself, but for his wife and child. An order for his arrest had been issued from the Privy Council. He fled with his family into Scotland, where he was kindly received, inasmuch as he had not become a Separatist like Robert Browne, who was there five years before, and whose antipathy to the Kirk in the northern kingdom was hardly less than to the Established Church in England.

Puritanism, such as Cartwright had testified for, was predominant in Scotland, and Penry was permitted to preach there.   In addition to his preaching, he translated from the Latin, and published, with a characteristic preface, a theological work entitled " Propositions and Principles of Divinity disputed in the University of Geneva."   But Queen Elizabeth thought that a fugitive for whose arrest an order had been issued from her Privy Council ought not to find safety by going beyond the Tweed, and, at her instigation,[1] the King of Scotland (afterward James I. of England) issued an order (Aug. 6, 1590) that " John Penry, Englishman," should depart from the kingdom within ten days, and not return under pain of death.   But by the friendly intervention of the Scottish clergy, the public proclamation which was necessary to make the order effective was in some way " staid ;" and the refugee remained in Scotland till he had printed for English readers another of his obnoxious books, " A Treatise wherein it is manifestly proved that Reformation, and those who are sincerely for the same, are unjustly charged with being enemies to her majesty and the state."

After more than three years in Scotland, he returned, with his family, to England.   He was not ignorant of the peril which he encountered, the order from the Privy Council for his arrest being still in force.   It had been in his thoughts to obtain, if possible, an interview with the queen—in whom he seems always to have had a most loyal confidence, and to beg of her the liberty of personally preaching the Gospel in his beloved Wales.   It was with some such expectation lingering in his mind that he arrived at London.   Till now

---

[1] In an autograph letter to her " deare brother the King of Scotland," Elizabeth, after entreating him to " stop the mouths, or make shorter the tongues of such ministers as dare to make oraison [prayer] in their pulpits for the persecuted in England for the Gospel," referred him to her messenger for particulars, " beseeching you," said she, "*not to give harbor room to ragabond traitors and seditious inventors, but to return them to me, or banish them your land.*"—Waddington, " Penry," p. 58.

(Sept., 1592) he had been only a Puritan, longing and striving for a further reformation of the National Church by national authority ; but now he was prepared to accept, in all its applications, the emancipating principle of " Reformation without tarrying for any."   Before he left Scotland, he had knowledge of the persecuted disciples at and around London, who, instead of agitating for a reformation of the state church, were attempting to reform themselves by instituting a voluntary church after the manner of the primitive disciples.   To their fellowship he was attracted by his religious sympathies.   When the church completed its organization, he was invited, notwithstanding the recency of his arrival among them, to become one of its officers ; but he declined the service.   " It hath been my purpose," he said, " to employ my small talent in my poor country of Wales, where I know that the poor people perish for want of knowledge ; and this was the only cause of my coming out of that country where I was, and might have stayed privately all my life —even because I saw myself bound in conscience to labor for the calling of my poor kindred and countrymen unto the knowledge of their salvation in Christ."   But though he sustained no office among his brethren, he was active to promote their spiritual welfare.   Sometimes he preached in their assemblies.   Sometimes their meetings were held in his house.   He could not print, but he wrote a " History of Korah, Dathan, and Abiram—applied to the prelacy, ministry, and church assemblies of England ;" which was circulated in manuscript copies, and was, at last, published in a printed edition fifteen years after the author's death.   That book, like his other works on the same theme, was addressed to the Parliament ; but the title of it implies that he no longer recognized the ecclesiastical establishment of England as a Christian church.

On the day which intervened between the indictment of Barrowe and Greenwood and their condemnation to death (March 22=31), Penry was arrested, the place of his concealment having been discovered by treachery.   A few days after his arrest, his wife, accompanied by a friend (a widow at whose house he had preached his last sermon), presented to the Lord Keeper of the Great Seal a humble petition in his behalf.   " Your suppliant's poor husband," said she, " is at this present kept close prisoner, . . . none suffered to come to him to bring him such things as are necessary for the preservation of his life and sustenance—he of himself being a very weak and sickly man, not able long to endure so hard and unreasonable imprisonment without hazard of his life."   " Most humbly, therefore, she beseecheth your honor, for God's cause, in consideration of her poor husband's sickly and weak state, that it would please you to grant your honor's warrant that she may have access unto her poor husband, to administer such necessaries unto him as she may, for the preservation of his life."   The petition was ineffectual; and the incident is on record that the widow who went with that sorrowful wife to stand by her when she presented her petition, was seized and committed to the Gate-house prison, simply for " being with Penry's wife when she presented the petition to the Lord Keeper."

It should, nevertheless, be told to the honor of the jailer, that he seems to have been as kind toward those who were imprisoned for conscience' sake as his responsibility to his superiors would permit him to be.   Penry himself, not long after his wife's unsuccessful petition, said of that keeper of the prison, " They do him injury who say that I have wanted either meat or drink competent since I was committed to his custody."   He thought himself more likely to perish with cold than with hunger.   " My wife, indeed," he added, " can not be permitted to come unto me; she knoweth not how I fare; and, therefore, she may be in fear that I am, in regard of meat and drink, hardlier used than I am or have been."

Having passed nearly two weeks in prison, and knowing what was before him, he began to write his latest counsels and farewells to his wife, to his little children, and to the church.   Strangely, and as if by some special providence of God, those memorials have been preserved to history.   Like the Second Epistle of Paul to Timothy, written from a prison, and when the writer could say, "I am now ready to be offered, and the time of my departure is at hand," they are full of what no devoutly Christian soul can fail to recognize as, in some true sense, a divine inspiration.   As we read them, we hear the sighing of the prisoner, we feel the beating of his heart, we catch, as from his eye, the gleam of his heroic constancy.   Those testamentary letters of his can hardly be matched in all the martyrology of Christendom for unaffected and unconscious grandeur of Christian faith, or for utterances of tenderness rippling the calm surface with gushes from "unsounded deeps" of human sorrow.

The letter to his wife was dated on the fifteenth day of his imprisonment (April 6).   While it is too long to be introduced without abridgment into this narrative, some portions of it must have place as illustrations of what the man was, and what the cause in which he suffered:

"To my beloved wife, Hellenor Penry, partaker with me in this life of the sufferings of the Gospel of the kingdom and patience of Jesus Christ, and resting with me in undoubted hope of that glory which shall be revealed—all strength and comfort, with all other spiritual graces, be multiplied through Jesus Christ my Lord.

"I see my blood laid for, my beloved, and so my days and testimony drawing to an end, for aught I know ; and therefore I think it my duty to leave behind me this testimony of my love to so dear a sister and so loving a wife, in the Lord, as you have been to me.

"First, then, I beseech you, stand fast in the truth which you and I profess at this present in much outward discouragement and danger.   Let nothing draw you to be subject unto Antichrist, in any of his ordinances.   Let your soul and your body be far from those assemblies which yield either

known or secret submission unto the ordinances of the 'beast'
—that is, to receive his 'mark' either in the right hand or
in the forehead." . . .

"Again, my beloved, continue a member of that holy society whereof you and I are; where the Lord in his ordinances reigneth: for here, and in all such assemblies, the
Lord dwelleth by the presence and power of his Spirit. Here
he is a mighty protector, and a defense ready at hand; and
his ordinances, you know, he hath commanded to be greatly observed. Our souls are to rejoice in those ways more
than in all substance and treasure, and the loving kindness
of the Eternal is forever toward them, and their seed, that remember his ordinances to do them." . . .

"My dear wife and sister, look not at any earthly thing;
consecrate yourself wholly—both soul and body, husband,
children, and whatsoever you have — unto the Lord your
God. Let them not be dearer unto you than God's service
and worship. Know it to be an unspeakable preferment for
you that he vouchsafeth to take either yourself or any of
yours to suffer afflictions with him and his Gospel. . . . Fear
not the want of outward things. He careth for you. The
Lord is my God and yours, and the God of our seed. I know,
if you and our poor children continue, that you shall see a
blessed reward in this life for those small and weak sufferings of ours for the interest and right of Christ Jesus; for I
am assured that the Lord will give a breathing time of comfortable rest unto his poor church in this life. In the mean
time, wait patiently the Lord's leisure." . . .

"Pray with your poor family and children morning and
evening, as you do. Instruct them and your maid in the good
ways of God, so that no day pass over your head wherein
you have not taught them (especially her) some one principle
of the truth. Think the time greatly gained, as I have often
told you, that is spent in the word of the Lord. Among
other places of the word wherein I would have you be conversant in regard of these times, I pray you read the 37th

Psalm; Isa. lx., and lxi., lxii., lxiii.; Matt. xx.; Exod. xxii., 22; Job xxiv. to xxvii." [1]

. . . "Above all things, pray that he would restore beauty unto the church, and overthrow the religion of the Roman Antichrist in every part thereof. Observe your own special infirmities and wants, and be earnest with the Lord that he would do them away and consume them by the power of his Spirit. Remember me also, and my brethren in bonds, that the Lord would assist us with the strength and comfort of his Spirit to keep a good conscience, and to bear a glorious testimony to the end. Yea, be not void of hope but I may be restored again by your prayers; and therefore, also, be earnest with him for my deliverance.

"If the Lord shall end my days in this testimony, . . . I am ready and content with his pleasure. Keep yourself, my good Helen, here with this poor church. You may make all good refuge and stay here, as any widow else, for your outward estate. Though you could not, yet I know that you had rather dwell under the wings of the God of Israel in poverty, with godly Ruth, than to possess kingdoms in the land of Moab; and what shift soever you make, keep our poor children with you, that you may bring them up yourself in the instruction and information of the Lord. I leave you and them, indeed, nothing in this life but the blessing of my God, and his blessed promises, made unto me, a poor, wretched sinner, that my seed, my habitation, and family should be blessed and happy on the earth; and this, my sister, I doubt not shall be found an ample portion both for you and them; though you know that in hunger often, in cold often, in poverty and nakedness, we must make account to profess the Gospel in this life. Teach them even now, I beseech you, in their youth, that lesson, indeed, which was the last that I taught them in word; that is, if they would reign

---

[1] If the reader will open his Bible at the passages thus referred to, he will find himself better acquainted than before with Penry's interior life.

with Christ, they must suffer with him. Teach them not to look for great things in this life, but every day to make account that they are to yield up their lives, and whatsoever they have, for their truth. While their affections are yet green, let them have instruction out of the Word, and corrections meet for them. Yet you know that parents must not be bitter unto their children; especially smite not the elder wench overhard, because you know the least word will restrain her. When they are capable of any hardy labor, I know you will not let them be idle. Let them learn both to read and also to work. Howsoever it be with them in your care—or under the hands of others—I, their father, do here charge them, when they come to years of discretion, as they will answer at that great day of judgment, that they join themselves with the true profession and church of Christ wherein I now go before them—the which charge of mine that they now keep, I beseech you, good wife, to put them often in mind of the same. . . . And withal, be careful, in case you should not be able to keep them all with you, that they are brought up with some of the church, with bread and water, rather than to be clad in gold with any, how forward soever they seem to please, that yield obedience unto the antichristian ordinances.

"I know, my good Helen, that the burden which I lay upon thee, of four infants, whereof the eldest is not four years old, will not seem in any way burdensome unto thee. Yea, thou shalt find that our God will be a father to the fatherless and a stay unto the widow. If, my dear sister, you are married again after my days, choose that, first, he with whom you marry be of the same faith and holy profession with you. Look not so much to wealth and estimation in the world; yet rather choose many blessings than one, if you may; but only respect the fear of God and the meetness of the party.

"Thus—having hitherto disburdened myself of my duty toward you, and care over you and our poor children, in some part—to come unto myself, I am, thank God, of great comfort in him, though under great trials of my weakness. . . . But in regard of men, and in respect of the cause of God wherein I stand, I fear not any power or strength of man whatsoever; and I am, this hour, most willing to lay down my life for the word of my testimony; and I trust I shall be unto the end."

Having narrated some of his experiences as a prisoner in the hands of the ecclesiastical authorities, he said: "They were so lamentably ignorant [of the Scriptures], and lay wait for blood so cruelly, that certainly the Lord's hand is not far off. The Lord show mercy unto us and them—from my heart I say it. I can not but think that they thirst after my blood, therefore pray for me, and desire all the church to do the same.

"And if I be offered upon this sacrifice, I pray thee, my good Helen, that all the dispersed papers which I have written in this cause, and are yet out of the enemies' hands, may be published unto the world after my death, together with the letters which I have written in the same cause, that are of any moment; though they be imperfect, yet the enemies' mouths will be stopped by that means, and no small light be given unto the cause." . . .

"To draw to an end, salute the whole church from me, especially those in bonds, and be you all much and heartily saluted. Let none of them be dismayed; the Lord will send a glorious issue unto Zion's troubles. Yet you must all be prepared for sufferings—I see likelihood. Let not those which are abroad [not yet imprisoned] miss to frequent their holy meetings.

"Salute my mother and yours in Wales, my brethren, sisters, and kindred there. My God knoweth—yea, yourself know—how earnestly and often I have desired that the Lord would vouchsafe my service in the Gospel among them, to the saving of their souls for evermore unto him. Salute your parents and mine, and our kindred in Northamptonshire—

with my poor kinsman, Jenkin Jones—and Mr. Davidd also, though I had not thought that any outward respect would have made him to withdraw his shoulders from the Lord's ways—but the Lord will draw him forward in his good time.   Salute all ours in Scotland, upon the borders, and every way northward. . . . Let it not be known unto any, save unto the party who shall read this unto you, that I have written at all as yet.   I got means, this day, to write this much, whereof no creature living knoweth."

To that letter, written "in great haste, with many tears, and yet in great spiritual comfort," he subscribed his name: "Your husband for a season, and your beloved brother for evermore, John Penry, an unworthy witness of Christ's testament against the abominations of the Roman Antichrist and his followers—sure of victory by the blood of the Lamb."

Were these to be his last words to his young wife, the heroic mother of those little children?   He could not send the letter without a postscript: "In any case, let it not be known that I have written unto you—be sure thereof.[1]   I would wish you to go to the judges for me, with your children, desiring them to consider your hard case and mine. Yea, and I would have you, if you can, go to the queen with them, beseeching her, for God's cause, to show her wonted clemency unto her subjects — with my lord treasurer and other of her council whom you think [likely] to regard your and my cries; for sure my life is sought for.   I am ready— pray for me, and desire the church to pray for me, much and earnestly.   The Lord comfort thee, good Helen, and strengthen thee.   Be not dismayed.   I know not how thou dost for outward things, but my God will provide.   My love be with thee now and ever, in Christ Jesus."

---

[1] Penry's anxiety on this point may have been lest he should compromise in some way the friend (possibly the jailer himself—see p. 169) to whom he was indebted for the privilege of writing.   "The party who shall read this unto" Mrs. Penry, may have been the same person, desirous of retaining in his own hands the evidence of his kindness toward the prisoner.

M

He found time and means for another letter to "good Helen," of which a fragment has been preserved. "I trust that my mother even will lay up some things for a store unto our poor children against they come of age—if they will give you and them nothing in the mean time. I will write unto them, if I can by any means, for this purpose. This is a cold and poor stay, my dear sister and wife, I leave you and my poor fatherless mess; but my God and yours (doubt you not) will provide abundantly for you and them if you serve him, as I doubt not but you will. But, my good wife, for his name's sake, and that with tears, take heed that neither you nor they return again into Egypt, whence, of the Lord's great favor, you and I am escaped—you know what I mean. Will you, or my children, join with the corruptions that are dyed with your husband's and father's blood? I am not jealous of you, my good wife, but warn you and my children. Oh! it is good to stay the Lord's leisure, and to suffer with him. In the mean time, he will overthrow Babel and build Zion again."

The advice which he gave to his wife concerning their children was not a sufficient expression of his paternal solicitude for them. Looking beyond the years of their fatherless childhood to the time when they would be able to appreciate and apply his dying counsels, he prepared a more elaborate epistle (April 10), addressed "To my daughters when they come to years of discretion and understanding." Dated only four days after the letter to his wife, and written as by stealth, it must have been the principal occupation of those intervening days. It begins with a few words, weighty and well chosen, concerning their personal trust in Christ and their obedience to the God of their father. It then warns them against "the ordinances and inventions of Antichrist's kingdom," and charges them "to be subject unto all that holy order which Christ Jesus hath appointed for the ruling of his church and members here upon earth." After reminding them of their father's six years' endurance of persecution for Christ, and of their mother's partnership with her husband in testimony and in suffering, it proceeds:

"Repay her, then, by your dutifulness and obedience, some part of that kindness which you owe unto her. Be obedient to her in word and in deed; and miss not to be the staff of her age who is now the only stay and support that is left unto you in your youth and infancy. I now leave four of you upon her, having nothing to speak of to leave her and you, save only that everlasting and durable fountain of the Lord's blessed providence and promises who relieveth the fatherless and the widow. The eldest of you is not yet four years old, and the youngest not four months; and therefore every way shall you be indebted to that mother who will think it no intolerable burden to bear and take the care of you all."

After advising them to be guided by their mother's advice in all things, and especially in bestowing themselves if God should grant them "the favor to enter into the holy state of matrimony," the testamentary epistle proceeds: "If she will place you in any service, think not honest labor too mean for you, nor wholesome diet too hard, nor clothing that may cover you and keep you warm over-base for you; but bless God that he provideth you food and raiment. . . . Whatsoever becometh of you in outward regard, keep yourselves in this poor church where I leave you, or in some other holy society of the saints. I doubt not but my God will stir up many of his children to show kindness unto my faithful sister and wife, your mother, and also unto you, even for my sake. Although you should be brought up in never so hard service, yet, my dear children, learn to read, that you may be conversant, day and night, in the word of the Lord. If your mother be able to keep you together, I doubt not but you shall learn both to write and read by her means. I have left you four Bibles, each of you one; being the sole and only patrimony that I have for you. . . . Frequent the holy exercises and meetings of the saints in any case; for there is the Lord most powerful in the holy ministry of his word;

and you must remember that the Lord regardeth, loveth, and blesseth the public worship more than any private exercise of religion whatsoever." . . .

"Show yourselves loving and kind unto all the saints of God, being ready to lay down your lives to do good unto the Lord's poor church and members here upon earth.   Whatsoever you have, bestow somewhat thereof for the relief of the church. Diminish from your diet and apparel, that you may bestow the same upon the church and members of Christ, for the maintenance of the true worship and service of God among them." . . .

In these testamentary counsels of the expectant martyr to his children, he did not forget his " people and kindred in the flesh."   Of the Welsh nation he said : " I trust the time is coming wherein God will show mercy unto them by caus-ing the true light of the Gospel to shine among them ; and, my good daughters, pray you earnestly unto the Lord—when you come to know what prayer is—for this, and be always ready to show yourselves helpful unto the least child of that poor country that shall stand in need of your loving support. In any case, repay the kindness, if you be able, which I owe unto my nearest kindred there—as to my mother, brethren, and sisters, and the others, who, I am persuaded, will be most kind toward you and your mother, unto their ability, even for my sake.   Be an especial comfort, in my stead, unto the gray hairs of my poor mother, whom the Lord used as the only means of my [support] in the beginning of my studies, whereby I have come unto the knowledge of that most pre-cious faith in Jesus Christ, in the defense whereof I stand."

Having exhorted them, in like manner, to pray much and often for the queen, under whose reign he had come to the knowledge of the truth for which he was to suffer—to show kindness to all strangers, especially to " the people of Scot-land, where," said he, " I, your mother, and a couple[1] of you

---

[1] Two, then, of the four children, had been born since his return from Scot-land, and were " not yet four months old."

lived as strangers"—to be "tender-hearted toward the widow and the fatherless," inasmuch as he was likely to leave them fatherless and their mother a widow; and having thus " unburdened [his] careful soul" in part, he brought that sad parental service to its close.   The broken phrases, the uncorrected lapses of the pen, betray the depth and conflict of his feelings.   "I have written this," he said, "in that scarcity of paper, ink, and time, that I could do it no otherwise than first it came into my mind and set it down, . . . but you may take instruction by it and follow it, that the blessing of God may light"—as "upon the posterity of Jonadab the son of Rechab," so—"upon the children of John Penry for the obedience they have yielded unto their father's godly commandment and counsel."   "Thus . . . while I am ready . . . not only to be imprisoned, but even to die for the name and truth of the Lord Jesus which I have maintained, and while I acknowledge with a loud and triumphant voice that the afflictions of this present life are not worthy of the glory which shall be revealed unto us, I betake you, my dear children, and your loving mother, unto your most undoubted and careful Redeemer in Jesus Christ our Lord, whom be blessed forever and ever."   Then, dating his letter "From close prison, with many tears, and yet in much joy of the Holy Ghost," he wrote his name, "John Penry, a poor witness in this life against the abominations of the Roman Babel."

On the day on which he subscribed that letter, the prisoner underwent, before two of the High Commissioners, a long examination, in which he witnessed a good confession.   His answers were prompt, clear, and resolute.   One of them may serve as a specimen.   In reply to the accusation, " You labor to draw her majesty's subjects from their obedience unto her laws, and from this Church of England," he said : " Nay, I persuade all men unto obedience to my prince and her laws; only I dissuade all the world from yielding obedience and submission unto the ordinances of the kingdom of Antichrist, and would persuade them to be subject unto Jesus Christ and his blessed laws.   And I know this enterprise to be so far from being repugnant unto her majesty's laws, as I assure myself that the same is warranted thereby.   Her majesty hath granted, in establishing and confirming the Great Charter of England (whereunto, as I take it, the kings and queens of this land are sworn when they come to the crown), that the Church of God, under her, should have all her rights and liberties inviolable forever.   Let the benefit of this law be granted unto me and others of my brethren, and it shall be found that we have done nothing but what is warrantable by her laws."   Standing on the *Magna Charta* as the supreme law of the land, the sacred compact between the sovereign and the people, renewed and sworn to at every coronation, he insisted that, under Queen Elizabeth, "the Church of God"—not the Roman power, nor the English prelacy and priesthood, but the Church as instituted by Christ himself, with "her rights and liberties" defined in the Scriptures—was free.

After that inquisitorial examination, he submitted to the commissioners a written profession of his loyalty toward the government and person of the queen, and of his faith toward God.   No man can read that document, so clear, so calm, so dignified in its earnestness, and not be convinced of its perfect sincerity.   In bringing it to a close, the heroic confessor said: "Death, I thank God, I fear not—in this cause especially—for I know that the sting of death is taken away, and that they are blessed which die in the Lord for witnessing against the former corruptions.   Life I desire not, if I be guilty of sedition—of defaming and disturbing her majesty's peaceable government."   But while thus professing his readiness to die, he went on to say: "I most humbly and earnestly beseech their honors and worships, in whose hands this writing of mine shall come, to consider that it is to no purpose that her majesty's subjects should bestow their time in learning—in study and meditation of the Word—in reading the writings and doings of learned men and of the holy martyrs which have been in former ages, especially the writings published by her majesty's authority—if they may not, without danger, profess and hold those truths which they learn out of them. . . . I beseech them also to consider what a lamentable case it is that we may hold fellowship with the Romish Church in the inventions thereof without all danger, and can not, without extreme peril, be permitted in judgment and practice to depart from the same. . . . I beseech them, in the bowels of Jesus Christ, to be a means unto her majesty and their honors, that my cause may be weighed in even balance. Imprisonments, indictments, arraignments, yea death itself, are no meet weapons to convince the conscience grounded upon the word of God and accompanied with so many witnesses of his famous servants and churches."

Penry had already said to his wife, "I see my blood laid for, and so my days and testimony drawing to an end." Yet he would not succumb so long as there was any effort to be made which he could make without compromising the truth for which he was Christ's witness. Expecting to be indicted, as Barrowe and Greenwood had been, for sedition, and that the indictment would be grounded, as in their case, on the books which he had published, he prepared (probably not without some aid of legal counsel) a paper showing what points might be insisted on in his defense against such an indictment. Thereupon another course was taken by those who intended his death. Among his private papers there had been found some imperfect notes of matters to be used in a memorial to the queen, which he had thought of preparing and presenting in person. In that private memorandum of something yet to be written, and with no evidence that it had ever been communicated to any human being, was the matter for which he was indicted. The trial, if trial it might be called where the prisoner was not permitted to be heard by counsel, took place at Westminster Hall, two months after his arrest (May 21 = 31); and of course he was convicted.

The next day he addressed to the queen's prime-minister, Lord Burleigh, a letter, with a formal "protestation," which none, of whatever party, can read at this time without rendering homage not only to the integrity of the man, but also to the Christian dignity of the martyr.   In the letter he says: "The cause is most lamentable, that the private observations of any student, being in a foreign land, and wishing well to his prince and country, should bring his life . . . unto a violent end; especially seeing they are most private, and so imperfect as they have no coherence at all in them, and, in most places, carry no true English. . . . Though mine innocency may stand me in no stead before an earthly tribunal, yet I know that I shall have the reward thereof before the judgment-seat of the Great King; and the merciful Lord, who relieveth the widow and fatherless, will reward my desolate orphans and friendless widow that I leave behind me, and even hear their cry—for he is merciful."   In the "protestation," after a conclusive argument to prove his innocence of the crime for which he was condemned, and the unreasonableness of the construction put upon his private papers, he told what the great business of his life had been, and what his aspirations had been: "I am a poor young man, born and bred in the mountains of Wales.   I am the first, since the last springing up of the Gospel in this latter age, that labored to have the blessed seed thereof sown in those barren mountains.   I have often rejoiced before my God, as he knoweth, that I had the favor to be born and live under her majesty, for the promoting of this work.   In the earnest desire I had to see the Gospel in my native country, and the contrary corruptions removed, I might well, as I confess in my published writings, . . . forget my own danger; but my loyalty to my prince did I never forget.   And being now to end my days before I am come to the one half of my years in the likely course of nature, I leave the success of my labors unto such of my countrymen as the Lord is to raise after me, for the accomplishing of that work which, in the calling of my country unto the knowledge of Christ's blessed Gospel, I began."

We linger in the martyr's prison cell while he is writing his final protestation, conscious that it is "the last writing which is likely to proceed from" him, and "looking not to live this week to an end." After an allusion to the attractions which life had for him, to the "poor, friendless widow" and the "four poor, fatherless infants" whom he was leaving, and to the comparative lowliness and poverty of the condition in which he had lived, he says: "Sufficiency I have had, with great outward troubles; but most contented was I with my lot; and content I am, and shall be, with my undeserved and untimely death, beseeching the Lord that it be not laid to the charge of any creature in this land. For I do, from my heart, forgive all those that seek my life, as I desire to be forgiven in that day of strict account—praying for them as for my own soul, that, although upon earth we can not accord, we may yet meet in heaven unto our eternal comfort and unity. . . . And if my death can procure any quietness to the church of God, or the state, I shall rejoice. I know not to what better use it [my life] could be employed if it were reserved; and therefore in this cause I desire not to spare the same. Thus have I lived toward the Lord and my prince; and thus I mean to die, by his grace. Many such subjects I wish unto my prince, though no such reward to any of them."

Having added his request, "as earnest as possibly I can utter the same, unto all those, both honorable and worshipful, unto whom this my last testimony may come, that her majesty may be acquainted herewith before my death—if it may be," he subscribes his name, "with that heart and that hand which never devised or wrote any thing to the discredit or defamation of my sovereign, Queen Elizabeth—I take it on my death, as I hope to have a life after this. By me, John Penry."

There is no reason to think that Elizabeth ever saw that protestation, or heard of it. It was submitted to the judges, as the queen's advisers; and their comment remains in the

State Paper Office.   "Penry," they said, "is not, as he pretendeth, a loyal subject, but a seditious disturber of her majesty's peaceable government.   [It] appeareth many ways." Among those "many ways," they alleged "his schismatical separation from the society of the Church of England, and joining with the hypocritical and schismatical conventicles of Barrowe and Greenwood," and also "his justifying of Barrowe and Greenwood, who, suffering worthily for their seditious writings and preachings, are nevertheless represented by him as holy martyrs."

Such was English liberty under the sceptre of Elizabeth. The voluntary association of Christian men for united worship and for mutual helpfulness in the Christian life — the quiet meeting, in fields and woods, or in private apartments, for the worship of God in any form or way not prescribed by the authority of that petticoated pope who called herself "Supreme Governor of the Church of England" — in one word, *Congregationalism*—was "sedition," to be punished by death.   Green be the memory, forever, of the men who, in that cruel age, with the gallows before them, and with the hangman's noose about their necks, asserted and obeyed a higher law.   To them, under God, do we owe it that in less than thirty years from that date there began to be a New England ; and that Old England itself, to-day, is free England.

Four days after trial and conviction, the prisoner was brought up and sentence of death was pronounced against him.   In the ordinary course of proceeding, execution would have followed on the second or third day after the sentence. For some reason there was a day's delay, and a respite began to be hoped for.   But on the fourth day (May 29 = June 7), Whitgift and other lords of the queen's council affixed their names to the death-warrant, the archbishop's name being the first.   At five o'clock, afternoon, the martyr was carried on a cart from his prison in Southwark to the usual place of execution for that county, at the second mile-stone on the Kent road, near a brook which, in memory of Thomas à Becket, was called St. Thomas-a-Watering.   An unexpected day and hour had been chosen for the execution, that his friends might have no opportunity of cheering him with their presence.   A few persons, who had seen the gallows so suddenly prepared, were standing around.   To them the martyr would have spoken; but not one word was he permitted to utter in their hearing.   It was almost sunset, and the sheriff and hangman were in haste.   They finished their work; and John Penry, in the thirty-fourth year of his age, having shared the ignominy of our Lord, who was hanged on a tree for sedition, went to be with Christ.[1]

---

[1] Dr. Waddington's "John Penry, the Pilgrim Martyr," gives all that is known concerning Penry, and clears his memory from the charge that would make him the author of the Marprelate tracts.

CHAPTER X.

PERSECUTION AND EXILE : THE CHURCH AT SCROOBY.

AT the time when Barrowe and Greenwood ended their testimony, a certain "Act to retain the queen's subjects in obedience" was passing through Parliament. On the day after their death, the bill, having been modified by Puritan influence in the Commons with the view of making it effectual against Separatists, "without peril of entrapping honest and loyal subjects," was passed into an act.[1] By that statute, banishment from the realm and forfeiture of goods became the punishment of every Separatist who, after suffering a three-months' imprisonment, should refuse to conform. The policy of Queen Elizabeth, in her attempted supremacy over the religion of her subjects (for it was distinctively *her* policy), had converted the men who at first were only anti-ritualists, scrupulous about certain ecclesiastical vestments and ceremonies, into resolute Puritans, demanding a presbyterian instead of a prelatical church government over the nation. It had converted Puritans into Separatists, and now it was compelling Separatists to become Pilgrims, and preparing them to become the founders of a new nationality.

Of course the new statute was first employed against the martyr church in London—or, more properly, in Southwark, for its place of assembling was on that side of the Thames. The pastor, Francis Johnson, had already been about four months a prisoner; and the teacher, John Greenwood, had just been released from his long imprisonment by being put to death. Many of the members among them, some who had

---

[1] The story of how that bill was carried through Parliament is well told by Mr. Punchard, "History of Congregationalism," iii., 193-200.

been clergymen in the Church of England, were suffering in filthy jails for their testimony in behalf of Christian liberty. Barrowe, their bold lay champion, had died on the same gallows with his friend Greenwood. The mockery of Penry's trial, followed by the cruelty of his death, was four weeks after the passage of the act, and seems to have been arranged for the purpose of striking terror into the Separatists, by showing them that the new law under which they were to be banished had not superseded the old law under which they might be hanged at the discretion of their enemies.

A letter from Johnson, the imprisoned pastor, to Lord Burleigh (Jan. 8, 1594), has come down to us. It shows that at the date of his writing he had been about fourteen months a close prisoner in one jail, and his brother George eleven months in another. He complained that his papers and books had been seized, and that all the papers, and some of the books (though published by authority), were still detained from him. A significant statement is made concerning one of the members of that persecuted church (William Smyth, formerly a clergyman in the Church of England), who had been examined by High Commissioners at Westminster a month before. He had been, at that time, eleven months a prisoner; and, at the date of Johnson's letter, he was still in prison. That unrelenting offender against the hierarchy was so bold as to tell the High Commissioners—by way of illustrating the absurdity of " dealing with men by imprisonment and other rigorous means, in matters of religion and conscience, rather than by more Christian and fit proceedings "—that " if he should, to please them, or to avoid trouble, submit to go to church, and to join with the public ministry of those assemblies as it now standeth, he being persuaded in conscience that it was utterly unlawful," his so doing would be mere dissimulation and hypocrisy ; to which the reply was, " Come to the church, and obey the queen's laws, and be a dissembler, be a hypocrite or a devil, if thou wilt."

Two of the many prisoners (Johnson knew not who, but might reasonably suppose himself to be one) were to be indicted, and Lord Burleigh's powerful influence was invoked in their behalf.   " We suffer these things," said he, " only for refusing to have spiritual communion with the antichristian prelacy and other clergy abiding in this land, and for laboring, in all holy and peaceable manner, to obey the Lord Jesus Christ in his own ordinance of ministry and worship. . . . Wherein if we did err, yet prisons and gallows were no fit means to convince and persuade our consciences; but rather a quiet and godly conference, or discussing of the matter by deliberate writing before equal judges."   He asked for such a conference, not as implying that he and his fellow-prisoners were not ready to die for the truth intrusted to them, " but to the end that, the truth being found out and made manifest, the false offices, callings, and works of the prelacy and other clergy of this land might be quite abolished out of it; and their lordships and possessions might be converted to her majesty's civil uses (to whom of right they belong), as were, not long since, the like livings of the abbots, monks, and friars in these dominions, that thus there might be more free passage to the Gospel of Christ, and more peace to the church."

Inclosed in the letter was a paper, drawn with an acuteness worthy of a practiced lawyer, and designed to show "That F. J., for his writings, is not under the danger of the statute of 35 Eliz., cap.1, made to retain the queen's subjects in their due obedience."   Some of the points taken are historically important for the light which they throw on the position of those sufferers, not only in relation to principles of universal religious freedom, but also in relation to the fundamental principles of English law and the chartered liberty of English subjects.

After a reference to the Act of Supremacy as defining the queen's authority in ecclesiastical matters, the question was raised, for the " prelates and ministers " to answer, " Whether

her majesty, with the consent of the Parliament, may suppress and abolish the present prelacy and ministry of the land, and transfer their revenues and possessions to her own civil uses, as her father, of famous memory, Henry VIII., did with abbots, monks, etc., and with their livings?" Obviously, the bishops, had they been required to answer that question, would have been as much perplexed as were the chief-priests of Judaism when required to answer whether the baptism of John was from heaven or of men. If the answer were No—where would be the queen's supremacy over the Church of England as by law established? If the answer were Yes—then there was no crime in Johnson's writings against the ecclesiastical establishment then existing.

The next point was that his writings were only in defense of the doctrines maintained by "the holy servants and martyrs of Christ in former days," whose doctrines, "as being against the canonical functions of the pope, were accounted Lollardy and heresy." If the new statute is to be construed as making those doctrines criminal for which the martyrs before the Reformation suffered, then it must be construed as virtually repealing the act by which (in the first year of Edward VI.) the old statutes against Lollardy had been abrogated.

Another point was that Johnson's writings were "in defense of the right and liberty of the Church of Christ; which the great charter of England granteth shall be free, and have all her whole rights and liberties inviolable." The question as to the legitimate meaning of Magna Charta in the clause referred to might have been argued, before learned and impartial judges, with great effect. No Protestant Englishman could reasonably maintain that the "Church" to which "all her rights and liberties" were guaranteed by that instrument was the Roman Catholic Church, the hierarchy unified and centralized in the pope. What was commonly recognized as the Church when the barons at Runnymede

extorted from King John the great security for the rights of
Englishmen, was afterward reformed by Henry VIII. and
Edward VI., and again by Elizabeth—many of its most valued institutions were suppressed—great portions of its wealth
were seized and appropriated to other uses—its forms of worship were revised and simplified; and all this was done pro-
fessedly in the interest of the true Church of Christ in England. Evidently the reforming sovereigns and Parliaments
had proceeded on the theory that the Church to which rights
and liberties had been guaranteed by the charter of the kingdom was none other than that institution which Christ founded. Christ's own institution, then—the Church as Christ
and his apostles made it—the Church of the New Testament Scriptures—was the institution to which the fundamental law of England had granted freedom. Johnson's
writings were in defense of freedom for the Church of Christ.
His interpretation (without which every step of what was
called the Reformation had been a violation of the sovereign's coronation oath) would have made the Magna Charta,
just what the church polity of the New Testament is, a charter of religious liberty.

Other points in the line of his defense were these: "He
never did, nor doth, obstinately, without lawful cause, refuse
to hear and to have spiritual communion with the public
ministry of these [parish] assemblies;" but he refuses only
upon conscience grounded upon God's word" ("which her
majesty protecteth and defendeth"), "and approved by consent of the confessions of the Reformed churches, and of
the faithful martyrs of Christ;" and, finally, "having been
close prisoner ever since long before this statute was made,
he can not, in regard of his writings or any other thing whatsoever, be lawfully convicted to have offended against this
statute."[1]

But no such argument—no appeal from the letter of the

---

[1] Strype, "Annals," iv., 134–138.

new statute to Magna Charta or to universal principles of justice—was allowed to prevail against the necessity of the most efficient measures to suppress the crime of separation from the National Church. Since the death of the three martyrs, Johnson was not only most conspicuous by his official position in the Separatists' church, but also most obnoxious by his writings. He might have been indicted and convicted under the same statute which had been used as the means of bringing his brethren to the gallows, but for some reason —perhaps because it was seen that the hanging of those martyrs had made their testimony more effective—he was proceeded against under the new statute, and, having been convicted in legal form, was compelled to " abjure the realm." In other words, he was banished for life, but not till he had passed more than another weary half-year in the foul prison. Others of the persecuted flock were in like manner dismissed from the prisons into life-long banishment, and were accompanied or followed in their exile by such as were willing to dispense with the process of imprisonment, indictment, and sentence. Amsterdam became to many of these their city of refuge. A church of English exiles was formed there, with Johnson for pastor, and the learned Henry Ainsworth for teacher. It was indeed the London or Southwark church, dispersed by persecution, driven beyond sea, and gathered again in a strange land.

This was in conformity with advice which Penry had given in anticipation of his death. Among the letters written by him from his prison was one, full of affectionate and sagacious counsel, " to the distressed faithful congregation of Christ in London, and all the members thereof, whether in bonds or at liberty." The bill for the " Act to retain the queen's subjects in obedience " had not yet become a law when that letter was written; but it was undergoing discussion and amendment in order to its passage, and they all knew that " on the side of their oppressors there was power." They knew that, in one way or another, the purpose of the

N

bill was likely to be executed. "My good brethren," said Penry, "seeing banishment with loss of goods is likely to betide you all, prepare yourselves for this hard entreaty." After warning them against the temptation to shift every man for himself in the impending calamity, and entreating them to take care that the church should not be broken up, but should go whithersoever it might please God to send them, he assured them, as with prophetic inspiration, "The blessing will be great that shall ensue this care; whereas, if you go, every man to provide for his own house and to look for his own family first, neglecting poor Zion, the Lord will set his face against you, and scatter you from the one end of heaven to the other. . . . You shall yet find days of peace and rest, if you continue faithful. This stamping and treading of us under his feet, this subverting of our cause and right in judgment, is done by him to the end that we should search and try our ways, and repent; . . . but he will yet maintain the cause of our souls, and redeem our lives if we return to him."

Then, having entreated those of them who had either some property or some trade by which they might win the means of living, that they should not permit "the poor ones" to struggle alone, "or to end their days in sorrow and mourning for want of outward and inward comforts in the land of strangers," the martyr advised that there should be consultation "with the whole church, yea, with the brethren in other places, how the church may be kept together," so that their banishment should not be dispersion; and he added: "Let not the poor and the friendless be forced to stay behind here, and to break a good conscience, for want of your support and kindness unto them that they may go with you." Nor could he forget how closely some of "the poor and the friendless" were related to him. "I beseech you that you would take my poor and desolate widow, and my mess of fatherless and friendless orphans, with you into exile, whithersoever you go. . . . Let them not continue after you in this land, where they must be enforced to go again into Egypt." He had also a word of loving remembrance for two by name: "Be every way comfortable unto the sister and wife of the dead, I mean unto my beloved M. Barrowe and M. Greenwood, whom I most heartily salute, and desire much to be comforted in their God, who, by his blessings from above, will countervail unto them the want of so notable a brother and husband." [1]

He had already made reference to "the brethren in other places;" but, before closing his letter, he mentioned them again, more distinctly, and in words of great significance.

"I would wish you earnestly to write—yea, to send, if you may, to comfort the brethren in the west and north countries, [2] that they faint not in these troubles, and that also you may have of their advice, and they of yours, what to do in these desolate times. And, if you think it any thing for their further comfort and direction, send them conveniently a copy of this my letter, and of the declaration of my faith and allegiance, wishing them, before whomsoever they be called, that their own mouths be not had in witness against them in any thing. Yea, I would wish you and them to be together, if you may, whithersoever you shall be banished; and, to this purpose, to bethink you beforehand where to be; yea, to send some who may be meet to prepare you some resting-place; and be all of you assured that he who is your God in England will be your God in any land under the whole heaven; for the earth and the fullness thereof are his, and blessed are they that, for his cause, are bereaved of any part of the same."

---

[1] Penry's letter to the church was written under the supposition that Barrowe and Greenwood had already suffered death. It was dated April 24, the day on which those martyrs were first brought forth for execution "early in the morning," and then respited. The news of that respite had not reached the prison in which Penry was confined.

[2] Some readers may not be aware that "county" and "country" were originally the same word.

This remarkable passage gives us a glimpse, first, of the fact that the suffering church in London was in relations of correspondence with suffering brethren in the western and northern counties of England; and then of the fact that, while the "Act for retaining the queen's subjects in obedience" was passing through Parliament, those persecuted Christians, in city and country, were beginning to consult on the possibility and the method of keeping themselves together as a distinct community in some strange land.   It was in the debate on the bill then pending that Sir Walter Raleigh estimated the Brownists scattered over England at twenty thousand.   Among the twenty thousand were those "brethren in the west and north countries" so affectionately remembered by Penry.   Who were they?   It happens that some of them were men in whom we have a special interest, and of whom some knowledge has come down to us.

We change the scene, then, from the narrow streets of old London and Southwark—from the filthy and crowded prisons of the metropolis—from the gallows at Tyburn and that at the brook on the road which Chaucer's Canterbury pilgrims traveled—to another part of England, nearly a hundred and fifty miles northward, where the three "countries" of Lincolnshire, Yorkshire, and Nottinghamshire border on each other.

Four years[1] before the hanging of the three Separatist martyrs, William Brewster, then about twenty-three years of age, came to reside with his father at a certain old manor-house, near the northern boundary of Nottinghamshire.   Born of an ancient family, and educated at the University of Cambridge, he was acquainted with the splendid court of Elizabeth, and conversant with public affairs.   He had been in the employment of William Davison, who, though he was a Puritan, was a trusted servant of the queen, her embassador in the Netherlands on a mission of great importance, and afterward one of her secretaries of state.   His relations with his patron, both in the embassy and in the

---

[1] For this date, heretofore uncertain, I am indebted to Dr. H. M. Dexter.

court at home, had been intimate and confidential. The secretary "trusted him above all others that were about him," "employed him in matters of greatest trust and secrecy," "esteemed him rather as a son than a servant; and for his wisdom and godliness, [in private] he would converse with him more like a friend and familiar than a master."[1] It is quite natural, then, to find that when, after many years of faithful service, Secretary Davison, by one of the queen's most conscienceless and most dishonorable strokes of policy, was disgraced, robbed of all he had, and imprisoned in the Tower, under the pretense that he had acted contrary to her will in the matter of the execution of Mary Queen of Scots (February, 1587), Brewster "remained with him some good time after that he was put from his place, doing him many faithful offices of service in the time of his troubles." Just how long after the downfall of his patron he remained in London does not appear. Nor do we know whether he had any personal acquaintance among the suffering Separatists there. Two years after the beginning of Davison's imprisonment, William Brewster was at the stately old manorhouse of Scrooby, acting for his infirm father, who held an office there in the service of the queen. Five years later we find that he was himself the "post," or postmaster at Scrooby, which was on the great road from London to York, and thence into Scotland. There he lived "in good esteem among his friends and the gentlemen of those parts, especially the godly and religious." He seems to have become an earnestly religious man, and to have accepted Puritan views at the university; for there it was that "the seeds of grace and virtue" were effectually planted in his mind. He did much for the advancement of religion "in the country where he lived." He was active in the Puritan way of doing good, "by procuring good preachers to the places thereabout, and drawing on of others to assist and help for-

---

[1] Bradford, "History of Plymouth Plantation," p. 409.

ward in such a work," contributing sometimes beyond his ability. "In this state he continued many years, doing the best good he could, and walking according to the light he saw, till the Lord revealed further unto him." More briefly, the queen's "master of the posts" at Scrooby was a gentleman of Puritan sympathies, working to promote the preaching of the Gospel in the Church of England, and hoping that the remaining superstitions would soon be reformed by authority.

But in that region the idea of "reformation without tarrying for any" was beginning to take effect. Men were beginning to learn that there might be individual and personal reformation, voluntary conformity to the rules and principles given in the New Testament, without waiting for a reformation of the National Church by the national government. How this came to pass, and by what stages of progress, may be best told by one who had himself no small part in the story. Tracing the movement from an undefined beginning, he tells us that " by the travail and diligence of some godly and zealous preachers, as in other places of the land, so in the north parts, many became enlightened by the word of God, and had their ignorance and sins discovered by the word of God's grace, and began to reform their lives and make conscience of their ways." In other words, they began to be conscientious in all things, and were earnest to know the will of God that they might obey it. This was nothing else than private judgment in religion—the practical recognition of individual responsibility to God—the first stage of " reformation without tarrying for any." Individuals, one by one, were beginning to reform themselves under the guidance of the Scriptures. What next? As soon as " the work of God," moving them to live soberly, righteously, and godly, became manifest in them, " they were both scoffed and scorned by the profane multitude; and the ministers," among whose hearers such changes were taking place, began to experience the oppressive urgency of the queen's hierarchy. Those ministers must submit to "the yoke of subscription," or be silenced. Nor was this all. Scoffs and scorn might be endured. The silencing of Nonconformist clergymen—if it had merely debarred them from preaching in the pulpits of the state church—would not have been an intolerable hardship, so long as there were private houses in which they could meet quietly those who desired to hear them. But the queen's supremacy gave them no such liberty; and the enginery of ecclesiastical oppression was brought to bear on the hearers as well as the preachers. "The poor *people* were so urged with apparitors and pursuivants and the commissary courts, as truly their affliction was not small."[1]

In other words, the same sort of ecclesiastical discipline by which John Copping, because of some conscientious irregularity in his manner of worshiping God, had been shut up in the jail of Bury St. Edmunds year after year, till, at last, he was hanged for a pretended felony,[2] and by which so many reformers on the voluntary principle had been made to suffer like things in London, was employed upon these self-reforming disciples of Christ in the north of England. Nor is there any reason to doubt that such proceedings began as early there as in the diocese of Norwich or in that of London.

We can easily believe that "truly their affliction was not small." But after they had borne it "sundry years with much patience," it had the effect of opening their minds to receive additional light on the ecclesiastical questions of those times—an effect which Elizabeth and her prelates had not expected. In the quaint phrase of their own chronicler, "they were occasioned by the continuance and increase of these troubles, and other means which the Lord raised up in those days, to see further into these things by the light of the word of God." At first they were simply Puritans—nonconforming members of a National Church which had not

---

[1] Bradford, p. 8. [2] *Ante*, chap. v.

been sufficiently reformed in its ritual—devout men, conscientiously omitting certain prescribed ceremonies in public worship, and occasionally seeking to supply the hunger of their souls elsewhere than in their own parish churches—loyal Protestants, lamenting the compromises which had been made with popery, and hoping for a time when the obnoxious vestments and ceremonies should be abolished.   But by the force of persecution stimulating their attention, and by the progress of inquiry and discussion, they were brought to see " that not only those base, beggarly ceremonies were unlawful, but *also* that the lordly, tyrannous power of the prelates ought not to be submitted to."   Taught and stimulated by " apparitors and pursuivants and commissary courts," they learned that the entire structure of the state church made " a profane mixture of persons and things in the worship of God," and that not only certain phrases and rubrics in the prescribed forms of public worship, but the very " offices and callings " of the established clergy, their " courts and canons," and all their distinctive authority and rule, " were unlawful and antichristian."

With these premises settled in their minds, it was not difficult for them, especially when urged by continual persecution, to make another stage of progress.   They were brought to the conclusion that, whatever might be the Christian character of some congregations in the parishes of England, and however numerous the true followers of Christ and members of his body might be among the English people, the ecclesiastico - political institution called " the Church of England " was not at all a church in any New Testament meaning of the word, but was (as their experience had proved) a positively antichristian institution.   Having arrived at this conclusion, they could no longer be Puritans merely, waiting and protesting in the hope of a new reformation to be made by national authority in the National Church.   They found incumbent on them a personal duty of reformation — even of church reformation—" without tarrying for any."   As on

the first Christians in Antioch and in Rome, before churches
existed there, the duty was incumbent of *forming* churches
according to the mind of Christ; so on them, in England,
where Christ's institution had been subverted, and a different institution set up in its place, there was incumbent a
duty of *re-formation* of churches.

How long the time was in which they were passing through
these successive stages of reformation, and at what date
they, or any of them, adopted definitely the principle of separation from the state church, we have no means of knowing exactly.   Some of "the brethren in the north countries,"
to whom Penry sent his dying testimony and advice, may
have been dwelling in the neighborhood of Scrooby, and
may have had personal intercourse with him as he passed
on the road to Scotland, or as he returned.   At the date
of his return, Brewster was already at home in the great
manor-house there.   But Penry himself had not then become
a member of a Separatist church; and it may be that those
brethren were at that time no further advanced than he.   We
know, however, on good authority, that, nine years after Penry's death (1602), "divers godly Christians in the north of
England, being studious of reformation, and therefore not
only witnessing against human inventions and additions in
the worship of God"—as the Puritans did in one way or another—"but minding most the positive and practical part of
divine institutions, . . . entered into covenant to walk with
God, and one with another, in the enjoyment of the ordinances of God, according to the primitive pattern in the
word of God." [1]   Or, in the words of the earlier historian,
"they shook off the yoke of antichristian bondage, and, as
the Lord's free people, joined themselves by a covenant of
the Lord, into a church estate in the fellowship of the Gospel, to walk in all his ways made known, or to be made
known to them, according to their best endeavors, whatever

---

[1] Morton, "New England's Memorial," p. 9, 10 (Boston, 1855).

it should cost them. . . . And"—with a vivid memory of all the way in which they had been led for more than forty years of persecution, flight, exile, and conflict with the hardships of a wilderness, the chronicler added, significantly— "that it cost them something this ensuing history will declare."

This was not far from the time when Queen Elizabeth, after a reign of forty-four years, was succeeded by James I. (March, 1603), who had been king in Scotland from the time when his mother, Mary, had been deposed by her subjects. A crowned king while yet an infant, he was entirely in the hands of the Protestant nobles who governed in his name. He was carefully educated for his kingly office, under the strictest discipline, and with all the culture of which his nature was capable.   In the old age of Elizabeth, there was naturally some relaxation of the severity with which offenders against the Act of Uniformity had been persecuted; for it was possible that the king of Presbyterian Scotland, succeeding to the headship of the National Church in England, might inaugurate a new reformation.   The Puritans were hoping not only that the mediæval ritualism — which had been so dear to Elizabeth, and so odious to scrupulous consciences— would be purged out of the national worship, but that the ecclesiastical government of the realm would be reconstructed according to the pattern which Cartwright had seen in the mount.   Even the Separatists could not but hope for some relief from a new sovereign who had made ostentatious professions of Protestantism.   But all such hopes were speedily disappointed.   James Stuart's experience of Puritanism in Scotland had not made him a Puritan.   He had played the hypocrite long enough in the presence of court preachers so much like John the Baptist as those to whom, from his youth up, he had listened with some show of deference; and great was his joy to find himself surrounded by obsequious prelates, who assured him that he spoke " by the special assistance of God's Spirit," and on their knees professed their joy that God had given them "such a king as since Christ's time had not been." The policy of Elizabeth, as supreme ruler of the National Church, was maintained with renewed zeal by the king and his prelates. Archbishop Whitgift, the conscientious and therefore relentless persecutor of nonconformity, lived only to see the "Scotch mist," which he had feared, dissolving into sunshine for the hierarchy, and was succeeded by Bancroft, a man of the same sort, but less worthy of respect—less conscientious, perhaps, but not less a persecutor.

It was at the period of transition from the reign of Elizabeth to that of James I., and from the primacy of Whitgift to that of Bancroft, that those "brethren in the north countries," assuming their rights "as the Lord's free people," became, by their covenant with each other and with God, a church of Christ, and determinately "shook off the yoke of antichristian bondage."

Four years later (1607), the people who were thus intent upon "the positive and practical part of divine institutions," became "two distinct bodies or churches" for the sake of convenience in holding their assemblies; inasmuch as their homes were dispersed over a territory too wide for their meeting in one place, especially in those times. After the division, one of the two churches met, ordinarily, in the manor-house of Scrooby. As at Colosse there was a church in the house of Philemon, and at Laodicea a church in the house of Nymphas—as at Corinth there was a church in the house of Aquila and Priscilla, and afterward another in their house at Rome, when they had removed their residence to the imperial city [1]—so this church, instituted without asking Cæsar's permission, might have been called the church that is in the house of William Brewster. There was the germ of New England.

Through many generations that place of meeting was un-

---

[1] Philem. 2; Col. iv., 15; 1 Cor. xvi., 19; Rom. xvi., 5.

known.   Early historians had described it in general terms
as on the borders of three counties, had (by a misprint)
named "Ansterfield" as Bradford's birthplace, and had said
that Brewster's house was "a manor of the bishop's," but
had not mentioned Scrooby by name.   Only a few years
ago, the place was identified beyond all doubt by an English
antiquary.[1]   The village church of Scrooby is there, as in the
old time, with its gray spire.   The little river Idle winds its
way over the plain.   Rich crops of grain, in fields divided
by green hedges, testify that now, as of old, the people are
employed in "the innocent trade of husbandry."   The hamlet
of Austerfield is only two or three miles away, its little
"chapelry" (where, as the record testifies, "William the son
of William Bradfourth was baptized in March, 1590") just
out of sight behind the trees.   On the lower grounds, once
marshy and waste, and inhabited by wild fowl and other
game, but now reclaimed, are green meadows with grazing
cattle.   Close by the village, divided from its little garden
patches by an ancient moat now dry, are the traces of the
old Scrooby manor, though the building has passed away.

As long ago as the age of William the Conqueror, the
place belonged to the archbishops of York; and from early
times it was an occasional residence of theirs—a hunting-
lodge, or a resting-place in their journeys.   Sometimes it received royal visitors.   Margaret, Queen of Scotland, daughter
of Henry VII. of England, lodged there for a night on her
way to her husband.[2]   Cardinal Wolsey, when, having lost

---

[1] Rev. Joseph Hunter, of London, published in 1849 a pamphlet entitled,
"The Founders of New Plymouth."   Since that publication, Scrooby and
the historic localities of its neighborhood have been sought out by many a
reverent pilgrim.   That beautifully illustrated volume, "The Pilgrim Fathers," by the artist W. H. Bartlett, has made many of the places associated
with the story of the Fathers familiar to the eyes of their descendants.

[2] James I. succeeded to the throne of England because that English
princess, Queen Elizabeth's aunt Margaret, was his grandmother, and every British monarch since that time has been her descendant.   The latest

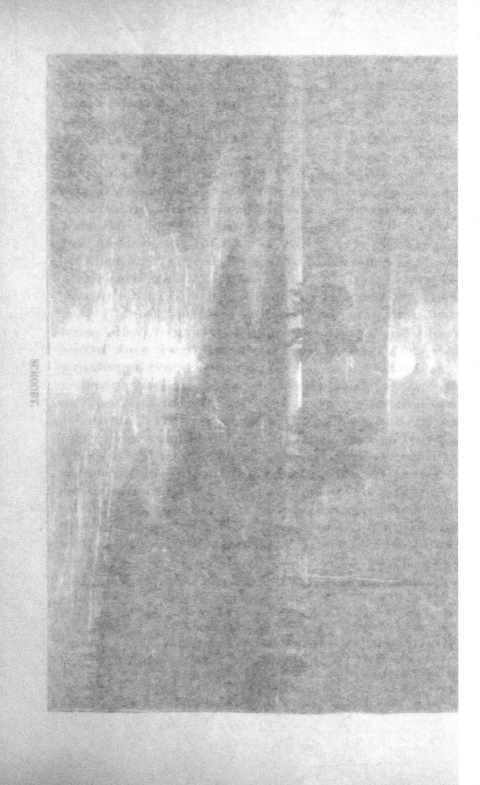

SCROOBY.

the favor of his sovereign, he was sent from court to his diocese of York, lingered for weeks at Scrooby; and there that
sovereign himself, Henry VIII., lodged not long afterward.
It seems a strange thing that a mansion so stately, and with
such a history, became the meeting-place of a Separatist
church in which every worshiper was liable to penalties of
fine and imprisonment.

Queen Elizabeth's zeal for the Church of England, as an
institution of which she was the supreme ruler, did not always restrain her from coveting, in behalf of her courtiers,
its superfluous endowments.   Sometimes a bishop was induced by a request from the queen—or, if the request were
ineffectual, by a peremptory letter threatening with an oath
that she would "unfrock" him—to alienate a town residence,
or a manor, or some other valuable property, by means of a
lease, perpetual or for a long term of years, to whomsoever
her majesty had undertaken to befriend in that way.   Thus
Cox, bishop of Ely, was compelled to surrender his town
garden to the queen's favorite, Hatton.   Samuel Sandys,
archbishop of York—a prelate who had Puritan sympathies
—stood out bravely against a demand for "the great manors
of Southwell and Scrooby," and for some reason was not
coerced into submission.   He declared that "the granting
of such a lease would highly displease God, kill his conscience, and spoil the church of York."   Some years afterward he made a similar resistance when a similar demand

English ancestor of the queen now reigning was that same sister of Henry
VIII.   James I. was a Scotchman, and his wife a Dane.   Their daughter,
Elizabeth Stuart, married a German, the Elector Palatine; and she became,
through the German marriage of her daughter Sophia, the grandmother of
George I.   The dynasty of the Georges was purely German, save only the
drop of English blood which came from Margaret.   Queen Victoria's mother
was a German.   Her husband was a German; and the Prince of Wales—so
far as lineage and blood can determine a man's nationality—is hardly more
an Englishman than the son of naturalized Celtic parents is a Yankee by
virtue of his having been born in New England.

was made for his house in London. "These be marvelous times," said he; "the patrimony of the church is laid open as a prey to all the world." Accordingly, it was inscribed on his monument, in sonorous Latin, that "he defended the patrimony of the church as a thing consecrated to God."[1] Yet it is among the mysterious incidents of the Elizabethan reformation that by this same archbishop, who so heroically defended "the church's patrimony" against the importunity of the queen herself, the manor of Scrooby—with its parks, mills, and woods—after having been for more than five hundred years a possession of the church, was leased to his eldest son, Sir Samuel Sandys.[2] Under him the stately house, which had been "a manor of the bishops," was occupied by William Brewster. Sir Edwin Sandys, another son of the archbishop, was a friend of Brewster in later years, and was doubtless acquainted with him before the downfall of Secretary Davison.[3] It may have been by the friendship of Sir Edwin that Brewster, after losing his place at court by the unmerited disgrace of his patron, came to reside at Scrooby as a servant of the queen, and so became, like Gaius at Corinth, "the host of the whole church." As his guests the little church assembled on the Lord's day—its members dropping in quietly, one by one, or two or three in company, careful not to attract too much attention, till some fit apartment of the great mansion was filled with worshipers. Long afterward, and far away, they remembered their meetings in his house, and that "with great love he entertained them when they came, making provision for them to his great charge."

How came there to be, just there, the materials out of

---

[1] Strype, "Whitgift," i., 286, 287; "Annals," iii., pt. ii., 550, 551.

[2] Steele, "Chief of the Pilgrims," p. 106.

[3] George Cranmer, a grand-nephew of Archbishop Cranmer, was Sir Edwin's very intimate friend at Oxford and in travels on the Continent, and was associated with Brewster in the service of Secretary Davison.

which these two congregations of Separatists could be gathered? We can understand more readily the growth of an advanced Protestantism in London, and in other centres of influence and of intercourse; but how came there to be in these rural parishes and scattered villages, among a people so remote from the places where agitation and progress would be natural, so much of thought on religious themes, so much of spiritual quickening, so much of movement toward ecclesiastical liberty? Are not these the people who might be expected either to hold fast the ancient superstitions, or to accept, without a murmur of inquiry, whatever may be determined by the queen? The question is answered when the chronicler tells us of the " godly and zealous preachers " who had propagated in those parts the doctrines of the religious reformation. It was by the preaching of that ancient Gospel, " repentance toward God and faith toward our Lord Jesus Christ," that so many of the plain country people, far away from the court and the universities and from the great trading towns, had become thoughtful students of the Bible, earnestly inquiring after God's truth, and resolutely determined on personal reformation at whatever cost. It happens that we know who and what some of those preachers were.

We have seen[1] that in the early years of Queen Elizabeth, under the reaction against the atrocities of the preceding reign and the manifold necessity of making England a Protestant country, there was some measure of connivance, on the part of the government, at the ecclesiastical irregularities of clergymen whose Protestantism protested against the " rags of popery." In various dioceses the bishops were themselves Puritans in theory, though they accepted for the time the existing regulations. Under some such influences in the dioceses of York and Lincoln, evangelical Protestantism, as it would now be called, took deep root and spread itself among

---

[1] *Ante*, chap. iv.

O

the people.   But when the queen began to be more urgent
in her demand for the strictest and minutest uniformity in
ecclesiastical ceremonies and vestments, and when the first
generation of her bishops—of whom many had been confessors and exiles for the Protestant faith — began to be succeeded by men of another sort, then it was that " the ministers," the "godly and zealous preachers," were "urged with
the yoke of subscription or else must be silenced," were summoned into the ecclesiastical courts to give account of their
ritual irregularities, were fined, were imprisoned, were deprived of their livings; and then it was that the nonconforming laity also found themselves at the mercy of malignant informers, and "were so vexed with apparitors and
pursuivants and the commissary courts as truly their affliction was not small."   Then, too, it was that some of the
preachers, and some of their hearers and converts, began to
advance from Puritanism into Separatism.

One of those clergymen was John Smyth, who had been
a fellow in one of the colleges at Cambridge, and had there
been put upon his defense before the Vice-Chancellor of the
University for having affirmed in a sermon the unlawfulness
of sports on the Lord's day.   He appears to have been a
preacher (probably a lecturer) in the city of Lincoln, and afterward to have held a benefice at Gainsborough, about twelve
miles distant from Scrooby.   He is described as "a man of able
gifts, and a good preacher;" but not many of the Puritans
were more likely than he to come into collision with the ecclesiastical authorities, or to be deprived and silenced.   Progress
from Puritanism into separation was natural to such a mind
as his, especially under the stimulus of persecution; but he
is said to have spent nine months in study of the questions
about conformity, and to have held a disputation with some
of the most conspicuous of the Puritan divines on those
questions, before his renunciation of the National Church.
He was chosen pastor of one of the two Separatist churches
—the one which ordinarily met at Gainsborough.

Another of the "godly and zealous preachers" was Richard Clyfton, who had been vicar of Marnham, near Newark,
in Nottinghamshire, and afterward rector of Babworth, a
village not far from Scrooby.   His ministry at Babworth
began about twenty years before the Scrooby church was
instituted.   Bradford, whose early religious experience was
associated with his ministry, affectionately testifies that he
"by his pains and diligence had done much good, and under
God had been a means of the conversion of many."   That
"grave and reverend preacher," having been pushed on from
Nonconformity to Separation, was chosen pastor of the
Scrooby church; and very naturally, for that church must
have consisted chiefly of those who already loved and honored him for his work's sake.

With him was associated, in the office of teacher, a young
man about twenty-five years of age, born in that part of England, a Master of Arts in the University of Cambridge, and
recently a fellow of Corpus Christi College there, who, after leaving the university, had received "deacon's orders"
in the Church of England, and had performed some work as
a minister of Christ in the city of Norwich and elsewhere in
the county of Norfolk.   That younger minister—"a man of
a learned, polished, and modest spirit, pious and studious of
the truth, largely accomplished with suitable gifts and qualifications"—bore the name which has become so venerable in
the history of New England, John Robinson.   Certainly it
was a rare privilege given to that little band of worshipers
that, while they had the experienced Clyfton for their pastor,
ministering to them in their assemblies the word of consola-
tion, they had also for their teacher, ministering the word of
doctrine, a man so gifted as Robinson, and of so sweet and
loving a spirit.

At a later period, the judicious and large-minded Brewster—the man whose diversified experience in affairs, as well
as his general culture and his weight of character, had most
conspicuously qualified him for the presidency in that Chris-

tian community, though he did not recognize in himself any special vocation to the ministry of the word—was chosen to be ruling elder; and thus the threefold eldership in the church—pastor, teacher, and ruler—the presbytery within the church, not outside of it and over it—was completed.

But such proceedings as these, the definite organization of two distinct churches near to each other, and their stated assemblies for worship—however conformable to apostolic precedents and to the law of Christ — were obviously contrary to the Act of Uniformity.   The policy which would have no church in England but the state church, and no worship but that which James Stuart had authorized, could not endure such an assertion of religious liberty.   No matter how peaceable and quiet, or how blameless in other respects, the men might be who dared to associate themselves under the law of Christ "as the Lord's free people," they were insubordinate under the hierarchy which Queen Elizabeth had established, and which her successor was resolved to maintain.

The story of what their undertaking cost them begins with their experience of more violent persecution.   It could not be expected that their definite organization of churches renouncing all dependence on the hierarchy or the state, and their stated meeting on the Lord's day for worship in a manner forbidden by the ruling powers, would escape the notice of their enemies.   Of course, they found themselves "hunted and persecuted on every side;" for they had none to befriend them.   "Some were taken and clapped up in prison, others had their houses beset and watched night and day [by apparitors and pursuivants], and hardly escaped their hands; and the most were fain to flee, and leave their houses and habitations and the means of their livelihood."   All this was no more than what their minds, strong in faith, and willing to suffer for Christ, were in some sort prepared for.   But it soon became a grave question how long all this could be endured.   They could not but inquire what refuge there was for their church, the organization in which their testimony for Christ and Christian liberty was embodied. Only a few leagues distant from the eastern shore of England, just opposite the low and fenny lands of Lincolnshire, there was a country where, if they were willing to lose all things else, they might enjoy their religious convictions. In the United States of the Netherlands, as the Dutch republic was then called, there was "a church without a bishop and a state without a king;" and there they might find "freedom to worship God." They had "heard that in the Low Countries was freedom of religion for all men; as also how sundry, from London and other parts of the land, had been exiled and persecuted for the same cause and were gone thither." Why might they not make that foreign land their refuge till better times should come in England? "By a joint consent, they resolved to go into the Low Countries." Not as individual exiles, fleeing in all directions on the plan of "save himself who can;" but as a church, for which their native country had no place of rest, they were to go beyond the sea. For about a year from the date of the friendly division into two distinct churches, they had continued to meet on the first day of the week, though not always in Brewster's house, and had, in that respect, baffled the diligent malice of their adversaries; but they could do so no longer, and they must get over into Holland as they could.

It was a brave resolve, for they knew the meaning of it. "To go into a country they knew not but by hearsay, where they must learn a new language, and get their livings they knew not how," and where many years of war had made all the necessaries of life oppressively dear—seemed "an adventure almost desperate." Moreover, they "had only been used to a plain country life and the innocent trade of husbandry;" and they were to take their chances among a people subsisting by manufactures and commerce. "But these things did not dismay them, although they did sometimes trouble them; for their desires were set on the ways of God, and to enjoy his ordinances. They rested on his providence, and knew whom they had believed." So beautifully did they obey the precept, "In all thy ways, acknowledge God;" and, more wisely and lovingly than they knew, the promise was performed—"He will direct thy paths."

That resolve, however, was not easily carried into effect; "for, though they could not stay, yet were they not suffered to go." On the one hand, the "Act to retain the queen's subjects in obedience" would not permit them to stay; for under it their goods would be forfeited, and they would be compelled to abjure the realm. On the other hand, the statesmanship which said of the Puritans, "I will make them conform, or I will harry them out of this land," was afraid that Nonconformists, when "harried" out of England, would take refuge in American wildernesses; and therefore a royal proclamation had been issued forbidding Englishmen to transport themselves into Virginia without a license.[1] Probably it was by force of that proclamation that the ports were shut against Separatists seeking to escape into Holland, for what security was there that they would not find their way from Holland to Virginia? Liable as such persons were to banishment, they must not be permitted to banish themselves. They were constrained to smuggle themselves out of their own country as if they had been runaway slaves.

Boston (or, if "writ large," St. Botolph's town), in Lincolnshire, about fifty miles distant from their homes, was the port from which a large company of them intended to sail. Brewster was one of them. He had relinquished his office (Sept., 1607), and, having prepared his books and other chattels for transportation, he bade farewell to Scrooby. He and his friends had hired a vessel for their purpose, and had arranged with the master for their embarkation at an appointed time and place. The shipmaster proved himself a knave. First, he involved them in delay and expense by not being ready at the time. Afterward, when he had them and their

---

[1] Palfrey, "History of New England," i., 138.

goods on board, he betrayed them into the hands of their enemies, with whom he had conspired against them. It was night; for the emigrants were hoping to escape into exile under cover of darkness. But just as they began to feel that they were safe — the ship riding at anchor — and that soon they would be beyond the reach of apparitors and pursuivants, they were arrested, taken from the ship into open boats, rifled of whatever they had about them, and searched to their shirts by ruffianly officers, who even insulted the modesty of the women. In the morning they were brought back into the town, " a spectacle and wonder to the multitude who came flocking on all sides to behold them," and were presented to the magistrates. It does not appear that Separatism had made any lodgment in Boston; but Puritanism was almost dominant there. Ecclesiastical officers other than simply ministers of the Gospel were not held in high esteem, and the persecution of honest and religious people for nonconformity was not much encouraged by citizens of the better sort in that old borough. So when the captured Separatists were brought before the civic magistrates, they were treated with respect, and would have been set at liberty, had not messengers been already sent to the lords of the council with information of so important an arrest. After a month of imprisonment, the messengers having had time to go and return, Brewster and six others were bound over for trial and detained in prison, while the others were discharged. What came of the trial, and how long those seven remained in prison, does not appear.

Some men would have been quite vanquished by such a defeat. It was not so with these men. About six months later, having quietly recruited their strength and renewed their preparation for removal, they made another attempt. In some way they had been brought into communication with a Dutchman at Hull, who had a ship of his own under the Dutch flag. Finding reason to trust him, they frankly informed him of their condition, and made an agreement with

him for their passage over to his country.   He was to take
them on board at a point on the Humber between Hull and
Grimsby.   The place, "a large common, a good way distant
from any town," seemed to promise them a safe embarkation.
When the appointed time drew near, the women and children of the company, with the goods, were sent, probably
from Hull, in a small bark which had been hired for the purpose; and the men went by land to meet them.   They were
a day too early for the ship; and as the sea, driven by an
easterly wind, rolled up the broad Humber, the women were
distressed with sea-sickness, and for their relief the little craft
put into a creek hard by, where the outgoing tide left her
aground.   The ship came early the next day; but the bark,
with so many of the passengers and all the freight, was fast
in the mud, and must wait till about noon for the tide.
Meanwhile the skipper, to save time, sent his boat for the
men, whom he saw walking about on the shore.   But when
the boat had gone once and returned full of passengers, and
was ready to go the second time—behold! "a great company, both horse and foot, with bills and guns and other weapons!"   The dangerous fugitives had been tracked, and the
posse comitatus had been called out to capture them.   It
was beginning to be a serious affair for the captain and his
ship as well as for his intended passengers.   To him the sight
of that armed force, "horse and foot," was a suggestion of
seizure and of proceedings in admiralty.   Thereupon he swore
a great Dutch oath, "and, having the wind fair, weighed his
anchor, hoisted sails, and away."   No time had he for considering what the condition would be of the few passengers
—one boat-load—whom he had on board.   There they were,
suddenly and helplessly parted from their wives and children, whom they saw falling into the hands of enemies.
They had nothing for their voyage—nothing for their settlement in a foreign country, save the clothes they wore: all
that they had prepared for their removal being on board the
bark.   But "there was no remedy: they must thus sadly

part." The men who were left on shore escaped the pursu-
ers; those only remaining whose presence might be some protection or help to the women. "But pitiful it was to see the
heavy case of these poor women—what weeping and crying
on every side; some for their husbands that were carried
away in the ship; others not knowing what should become of
them and their little ones; others, again, melted in tears, seeing their poor little ones hanging about them, crying for fear
and quaking with cold." But, after all, the capture of so
many women and children was no great achievement. It
was something that the emigrating expedition had been defeated; but what were the captors to do with their captives?
After going from one justice to another in vain, they began
to be embarrassed. "To imprison so many women and innocent children for no other cause (many of them) but that
they must go with their husbands, seemed to be unreasonable, and all would cry out of them; and to send them home
again was as difficult," for their homes had been broken up
in order to their migration. "In the end necessity forced a
way for them," and they were released without being imprisoned.

Meanwhile the few men—"the first boat-load"—carried
away in the ship against their will were driven by a tempest,
far northward, to the coast of Norway. Instead of the few
hours which should have sufficed for their voyage to Holland, they were fourteen days at sea; and for seven days
"they saw neither sun, moon, nor stars." At one time the
ship seemed to be foundering, and the sailors despaired. But
she righted in a moment, and just then the storm began to
abate. It was only after such perils that they arrived at
their destination. Bradford, who was one of them, retained
in his old age a vivid remembrance of that voyage—how earnestly and believingly they prayed while the tempest was
roaring; and how, "when man's hope and help failed, the
Lord's power and mercy appeared" for them. "Blessed are
the pure in heart, for they shall see God." They, in the sim-

plicity of their trust and the purity of their devout affection, saw God in the tempest, and to him they cried. They saw him in the calm; and he "filled their afflicted minds with such comforts as every one can not understand." No scientist of to-day believes in the immutability of natural law and the conservation of force more firmly than they believed in the immutability of the divine purposes. In their theory of the universe, the storm and the hush, the billows and the ship that rode upon their surges, the peril and the deliverance, were equally determined from eternity. They did not expect that their words, thrown out upon the wind, would change God's purpose; yet they prayed, for, to their thought, the prayer was itself included in the decree of the Ineffable Love that had loved them from before the foundation of the world. Scientists may perplex themselves about what prayer has to do with events, for science knows only what is limited by time and space; but faith, taking hold of the infinite, and recognizing in events the evolution of an eternal thought and purpose, walks with God, speaks to him, listens for his voice, accepts his determinations, and sees him even in "the stormy wind fulfilling his word."

Baffled in two attempts, the members of the Scrooby church seem to have abandoned their plan of emigrating in a body, as Israel went out of Egypt. Some of their most active men having been, by the last disaster, carried into Holland, were able to serve as pioneers for the company, and to make such arrangements for them as were possible after their losses. Amsterdam was the rendezvous of the fugitives as they made their escape out of England, one by one, or in families. "In the end, they all got over, some at one time and some at another, and met together again with no small rejoicing." Meanwhile, by the troubles they had suffered, "their cause became famous." Their Christian behavior under persecution "left a deep impression on the minds of many." In many a thoughtful mind the inquiry was raised, "Who and what are these men? What evil have they done? What

is it for which they suffer so meekly, and yet so perseveringly?"

Who and what were they? Whatever ecclesiastical or
political prejudice against them may linger in some quarters,
no intelligent reader of history can think of them as frantic
enthusiasts, as dupes of knavish leaders, or as in any way
dangerous members of society. Some of them were men
trained at the English universities, and skilled in the learning and the controversies of their time. Some were not without experience of life in the great world, and in connection
with public affairs; others were plain people of the old English yeomanry, who had lived on their hereditary acres—
the type and original of our New England farmers. All had
gained the intelligence that comes from the diligent study
of the Bible, and all were honest and earnest believers in the
Christ of the New Testament. Such were the men and the
women who were thus driven out of their native England,
yet hunted and intercepted in their flight, as if they were
criminals escaping from justice. Why did they suffer the
spoiling of their goods, arrest, imprisonment, exile? Their
only crime was that, while they rendered to Cæsar the things
that are Cæsar's, they would not render to Cæsar the things
that are God's. They had caught from the Bible the idea of
a church independent alike of the pope and the queen, independent of Parliament as well as of prelates, and dependent only on Christ. It was their mission to work out and
organize that idea; and, in so doing, they wrought and suffered for their posterity in all ages and for the world.

CHAPTER XI.

THE SEPARATISTS IN AMSTERDAM.

THE Separatists of Scrooby, having made their escape from their native country, had become literally "strangers and pilgrims on the earth." Holland was to them only "a strange country," not the land of promise. In Bradford's report of the impressions which that country made upon them when they saw it, there is a picturesque effect which shows how he felt as one of them. He was at that time a youth of not more than twenty years — a plain north-country Englishman, whose knowledge of the world beyond the seas was only so much as he had been able to gain from vague report with the aid of a few books, and who had probably never seen any larger town than Boston, in Lincolnshire, and Hull, in Yorkshire. His own words, for himself and his fellow-exiles, are the best in which to tell the story:

"Being now come into the Low Countries, they saw many goodly and fortified cities, strongly walled, and guarded with troops of armed men. Also they heard a strange and uncouth language, and beheld the different manners and customs of the people, with their strange fashions and attires; all so far differing from that of their plain country villages, wherein they were bred and had so long lived, as it seemed they were come into a new world. But these were not the things they much looked on, or which long took up their thoughts; for they had other work in hand, and another kind of war to wage and maintain. For though they saw fair and beautiful cities flowing with abundance of all sorts of wealth and riches, it was not long before they saw the grim and grisly face of poverty coming upon them like an armed man, with whom they must buckle and encounter, and from whom they could not fly.   But they were armed with faith and patience against him ; and though they were some- times foiled, yet, by God's assistance, they prevailed and got the victory."

They were not entirely without friends in Amsterdam, the place of their first residence after their migration. Others of their countrymen, exiles like them, were there be- fore them.   Besides the recognized congregations of English subjects, which had been established in various cities, and which—purporting to be of the Church of England, though generally served by Puritan ministers[1] — were under the protection of a treaty, there was at Amsterdam (as former- ly, under Robert Browne, there had been at Middleburg) an organized congregation of English Separatists.   In that more ancient church, the exiles from Scrooby found some of their former friends.   They also found in Amsterdam their old neighbor John Smyth, and many who had been members of the church under his guidance at Gainsborough, and who, with him, had escaped from England a year or two earlier than they.   It was natural for them to sit down, at first, among their countrymen and friends in that great commer- cial city, till they could intelligently form their plans for a more permanent residence.

They soon discovered that, among the English Separatists at Amsterdam, there were elements of discord, tending to dissolution.   Already there had been a painful agitation in the church under the pastoral care of Francis Johnson ; and it had resulted in the excommunication of two conspicuous members.   The story is worth telling, not only because it gives us a glimpse into the interior of a Separatist church in those days, but also because there is something of a moral in it.   It began with a complaint against the pastor's wife.

---

[1] Such was the position of Francis Johnson when he was "preacher to the Company of English of the Staple at Middleburg."   *Ante*, p. 129.

When the Scrooby exiles knew her, she was, as they testify, a grave matron, modest in dress and demeanor, ready to all good works in her place, especially helpful to the poor, and an ornament to her husband's pastoral office.   In her youth she had been a merchant's wife and widow; and she was still young when Johnson married her—"a godly woman" with "a good estate."   But she was blamed by some "because she wore such apparel as she had been formerly used to," which certainly was not very extravagant.   They found fault with "her wearing of some whalebone in the bodice and sleeves of her gown," also with her corked shoes, and "other such like things as citizens of her rank used to wear." The pastor and his wife, in deference to such scruples, were willing to reform the objectionable conformity to fashion, "so far as might be without spoiling of their garments;" but the fault-finders would accept no compromise.   Pitiful it seems to us that the peace of a church should be disturbed by a conflict of opinions about the whalebone in a lady's bodice and the cork in the heels of her shoes.   Pitiful it seemed to those who under the teaching of Clyfton and Robinson had added to their faith virtue, and to virtue knowledge; but "such," said they, "was the strictness of some in those times," who could tolerate no Christian brother unless he "came full up to their size."

The chief complainants against the "outward adorning" of the pastor's wife were the pastor's father and brother. Probably some domestic feud was the cause of the church difficulty.   The good sense of the majority is shown in the fact that the pastor was not dismissed, nor his wife put under censure; while the fidelity of the church appears in the fact that the two leading agitators, "after long patience toward them and much pains taken with them," were excluded from communion "for their unreasonable and endless opposition, and such things as did accompany the same."[1]   The scars

---

[1] Bradford's "Dialogue," in Young's "Chronicles of the Pilgrims," p. 446.

of that conflict must have remained till after the arrival of the exiles from Scrooby.

At the same time another trouble was impending. Smyth, "a man of able gifts and a good preacher," was also a man of "inconstancy and unstable judgment." He had, of course, much influence among those who came with him out of England, having been under his pastoral care at Gainsborough; and he was beginning to entertain and broach opinions which were likely to raise a controversy. Robinson, and "some others of best discerning" in the church that came from Scrooby, "seeing how Mr. John Smyth and his company were already fallen into contention with the church that was there before them," and finding reason to believe "that no means they could use would do any good to cure the same," were naturally averse from the thought of a permanent residence in Amsterdam. "Flames of contention," kindled by other causes, seemed "likely to break out in that ancient church itself." Robinson, therefore, and Brewster, and others in their company, felt that they must make another removal, "though they knew it would be much to the prejudice of their outward estate." Their "outward estate" was not the main thing in their estimate of life; for they were "strangers and pilgrims on the earth."

Is there not in that unwillingness of theirs to remain among their fellow-exiles at Amsterdam a noteworthy indication of their character as a community? There was no persecution to drive them away. There was no prospect of their obtaining more lucrative employment or better support for their families elsewhere. We have evidence that there was no lack of friendliness between them and their brethren in exile. But they saw that, in Amsterdam, they were likely to be troubled with the whimsies of erratic and inconstant men; that ultra-Separatists, crotchety inventors of new opinions, and restless agitators of all sorts, would be continually attracted to that centre, and that in some other place they could have more peace in their communion with each other, and better opportunities for mutual edification and the cultivation of Christian character.

"For these and other reasons," says Bradford, "they removed to Leyden, a fair and beautiful city, and of a sweet situation, but made more famous by the university with which it is adorned." Such were the attractions which they felt when selecting the place of their abode—the beautiful city—the pleasant situation—the famous university with its resort of learned men. Against attractions so potent, the consideration that Leyden, "wanting that traffic by sea which Amsterdam enjoyed, was not so beneficial for their outward means of living," had no preponderating force.

The history of the church under the care of Johnson and Ainsworth verified the forebodings which induced the Pilgrims to seek another place of refuge. In some respects that church seemed to prosper. Exiles from England, making a fair profession, and sufferers for conscience' sake, were continually gathered into its communion; so that for a time it had about three hundred members. It was served by a full staff of able officers—pastor, teacher, ruling elders, deacons, and deaconess.[1] Its worship, conducted by Johnson, was edifying and impressive, not with ritual ornament, but with

---

[1] The "Ancient Men," in Bradford's "Dialogue," say : "At Amsterdam, before their division and breach, they were about three hundred communicants; and they had for their pastor and teacher those two eminent men before named, and in our time four grave men for ruling elders, and three able and godly men for deacons, [also] one ancient widow for a deaconess, who did them service many years, though she was sixty years of age when she was chosen. She honored her place and was an ornament to the congregation. She usually sat in a convenient place in the congregation with a little birchen rod in her hand, and kept little children in great awe from disturbing the congregation. She did frequently visit the sick and weak, and especially women, and, as there was need, called out maids and young women to watch and do them helps as their necessity did require ; and, if they were poor, she would gather relief for them of those that were able, or acquaint the deacons ; and she was obeyed as a mother in Israel and an officer of Christ."—Young, p. 455, 456.

spiritual beauty of simplicity.[1]   But it was the unhappiness
of that church to be infested with too many of those eccen-
tric and restless persons who, either by their superficial enthusiasm and impulsive instability, or by their conscientious
narrowness, or perhaps by their stubborn impracticableness,
are more troublesome than profitable to any church that has
them among its members.   Such men are indigenous every
where; and in times of persecution many of them are found
among the persecuted.   Amsterdam was the most convenient
and attractive refuge for all sorts of persons who could find
no toleration at home for their religious opinions or their
modes of worship; and consequently the church of English
exiles there had more than it could well bear of those members who become apostates and enemies, as well as of those
who, wherever they may be, and under whatever ecclesiastical forms, disturb the peace of the church, and make its
edification almost or altogether impossible.

Those troubles began very early.   While Johnson, the pastor, was still in prison at London, some of the exiled members of his flock fell into we know not what extravagant
opinions of the Dutch Anabaptists, and were excommunicated
by the others.   Not much later, " many others—some older,
some younger, even too many, though not the half—fell into
a schism from the rest; and so many of them as continued
therein were cast out; divers of them repenting and returning before excommunication, and divers of them after."[2]
Then, after Johnson himself had passed from prison into exile, there arose the great conflict concerning the whalebone
in Mrs. Johnson's too fashionable bodice and the corks of her
high-heeled shoes.   An unhappy notoriety was given to that
conflict by the indomitable George Johnson, who, after he

---

[1] " A very grave man he was, and an able teacher, and was the most solemn in all his administrations that we have seen any, and especially in dispensing the seals of the covenant, both baptism and the Lord's Supper."
Bradford's " Dialogue," in Young, p. 445.

[2] Johnson, in Hanbury, i., 110, 111.

had been cast out of the church " for lying, slandering, false accusation, and contention," found means to print his version of the story in a volume, which, of course, found currency among the enemies of Separation, whether Puritans or Prelatists.[1]

In other instances the church was vexed with defamatory pamphlets by apostate members. One such pamphlet, of which a copy is still extant, seems to have been considered, like George Johnson's, unworthy of a reply ; but, in another case, a public and authentic contradiction was thought necessary, not only for the reputation of the church, but rather for the defense of the principle of Separation.[2] All these conflicts and assaults had preceded the arrival of the Pilgrims at Amsterdam.

John Smyth was almost the last man whom a judicious adviser would have selected to neutralize the elements of discord in such a church. Evidently, there was a sort of magnetism in his enthusiastic nature. He was not only a good preacher, but had also other " able gifts." In his moral character he seems to have been unblamable. The fearlessness with which he sought for truth, and the fidelity with which he obeyed his convictions, could not but command respect. But with all his " able gifts" and estimable qualities, he had not the gift of good common-sense ; his mind's eye was mi-

---

[1] " Discourse of certain Troubles and Excommunications in the Banished English Church at Amsterdam, etc.   1603."   Hanbury, i., 99.

[2] " Brownism turned the Inside outward : Being a Parallel between the Profession and Practice of the Brownists' Religion.   By Christopher Lawne. lately returned from that wicked Separation.   London, 1603."   Hanbury. i., 100.

" A Discovery of Brownism : Or a brief Declaration of some of the Errors and Abominations daily practiced and increased among the English Company of the Separation remaining for the present at Amsterdam, in Holland. By Thomas White.   London, 1605."   Hanbury, i., 107.

" An Inquiry and Answer of Thomas White in his ' Discovery of Brownism.'   By Francis Johnson, Pastor of the Exiled English Church at Amsterdam, in Holland.   1606."   Hanbury, ibid.

croscopic, incapable of seeing things in their perspective and proportions. Such a man could not but bring with him, into such a community as that of the English exiles at Amsterdam, new questions to be debated and new contentions.

At this day, it weighs not much in proof of Smyth's instability, or against the soundness of his judgment, when we are told that he adopted those theological opinions which Arminius had maintained in opposition to Gomarus, and which were favored in England by divines like Laud and Bancroft. Nor can we certainly conclude against him when we are told that he became scrupulous about baptism, and denied that it could be properly administered to the children of Christian parents. But when we find what the beginning was of his quarrel with the Amsterdam church, we see what ailed him. "He, with his followers," says Ainsworth in behalf of the church, "breaking off communion with us, charged us with sin for using our English Bibles in the worship of God." His position was that the official ministers of a church —the pastor and teacher—"should bring the originals, the Hebrew and Greek, and out of them translate by voice." Withdrawing from the church, for this reason, with his adherents, he afterward discovered that what he called "the tri-formed presbytery" (consisting of pastor, teacher, and ruling elders) was "a false ministry," and he denounced it accordingly. Then he learned that, "in contributing to the church treasury, there ought to be a separation from them that are without," inasmuch as the contribution is a religious communion. Another of his crotchets was that the singing of improvised compositions (the tune and the hymn coming "by gift of the Spirit") is "a part of God's proper worship in the New Testament;" and on that ground, also, he quarreled with his former brethren, "who contented themselves with joint harmonious singing of the Psalms of Holy Scripture." Evidently the man was, in Ainsworth's phrase, and more literally than Ainsworth thought, "benumbed in mind." Yet such were the materials of the Amsterdam church, and such was the man's personal influence, especially over those who had come with him out of England, that in his secession he drew after him a considerable body of followers.[1] He died not long after that secession; but the church which he gathered—sometimes called "the remainders of Mr. Smyth's company"—outlived him, and, after a while, returned into England to testify and to suffer there in the great cause of religious liberty.

At a later date, the Amsterdam church was agitated, and finally rent in twain, by another controversy—probably the one which Robinson "and others of the best discerning" in his church had foreseen as "likely to break out," and from which they desired to escape. The question arose whether the church should be self-governed, or governed by what Smyth had called "the tri-formed presbytery." Whether there should be elders in the church was not disputed; nor whether, in addition to the pastor and teacher, known as the "teaching elders," there should be other elders, sharing equally with them in the duty of overseeing and ruling the congregation. All this was agreed to on both sides as the obvious interpretation of apostolic precept and example. The elders, including the pastor and the teacher, were to rule, and were all equal in the function of ruling; but in what sense were they to rule? Were they executive officers merely, presiding in the assembled church, conducting its worship, preparing matters for its consideration, guiding its deliberations, but concluding nothing save with the consent of the

---

[1] The church which Smyth gathered does not appear to have been a Baptist Church, as that name is commonly understood. Had he insisted on immersion as the only baptism, there would have been some traces of a controversy on that point between him and Ainsworth, or between him and Robinson. He and his party held that those who had been baptized in their infancy must be rebaptized on a personal profession of faith, and, in that sense, they were *Ana*-baptists. Smyth is sometimes called "the *Se*-baptist," because, when he renounced his former baptism, he baptized himself before proceeding to baptize his followers. Robinson's Works, i., 452; iii., 168, 169.

brethren?   Or, on the other hand, were they to open and
shut, to censure and absolve, to direct and control all things
according to their own judgment and without appeal, the
only duty of the brotherhood in such matters being the duty
of submission?

On this question, the pastor and the teacher were opposed
to each other.   Johnson, as a Puritan, had adopted Cartwright's ideal of ecclesiastical polity; and, when he separated from the National Church, he might very naturally
carry with him, into his new relations, the Presbyterian feeling that a congregation ought not to govern itself as an
equal brotherhood, but ought rather to be governed by its
officers in a consistory or session.   Ainsworth had never been
a member of the clerical order in England; and, naturally,
he had no hierarchical prejudices.   He was only a Christian
scholar, profoundly and minutely learned, whom the church,
because of his gifts, had chosen to be one of its elders, laboring in word and doctrine, as it had chosen Johnson to be
another.   It was easy for him to understand that the elders,
whether ruling only, or ruling and teaching, were not lords
over God's heritage, but servants of the church, responsible
to their constituency for their official acts, and governing
not by power but by light, and with the free consent of the
brotherhood to every act of government.   After much contention, the "Ainsworthians," as they were called, withdrew
from the "Johnsonians," and the church was finally divided.
(Dec., 1610).[1]

Which of the two parties was the more numerous does
not appear.   It is said that Johnson and his adherents removed, after a while, from Amsterdam to Embden, in the
neighboring province of Friesland; and that there his church,
claiming to be the same with the old Southwark church of
which he was the pastor and Greenwood the teacher, dwin-
dled in its loneliness, till not far from the time of his death

---

[1] Hanbury, i., 240-256.

it became extinct. The other fragment, under the ministry
of Ainsworth, remained at the old place, and afterward was
known as "the ancient English Church in Amsterdam." After
his death it lived on, not without some experience of internal
dissensions, and, even half a century later (1671), there were
said to be "some remains" of it. The "blind lane" in which
the English Separatists had their meeting-place was probably
that which is now called "Brownists' Lane," and which is the
only remaining trace in Amsterdam of "that ancient church."

But "the bush was not consumed." Before the death of
Johnson the church of the martyrs had begun to live again
in Southwark. Henry Jacob, a beneficed minister of the
National Church, had suffered for nonconformity, and, like
many other clergymen obnoxious to the ecclesiastical courts,
had escaped into Holland, where he gathered a congregation
of English sojourners, using their liberty of worship, but professing not to separate from the National Church of their
own country. As a Puritan he had earnestly opposed the
extreme opinions of the Separatists, and had been, in more
than one published discussion, the antagonist of Johnson;
but, like Johnson, he had yielded to arguments which he
could not refute, and had become himself a Separatist. He
had ventured on returning into England; and, perhaps with
the aid of some who had been members of the church in Amsterdam, he sought out and gathered into a new church (1616)
the hidden ones who had maintained their fidelity to the
cause through those years of persecution. It was a new
church, constituted partly from what remained in London of
that martyr church which, after giving Greenwood, Penry,
and Barrowe to the gallows, had been driven into exile. It
was the church of the martyrs, renewing its life at its birthplace. A few brethren, in whom the spirit of the martyrs
lived, assembled in private for a day of prayer and fasting.
At the close of the day, each of them in succession made
profession of his faith in Christ. Then, standing together,
hand clasped in hand, they covenanted with each other and

with God that they would walk together as a church of
Christ "in all God's ways and ordinances, according as he
had already revealed *or should further make them known to
them.*" To complete the organization, church officers must be
chosen and inducted.   Henry Jacob was designated pastor
by the uplifted hands of the brotherhood, and others, by the
same formality, were chosen deacons.   Then pastor and deacons were ordained by prayer and the laying on of hands.[1]

The church in Southwark thus reconstituted has outlived
persecution, and is now the mother church of the thousands
of Congregational churches in the British Empire.

---

[1] Neal, vol. i., 262; Hanbury, i., 292, 293; Robinson's Works, iii., 444–446.
The church is that of which Dr. Waddington was lately pastor, and from
which he has retired to pursue his work in "Congregational History."

CHAPTER XII.

THE SOJOURN AT LEYDEN.—JOHN ROBINSON A PASTOR AND AN AUTHOR.

In the archives of the city of Leyden there has been preserved a memorial addressed by the Pilgrims (Feb. 12=22, 1609) to "the Honorable the Burgomasters and Court of the City." The memorialists, "to the number of one hundred or thereabout, men and women, represent that they are desirous of coming to live in this city, by the first of May next, and to have the freedom thereof in carrying on their trades, without being a burden in the least to any one;" and their humble petition is that they may have "free consent" to do so. The reply of the civic authorities was "that they refuse no honest persons free ingress to come and have their residence in this city, provided that such persons behave themselves and submit to the laws and ordinances; and therefore the coming of the memorialists will be agreeable and welcome."

That "first of May," then, was their "moving-day." Leaving the friends whom they had found in Amsterdam, and making their escape from the conflicts that seemed to be impending there, they came to the more quiet city which was to be for a while their home. There, in a community by themselves, bound to each other by intimate sympathies and by mutual helpfulness, they could wait for some such change in the policy of the English government as would give them toleration in their native land. Accordingly "they fell to such trades and employments as they best could, valuing peace and their spiritual comfort above any other riches." In respect to trades and employments, the place of their abode was wisely chosen. Leyden was a great hive of manufacturing industry—not like a manufacturing city of to-day, but as such industry was before the age of machinery; and at that time the products of Dutch handicraft went into all the markets of the world.

Most of the Pilgrims had been, in England, simple husbandmen. Their brief residence in Amsterdam had given them scanty opportunity for becoming skillful in new employments. If they were to live in Leyden, they must learn such trades as would yield them a subsistence there; and however willing they might be to labor, their earnings must needs be small at first. Yet they redeemed their promise to sustain themselves "without being a burden in the least to any one." With brave hearts they betook themselves to such employments as they could find; "and at length they came to raise a competent and comfortable living, but with hard and continual labor." A few of them (not more than five) seem to have had so much capital as enabled them to engage in commerce, and are named in the city records as "merchants." One was a "physician," whose gift of healing was employed, no doubt, chiefly among the members of the Pilgrim community. Others were "silk-workers," "fustian-makers," "wool-carders," and artisans in similar branches of manufacture. Three were printers, there being (as we have seen) much occasion for the printing of English books in the Netherlands. One was a mason, one a carpenter, one a smith, and one a tailor; and these might have brought their trades with them out of England. Bradford is mentioned in the records as a fustian-maker. But another authority tells us that while he was at Amsterdam, he "stooped to difficulties in learning and serving of a Frenchman at the working of silks;" and that when he came of age—which was after their arrival at Leyden—he sold his estate in England and "set up for himself" in some business (perhaps the same "working of silks"), which proved to him unfortunate.[1] Brewster, the scholar and courtier, who had for-

---

[1] Mather, "Magnalia," i., 111.

merly passed through the cities of Holland as an attaché of the English embassy, "suffered much hardship after he had spent the most of his means, having a great charge and many children," and being, because of his former condition and course of life, "not so fit for many employments as others were, especially such as were toilsome and laborious." Yet he was always cheerful and contented.   After a few years, his familiarity with Latin enabled him to support himself comfortably by teaching English to students in the university, "both Danes and Germans," for whom he seems to have drawn up an English grammar in Latin.   He also obtained means to establish a printing-office, where books were printed in Latin and in English, the English books being sometimes such as could not be safely printed in England.[1] Though it can hardly be supposed that he was either compositor or pressman, he was so much of a printer that the books from his establishment attest his skill in the art.   His partner in that business—apparently a sleeping partner who supplied the capital—was Thomas Brewer, "a gentleman of a good house, both of land and living," who was himself a sojourner in the Netherlands for conscience' sake, who had many friends there, and had become a member of the university in Leyden, and who was expending his wealth freely in the service of religion.[2]

When the Pilgrims had established themselves in Leyden, the office of pastor in their church was vacant.   At Scrooby they had Clyfton for pastor and Robinson for teacher.   So while they sojourned at Amsterdam, if they assembled by themselves instead of joining temporarily with the church already there, they had the same officers.   But when they determined to make another removal, Clyfton was unwilling to remove with them.   He was beginning to be an old man, though he was not so old as he seemed to his younger and

---

[1] Bradford, p. 412, 413.
[2] Waddington, "Hidden Church," p. 210-227.

more enterprising brethren.   Bradford, who revered him as
his spiritual father, and, while yet a child, had been under
his earnest ministry, says of him : " He was a grave and fa-
therly old man when he first came into Holland, having a
great white beard ; and pity it was that such a reverend old
man should be forced to leave his country, and at those years
to go into exile.   But it was his lot ; and he bore it patiently."   At the age of fifty-six, he did not feel that he was
called to make another removal.   Perhaps he differed from
Robinson and others of that company in their foresight of
" the flames of contention that were like to break out " between Johnson and Ainsworth ; for afterward, when that
contention had arrived at its crisis, he and the church, in
which he once held the foremost place, were on opposite
sides.   Certainly he was " settled at Amsterdam " so much
to his own satisfaction that " he was loath to remove any
more."   When the Pilgrims removed from that city, he was
amicably dismissed to the ancient church ; and there, some
three years later, he succeeded Ainsworth in the office of
teacher.

The vacancy made by the dismissal of Clyfton was filled
by the election of Robinson to the office of pastor.   Although
the pastor-elect had been " in holy orders " before he became
a Separatist, and had been ordained again when the church
called him to minister as its teacher, his induction to another
office required (in his opinion and in that of the church) a
new ordination.   Instead of being " installed " over the
church, he was ordained to a definite office in the church.
A minister who is already a member in a classical presbytery may be publicly put in charge of one of the congregations governed by that presbytery, and the ceremony will
be an installation ; but such was not the introduction of the
Pilgrim pastor into his office.   Having been designated by
the uplifted hands of the brotherhood (χειροτονία), he received
also " the laying on of hands " (χειροθεσία) by the authority
which Christ had given to the church itself.   The office of

teacher, made vacant when Robinson became pastor, was not filled—probably because no other man among them had received the education which they required as a qualification for the work of a teaching elder.   Brewster was thenceforward (perhaps had been before) the ruling elder, and in that capacity he was a colleague-bishop with the pastor.   They had also "three able men for deacons."   John Carver was one of them, and Samuel Fuller, their physician, was another.[1]

As, in England, their place of meeting had been Brewster's great manor-house, so, in Leyden, not long after their removal thither, a large house was purchased by John Robinson and three others—whether with their private means or as agents for the community, we can only conjecture; and that house seems to have been at once the pastor's residence and the meeting-house of the church.   Recent investigations have ascertained the locality with great exactness.[2]   It was near the Peter's-church, being just across the street from the "clock-house" (or campanile) of that grand old edifice— a cathedral which then had stood five hundred years, and which, even now, may stand five hundred years more.   A few rods distant, in one direction, was Brewster's printing-

---

[1] Robinson, Works, vol. i., "Memoir," p. xxix., xxx. ; also p. 452, 453; Bradford, p. 17, 413.   Bradford says of the ruling elder Brewster: "When the church had no other minister, he taught twice every Sabbath, and that both powerfully and profitably."   Teaching was not an ordinary function of a ruling elder, but in the absence of pastor and teacher, he presided in public worship, and the gift of public speech was regarded as an important qualification for his office.   Robinson says (Works, ii., 131): "We make no dumb ministers; neither dare we admit of any man either for a teaching or governing elder of whose ability in prayer, prophesying, and debating of church matters we have not had good experience."

[2] The late George Sumner led the way in exploring Leyden and its archives for traces of the Pilgrims in their residence there, and gave his results in "Memoirs of the Pilgrims at Leyden."   Among those who have followed him, none have been more diligent or more successful than Prof. George E. Day, of New Haven, and Dr. Henry M. Dexter, of Boston.

office, and near by, in another direction, his residence.   Not much farther off was Bradford's house, very near the old pile known as the university; for, though the Leyden university was then a modern institution, it occupied a building of the Middle Ages, which, till the Reformation, had been a monastery.

The Pilgrims received kind and hospitable treatment in Leyden, and enjoyed their sojourn there, notwithstanding their many hardships.   Sweet was the taste of liberty, though in a land of strangers; and sweet was their communion with each other and with God, while in their allotted measure they were " filling up that which is behind of the afflictions of Christ."   All that they had suffered together endeared them to each other, and was the first stage—as those years of " peace and spiritual comfort " were the second—of their training for a destiny of which they had, as yet, no definite anticipation.   Long afterward, when they had begun to inhabit a wilderness which, in some sense, they could call their own, they cherished a grateful and tender memory of Leyden.   "Being thus settled, after many difficulties, they continued many years in a comfortable condition, enjoying much sweet and delightful society and spiritual comfort together in the ways of God, . . . so as they grew in knowledge and other gifts and graces of the Spirit of God, and lived together in peace and love and holiness."   Nor were they without increase of numbers; for the report of their peace and spiritual prosperity went abroad among the Separatists still persecuted in their native country.   "Many came to them from England, so as they grew a great congregation," hardly less numerous than that in Amsterdam.   "And if at any time any differences did arise, or offenses broke out (as it can not be but that sometimes there will even among the best of men), they were ever so met with and nipped in the head betimes, or otherwise so well composed, as still love, peace, and communion was continued; or else the church [was] purged of those that were incurable and incorrigible, when, after much patience used, no other means would serve—which seldom comes to pass." [1]

Maintaining a fraternal intercourse with their fellow-exiles at Amsterdam, they could not but have some share in the troubles which came upon that less-favored community. The Amsterdam church—partly by reason of its locality, partly, perhaps, by the force of some elective affinity—drew to itself many of those fugitives or exiles who, having been Puritan clergymen in the Church of England, had advanced from Puritanism to Separation. Some of these—for example, Clyfton—were never liable to any charge of defection from evangelical doctrine or of instability. Others—such as Smyth—were erratic, and driven by every wind of doctrine. Others were of the same sort with Robert Browne, zealous for a while, then relapsing into Anglicanism, and, sometimes at least, assailing the persecuted church with malignant slanders. The Leyden church was "not at all inferior in able men;" but its able men were of another sort—men of broad views and generous culture, like Robinson—men of wide experience in affairs, like Brewster—practical men, like Carver and Bradford. Thus exempted from the disturbing influence of men who live in speculations and disputes, and who seem to regard religion itself as something to quarrel about, they were trained into the simplest and purest style of Christian character; "and, that which was a crown unto them, they lived together in peace and love all their days without any considerable differences, or any disturbance that grew there by but such as was easily healed in love." Yet let it not be thought that all the able men in the church at Amsterdam were contentious. "Many worthy and able men there were in both places, who lived and died in obscurity in respect of the world, as private Christians, yet were they precious in the eyes of the Lord, and also in the eyes of such as knew them—whose virtues we," said the "ancient men"

---

[1] Bradford, p. 17, 18.

at Plymouth, "with such of you as are their children, do follow."

Among the Pilgrims there was no serious division on that question about the powers of elders or church-overseers which was so contentiously debated at Amsterdam.[1] When the contention had become chronic, the minority (for so we may call the party opposing Johnson's claim of power) proposed that the church at Leyden should be sent for to hear the question debated and to give advice. This proposal was, substantially, a request for a mutual council; but the majority preferred that the Leyden church should either interpose uninvited, or come at the invitation of the discontented party. After some hesitation, about thirty members of the Amsterdam church subscribed a letter inviting the Leyden church to come, to hear all parties, and to give such advice as might be needful. In other words, the minority called an *ex parte* council. They thought that their teacher, Ainsworth, though disliking their pastor's new doctrine, was not sufficiently resolute in his opposition to it, "hoping rather to pacify his colleague by moderation, than by opposition to stop him in his intended course, and fearing lest he should give encouragement to the too violent oppositions of some brethren" with whom he agreed in opinion on the main question. But the Leyden church was reluctant. Instead of complying at once with the invitation, they wrote to the church at Amsterdam, asking for information, and "signifying their unwillingness to interpose save upon a due and necessary calling, and under the conditions of best hope of success." At last, Robinson and Brewster went, first of themselves, and afterward at the request of Ainsworth and his friends, being sent by the church of which they were the elders, and "delivering the church's message," reproving what they judged evil in the Amsterdam church, "and that" —as they confess in a review of the whole story—"with

---

[1] See chap. xi.

Q

some vehemence." The result of that neighborly visit was an agreement—somewhat informal perhaps, but proposed by Johnson, and distinctly approved by the other church—that those of the minority who could not with a good conscience submit to the presbyterian rule which their pastor was introducing, should be freely dismissed to the church at Leyden. But when it appeared that the persons thus dismissed would hold themselves free to reside still at Amsterdam, the agreement was repudiated by Johnson and his friends. Other proposals for accommodation were subsequently discussed in letters between the two churches, and the correspondence was continued till Ainsworth and his friends withdrew, and became another church in Amsterdam.

The story of this appeal from one church to another, and of the response, is significant of the relations which were to exist among voluntary churches, mutually independent, as well as independent of thrones and hierarchies. Churches which have no other charter than the New Testament, which derive their authority, each for itself, directly from Christ, and which profess that to its own master each must stand or fall, may nevertheless acknowledge a fraternal responsibility to each other—may ask one of another, and may give advice or other help in case of need—may fraternally admonish or rebuke each other in case of fault—may co-operate by mutual helpfulness or combined effort in behalf of common interests—without any surrender of their independence, and without organizing a superior and centralized government over all.

It was for the sake of assembling freely to worship God according to the simplicity and purity of the New Testament, and to be edified by the ministry of the word, that the pilgrims had escaped out of England into that land of strangers. What, then, were their advantages and means of Christian culture? As a religious community in Leyden, they were almost isolated. The church at Amsterdam was forty miles away; and while they recognized the fraternal bond of communion with it, they did not long for a closer proximity to it. Simultaneously with their coming to the city, a Scotch congregation was established there, with Robert Durie as its minister; but though, since the death of Queen Elizabeth, the King of Scots had been also King of England, the two kingdoms were not yet united, and the natives of each were foreigners to the other. English Puritans might fraternize with the National Church of Scotland, but both alike abhorred what they called Brownism. The relation of the Pilgrims to their Dutch neighbors seems to have been always friendly; but the diversity of language was, for the first few years at least, a bar to religious communion with them; and though Robinson acknowledged that the Dutch churches were formed on the principle of separation from the world, he nevertheless testified, and his church with him, against certain deviations from primitive simplicity and purity in the practice of those churches. Ecclesiastically, the Pilgrims at Leyden were alone. They had none of the strength that comes with the consciousness of being comprehended in a wide and powerful organization. All their strength was in their principles, and in the confidence that God would sustain their testimony for the liberty and purity of his church.

And what were their arrangements and order as a worshiping assembly? How frequently they met for prayer and informal conference in order to mutual edification can not be definitely known; but we know that to them, not less than to the Puritans who disowned them, the first day of the week was a holy Sabbath. They observed that day with a stricter abstinence from labor and amusements than was practiced by the Calvinists of Holland. Coming together on that day in their pastor's house, they felt, as few congregations can feel, the closeness of the bond which made them one in Christ. On other days and in other places they heard on all sides, and were learning to speak, " a strange and uncouth language;" but in that meeting-place, every word on

their lips or in their ears was their own dear mother tongue—
dearer for their being in a land of strangers, and dearer yet
for the liberty they had gained by exile.   One in the most
intimate fellowship of faith, and in the fellowship of suffering for Christ, they were most tenderly conscious of their
unity when, coming together as "strangers and pilgrims,"
they felt most deeply their seclusion from all the world without.   The arrangements of the room when they met for worship gave it an informal consecration, and presented to their
eyes the simple order of their church.   Official seats were
there for the elders (Robinson and Brewster), raised on some
slight platform, and for the deacons at the sacramental table.   Nor was the congregation seated without arrangement,
for we may assume that they had even then a custom of as-
signing a seat to every worshiper in some orderly method.
At the appointed hour the pastor "led the assembly in prayer
and the giving of thanks," according to the Pauline rubric:
"that, first of all, supplications, prayers, intercessions, and
giving of thanks be made for all men."   Then their voices
were blended in one of the Old Testament psalms, translated
by Henry Ainsworth out of the Hebrew into English stan-
zas, with great fidelity, but with little felicity of versification.
Next came "the exercise of the Word," in conformity with
another rubric: "Give attendance to reading, to exhortation,
to doctrine."[1]   Two or three chapters of Holy Scripture were
read, "with a brief explanation of their meaning."   The pastor — in those years the only teaching elder — taking some
passage for a text, expounded and enforced it in a sermon.
But, in that church, a ministry of gifts was recognized as
well as a ministry of offices; and, under the presidency of
the elders, brethren not in office might "prophesy."   The
truth held forth by the pastor might be further illustrated
and applied, sometimes by respectful questions on one point
or another, sometimes by a word of testimony or of exhorta-

---

[1] 1 Tim. ii., 1 ; iv., 13.

tion.   Another psalm followed "the exercise of the Word." Then came the ministration of baptism or the Lord's Supper; for to believing hearers the promises of the Word were "sealed" in the sacraments.   Nor was their worship ended without the contribution; for that act of sacrifice—each giving according to his ability and his readiness of mind to the support of the church and the relief of its poor—was necessary to the completeness of the service.

Besides the two services on the Lord's day every week, there was a similar service on a secular day, for it is in the record of the pastor's labors that "he taught thrice a week." A church so conducted was a school of religious knowledge and of intellectual discipline as well as of devotion.   Preaching in those days and in that church was not rhetoric nor sentiment alone, but literally "teaching."   That church was in some sort a school of the prophets—for it discovered and tested, and at the same time cultivated, the gifts of wisdom and of utterance in its members by its "exercise of prophecy."[1]   We may well believe that the members of that

---

[1] What the "exercise of prophecy" was, in the church at Leyden, is explained in Robinson's Catechism.   To the question, "Who are to open and apply the Scriptures in the church?" the answer is: "1. Principally, the bishops or elders, who, by the Word of Life, are to feed the flock both by teaching and government.—Acts xx., 28.   2. Such as are out of office, in the exercise of prophecy."   Several arguments from the Scriptures are given in proof of that exercise, the fourth and last being an enumeration of "the excellent ends which, by this means, are to be obtained: as, 1. The glory of God in the manifestation of his manifold graces.—1 Pet. iv., 10, 11.   2. That the gifts of the Spirit in men be not quenched.—1 Thess. v., 19.   3. For the fitting and trial of men for the ministry.—1 Tim. iii., 2.   4. For the preserving pure of the doctrine of the church, which is more endangered if some one or two alone may only be heard and speak.—1 Cor. xiv., 24, 25. 5. For debating and satisfying of doubts, if any do arise.   6. For the edifying of the church and the conversion of others.—Acts ii., 42; Luke iv., 21–23."   "A prophet in this sense" is "he that hath a gift of the Spirit to speak unto edification, exhortation, and comfort."—1 Cor. xiv., 4, 24, 25. "The order of this exercise" is "that it be performed after the public ministry by the teachers, and under their direction and moderation, whose duty

church, with Robinson for pastor and teacher, "grew in knowledge and other gifts and graces."[1]

It was truly a great work which Robinson was performing in those years of exile, training the Pilgrims for their destiny of suffering and of achievement. What his influence was upon them is testified by their own chronicler in words too full of pathos not to be transcribed: "Such was the mutual love and reciprocal respect that this worthy man had to his flock and his flock to him . . . that it was hard to judge whether he delighted more in having such a people, or they in having such a pastor. His love was great toward them, and his care was always bent for their best good both for soul and body. For, besides his singular abilities in divine things, wherein he excelled, he was also very able to give directions in civil affairs; by which means he was very helpful to their outward estates, and so was every way as a common father unto them. And none did more offend him than those that were close and cleaving to themselves, and retired from the common good; as also such as would be stiff and rigid in matters of outward order, and inveigh against the evil of others, and yet be remiss in themselves, and not so careful to express a virtuous conversation. The church, in like manner, had ever a reverent regard to him, and had him in precious estimation as his worth and wisdom did deserve; and though they esteemed him highly while he lived and labored among them, yet much more [did they] after his death when they came to feel the want of his

---

it is, if any thing be obscure, to open it; if doubtful, to clear it; if unsound, to refuse it; if unprofitable, to supply what is wanting, as they are able.—1 Cor. xiv., 3, 37; Acts xiii., 15."—Works, iii., 432, 433.

[1] An account of the order of public worship in the Amsterdam church is found in the Appendix to Robinson's Works, iii., 485. It is a statement which Clyfton made while he was teacher of that church after the withdrawal of Ainsworth and his friends. It omits "the exercise of prophecy;" and that omission was, probably, a characteristic of Johnson's church as distinguished from Robinson's and from Ainsworth's.

help, and saw, by woeful experience, what a treasure they had lost." [1]

When the Pilgrims had become established in Leyden, their pastor began to frequent the lectures in the university —especially the lectures by the two professors of theology. The controversy in which Arminius and Gomarus had been antagonists at first, was still kept up in the universities, and nowhere more learnedly or more persistently than there, where Arminius himself had propounded the doctrines which afterward were called by his name. The two professors of theology, Polyander, defender of the old Calvinism, and Episcopius, champion of the obnoxious novelties in doctrine, were agitating the university with disputes and controversial lectures. Robinson, by carefully hearing both sides, by familiar conference with the Leyden divines, and by his own profound and accurate thinking, made himself master of the questions at issue. He saw, or thought he saw, that the Arminian theories concerning the relation of God's purpose and power to the going on of nature and of human history, were shallow; and it began to be understood that "the preacher of the English Society by the Belfry" was an acute and strenuous disputant. In the progress of that war of dogmas, Episcopius, confident in himself and in his cause, resorted to an expedient which had not then become obsolete in universities. He set forth a series of theses, or propositions challenging dispute, which he was to defend against whoever might assail them. Such was his intellectual stature and weight, and such his "nimbleness" in that sort of fencing, that Polyander, and "the chief preachers of the city," not choosing to encounter in their own persons the chances of defeat, entreated Robinson to enter the lists against the challenger. Declining their request at first with the modesty of " a stranger," he yielded to their importunity, and " prepared himself against the

---

[1] Bradford, p. 18.

time." The disputation was, of course, in Latin, the university language; so that the Dutchman had no accidental advantage over the Englishman. On the appointed day there was "a great and public audience" as at a commencement; and the firm belief of the Pilgrims, long cherished in their loving memory, was that, by the help of the Lord, their pastor, in his defense of the truth, foiled that great adversary, and "put him to an apparent nonplus." It was also affirmed that on two similar occasions he achieved a similar success. "The which," says Bradford, "as it caused many to praise God that the truth had so famous victory, so it procured him much honor and respect from those learned men, and others that loved the truth."[1]

The records of the university show that Robinson was in due form—but not till he had been six years a resident in Leyden—incorporated with that renowned society of learned men, and so became a partner in its privileges. Thenceforth he was no longer subject to the city magistrates, and was so far exempted from taxation that he might have, free of town and state duties, half a tun of beer every month, and about ten gallons of wine every three months.[2]

Hoornbeek, a learned theologian of that age, himself a professor in the same university, confirms the testimony of the Pilgrims as to the estimation in which their pastor was held among the learned men of Leyden. He says: "John Robinson was most dear to us while he lived, was on familiar terms with the Leyden theologians, and was greatly esteemed by them. He wrote, moreover, in a variety of ways against the Arminians, and was the frequent opponent and bold antagonist of Episcopius himself in the university."

---

[1] Bradford, p. 20, 21.
[2] Sumner, p. 18, 19.   The record, as transcribed by Mr. Sumner is:
1615
    Sep. 5°   JOANNES ROBINTSONUS.   Anglus.
coss. permissu.   Ann. xxxix.
                                      Stud. Theol. alit familiam.

It was not till after his removal into Holland that Robinson began to be an author. His first publication was almost coincident in date with his settlement in Leyden. Joseph Hall, who had been a companion with him at the university, and who afterward became bishop of Norwich, published (1608), when the Pilgrims had just escaped from their persecutors, a letter of rebuke and admonition addressed to Smyth and Robinson as "ringleaders of the late separation at Amsterdam." To that "censorious epistle" Robinson replied with manifest ability, and with more of calmness and courtesy than was usual in the controversial writings of that age. Hall made his answer in an elaborate work, entitled, "A Common Apologie of the Church of England against the Unjust Challenges of the Overjust Sect commonly called Brownists"—a work of which Robinson took no public notice save in the preface of his reply to another and more earnest adversary, but upon which John Milton made some scorching observations, at a later period, in his controversy with the same author. Notwithstanding the position of Bishop Hall in English literature, as well as in the Church of England, he exhibits no superiority in the controversy with Robinson, save the superiority of arrogance. In argument, in style, in courtesy, and in charity, the Pilgrim pastor has the advantage over his flippant and insolent adversary. One sentence from the last page of the "Common Apologie" may suffice to show what sort of an adversary Hall was: "The mastership of the hospital at Norwich, or a lease from that city—sued for with repulse—might have procured that this separation from the communion, government, and worship of the Church of England should not have been made by John Robinson." Well said! rector of Halstead, looking for preferment! Is it not a manly and charitable imputation? Why was it that John Robinson, instead of aspiring to some fat rectory, sued for the mastership of that hospital? Why was it that he could not have the humble place for which he sued? If he were governed by mercenary considerations, what hindered him from taking the side which had mercenary considerations to offer?   By taking that side, *you* are prospering in the world, and are to be—ere long—a bishop and a peer of the realm; while *he*, by taking the other side, has suffered the loss of all that you have or hope for in this life, and has become an outlaw and an exile.

Something is added to our knowledge of what Robinson must have been to the Pilgrims, as their pastor and teacher, by the series of his published writings, beginning with the first year of his exile and ending with the year of his death. Two of his most elaborate works were written to defend the position of the Separatists against Puritan assailants—"Reformists," he called them, in distinction from "Conformists." [1] Another, originally published in Latin and afterward translated by himself, was especially designed to show both the differences and the agreement between the churches of the English exiles called Brownists and the Reformed Dutch churches. [2]   Other works of his—some very elaborate—were written in controversy with Separatists who carried their

---

[1] "A Justification of Separation from the Church of England, against Mr. Richard Bernard his Invective, entituled 'The Separatists' Schisme.   By John Robinson.   'And God saw that the light was good, and God separated between the light and between the darkness.'   Gen. i., 4.   'What communion hath light with darkness?'   2 Cor. vi., 14.   Anno D. 1610."

"The People's Plea for the Exercise of Prophecy, against Mr. John Yates his Monopolie.   By John Robinson.   'Follow after charity, and desire spiritual gifts, but rather that yee may prophesy.'   1 Cor. xiv., 1.   Printed in the yeare 1618."

[2] "A Just and Necessarie Apologie of Certain Christians, no less contumeliously than commonly called Brownists or Barrowists.   By Mr. John Robinson, Pastor of the English Church at Leyden, first published in Latin, in his and the church's name over which he was set, after translated into English by himself, and now republished for the special and common good of our own countrimen.   'O blessed is he that prudently attendeth to the poore weakling.'   Psalm xli., 2.   Printed in the yeere of our Lord MDC.XXV."

The title of the original work was, "Apologia justa et necessaria quorundam Christianorum, æque contumeliose ac communiter dictorum Brownistarum sive Barrowistarum, per Johannem Robinsonum, Anglo-Leidenensem,

separation too far, and had gone beyond the true landmarks in matters of Christian doctrine or of Christian fellowship. Perhaps his works in this line—though now of little value save as historic documents—were in their immediate influence and in their remoter effects more important than any other productions of his pen.[1] He opposed, and in a good measure subdued, the ultraism of some who had preceded him, or who were his contemporaries. The extravagant vehemence of Robert Browne, and the tremendous invectives of Barrowe, found no place on his pages.

Thus he became a reformer of the Separation; and to him is the honor due of having introduced into Congregationalism that more catholic spirit, those broader views of the kingdom of Christ, and that more conservative tendency, by which it is distinguished from the strict Independency which held no sort of religious communion with any who had not renounced and forsaken the national churches.

---

suo et ecclesiæ nomine cui præficitur.   Psa xli., 2: 'Beatus qui attendit ad attenuatum.'   Anno Domini 1619."

[1] "Of Religious Communion, Private and Public.   With the silencing of the clamors raised by Mr. Thomas Helwisse against our retaining the Baptism received in England and administering of Baptism unto infants.   As also, A Survey of the Confession of Faith published in certain conclusions by the remainders of Mr. Smith's company.   By John Robinson.   'The simple believeth every word: but the prudent looketh well to his going.' Prov. xiv., 15.   Printed anno 1614."

"A Defense of the Doctrine propounded by the Synode at Dort, against John Murton and his associates in a treatise entituled 'A Description what God,' etc., with the Refutation of their Answer to a writing touching Baptism.   By John Robinson.   Printed in the year 1624."

"A Treatise of the Lawfulness of Hearing of the Ministers in the Church of England.   Penned by that Learned and Reverent Divine, Mr. John Robinz, late Pastor to the English Church of God in Leyden.   Printed according to the copie that was found in his studie after his decease, and now published for the common good.   Together with a Letter written by the same Authour, and approved by his Church, which followeth after this Treatise. 'Judge not according to pearance, but judge righteous judgment.'   John vii., 24.   Printed anno 1634."

The only one of Robinson's works which was not controversial, or in some other way occasional, was published in
the year of his death; and, inasmuch as it bears no indication of its being posthumous, the revision of it, while it was
in press, must have been almost the latest labor of his life.[1]
His "Essays, or Observations Divine and Moral," are weighty
with thought, rich in knowledge of mankind, adorned with
allusions to all sorts of authors, ancient or contemporaneous,
and sparkling occasionally with a kind of grave wit.   Their
style is sententious, epigrammatic, and more polished than
the author uses in his controversial writings.   An intelligent
reader can hardly avoid thinking that somehow they resem-
ble those incomparable Essays by Lord Bacon which Archbishop Whately has so largely expounded. Nor would it
be easy to say why they are not as worthy of a permanent
place in English literature as the Essays of Bishop Hall, the
"censorious" opponent of the exiled Separatist.

Robinson's "Essays" are, probably, of all his writings that
remain to us, the most significant in relation to the quality of
his official "teaching."   It is not likely that any of his sermons were committed to writing; certainly no specimen of
them has been preserved.   His controversial works show
great familiarity with the text-book of all Christian teaching, a common-sense faculty of interpretation, a habit of logical exactness and acuteness which is nowhere more important than in the preparation of sermons, and a practiced ability in dealing with the profoundest themes of theology.   But

---

[1] "New Essays; or Observations Divine and Moral, collected out of the
Holy Scriptures, ancient and modern writers both divine and human; as also
out of the great volume of men's manners: Tending to the furtherance of
knowledge and virtue.   By John Robinson.   'Give instruction to a wise
man, and he will be yet wiser; teach a just man, and he will increase in
learning.'   Prov. ix., 9.   'Experientia docet aut nocet.'   Printed in the
year 1638."

Three editions, at least, of this work were published in seventeen years.
The foregoing is the title of the second edition.

it is difficult to believe that his "teaching" in the church was always or often in the same strain with his "Defense of the Doctrine propounded by the Synod at Dort." The "Essays," on the contrary, seem as if he had condensed into them the thoughts given out or to be given out, more diffusely and more familiarly, in his sacred work of teaching. Some of them are theological; all, with hardly an exception, are strictly religious in theme and spirit. We might even take them as digested from the notes or briefs which (not lying before him, but retained in memory) were his preparation for feeding his flock with divine knowledge.

For specimens, then, of the matter and quality of the discourses which the Pilgrims in Leyden heard from their pastor, we turn to those "Essays." Thus we learn that while he did not refrain from teaching in the church those transcendent truths concerning God's eternal thought and will which are in all ages the themes of insatiable speculation, he could nevertheless set forth in lucid and winning statement the love of God.

"Love in the creature," said he, "ever presupposeth some good, true or apparent, in the thing loved, by which that affection of union is drawn, as the iron by the loadstone; but the love of God, on the contrary, causeth all good, wrought or to be wrought, in the creature. He first loveth us in the free purpose of his will, and thence worketh good for and in us; and then loves us actually for his own good work for and in us; and so still more and more for his own further work. And hence ariseth the unchangeableness of God's love toward us, because it is founded in himself and in the stableness of the good pleasure of his own will. And although the arguments of comfort be great which we draw from the certain knowledge of our love to him, yet are those infinitely greater which are taken from the consideration of his love to us. . . . And hereupon it was that the sisters of Lazarus, seeking help for their sick brother, sent Christ word, not that he who loved him (though that were not nothing),

but that 'he whom he loved was sick.' . . . He whom God
loves, though he know it not, is a happy man; he that knows
it, knows himself to be happy.   Which caused the apostle to
make, in his own name, and in the names of all the 'beloved
of God' (Rom. viii., 35–39), that glorious insultation over all
the enemies of his and their happiness, that they could not
separate him or them—not from the power, or wisdom, or
holiness, but not—'from the love of God which is in Christ
Jesus.'   From this 'love of God,' as from a springhead, issu-
eth all good, both for grace and glory.   Yea, by it (which is
more), all evil, by all creatures intended or done against us,
is turned to good to us. . . . By reason of it 'the stones of the
field are at league with us, and the beasts of the field are at
peace with us;' yea, even the very sword that killeth us, the
fire that burneth us, and the water that drowneth us, is in a
kind of spiritual and invisible league with us, to do us good.
. . . As we may certainly know that the sun shines, by the
beams and heat thereof below, though we climb not into
heaven to see, so we may have certain knowledge of God's
gracious love toward us without searching farther than our
own hearts and ways, and by finding them truly and effectually turned from sin to God."[1]

See in what terms the pastor, teaching his flock what
" faith, hope, and charity " ought to be in them, might speak
of Christian love:

" As love is the affection of union, so it makes, after a sort,
the loving and loved one; such being the force thereof as
that he that loveth suffereth a kind of conversion into that
which he loveth, and by frequent meditation of it uniteth it
with his understanding and affection.   Thus, to love God, is
to become godly, and to have the mind, after a sort, deified,
' being made partakers of the divine nature.' . . . Oh! how
happy is that man, who, by the sweet feeling of 'the love of
God shed abroad into his heart by the Holy Ghost,' is thereby,

---

[1] Works, i., 4–7.

as by the most strong cords of heaven, drawn effectually and with all the heart, to love God again who hath loved him first, and so becomes one with him, and rests upon him, for all good." . . .

"Love is the loadstone of love; and the most ready and compendious way to be beloved of others is to love them first. They, taking knowledge thereof, will be effectually drawn to answerable good-will, if they be not harder than iron, and such as have cast off the chains and bonds of common humanity; for even 'publicans and sinners love those that love them.' Yea, admit thy love of them never come to their knowledge, yet will God, by the invisible hand of his providence, bend their hearts by mutual affection unto thee, at least so far as is good for thee. . . . We must not be like the Pharisees who, instead of enlarging their own affections, straightened [narrowed] the law of loving their neighbors unto such as loved them or dwelt within a certain compass of them; but we must account all our neighbors that need pity or help from us; and our Christian neighbors and brethren also, if the Lord have received them, though they be neither minded in all things as we are, nor minded towards us as we are towards them."[1]

The Separatists were charged sometimes with heresy, always with schism. On the topic of "heresy and schism," the pastor of the Pilgrims might hold forth light in words like these:

"Men are often accounted heretics with greater sin through want of charity in the judges than in the judged through defect of faith. Of old, some have been branded heretics for holding antipodes; others for holding the original of the soul by traduction; others for thinking that Mary the mother of Christ had other children by her husband Joseph—the first being a certain truth; and the second a philosophical doubt; and the third, though an error, yet neither against

---

[1] Works, i., 64-66.

foundation nor post of the Scripture's building.   As there
are certain elements and foundations of the oracles of God
and of Christian faith, which must first be laid, and upon
which other truths are to be built, so must not the foundation be confounded with the walls or roof; nor [must] errors lightly be made fundamental or unavoidably damnable.
Yea, who can say with how little and imperfect faith in
Christ, both for degree and parts, God both can and doth
save the sincere in heart, whose salvation depends not upon
the perfection of the instrument, faith, but of the object,
Christ?   On the contrary, there are some vulgar and common errors, though less severely censured, which are apparently damnable—as, by name, for a man to believe and expect mercy from God and salvation by Christ, though going
on in affected ignorance of, or profane disobedience to God's
commandments."

. . . . "If only an uncharitable heart make an uncharitable person before God, and a proud heart a proud person, then he who, upon due examination and certain knowledge of his heart, finds and feels the same truly disposed to
union with all Christians so far as possibly he can see it
lawful—though through error or frailty he may step aside
into some by-path—yet hath that person a *supersedeas* from
the Lord in his bosom, securing him from being attached
as a schismatical person, and so found in the court of
heaven — what blame soever he may bear from men upon
earth, or correction from God, for his failing, upon infirmity,
therein.

"No man can endure to be withdrawn from, nor easily
dissented from by another, in his way of religion; in which,
above all other things, he makes account that he himself
draws nearest to God.   Therefore to do this causelessly (for
not the separation but the cause makes the schismatic),
though out of error or scrupulosity, is evil; more, to do it
out of wantonness of mind, or lust to contend, or affectation

of singularity; most of all, to do it out of proud contempt or cruel revenge against others."[1]

The last essay is "Of Death." To most of those who had loved and honored the writer as their pastor, the first reading of it must have been when they were "sorrowing most of all that they should see his face no more." Surely they must have seemed to hear some of his tones and cadences, as if

> " From the sky, serene and far,
> A voice fell like a falling star,"

while they read, through their tears, these latest words of teaching and of comfort from him who had so bravely borne with them the heat and burden of their day :

"'Precious in the sight of the Lord is the death of his saints,' when they die for, or in, faith and a good conscience; as the gold, melting and dissolving in the furnace, is as much esteemed by the goldsmith as any in his shop or purse. Precious also it is while they live, and that which God will not lightly suffer to befall them. And if he put their tears in his bottle, he will not neglect their blood, nor easily suffer it to be shed; neither doth death, when it comes, part him and them, though it part man and man, yea man and wife, yea man in himself, soul and body. Friends show themselves faithful in sticking to their friends in sickness and all other afflictions; but they, how affectionate soever, must leave them in death, and are glad to remove them, and have 'their dead buried out of their sight.' But the fruit of God's love reacheth unto death itself—in which he doth his beloved ones the greatest good, when friends can do no more for them.

"He that said, 'Before death and the funeral no man is happy,' spake the truth, as he meant, of the happiness which can be found in worldly things. But both he, and they who have so admired his saying, should have considered that he

---

[1] Works, i., 70, 72.

R

who is not happy before death in worldly things, can not be happy in them by it which deprives him of them all, and of life itself, which is better than they, and for which they are. But miserable, indeed, is the happiness whereof a man hath neither beginning nor certainty but by ceasing to be a man. The godly are truly happy both in life and death, the wicked in neither.

"We are not to mourn for the death of our Christian friends, as they which are without hope, either in regard of them or of ourselves;—not of them, because such as are asleep with Jesus, God will bring with him to a more glorious life, in which we (in our time and theirs) shall ever remain with the Lord and them;—not of ourselves, as if, because they had left us, God had left us also. But we should take occasion by their deaths to love this world the less, out of which they are taken, and heaven the more, whither they are gone before us, and where we shall ever enjoy them.   Amen."

CHAPTER XIII.

STRUGGLES AND SACRIFICES IN A GREAT ATTEMPT.

So long as the Pilgrims remained in Holland, they never ceased to feel that they were simply exiles from their country—strangers in a strange land. They were ever waiting, with hope deferred, for some such change in the policy of the English government as would permit them to go home. None of them could forget that the change of policy which took place when Mary was succeeded by her half-sister Elizabeth brought back hundreds of English fugitives from all parts of Europe. Who could tell how soon the providence of God, in whose hand is "the king's heart as the rivers of water, and he turneth it whithersoever he will," might open the way for their return? In that hope, they labored and struggled; they ate contentedly the bread of carefulness; they bore each other's burdens, fulfilling the law of Christ; they married and were given in marriage; they greeted the birth of children in their households, and gave them to God in baptism; they buried, in hope of "a better country, even a heavenly," many an associate in testimony and in suffering, whose eyes had failed with longing for the sight of dear old England. In that hope, the church for which they had suffered, and which encircled them with the bond of its covenant, grew dearer to them year by year; the simplicity and purity of its worship, the fidelity and efficacy of its discipline, and the constant wealth of "teaching" from its honored pastor, were more and more valued by them, as showing what might be in England if liberty were there. But gradually that hope was receding. While some had found their graves in that foreign soil, others were growing old. What was to become of their children? What would become of

their church?   The end of the twelve-years' truce, which had
interrupted the long and terrible war of the Dutch with
Spain for their independence and their religion, was drawing
near; and then—what?   "Taught by experience," they say,
"those prudent governors [Robinson and Brewster], with sundry of the sagest members, began both deeply to apprehend
their present dangers and wisely to foresee the future, and
think of timely remedy."

At first, these matters were discussed in private conference
among the leading minds of the community; and the more
they thought and talked in such conference, the stronger did
the arguments seem for attempting a removal.   Twenty-five
years earlier, even before the latest martyrs of Separation
were put to death, the thought of migration to America had
been entertained among the Separatists in England; and petition for liberty to form a Separatist colony in America had
been made to Queen Elizabeth (1592), whose government
was at that moment contriving the law by which every persistent Separatist should be compelled to abjure the realm
and go into banishment.[1]   There is no evidence that the petition was answered, nor that it received any attention from
the queen or from her ministers.   Evidently, those who, at
that time, were most intent on expelling the "Brownists"
from England, were unwilling to see them go without their
being first punished by imprisonment and plundered by forfeiture of all their goods—still more unwilling that they
should have their own schismatic way even in the wildernesses of America.   The persecution which followed the passage of the "Act to retain the Queen's subjects in obedience"
defeated the proposed migration, notwithstanding the suggestion of the petitioners that in the "far country" where
they desired to plant themselves, they, while worshiping
God "as in conscience persuaded by his word," might "also

---

[1] Editor's Preface to Morton's "Memorial" as published by the Congregational Board of Publication.   Boston. 1854.

do unto her majesty and country great good service, and in
time also annoy that bloody and persecuting Spaniard about
the Bay of Mexico." But, at last, the thought, which may
have been in Penry's mind when he sent his dying messages
to the brethren in the north countries, and which had been,
so long, like a seed buried too deep to grow, came into the
consultations of Robinson and Brewster, with other "sagest
members" of the Pilgrim church. In view of present and
impending dangers incident to their lot in Leyden, they were
thinking of "timely remedy;" and what remedy was there
but migration from that old world to the new? "Not out
of new-fangledness, or other such like giddy humor," were
they "inclined to the conclusion of removal." They found
themselves urged by "sundry weighty and solid reasons"
which belong to history, and which they have put upon record for us.

"First, they saw, and found by experience, the hardness
of the place to be such that few in comparison would come
to them, and fewer would bide it out and continue with
them. For many that came to them—and many more that
desired to be with them—could not endure that great labor
and hard fare, with other inconveniences, which they underwent and were contented with. But though they loved their
persons, approved their cause, and honored their sufferings,
yet they left them—as it were weeping—as Orphah did her
mother-in-law Naomi; or as those Romans did Cato in Utica,
who desired to be excused and borne with though they
could not all be Catos. Many—though they desired to enjoy the ordinances of God in their purity, and the liberty of
the Gospel with them—yet, alas! admitted of bondage, with
danger of conscience, rather than to endure these hardships:
yea, some preferred and chose the prisons in England rather
than liberty in Holland with these afflictions. It was thought,
therefore, that if a better and easier place of living could be
had, it would draw many, and take away these discouragements. Yea, their pastor would often say that many of those

who both wrote and preached against them, would practice as they did if they were in a place where they might have liberty and live comfortably."

Such, then, in their own simple statement, was the first consideration urging them to a removal.   Their foremost thought was for the cause in which they had suffered.   Ought they not to dare—and perhaps to suffer—greater things in the hope of making a refuge for others like-minded with themselves?   At the same time, other considerations, drawn from their own hardships, apparently so ineffective, and from their hopes and fears for their children, pointed in the same direction.

The second "weighty and solid reason" was: "They saw that, though the people generally bore all these difficulties very cheerfully, and with a resolute courage, being in the best and strength of their years, yet old age began to steal on many of them"—even before the time, hastened by "their great and continual labors, with other crosses and sorrows;" and it was becoming evident "that within a few years more they would be in danger to scatter by necessities pressing them, or to sink under their burdens, or both.   Therefore they—like skillful and beaten soldiers—thought it better to dislodge betimes to some place of better advantage and less danger, if any such could be found."   The few who were holding these consultations were leaders; their conference was like a council of war.   Willing as they were, and willing as their associates were, to struggle and suffer for the Gospel, they were not willing to throw their lives away with no advantage to the cause, if, by a timely retreat, they could gain a more hopeful position.

The third consideration was still more urgent.   What was to become of their children there in Holland?   "As necessity was a taskmaster over them, so they were forced to be taskmasters not only to their servants, but, in a sort, to their dearest children—which was not only painful to many a loving father and mother, but produced likewise sundry sad and sorrowful effects. Many of their children that were of best dispositions and gracious inclinations, having learned to bear the yoke in their youth, and willing to bear part of their parents' burden, were so oppressed with their heavy labors that, though their minds were free and willing, their bodies bowed under the weight and became decrepit, the vigor of nature being consumed, as it were, in the bud. But that which was more lamentable, and of all sorrows most heavy to be borne, was that many of their children, by these occasions and the great licentiousness of youth in that country, and the manifold temptations of the place, were drawn away by evil examples into extravagant and dangerous courses. . . . Some became soldiers, others took upon them far voyages by sea; and some others, worse courses tending to dissoluteness and the danger of their souls." With such sad facts before them, " they saw that their posterity would be in danger to degenerate and be corrupted."

Other considerations were not without weight in their deliberations. Exiles as they were, they could not forget that they were English; and little as they owed to king or parliament, they were loyal to their native country. They could not bear the thought of losing their nationality. After all, it was their desire "to live under the protection of England, and that their children after them should retain the language and the name of Englishmen."

Nor was that all. They wanted more for their children than the inheritance of their nationality. One incident of their poverty, in that foreign land, was "their inability to give their children such an education as they had themselves received." If they could have a country of their own, even though it were in a wilderness three thousand miles away, they might have English schools for all their children.

It was characteristic of the men that the religious value of the Christian Sabbath entered into their deliberations. They had been Puritans, and, in becoming Separatists, they had not surrendered the Puritan doctrine which made the first day of the week a day of holy rest, and recognized no other day as holy. A Continental Sunday, even among Calvinists, did not seem to them like God's institution in the Decalogue. How did their hearts long for the stillness of those rural Sabbaths in old England. "Their grief at the profanation of the Sabbath in Holland" made them weary of that land, with all the liberty it gave them. As they thought how tranquil and how full of heaven that day might be to them in a country all their own, the thought was like a vision of the rest that remaineth to the people of God.

But most inspiring of all the reasons for so bold an enterprise was the one which blended with every other, lifting their consultations up to a higher plane; and it would be unjust not to describe it in their words. It was "a great hope and inward zeal they had of laying some good foundation (or at least to make some way thereunto) for propagating and advancing the Gospel of the kingdom of Christ in those remote parts of the world; yea, though they should be but stepping-stones unto others for the performance of so great a work."[1]

After much thought and prayer, when Robinson and Brewster had taken counsel of such "sagest members" as Carver, Bradford, Winslow, Cushman, Allerton, and others, the question was brought before the church: Shall we attempt to found an English colony in America? Some caught at once the grand idea. Others doubted. There was a full comparison of opinions, and apparently a long debate. Fears and discouragements were set over against the greatness and seeming hopefulness of the proposal. We know something of what was said on one side and the other.

The more timid were appalled by the greatness of the design. It involved inconceivable dangers—the casualties of the sea—the hardships of the long voyage, unendurable by

---

[1] Bradford, p. 22–24; Winslow, in Young, p. 358 seq. Bradford's statement loses something of its effect if translated into nineteenth century English. I have ventured to make only very slight abridgment.

their aged and feeble men and women—the liability to famine and nakedness, and to the want of all things. The change
of air, too, and of food, and " the drinking of water " instead
of their customary beer, " would infect their bodies with sore
sickness." If any should escape or overcome such dangers,
they would yet be in continual danger from " savage people, cruel, barbarous, most treacherous, most furious in their
rage, and merciless where they overcome ;" and many were
the specifications of horrible torments to be inflicted by
those savages on such as might fall into their hands.

Objections of another sort were to be considered by prudent men. The cost of the voyage merely would be too
great for their almost exhausted resources. And what was
the cost of the voyage, and of personal outfit, compared with
the aggregate expenditure necessary to the founding of a
colony in so distant a wilderness ? Other attempts, with
larger means than they could hope to command, had resulted
in miserable failure. Ought not they to learn caution from
what they had already suffered, struggling for subsistence
in a civilized and hospitable country ? Did not their own
experience warn them against going forth—so ill-furnished as,
at the best, they must be—into a barbarous wilderness on
the other side of the ocean ?

These and other like objections were considered, and the
answer was, " All great and honorable actions are accompanied with difficulties that must be met and conquered with
corresponding courage. What though the dangers be great,
they are not desperate. What though the difficulties be
many, they are not invincible. Some of the things so greatly feared may never befall us ; others, by foresight, care, and
good use of means, may in a great measure be prevented ; and
all of them, by fortitude, patience, and God's help, can be
borne or overcome. Such attempts, it is true, are not to be
made without good ground and reason ; but have we not
good ground and honorable reasons ? Have we not, in the
providence of God, a lawful and urgent call to the proposed

undertaking?   May we not, therefore, look for God's blessing upon it?   Yea, though we should lose our lives in this
action, yet may we have comfort in the same, and our endeavors will be honorable."   In a word, the attempt was
worth dying for.

There was another aspect of the case, too obvious not to
be considered.   "What is to befall us if we remain where we
are?   We know not when or how the war, now soon to be
renewed, will end.   The Spaniard can be as cruel as the savages of America.   Famine and pestilence may be as terrible
here as in the wilderness; and if famine or pestilence come
upon us here, retreat may be dishonorable, and escape or
remedy impossible."

How long, and in how many meetings, the question was
debated, we know not; but in the end, "it was fully concluded by the major part to put this design in execution, and to
prosecute it by the best means they could."   Whether they
were to make the bold attempt was no longer an open question.

Other questions followed in their order.   First, to what
transatlantic country should they go?   Guiana, in South America — stretching along the coast between the Orinoco and
the Amazon—had been not long ago explored by Sir Walter Raleigh, and was represented by him, and by travelers
more recent, as a country which, "for health, good air, pleasure, and riches, . . . can not be equaled by any region either
in the east or west."   Some were impressed with the belief
that there was for them the land of promise.   "The country," they said, "was rich, fruitful, and blessed with a perpetual spring and a flourishing greenness, where vigorous
nature brought forth all things in abundance without any
great labor or art of man.   It must needs make the inhabitants rich, seeing less provision of clothing and other things
would serve than in colder and less fruitful countries must
be had.   The Spaniards, having much more than they could
possess, had not yet planted there, nor any where near."   But

the sturdy sense of the majority prevailed against these po-
etic visions. Born and bred in England, they could not
endure the heat and diseases of a tropical climate. "The
jealous Spaniard—if they should live there and do well—
would never suffer them long, but would displant or overthrow them (as he did the French in Florida, who were seated farther from his richest countries); and the sooner, because they should have none to protect them, and their own
strength would be too small to resist so potent an enemy."

On the other hand, Virginia was proposed. It was a region of which they had little knowledge; but it was within
the northern temperate zone, it was claimed by the King of
England, and there "the English had already made entrance
and beginning." The king had created, more than ten years
ago, two great colonizing corporations, dividing to them a
thousand miles of sea-coast, that, by their regulated compe-
tition, the empty claim of dominion might be converted into
a substantial English empire in America. One of those two
corporations, or Virginia companies, was established in London, the other at Plymouth. Under the patronage of that
Lord Chief Justice Popham who sentenced Penry to the
gallows, there had been an abortive attempt, in behalf of
the Plymouth Council, to establish a colony near the mouth
of the Sagadehock, in what was then known as North Virginia. A more costly attempt, by the London Council, to
plant a colony on the James River, in South Virginia, had
been continued through the struggles and disasters of ten
years; but had hardly ceased to be doubtful. So much of
"entrance and beginning" had England made in that great
field of colonization. Virginia, therefore, measured off on the
map from Cape Fear to Passamaquoddy Bay, was English;
and the Spanish power was far away. But, on the other
hand, the Church of England—the National Church, identified with the state—was there; and there, as in England, separation from the National Church, and conformity to the
New Testament in the worship of God, would be under the

ban of the law.   Might not the Pilgrims find even less of safety and religious freedom there than in England itself?

Their inquiries terminated in this conclusion: They would apply to the Virginia Company of London for a grant of territory on which they could settle as a distinct community "under the general government of Virginia;" and, by the mediation of their friends, they would "sue to his majesty that he would be pleased to grant them freedom of religion." Friends they had, "of good rank and quality," who had encouraged them to hope for success, and whose influence in their behalf they thought would be effectual, not only with the company, but with the king. Especially do they seem to have relied on the friendship of that "religious gentleman," Sir Edwin Sandys,[1] who, since the time when Brewster was placed as postmaster for Queen Elizabeth in the manor-house of Scrooby, had become conspicuous in Parliament and elsewhere. We may assume that there had already been some communication, direct or indirect, from him to them.

Accordingly, two of the Pilgrims, John Carver and Robert Cushman, were sent to negotiate with the council of the Virginia Company at London, and to present the petition of the exiles to the king (Sept., 1617). They found the Company ready enough to grant all that the Church asked for. In that quarter, Sir Edwin Sandys had influence; and it was easy for him, as a member of the London Council, to convince his colleagues that the exiles at Leyden, notwithstanding their antipathy to national churches, were the right men for that work of colonization. But the application to the king "for liberty in religion" was unsuccessful. Their friends in the Virginia Company had been confident that so simple a request would be granted, and that the grant would be "confirmed under the king's broad seal." In that confidence, they undertook to have the petition laid before his majesty.

---

[1] *Ante*, p. 204.

Some men, who were thought to have influence, "labored with the king to obtain it," while others "wrought with the archbishop to give way thereunto; but it proved all in vain." Neither the archbishop nor the king could be made to see that men who denied the theory of national churches, and whom they called, in contumely, Brownists and Barrowists, might be tolerated, even under the condition of their transporting themselves into the transatlantic wilderness.

The commissioners, Carver and Cushman, returned to Leyden (in November), having concluded nothing, but bringing with them a friendly letter from Sir Edwin Sandys, who commended the discretion with which they had conducted the business committed to them, promised that he and his associates in the Virginia Council would forward the proposed migration "in the best sort which with reason may be expected," and religiously expressed his confidence that "the design is verily the work of God." A second embassy (Carver and "a gentleman of our company") was sent after a few days (Dec. 15 = 25), bearing a letter from Robinson and Brewster to their "right worshipful" friend, Sir Edwin. In that letter, the pastor and ruling elder, speaking for the Church to encourage their "godly and loving" patron's endeavors for them "in this weighty business about Virginia," gave him, as they said, "these instances of inducement." Their own words are the best illustration of the story:

"1. We verily believe and trust the Lord is with us, to whom and whose service we have given ourselves in many trials; and that he will graciously prosper our endeavors according to the simplicity of our hearts therein.

"2. We are well weaned from the delicate milk of our mother country, and are inured to the difficulties of a strange and hard land, which yet, in a great part, we have by patience overcome.

"3. The people are, for the body of them, industrious and frugal, we think we may safely say, as any company of people in the world.

"4. We are knit together as a body in a most strict and sacred bond and covenant of the Lord, of the violation whereof we make great conscience, and by virtue whereof we do hold ourselves straitly tied to all care of each other's good, and of the whole by every one, and so mutually.

"5. Lastly, it is not with us as with other men whom small things can discourage, or small discontentments cause to wish themselves at home again. We know our entertainment in England and in Holland; we shall much prejudice both our arts and means by removal; [and] if we should be driven to return, we should not hope to recover our present helps and comforts, neither indeed look ever, for ourselves, to attain unto the like in any other place during our lives, which are now drawing toward their periods."

While the letter makes no allusion to any former acquaintance which the writers, or either of them, may have had with Sir Edwin, it expresses, nevertheless, a most affectionate confidence in his Christian sympathy with them in their undertaking. Referring gratefully to what he had done for them, they told him, "Under God, above all persons and things in the world, we rely upon you, expecting the care of your love, counsel of your wisdom, and the help and countenance of your authority." The foregoing "instances of inducement" were set down, not so much for the sake of increasing his confidence in their fitness for the work in question, as for the sake of suggesting to him what he in his wisdom might impart to other "worshipful friends" in the council.

It must be remembered that the agents of the church, though kindly received by the council of the Virginia Company, found their way blocked up in the Privy Council. When Carver went to England for the first time, having Cushman for his colleague, it was well understood that certain prejudices against them as "Brownists" must be overcome. For that reason, a statement in "seven articles," intended as a disavowal of certain opinions currently imputed to the exiles, and as a profession of loyalty and of Protestant orthodoxy, was prepared and subscribed by the elders in behalf of the church; and it was hoped that, with so authentic a document in their hands, the agents would be able to make friends both in the council of the Virginia Company and among the advisers of the king.　That document is so important to the business then in hand, and exhibits so clearly the character and spirit of the Pilgrims, that a full statement of its substance and meaning seems essential to our story. [1]　　　　　　　　　　　　●

In the first of the "seven articles," the church professed their concurrence with the Reformed Churches of Holland in assenting "to the confession of faith published in the name of the Church of England."　In the second they acknowledged, not that the parishes in England were churches of Christ, but that "the doctrine of faith," in the confession before mentioned, was effectual in England "to the begetting of saving faith in thousands" who adhered to the National Church, "conformists and reformists;" and there was added a guarded expression of their "desire to keep spiritual communion," not only with their "own brethren," but also with such non-separating believers "in all lawful things." The third article was an acknowledgment of the king as "supreme governor in his dominion"—whether England, Scotland, Ireland, or Virginia—"in all causes and over all persons;" a denial of any right to "appeal from his authority and judgment in any cause whatever;" and a profession "that in all things obedience is due to him, either active— if the thing commanded be not against God's word—or pas-

---

[1] This document is mentioned by Sir Edwin Sandys in his letter to Robinson and Brewster (*Ante*, p. 263), but was not known to be in existence till it was discovered, a few years ago, in the State Paper Office of the British government by Mr. Bancroft.　A copy of it was communicated by him to the New York Historical Society, and was published in the Collections of that society, 2d series, vol. iii., p. 295–302.　It may be found entire in Mr. Punchard's History, iii., 454.

sive—if it be—except pardon can be obtained."   In other words, the Roman Catholic doctrine of the supremacy of the pope over the civil power was unequivocally repudiated, and with it all the John-of-Munster or so-called "Anabaptist" doctrines often imputed to the Separatists; while, on the other hand, the right of private judgment, the sacredness of individual conscience, and the majesty of God's law, were reserved and guarded against the decrees of Nero or of Nebuchadnezzar, by the intimation that only a "passive obedience," the unresisting endurance of penalties, is due to the king's authority in conflict with the Word of God.   The fourth article admits that it is "lawful for his majesty"—the supreme power in the state—"to appoint bishops, civil overseers, or officers in authority under him, . . . to oversee the churches and govern them civilly according to the laws of the land;" and that to such officers for civil or secular government the churches "are in all things to give an account." The fifth acknowledges "the authority of the present bishops" in England, "so far forth as the same is indeed derived from his majesty unto them, and as they proceed in his name."   The sixth, disavowing the doctrine of Cartwright and of Puritanism in Scotland, affirms "that no synod, classis, convocation, or assembly of ecclesiastical officers hath any power or authority at all, but as the same is by the magistrate given unto them."   The seventh can not be abridged, and need not be explained.   "Lastly, we desire to give unto all superiors due honor; to preserve the unity of the spirit with all that fear God; to have peace with all men, what in us lieth; and, wherein we err, to be instructed by any."

Such was the document of which Sir Edwin Sandys testified that, to "divers select gentlemen of his majesty's council for Virginia," it was so far satisfactory that, "for the public good," they were resolved to aid the undertaking.   But his majesty's Privy Council was not like "his majesty's council for Virginia."   How to have a thriving colony, and what men could be had that were likely to begin another England in America? were the sort of questions for Sandys and his associates of the Virginia Company. In the more august deliberations of the Privy Council, the right of the National Church to dominion over the conscience and religion of all Englishmen, in all parts of the world, seemed too evident to be doubted, and too sacred to be compromised as it would be if Brownists should be permitted, any where under the king's protection, to worship God in their own way with impunity. To mitred lords, though they might be Calvinists in doctrine, as Archbishop Abbott was, the "seven articles" were not satisfactory. Might there not be offered, in behalf of the church, some additional explanation which would help their friends of the Virginia Company in dealing with members of the Privy Council? A letter was addressed by Robinson and Brewster (1618, Jan. 27 = Feb. 6) to Sir John Wolstenholme, a principal member of the Virginia Company, who had used "singular care and pains" in behalf of the application from Leyden. He may have been one of those who "labored with the king," possibly one of those who "wrought with the archbishop." To him, therefore, the two elders, officially representing the church, sent the additional explanation. "Some of his majesty's honorable Privy Council" had specified three points on which the seven articles were not sufficiently clear—"the ecclesiastical ministry," the sacraments, and the oath of supremacy. Concerning these points the Leyden petitioners had not thoroughly purged themselves of opinions and practices too dangerous to be tolerated even three thousand miles away. "Though it be grievous to us," said the elders, "that such unjust insinuations are made against us, yet we are most glad of the occasion of making our purgation unto so honorable personages." They inclosed their "further explanation" in two forms— "the one more brief and general," which in their judgment was "the fitter to be presented;" "the other something more large," and expressing "some small accidental differences" between their own churches and those of the French Prot-

S

estants.   Sir John, "and other of the worshipful friends"
who had the matter in their charge, might send either form
of the explanation, as to them might seem good; and from
him they hoped to receive " knowledge of the success of the
business with his majesty's Privy Council."   From the messenger who delivered the letter to Sir John, and who waited
while he read both the letter and the explanation, we have
an almost dramatic rehearsal of the interview.   Writing to
Robinson and Brewster (Feb. 14), he reports:

"There were two papers inclosed : he read them to himself, as also the letter, and in the reading he spake to me
and said, 'Who shall make them ?'"—*videlicet*, the ministers.

" I answered his worship that the power of making was
in the church, [and that the ministers were] to be ordained
by the imposition of hands by the fittest instruments they
had.   It [the power of making and ordaining ministers] must
be in the church or from the pope, and the pope is Antichrist.

"' Ho !' said Sir John, ' what the pope holds [that is true
and] good—as in the Trinity, that we do well to assent to.
But,' said he, ' we will not enter into dispute now.'

" As for your letters, he would not show them at any
hand, lest he should spoil all.   He expected you should have
been of the archbishop's mind for the calling of ministers;
but it seems you differed."

Sir John Wolstenholme was shrewd enough to see that
the more his Leyden friends explained themselves " touching
the ecclesiastical ministry" and " the two sacraments," the
more manifest would the difference be between their judgment and " the archbishop's mind."   Their view of Christianity excluded the theory of a sacerdotal order ruling the
universal church of God, dispensing God's grace by manipulation of the sacraments, and perpetuating itself by the mysterious efficacy of ordination.   No priesthood would they
acknowledge save the High-priesthood of Christ, and the
universal priesthood of his followers, all brethren, and all

kings and priests unto God.   On the other hand, sacerdotalism and sacramentalism were essential to Christianity according to Bancroft.   First, a priesthood, mediating between
God and the souls of men, and lording it over God's heritage—then sacraments, operating not by their significance
to the intelligent mind and devout sensibilities of the believer, but by their validity in priestly hands—were the Jachin
and Boaz of that national temple wherein King James was
the Solomon, and "my Lord's Grace of Canterbury" the high-
priest.   The elders of the Leyden Church knew what the explanation was which their opponents in the Privy Council
expected on those two points—"the ecclesiastical ministry"
and "the sacraments;" and, therefore, instead of rushing
into a dispute which might be fatal to their cause, they simply professed their agreement on both points with the French
Reformed churches.   Sir John, on the other hand, finding
that they would not profess to be "of the archbishop's
mind" on either point, promptly decided that neither form
of their "further explanation" should be submitted to the
Privy Council.   He thought he had already gained at least
as much as was likely to be gained by more protracted negotiation.   "The king's majesty and the bishops," he said, had
"consented."   But what they had consented to, he did not
venture to tell.   He would go to the chancellor that day;
and "next week" the messenger who had brought him that
letter from Leyden "should know more."   Probably he was
then hoping for what, as afterward appeared, could not be
obtained.   All negotiations with the Privy Council to obtain
for the Pilgrims a valid permission to organize their own religious institutions, and to worship God according to their
own convictions, in a colony by themselves under the general government of the Virginia Company, were baffled by
the obstinacy of the archbishop and the folly of the king.
What "the king's majesty and the bishops" consented to
was a vague promise, in words which were only breath, that
James Stuart, whose reputation for fidelity to such engage-

ments was not good, "would connive at them, and not molest them, provided they carried themselves peaceably." This was all that could be gained for them.   Yet the chief men of the Virginia Company, and other friends of theirs in England, advised them to proceed with their plan of removal, "presuming" that they would not be troubled.

Four months, at least, had passed in these negotiations; and nothing had been concluded.   When Carver and his associate returned from that second mission in England, their report "made a damp in the business."   Some of the church could not see that it was right to proceed under such conditions.   Ought they to detach themselves from their homes and occupations, to dispose of their property, and to remove into the wilderness beyond the ocean, all uncertain whether they would not there, as in England, be "vexed with apparitors and pursuivants and commissary courts" enforcing the Act of Uniformity, and equally uncertain whether they would not find themselves again under the High Commission for causes ecclesiastical?   Better would it have been to go without making any request to the king, than to go now, having had their petition considered in the Privy Council and rejected.   But, on the other hand, it was said that the king, as their best friends in England had advised them, "was willing enough to suffer them without molestation, though for other reasons"—for the sake of consistency, and for the sake of pleasing the bishops—"he would not confirm" that verbal and indefinite promise "by any public act."   That promise, or less than promise, of mere connivance they at last concluded to accept, "resting on God's providence as they had done in other things;" and wisely comforting themselves with the argument that, "if there were no security in the promise intimated, there would be no great certainty in a further confirmation of the same."   It was evident that, had their petition been granted, "if afterward there should be a purpose or desire to wrong them, though they had a seal as broad as the house floor, it would not serve the turn, for there would be means enough found to recall or reverse it."

Having arrived at this conclusion, they were ready to finish their negotiation with the Virginia Company; and Brewster and Cushman were sent to London as agents for the church in that transaction. They were "to procure a patent with as good and ample conditions as they might by any good means obtain." At the same time they were empowered "to treat and conclude with" certain "merchants and other friends" who had intimated their willingness to adventure capital in the undertaking. But their commission, especially in regard to a contract with the capitalists, was carefully limited. If the conditions on which the Pilgrims insisted were not consented to on the other side, they were to conclude nothing without new instructions.

We have some remarkable evidences of how quietly and cautiously those agents went about their business. Their going from Leyden seems to have been as secret as if they had been criminals escaping from justice. They had not been long absent when Sir Dudley Carleton, the English embassador, is found taking measures to have Brewster, as printer, and Brewer, as proprietor of the press, arrested for the offense of printing certain books of a sort which had been prohibited in Scotland by royal authority. King James had been at work for some time, in his arbitrary and blundering way, to subvert the Presbyterian government of the National Church in his native kingdom, and to establish there the ecclesiastical system which he admired in England, and which he had found so subservient to his vanity and to his passion for governing by a divine right superior to all human laws. In the prosecution of that design, he had suppressed the printing of Presbyterian books in Scotland. Consequently, books of that sort, written in Scotland, were printed in the free Netherlands. Two were supposed to have been printed by Brewster. At that crisis, the Dutch republic could ill afford to quarrel with the King of England and Scotland on a point of international law, and it was prudent for the authorities to make some show, at least, of compliance with his wishes intimated through his embassador.   On the 9th (=19th) of July, an agent of Sir Dudley reported from Amsterdam that, after diligent inquiry there concerning Brewster among those who knew him well, there was no evidence that he was not still "dwelling and resident at Leyden;" furthermore, that there was no probability of his removing to Amsterdam, inasmuch as another Brownist printer was already settled in that city; and the discouraging hint was added, "If he lurk here for fear of apprehension, it will be hard to find him."   Three days later (July 12=22) the embassador wrote that "within three weeks" Brewster had removed from Leyden, and gone back to live in London, where he might be "found out and examined."   On the 10th (=20th) of August, he had made good inquiry at Leyden, and was well assured that the subject of the inquiry had not returned to that place, but had removed his family and goods.   Three weeks later (Sept. 2=12), he had, in a previous dispatch, announced "that Brewster was taken at Leyden," and was then under the disagreeable necessity of contradicting that report, because the officer making the arrest had "taken one man for another."   At the end of another week (Sept. 9=19), the municipal authorities of Leyden believed that Brewster was "in town at present, but sick." In four days more (Sept. 13=23), having made an attempt (feigned or earnest) to arrest him, they found that he "had already left" the city.[1]

All that while the undiscoverable printer had been just where we might suppose the English government would most easily find him; and letters had been occasionally exchanged between him and his friends at Leyden.   Just about four months before the dispatch in which Sir Dudley mistakenly announced to his majesty's secretary of state " that

---

[1] Waddington, "Hidden Church," p. 210–227.

Brewster was taken at Leyden " (May 8 = 18), the two agents for the Pilgrims had been in London long enough to have completed their business had they not been hindered by troubles arising in the Virginia Company.   At that time, "Mr. Brewster " was "not well ;" but whether he would go back to Leyden, " or go into the north," his colleague in the mission did not know.   Such were the factions and contentions in the council and among the members of the Virginia Company that no business could be transacted with them. Ill tidings, too, from the unfortunate colony in Virginia darkened the prospect.   Cushman was going "down into Kent," and would "come up again " in two or three weeks, expecting that then the business on which he had been sent would be soon finished—unless, in consideration of all these discouragements, it should be abandoned.

How long they were thus hindered does not appear.   At last, after "their long attendance," the Company having been brought again into working order, the desired patent was granted and "confirmed under the Company's seal."   But the delay, and the "divisions and distractions " that caused it, had estranged some who might otherwise have continued to befriend them, and on whose offers of capital for the enterprise they had relied.   Yet one member of the Company lent them three hundred pounds without interest for three years—a loan which, notwithstanding their poverty, was honestly repaid.[1]

---

[1] Winslow, in Young, p. 383.   Bradford says : "By the advice of some friends, this patent was not taken in the name of any of their own, but in the name of Mr. John Wincob (a religious gentleman then belonging to the Countess of Lincoln), who intended to go with them.   But God so disposed as he never went, nor they ever made use of this patent, which had cost them so much labor and charge."

Perhaps the odium attached to the names of the Leyden Pilgrims, as declared and exiled Separatists, was the reason of the advice that only the name of "a religious gentleman then belonging to the Countess of Lincoln" should appear in the patent.   This is the first but not the last mention of that noble family in the story of New England.

It must have been, at the earliest, late in the autumn (more than two years after the first attempt at negotiation) when Cushman, leaving Brewster in England, returned to Leyden with the long-desired patent.   He reported, also, to the church the progress which he and his associate in the agency had been able to make in matters which were really more important.   Brethren had been found in England who were proposing to go with the Pilgrims.   Friends had been found who would make a venture of capital, where they were expecting to adventure, not only all their worldly estate, but their lives also—and lives dearer to them than their own. Certain merchants, "on whom they did chiefly depend for shipping and means," had made "large proffers"—especially "one Mr. Thomas Weston"—and the church was invited to make ready with all speed for its intended migration.

The question had become more definite than on any former occasion.   Shall we accept these "large proffers," and enter into the partnership to which those London merchants and other friends invite us?   Before deciding the question, "they had a solemn meeting and a day of humiliation to seek the Lord for his direction."   Their pastor's discourse to them, on that fast-day, was from the text, "And David's men said unto him, See, we be afraid here in Judah: how much more if we come to Keilah against the host of the Philistines?

It is not strange that no copy of that patent has been found.   As the Pilgrims were unable to make it useful, they saw no reason for preserving the worthless parchment.   Its only value to them was that it made them (had they been able to use it) the legal proprietors—against all English claimants—of a definite though unknown territory, in which they might become a distinct community under the general government of the Virginia Company in London, and under such protection as that corporation might be able to give them.

The territory granted to them by the company is believed to have been near the mouth of the Hudson, where the Dutch had already made a beginning.   Had they prospered according to their hopes, "Plymouth Rock" might have been, perhaps, somewhere in what is now the State of New Jersey.

Then David asked counsel of the Lord again. And the Lord answered him and said, Arise, go down to Keilah, for I will deliver the Philistines into thine hand."[1] It was long remembered by the hearers that, from that text, "he taught many things very aptly, and befitting their present occasion and condition, strengthening them against their fears and perplexities, and encouraging them in their resolutions."

After that religious preparation, the question was, Who shall go first? The entire body of the church could not go at once; for so large an expedition was beyond their means, and was every way inexpedient. Some were too old, or otherwise too feeble, for the hardships which the pioneers of a new colony must encounter. Others could not immediately withdraw themselves from their affairs in Leyden. From among those who were willing to go first, and could speedily complete their preparation for going, a competent number (as they judged) were selected for the first expedition. The majority were to remain behind for a time, and it was their desire that the pastor should remain with them, —which was the more readily agreed to, because for some other reason it was inconvenient for him to remove just then. On the other hand, the pioneers obtained the privilege of being accompanied by the pastor's colleague in the oversight of the flock, Brewster, who was still in England.

The question was considered whether, when divided, at least for a time, by the breadth of the Atlantic Ocean, they were to be two churches or only one. Should those who were going out be dismissed, and so become a new church,

---

[1] 1 Sam. xxiii., 3, 4.　Bradford's quotations from the Bible are in the words of the Geneva translation. The translation now in use (made by order of King James) was a novelty to the exiles at Leyden; and the authority by which it was made ("his majesty's special command"), and "appointed to be read in churches," did not very much commend it to their prejudices. The introduction of King James's version into the churches and families of the Separatists was effected gradually, as the former translations ceased to be reprinted.

to which those who were to follow might come with letters of commendation and dismissal, till the Leyden church, in which their fellowship had been so pleasant and so profitable, should be extinct?   Under the guidance of Robinson, they disposed of that question, and of all future questions about the identity of the church that was to exist in the colony with the church of their exile at Leyden and of their earlier afflictions at Scrooby.   Their mutual understanding was that, while the migration should be in progress, neither portion of the church should be subordinate to the other; that the majority, on whichever side of the ocean, should not govern the minority on the other side; that each portion, whether majority or minority, should be the church to the members present with it, and should perform toward them—and they toward each other—all the duties of their sacred fraternity; and that members migrating to the colony, or returning thence, should be received without dismissal or testimonial, till the entire church should have passed over into its land of promise.   Thus Brewster, going over in the first expedition, would be ruling elder in the colony, and Robinson—whenever he might follow—would be pastor, without any new ordination or election.

Not long before these preparations were begun, the Pilgrims were favored with a visit from "one Mr. Thomas Weston," a London merchant with whom some of them had been acquainted, and who had given them some aid in their former proceedings.   He came with a plausible appearance of friendship and of godliness—greatly interested in their heroic enterprise, and seemingly ready to make large sacrifices for it. He gained their confidence, and was especially trusted by Robinson.   At his persuasion, they declined the invitation which they had received from a trading company at Amsterdam to settle under Dutch protection and patronage in the New Netherlands.   He advised them not to depend too much on the Virginia Company for assistance in founding their colony, and assured them that should their hopes in that

quarter fail, they need not be discouraged.   Let them resolutely use their own means, and "he and such merchants as
were his friends would set them forth."   He promised that
what they could not provide from their own resources should
be provided for them ; therefore "they should make ready,
and neither fear want of shipping nor of money."   At his
suggestion, a prospectus was drawn up, entitled "Articles of
Agreement," and exhibiting the formal contract which the
Pilgrims were willing to make with him and "such friends
as he should procure to adventure in this business."

Those articles, having been approved by him as sufficient
for his purpose of inducing his friends to venture capital in
the enterprise, were deliberately sanctioned by the Pilgrim
community as a statement of the responsibilities which were
to be assumed on their part.   Carver was sent into England
to be associated with Cushman in making the proposed contract, in receiving the money which "the Adventurers" were
to contribute, in purchasing or hiring vessels for the transportation of the first company, and in making all necessary
provisions and arrangements for their voyage and their settlement.   At the same time a committee was chosen to superintend the enterprise at Leyden.   Those who were to go in
the first expedition "sold off their estates;" and whatever
they had, more than was necessary to their personal outfit or
that of their families, was put into "the common stock"
which was to be for the common benefit of the colony.
Every family had, of course, its own perplexities in deciding
what of its household stuff to dispose of and what to retain
for a new home.   Often, when the question, Can we part
with this, and do without it in the wild country we are go-.
ing to ? had been answered with a resolute No, a more im-
perative No would answer the other question, Can there be
found room for it in the crowded vessel ?   Day by day, all
hands were busy in the various work of preparation.   Day
and night, all their hearts — sometimes aching in sadness,
sometimes exultant in hope—were full of one great thought,

removal from that familiar city to an unknown wilderness. That one thought was the burden of prayer in their holy assemblies, and in every worshiping household; for they acknowledged God in all their ways. It is only by calling up before our minds such details as these that we can see the true and interior meaning of the story.

Meanwhile an event, supposed to be of much significance, was taking place in England. The second, or Plymouth, Virginia Company, incorporated to colonize "the north parts of Virginia," was obtaining from the king a new charter of incorporation, reviving it under another corporate name, and giving to the territory over which its authority was to extend a name which had been recently proposed by Captain John Smith, with the approval of "Charles, Prince of Wales." Thenceforth the region which had been called "the North Parts of Virginia," extending from the forty-first degree of north latitude to the forty-fifth, was to be the domain of "the council established at Plymouth in the county of Devon, for the planting, ruling, ordering, and governing of NEW ENGLAND in America." Wild dreams of infinite gold and silver —like the stream of treasure which for a century had been enriching and enfeebling Spain—had been, partly at least, dispelled; and English mariners and merchants had begun to know that the fisheries on that northern coast, and the furs from those northern forests, might become to English enterprise a mine of wealth. Thomas Weston and others of the Londoners, without whose money nothing could be done, had set their minds upon the profits of the fisheries and of the fur-trade with the Indians; and, at Leyden also, it began to be said by some of the leading men that, inasmuch as the empty patent was all they had obtained, or were likely to obtain from the Virginia Company, it might be best for them, after all, to settle in New England under the patronage of the "honorable lords" who were to be incorporated as the Plymouth Council. As yet, however, the question whether their place of settlement should be north or south of a certain degree of latitude was of no immediate importance. The business on hand was to complete their preparation, so that they might make their voyage at the favorable season.

But while the Pilgrims at Leyden were doing their part, their agents in England encountered various disheartening difficulties. The first disappointment was that some of the friends there, who had been expected to go in the first expedition, contributing themselves and their families to the personal strength of the colony, and adding their means to the capital of the joint-stock company, "fell off, and would not go." They preferred the chances of persecution in their native country to the perils of the ocean and the wilderness. The faith and hope which glowed at Leyden had not kindled in them the enthusiasm needful to so great an enterprise.

Another disappointment came from "merchants and friends that had offered to adventure their money," but, when solicited to take stock in the company, "withdrew, and pretended many excuses." All know how it is when men, partially committed, want to withdraw from an undertaking which they fear will not yield the dividends it seemed at the first view to promise. Some excused themselves because the colony was not to be planted in Guiana. Others must have security that it should be nowhere else than in Virginia. Others, again, had seen and heard enough of disastrous attempts at colonization under the Virginia Company, and would do nothing without a pledge that the colony should not be planted any where within the jurisdiction of that unlucky and ill-managed corporation. When these things were reported at Leyden, there were serious questionings. To men who had disposed of their property with reference to an immediate removal, the prospect was by no means encouraging. It was doubtful "what issue these things would come to." Should they forego the advantages which their patent from the Virginia Company gave them? It does not appear that there was any formal decision; but some of them, surely, had read Captain John Smith's "Description of New England," and "at length the generality was swayed to the opinion" that "for the hope of present profit to be made by the fishing in that country," it was best for them to plant their colony there, and to negotiate afterward for a patent from the reincorporated Plymouth Council.

There was a much greater difficulty. The compact to be made between "the Adventurers" and "the Planters" was in those Articles of Agreement which had been drawn up at Leyden, and to which Weston had given, unequivocally, his approval and consent. But after the Pilgrims had committed themselves irretrievably, and when they were in the midst of their preparation for the voyage, Weston and some others of the Adventurers insisted on a change. Their pretense was that the articles, as agreed upon at Leyden, were not satisfactory to some whose co-operation was important, and to whom the proposed change would be a sufficient inducement. But the sequel of the story seems to prove that Weston, at least, was one of those traders who take every possible advantage in a bargain. He knew that the Pilgrims were in his power; for they must either relinquish in despair the undertaking to which they had committed their fortunes and their lives, or submit to whatever conditions the Adventurers might impose upon them. The two agents saw that there was no help, and reluctantly submitted. Cushman,[1] always quick to discern the practicable and the inevitable, always prompt to act for himself or for others when action was required, took the responsibility. He, therefore, rather than Carver, had to bear the brunt of the "many querimonies and complaints" that came from his brethren at Leyden. It was natural for them to complain that he had been "making conditions fitter for thieves and bond-slaves than honest men;" but they, too, in their turn submitted to the

---

[1] "A good man, and of special abilities in his kind, yet most unfit to deal for other men by reason of his singularity and too great indifferency for any conditions."— Robinson, in Bradford, p. 48.

inevitable. They felt, as he did, that it was better to proceed under "conditions fit for thieves and bond-slaves," than to abandon their enterprise after having gone so far.

The Pilgrims had hoped to make a better bargain with their friends in London; for, after all, the Adventurers generally were their friends, whatever might be true of Weston and some others, whose thoughts were of codfish and beaver, and who—under a show of sympathizing zeal—cared more for large profits on their investment than for the Gospel and the kingdom of Christ. Evidently, the influence which had demanded and obtained those new conditions was that of "the merchants" in the copartnership of Adventurers—the men of business, with whom "business was business," who regarded the whole affair as a commercial venture, and whose calculation was that the godliness of these self-sacrificing Pilgrims would yield to the company the promise of this life, while the other party would have for their share the promise of the life to come. Other members of the company—probably a numerical majority—were actuated by higher motives, and were more intent on planting a Christian colony than on making large profits. That Thomas Brewer who had been Brewster's partner in the printing-office at Leyden—and who, "being a man of good estate," was afterward denounced as "the general patron of the Kentish Brownists," and imprisoned fourteen years for his efforts in that cause[1]—was one of them. Others were like-minded with him. But Weston, by his forwardness, and perhaps by his greater acquaintance with commercial affairs, obtained a controlling influence; and the business of the company seems to have been managed for a time by his will. Thus it was that the Pilgrims found themselves under the necessity of submitting to conditions against which not only their judgment but their self-respect protested, and which they would not formally accept.

[1] Waddington, "Hidden Church," p. 226. Brewer was one of Laud's prisoners, and was released by an order of the House of Commons, November 28, 1640.

Briefly stated, the plan was this. There were two distinct parties, joint proprietors of the intended colony. One party was the Adventurers, residing in London and its vicinity, who raised the capital to begin and supply the colony, and were to manage the affairs of the partnership considered as a commercial adventure. They were "about seventy—some gentlemen, some merchants, some handicraftsmen ; some adventuring great sums, some small, as their estates and affections served." They were not a legal corporation, but were "knit together by a voluntary combination in a society without constraint or penalty, aiming to do good and to plant religion."[1] The other party was the Planters, members of the Leyden church, with a few more, recruited from Essex and some other parts of England. According to the Articles of Agreement, the partnership between the Adventurers and Planters was a joint-stock company, to continue seven years unless dissolved earlier by general consent. The number of shares was unlimited, at ten pounds each. Every settler in the colony, if not less than sixteen years of age, was to be considered as having contributed one share ; and, if self-provided with an outfit of not less than ten pounds' value, two shares. Every child over ten years of age and under sixteen was to be rated at half a share. There was to be no dividend of profits till the end of the seven years ; and, in the mean time, every person in the colony was to be supported out of the common stock, and to labor under direction, without wages, for the benefit of the great partnership. At the winding up of the concern, all the capital, with the accumulated profits (including the colony itself, with its lands and houses, and not excepting even household goods), was to be divided among the stockholders in proportion to their shares.[2]

---

[1] Captain John Smith's "General History of Virginia " (1624), quoted in Young, p. 81, 82.

[2] Other articles in the contract were, that "such children as now go, and are under the age of ten years, have no other share in the division but only fifty acres of unmanured (uncleared) land ;" and that "such persons as die

In other words, the Pilgrims—men, women, and little ones— were to be bond-servants to the company for seven years; in all that time, no man of them was to labor, spend, or save for himself or for his wife and children; and, at the end, he was to receive for his seven years of labor and hardship in the wilderness, and of peril by sea and land, just the same share of the total product with the man who had contributed ten pounds, and lived quietly all the while in London.   It was a hard bargain, but they submitted to the harsh conditions, because there was no other way in which they could pursue their heroic enterprise.

before the seven years be expired, their executors to have their part or share at the division, proportionately to the time of their life in the colony."

In drawing up the Articles of Agreement, the Pilgrims stipulated that the houses and the land under cultivation—especially gardens and home lots— should be, at the end of the seven years' partnership, the property of the planters; and also that every man—especially such as had families—should be at liberty, two days in a week, to work for himself.   These were the two stipulations which the merchants, against the protest of the Pilgrims, insisted on striking out of the contract.

T

CHAPTER XIV.

FROM LEYDEN TO SOUTHAMPTON.—ROBINSON'S PASTORAL LET-
TER.—THE PILGRIMS THE REFORMERS OF SEPARATISM.

HARDLY less than three years had passed since the resolution was taken at Leyden to attempt the founding of a colony, and the first expedition was not yet ready. It ought
to have been set forth early in the summer, so that there
should be time after its arrival to make preparation for the
winter. But so many were the hinderances to be overcome
by the agents in England, that the longest day of summer
(June 11 = 21, 1620) had come, when Cushman wrote from
London, "I hope we shall get all here ready in fourteen
days." He and Weston had resolved to hire a ship, and had
obtained the refusal of one for a day or two—not so large as
would be desirable, only about a hundred and eighty tons;
"for a greater one," said he, "we can not get, except it be
too great; but a fine ship it is." It was the MAYFLOWER.

At the same time a much smaller vessel—the *Speedwell*, of
sixty tons—was purchased and fitted in Holland. She was
to accompany the *Mayflower* as a transport, and was then to
remain in the service of the colony as a fishing and coasting
vessel. She was first to be employed in conveying the Leyden part of the expedition to Southampton, in England, the
port whence they were to sail for America. Once more the
pioneer Pilgrims were to see the green fields of their native
land.

When all other preparations had been completed, the
church again devoted a day to humiliation and united prayer
(July 11 = 21), the crowning preparation. Their pastor "spent
a good part of the day very profitably and suitably to their
present occasion," preaching—or, rather, teaching—from an

apposite and ever-remembered text: "And there at the riv-er by Ahava, I proclaimed a fast, that we might humble our-selves before our God, and seek of him a right way for us, and for our children, and for all our substance."[1]   Prayers were offered "with great fervency, mixed with abundance of tears."   The fasting was followed by a frugal feast; "they that stayed at Leyden," says one who was there, "feasted us that were to go at our pastor's house (being large), where we refreshed ourselves, after our tears, with singing of psalms, making joyful melody in our hearts as well as with the voice (there being many of the congregation very expert in music), and indeed it was the sweetest melody that ever mine ears heard."   It was fit that the evening hours, after that day of prayer and tears, be cheered with sacred song.

The day had come when they must depart.   But those who were to embark were accompanied by most of their brethren, about fourteen miles, to Delft-Haven, where the *Speedwell* lay ready to receive them.   "So," floating in Dutch canal-boats, "they left the goodly and pleasant city which had been their resting-place near twelve years."   As the huge pile of the Peter's-church lessened in the distance and sank below the horizon, they could not but feel how dear Leyden was to them; "but they knew they were pilgrims, and looked not much on these things."   Other friends, who could not accompany them, followed at a later hour, and even from Amsterdam some came to see their embarkation and to say farewell.   "That night was spent with little sleep by the most, but with friendly entertainment and Christian discourse, and other real expressions of Christian love," for "there," says Winslow, "they feasted us again."   Those men were neither sour nor grim; they could fast or feast as oc-casion might require; and on that occasion the joy of hope, and of a grand endeavor auspiciously begun, was mingled with the tender sadness of their parting.

---

[1] Ezra viii., 21—Geneva Version.

"The next day, the wind being fair, they went aboard," after prayer had been offered by the revered pastor, who was hoping soon to be with them again on the other side of the ocean.   "Then," says Winslow, "they accompanied us to the ship, but were not able to speak one to another for the abundance of sorrow to part."   A few moments, while "the tide which waits for no man was calling them away," the voyagers on board and their friends on the quay linger- ed in silence.   Heads are reverently uncovered; all kneel for worship; and once more Robinson, with tremulous voice, commends the departing Pilgrims to Him who rules the winds and the sea.   The little vessel swings from the quay into the broad channel, spreads her sails to the "prosperous wind," and gives her parting salute.   "We gave them," says Winslow, "a volley of small shot, and three pieces of ord- nance; and so, lifting up our hands to each other, and our hearts for each other to the Lord our God, we departed, and found his presence with us."

Something of what was going on that day had been told among the people of Delft-Haven; and the sailing of the *Speedwell*, with religious exiles from England to begin a colony in America, drew some Dutch strangers to the river- side, whose tears attested their sympathy.   Years afterward — yet long before the importance of the event in relation to the world's history was known or suspected in Europe —the embarkation of the Pilgrims was freshly remembered there.

With that favoring wind, a few hours' sailing brought them to Southampton, where the *Mayflower* was lying, and where the rest of their company were ready.   There was a joyful welcome, with mutual congratulations and friendly en- tertainment, and then the question was how to get off most expeditiously on their long voyage.   But that question in- volved a parley with their agents about the change in the Articles of Agreement.   Carver referred them to Cushman, whose defense was "necessity:" if he had stood out against

THE EXHIBITION AT DENT MAJEN.

THE EMBARKATION AT DELFT-HAVEN.

Weston and the others, who insisted on the change, "all had been dashed, and many undone." A protracted altercation between the Planters and the Adventurers would hinder the business; and already they had been too long delayed, as "he feared they would find to their cost." But, though it was admitted that Cushman had intended to do what he thought was best to be done, "these things gave not content at present." Weston came from London to expedite their sailing, "and to have the conditions confirmed." But they would ratify no alteration of the original agreement, and Weston went home in displeasure, refusing to disburse a penny for them, though they needed nearly a hundred pounds "to clear things at their going away." They were not to be overcome by any such proceeding on the part of Mr. Thomas Weston. Instead of succumbing at his intimation that, till they should consent to the new conditions, "they must look to stand on their own legs," they immediately "stopped the gap" by selling off sixty or eighty firkins of butter which had been provided for them by their agents, but which seemed, in that strait, not quite indispensable. Having made this attempt to "stand on their own legs," they addressed a resolute but courteous letter (Aug. 3 = 13) to "the merchants and adventurers," insisting that Cushman had no power from them to modify the articles deliberately agreed upon between them and Weston (whose share in the capital was greater, they said, than that of any other Adventurer), persistently refusing to ratify those new conditions, yet proposing a substitute which they hoped would be acceptable, because they had been assured that not more than one fourth of the stock had been subscribed by the men for whose sake the obnoxious clauses had been interpolated into the contract. In the close of that letter they said: "We are in such a strait at present, as we are forced to sell away sixty pounds' worth of our provisions to clear the haven, and withal put ourselves upon great extremities — scarce having any butter, no oil, not a sole to mend a shoe, nor every man a sword to his side—wanting many muskets, much armor, etc.   And yet we are willing to expose ourselves to such eminent dangers as are like to ensue, and trust to the good providence of God, rather than his name and truth be evil spoken of for us.   Thus saluting all of you in love, and beseeching the Lord to give a blessing to our endeavor, and keep all our hearts in the bonds of peace and love, we take leave."

Embarrassed as they were by Weston's angry refusal to help them "clear things at their going away," so that God's name and truth should not be evil spoken of on their account, they succeeded in clearing things ; and, in little more than a week after their arrival, all accounts were settled, the freight and the passengers were properly divided between the two vessels, and all were ready.   A governor and two or three assistants were chosen for each ship, with power to order the people on the voyage, to superintend the distribution of their provisions, and in general to take care of the little commonwealth—the masters of the vessels consenting to these arrangements, and giving to them the sanction of their own authority over their passengers at sea.

But before those last arrangements, and by way of preparation for them, the Pilgrims—formally assembled, as we may presume, under the presidency of their ruling elder, now with them—received a communication from their pastor.   They knew how entirely his heart went with them ; and that the great idea which they were attempting to realize by their migration to the new world beyond the ocean was his conception.   His official counsel on that occasion—the pastoral letter, "which had good acceptation with all, and after-fruit with many"—is a material part of the history.   It is itself an event to be studied, not only because it exhibits the religious character and principles of the writer, but also because it illustrates the spirit and the structure of the church which, having been so carefully trained by him, was then passing over to plant itself in America :

"LOVING CHRISTIAN FRIENDS,—I do heartily and in the Lord salute you, as being those with whom I am present in my best affections and most earnest longings after you, though I be constrained for a while to be bodily absent from you. I say 'constrained,' God knowing how willingly, and much rather than otherwise, I would have borne my part with you in this first brunt, were I not by strong necessity held back for the present. Make account of me, in the mean while, as of a man divided in myself with great pain, and as (natural bonds set aside) having my better part with you. And though I doubt not but in your godly wisdom you both foresee and resolve upon that which concerneth your present state and condition, both severally and jointly, yet I have thought it but my duty to add some further spur of provocation to them that run well already—if not because you need it, yet because I owe it in love and duty.

"And, first, as we are daily to renew our repentance with our God, especially for our sins known, and generally for our unknown trespasses, so doth the Lord call us in a singular manner, upon occasions of such difficulty and danger as lieth upon you, to a both more narrow search and careful reformation of our ways in his sight; lest he, calling to remembrance our sins forgotten by us or unrepented of, take advantage against us, and in judgment leave us for the same to be swallowed up in one danger or other. Whereas, on the contrary, sin being taken away by earnest repentance, and the pardon thereof from the Lord sealed up unto a man's conscience by his Spirit, great shall be his security and peace in all dangers, sweet his comforts in all distresses, with happy deliverance from all evil, whether in life or in death.

"Now, next after this heavenly peace with God and our own consciences, we are carefully to provide for peace with all men, what in us lieth, especially with our associates; and for that end watchfulness must be had, that we neither at all in ourselves do give [offense]—no, nor easily take offense be-

ing given by others.   Woe be unto the world for offenses;
for though it be necessary (considering the malice of Satan
and man's corruption) that offenses come, yet woe unto the
man, or woman either, by whom the offense cometh, saith
Christ (Matt. xviii., 7).   And if offenses in the unseasonable
use of things in themselves indifferent be more to be feared
than death itself, as the apostle teacheth (1 Cor. ix., 15),
how much more in things simply evil, in which neither hon-
or of God nor love of man is thought worthy to be regarded.
Neither yet is it sufficient that we keep ourselves, by the
grace of God, from giving offense, except withal we be armed
against the taking of them when they be given by others.   For
how unperfect and lame is the work of grace in that person who
wants charity to cover a multitude of offenses, as the Scriptures
speak.   Neither are you to be exhorted to this grace only upon
the common grounds of Christianity, which are, that persons
ready to take offense either want charity to cover offenses, or
wisdom duly to weigh human frailties; or, lastly, are gross
though close hypocrites, as Christ our Lord teacheth (Matt.
vii., 1–5); as, indeed, in my own experience, few or none have
been found which sooner give offense than such as easily
take it; neither have they ever proved sound and profitable
members in societies, which have nourished this touchy humor.   But, besides these, there are divers motives provoking
you, above others, to great care and conscience this way.
As, first, you are many of you strangers, as to the persons,
so to the infirmities one of another, and so stand in need of
more watchfulness this way, lest, when such things fall out
in men and women as you suspected not, you be inordinately
affected with them—which doth require at your hands much
wisdom and charity for the covering and preventing of incident offenses that way.   And, lastly, your intended course
of civil community will minister continual occasion of offense, and will be as fuel for that fire, except you diligently
quench it with brotherly forbearance.

"And if taking of offense causelessly or easily at men's

doings be so carefully to be avoided, how much more heed is to be taken that we take not offense at God himself; which yet we certainly do so oft as we do murmur at his providence in our crosses, or bear impatiently such afflictions as wherewith he pleaseth to visit us. Store up, therefore, patience against the evil day, without which we take offense at the Lord himself in his holy and just works.

"A fourth thing there is carefully to be provided for, to wit: that with your common employments you join common affections, truly bent upon the general good; avoiding, as a plague of your both common and special comfort, all retiredness of mind for proper advantage, and all singularly affected any manner of way. Let every man repress in himself, and the whole body in each person, as so many rebels against the common good, all private respects of men's selves not sorting with the general conveniency.[1] And as men are careful not to have a new house shaken with any violence before it be well settled and the parts firmly knit, so be you, I beseech you, brethren, much more careful that the house of God, which you are, and are to be, be not shaken with unnecessary novelties or other oppositions, at the first settling thereof.

"Lastly, whereas you are to become a body politic, using

---

[1] Robinson, in this passage, refers to the Pilgrims' "intended course of civil community." Their labor (the whole of it, as Weston and others of the Adventurers contended—four days out of six, as they willingly conceded) was to go into the "common stock" for the founding of the colony. He knew what temptations were incidental to such a plan at the best, and that the temptations would be increased by the conflict of opinion which had arisen between the Adventurers and the Planters about those "common employments." He therefore counsels them to enter heartily into the spirit of their enterprise as involving self-denial for the general good, to avoid the withdrawing of their minds from the common interest toward any advantage proper to one's self and not common to all, and every consideration which "in any manner of way" affects the single and separate interest of the individual, or regards it as adverse to the interest of the colony which they are founding.

among yourselves civil government, and are not furnished
with any persons of special eminency above the rest to be
chosen by you into office of government, let your wisdom
and godliness appear not only in choosing such persons as do
entirely love and will diligently promote the common good,
but also in yielding unto them all due honor and obedience
in their lawful administrations; not beholding in them the
ordinariness of their persons, but God's ordinance for your
good; nor being like the foolish multitude, who honor more
the gay coat than either the virtuous mind of the man or [the]
glorious ordinance of the Lord.   But you know better things,
and that the image of the Lord's power and authority, which
the magistrate beareth, is honorable in how mean persons soever.   And this duty you may both the more willingly and
ought the more conscionably to perform, because you are, at
least for the present, to have only them for your ordinary
governors which yourselves shall make choice of for that
work.

"Sundry other things of importance I could put you in
mind of, and of those before mentioned in more words.   But
I will not so far wrong your godly minds as to think you
heedless of these things; there being also divers among you
so well able to admonish both themselves and others of what
concerneth them.   These few things, therefore, and the same
in few words, I do earnestly commend unto your care and
conscience, joining therewith my daily, incessant prayers unto
the Lord, that He who hath made the heavens and the earth,
the sea and all rivers of waters, and whose providence is
over all his works, especially over all his dear children for
good, would so guide and guard you in your ways—as inwardly by his Spirit, so outwardly by the hand of his power
—as that both you and we also, for and with you, may have
after-matter of praising his name all the days of your and
our lives.   Fare you well in Him in whom you trust, and
in whom I rest,—an unfeigned well-willer of your happy
success in this hopeful voyage,   JOHN ROBINSON."

The official communication must have been transmitted to Brewster as ruling elder, and by him communicated to the Pilgrim company. A private letter from Robinson to Carver was sent, apparently, by the same conveyance. That letter of personal affection was preserved for posterity to read—probably because "it was the last letter Mr. Carver lived to see from" his pastor. It is characteristic not only of the writer but of the enterprise (July 27=Aug. 6). "I have a true feeling of your perplexity of mind and toil of body; but I hope that you, who have always been able so plentifully to administer comfort to others in their trials, are so well furnished for yourself as that far greater difficulties than you have yet undergone (though I conceive them to have been great enough) can not oppress you, though they press you, as the apostle speaks. The spirit of a man (sustained by the Spirit of God) will sustain his infirmity; so, I doubt not, will yours. And the better, much, when you shall enjoy the presence and help of so many godly and wise brethren for the bearing of part of your burden, who also will not admit into their hearts the least thought of suspicion of any the least negligence, at least presumption, to have been in you, whatsoever they think in others. Now what shall I say or write unto you and your good wife my loving sister? Even only this: I desire, and always shall, unto you from the Lord as unto my own soul; and assure yourself that my heart is with you, and that I will not foreslow my bodily coming at the first opportunity. I have written a large letter to the whole, and am sorry I shall not rather speak than write to them; and the more, considering the want of a preacher, which I shall also make some spur to my hastening after you. I do ever commend my best affection unto you, which if I thought you made any doubt of, I would express in more—and the same more ample and full— words. And the Lord in whom you trust, and whom you serve ever in this business and journey, guide you with his hand, protect you with his wing, and show you and us his savation in the end, and bring us in the mean while together in the place desired, if such be his good will, for Christ's sake.   Amen."

These letters from the Pilgrim pastor to the voyagers are valuable to a discerning reader for their unconscious exhibition of the spirit and inner life of the church which was seeking a home for itself in the American wilderness.   For more than fourteen years — at Scrooby, at Amsterdam, and at Leyden — the church had been taught and trained by the writer of those letters.   Through all those years, in the constant study of the Scriptures, and under the discipline of duty and of suffering, he had been learning, and the church had been learning with him.   At first, the Separatists who held their meetings in the manor-house of Scrooby may have been like other Separatists in the strictness of their close communion.   Attempting to realize their fundamental idea that a church of Christ can exist only as a fellowship of kindred souls voluntarily separating themselves from the world that lieth in wickedness, they first found that the so-called Church of England was not constituted in that way, but was designed to comprehend all subjects of the English crown—men of Belial as well as saints of God—and was therefore not at all a church of Christ.   Next they found that the worship in the parish assemblies constituted by law was not only at variance with the rules and principles of the New Testament, but defiled by superstitious ceremonies and various compromises with idolatry.   Therefore they could not content themselves with merely denouncing the theory of what was called the Church of England.   To them that entire institution was Babylon; and they made haste to come out of it.   They testified against it by practicing, "as the Lord's free people," the "positive part of church reformation."   They would have no communion with the national worship, with sacraments in which the unholy and profane were not only permitted but by law required to be partakers; nor with prayers which, besides being prescribed and imposed, were superstitious in matter and ceremony, and were at the best only a substitute for prayer, as the homilies were a substitute for preaching.   Many of the early Separatists were so zealous against idolatry that they would have no religious intercourse with any who recognized the parish assemblies as churches of Christ, or worshiped in the established forms.   Some advanced Puritans absented themselves from the liturgical part of the service, but came to church in time for the sermon, and for the "free" or "conceived" prayer which the minister, if a Puritan, introduced into the order of public worship, after the reading from the Prayer-book and before the sermon.   Extreme Separatists held no communion with mere Puritans, however advanced.   Their judgment was that the National Church was not a Christian but an antichristian institution, and that all who worshiped in its assemblies, under whatever protest, were unfit for Christian communion.   Such was the position held, at first, by Robinson, and by the church over which he presided.

Their removal from Amsterdam, for the purpose of avoiding the contentions among the Separatists there, implied no change of opinion on the question of religious intercourse with adherents of the Church of England; but it may be regarded as the first step toward broader views and a more open communion.   In their church life at Leyden—so quiet, so full of mutual helpfulness, so blessed with advantages for edification — there was spiritual growth.   By their friendly intercourse with Christian brethren of another race and language, as well as by the intercourse of their pastor with the Reformed ministers of the city and the theologians and other learned men of the university, their minds were enlarged, and their religious sympathies were (in the true sense) liberalized.   In the early years of their sojourn at Leyden, we find Robinson maintaining against a fellow-exile (1612), the learned and honored Puritan, Dr. Ames,[1] that there ought to

[1] William Ames (often called, in the Latin form, Amesius), one of the most learned of the Puritan divines, avoided the penalties of nonconformity

be no visible communion—not even in a private meeting for prayer—between members of a true church and those who, though recognized as personally holy, are members only of a false church.   But though he defended his position with much logical skill, he, not long afterward, receded from it (1614), and acknowledged that he had learned a new lesson. He had learned to make a distinction between "personal" religious actions —"such as arise from, and are performed immediately by, the personal faith and other graces of God in the hearts of holy men"—and "church actions"—such as sacraments and censures, which imply "a church state and order."   Referring to what he had written in his correspondence with Ames, he says of this distinction, "It would have cleared the question to my conscience;" and it was that "with which I did wholly satisfy myself in this matter, when God gave me once to observe it."   His treatise, "Of Religious Communion, Private and Public," is founded on that distinction.   He says: "The thing I aim at in this whole discourse is, that we who profess a separation from the English national, provincial, diocesan, and parochial church and churches, in the whole formal state and order thereof, may,

by escaping from Archbishop Bancroft and the High Commission into Holland in 1609, and found employment as minister of an English congregation at the Hague.   Dismissed from that place in 1612, at the instigation of Archbishop Abbott, and by the intervention of the English embassador—and prevented, by the same influence, from being called to one of the theological professorships in Leyden—he was afterward, for twelve years, professor of theology in the University of Franeker.   Thence, in failing health, he removed to Rotterdam, where he was associated with Hugh Peters in the care of an Independent church.   In his character as professor in a Dutch university, he was a member of the Synod of Dort, and had a conspicuous part in the Arminian controversy.   He was highly esteemed by Puritans on both sides of the Atlantic; and, at the time of his decease, in 1633, he was expecting to remove to New England.   Two of his works, "Cases of Conscience," and "Medulla Theologiæ," were regarded as classical; and the latter, when Yale College was instituted, nearly seventy years after his death, was made a text-book of theology in the "collegiate school."

notwithstanding, lawfully communicate in private prayer and other the like holy exercises (not performed in their church communion, nor by their church power and ministry) with the godly among them, though remaining, of infirmity, members of the same church or churches—except some other extraordinary bar come in the way between them and us."[1]   The church in Leyden, accepting this distinction, took a position which the church in Amsterdam, then under Ainsworth's care, did not take.   Between the two churches there was, thenceforth, without any breach of fraternity, one marked difference.   At Amsterdam, the Separatist and the Puritan could not even pray together; but at Leyden, fellow-exiles, whether renouncing the Church of England or adhering to it, could unite in all those acts of worship or of mutual edification in which there is no necessary reference to a church or its ministry — "of which sort are private prayer, thanksgiving, and singing of psalms, profession of faith and confession of sins, reading or opening the Scriptures, and hearing them so read or opened, in the family or elsewhere, without any church power or ministry coming between."

Another extreme conclusion on the part of the early Separatists was that not only the idolatrous images and pictures in the edifices built for Roman Catholic worship, but the edifices themselves, were monuments and implements of idolatry, and as such ought to be destroyed.   Robinson's own language was: "As the temples, altars, and high places for those Baalims and other idols, were by godly kings to be rased down and taken away (Deut. xii., 1–3; 2 Kings x., 25 –28; xviii., 1, 3, 4), and no way to be employed to the true worship of God; so are the temples, with their appurtenances, built to the Virgin Mary, Peter, Paul and the rest— though true saints, yet the Papists' false gods and very Baalims — to be demolished and overthrown by the same lawful authority, and in the mean while to be avoided as exe-

---

[1] Robinson, Works, iii., 102, 105.

U

crable things by them which have none authority to deface
or demolish them." Such was the Pilgrim pastor's teaching,
on that point, in the early years (1610) of the sojourn at Leyden.   A few years later there was a controversy between
Ainsworth and John Paget (1618), minister of an English
Puritan congregation at Amsterdam.   Paget's church had
for its place of worship a "temple," described by Ainsworth
as "the Nuns' chapel, built for the worship of their breaden
god and other idols;" and that was one of many reasons
why the Separatists could not commune with it.   In reply
to this, Paget said, among other things: "Mr. Robinson,
though he have written in such high words against these
'temples,' . . . yet hath he, for this long time, tolerated Mr.
Brewster to hear the Word of God in such places; . . . and
now of late, this last month, . . . begins openly, in the midst of
his congregation, to plead for the lawful use of these 'temples.'" [1]   Paget's testimony is confirmed by Robinson himself.   In his "Apology," he says that if these "temples" are
not "monuments and snares of idolatry," there is no reason
why they should be destroyed; and he marks the distinction
between the temple regarded as a holy place by the superstitious multitude, and the temple regarded simply as a place
"in which the church may well and conveniently assemble
together." He adds: "The former use I deem altogether unlawful; the latter not so, but lawful, provided always that
the opinion of holiness be removed, and withal such blemishes

---

[1] Hanbury, i., 329, 333. Paget's argument, on this point, was entirely *ar-
gumentum ad hominem*. First, Ainsworth's church, at the time of their withdrawal from Johnson's, did not refuse to occupy what had been a Jewish
synagogue.   Secondly, The same church, after Johnson's company had been
dispossessed, was content to occupy that place.   Thirdly, The members of
the same church received alms from the Dutch in a place which they regarded as an idol temple.   Fourthly, Separatists were not of one mind nor
constant to one opinion on the question.   In proof of this last point, Robinson's change of opinion and practice is mentioned; and also the fact that
some of Ainsworth's church did "sometimes hear the Dutch ministers even
in those 'temples.'"

of superstition as wherewithal things lawful in themselves are usually stained."

These two points being gained in the direction of an enlarged intercourse with Christians still adhering to national churches, another step was taken in natural sequence. If members of a true church might have private communion with Christian souls not yet separated from the false church, and might unite with them in all religious actions not requiring nor implying the intervention of an organized church or an official ministry; and if Separatists, devoutly abhorring all the "monuments and snares of idolatry," might nevertheless regard a once idolatrous temple as nothing else than a place convenient for an assembly of Christian worshipers—especially when the majority of those assembling in it had ceased to honor it with superstitious veneration—still more when the structure, though built "for the worship of the breaden god," was really fit for the use of a parish assembly, instead of being a cathedral or minster " which for its magnificent building and superstitious form agrees far better to the Romish religion, pompous and idolatrous as it is, than to the reformed and apostolical simplicity "—then surely it might be lawful for a Separatist to hear a "lecture," or sermon, from an evangelical preacher in a parish church; nor would he, in so doing, lessen the force of his protest against superstition and ecclesiastical despotism. Robinson saw this clearly in his later years, and asserted it against the rigid Separatists of Amsterdam. His tract on " the Lawfulness of Hearing the Ministers in the Church of England," though not written till near the end of his life, nor published till after his death, expresses no sudden or recent conclusion. The principle on which the author stands is that, as the Athenians who heard Paul on Mars Hill did not by simply hearing him acknowledge his apostleship—as a stray hearer coming into any Christian assembly, and listening to a sermon, does not thereby recognize that assembly as a true church of Christ—so those who resort to the parish temple simply as hearers, knowing that the minister preaches the Gospel of Christ, do not thereby have any communion with what is antichristian in the constitution and hierarchy, or superstitious in the ritual of the Church of England.   His " learned, polished, and modest spirit " grew saintlier as he drew near to heaven; and in none of his writings does it manifest itself more attractively than in this.   To what breadth of Christian brotherly kindness he had attained, without compromising the great principle for which God had made him a witness, the closing sentences tell us.

" To conclude: For myself, thus I believe with my heart before God, and profess with my tongue, and have [professed] before the world :

" That I have one and the same faith, hope, spirit, baptism, and Lord which I had in the Church of England, and none other ;

" That I esteem so many in that church, of what state or order soever, as are truly partakers of that faith (as I account many thousands to be), for my Christian brethren, and my-self a fellow-member with them of that one mystical body of Christ scattered far and wide throughout the world ;

" That I have always, in spirit and affection, all Christian fellowship and communion with them, and am most ready— in all outward acts and exercises of religion, lawful and law-fully done—to express the same ;

" That I am persuaded the hearing of the Word of God there preached—in the manner and upon the grounds former-ly mentioned—is both lawful and (upon occasion) necessary for me and all true Christians withdrawing from that hie-rarchical order and church government and ministry, and [from the] appurtenances thereof, and uniting in the order and ordinances instituted by Christ, the only King and Lord of his church, and by all his disciples to be observed ;

" And, lastly, That I can not communicate with or submit unto the said church-order and ordinances there established, either in state or act, without being condemned of mine own heart, and therein provoking God, who is greater than my heart, to condemn me much more.

"And for my failings (which may easily be too many, one way or another) of ignorance herein, and so for all my other sins, I most humbly crave pardon, first and most at the hands of God—and so [at the hands] of all men whom I therein offend, or have offended any manner of way—even as they desire and look that God should pardon their offenses."[1]

It can not be doubted that, in all this progress, the Pilgrim Church as a whole, and the individual members of it, in proportion to their intelligence and the breadth of their spiritual sympathy, kept pace with the pastor whom they so loved and honored. As his views broadened, so did theirs. As he, in the growth of his Christian manliness, broke the shackles of a narrow and self-deluding Separatism, they too were by his teachings relieved and brought into freedom. We find him, in one instance, referring sadly to " the woeful experience of many years " which he had had with unreasonable and unteachable men among Separatists; " though," he adds, " not much, I thank the Lord, among them unto whom I have ministered."[2]

Edward Winslow was under Robinson's ministry for three years before the embarkation at Delft-Haven. He knew only by report that the pastor had been formerly " more rigid in his course and way;" but for those three years his testimony concerning what Robinson daily taught, or concerning the Catholic spirit and practice of that Pilgrim church, is as direct as it is explicit: " Never people upon earth lived more lovingly, and parted more sweetly than we, the church at Leyden, did." " That church," he says, " made no schism or separation from the Reformed churches, but held communion with them occasionally. . . . For the truth is, the Dutch and French churches, either of them being a people distinct from the world and gathered into a holy communion, and not na-

---

[1] Robinson, Works, iii., 337, 378.   [2] Works, iii., 355.

tiona. churches, . . . the difference is so small (if moderately pondered) between them and us, as we dare not for the world deny communion with them." So far, indeed, had the Pilgrim pastor and his church advanced toward what in earlier years they would have deemed a dangerous laxity, that on one occasion they were ready, as it might seem, "to hold communion with" the theoretically national Church of Scotland.[1]

The same witness reports "the wholesome counsel" which the Pilgrims received from their pastor "at their departure from him to begin the great work of plantation in New England." That wholesome counsel may have been given in the sermon on the day of prayer before the embarkation. It may have been spoken in more informal exhortation on

---

[1] Winslow, in Young, p. 388–396. "A godly divine coming over to Leyden, in Holland, where a book was printed anno 1619, as I take it, showing the nullity of the Perth Assembly [one of the books for which Brewer and Brewster were brought into trouble, see *ante*, p. 272], whom we judged to be the author of it, and hidden in Holland for a season to avoid the rage of those evil times, . . . this man being very conversant with our pastor, Mr. Robinson, and using to come to hear him on the Sabbath—after sermon ended, the church being to partake of the Lord's Supper, this minister stood up and desired he might, without offense, stay and see the manner of his administration and our participation in the ordinance. To whom our pastor answered in these very words, or to this effect: 'Reverend sir, you may not only stay to behold us, but partake with us if you please; for we acknowledge the churches of Scotland to be the churches of Christ,' etc. The minister also replied to this purpose, if not also in the same words, that for his part he could comfortably partake with the church, and willingly would, but that it is possible some of his brethren in Scotland might take offense at his act: which he desired to avoid in regard of the opinion the English churches, with which they held communion withal, had of us. However, he rendered thanks to Mr. Robinson, and desired, in that respect, to be only a spectator of us."

It should be observed here that, according to Winslow's report, Robinson, in giving the invitation, professed to acknowledge (not the National Church, but) the *churches* of Scotland, and that the Scotchman, in his reply, said nothing about the Church of England as having a bad opinion of Separatists, but mentioned " the English *churches*," meaning those parish assemblies in which there was a Puritan administration of the Gospel.

the day of their leaving Leyden, when, as Winslow tells, "the brethren that stayed feasted us that were to go," and the pastor's house, after their tears, resounded with psalms and joyful melody. It may have been a portion of what was uttered while they were in their last meeting at Delft-Haven. We may even suppose the reporter to have thrown together his recollections of what their wise and loving pastor said on various occasions in view of their expected departure. It is enough that we have it from a credible reporter, and that every word of it is not only accordant with Robinson's character and way of thinking, but might even be confirmed by quotations from his writings.

"We were ere long to part asunder; and whether ever he should live to see our faces again, was known to the Lord. But whether the Lord had appointed it or not, he charged us, before God and his blessed angels, to follow him no further than he followed Christ; and, if God should reveal any thing to us by any other instrument of his, to be as ready to receive it as ever we were to receive any truth by his ministry; for he was very confident the Lord had more truth and light yet to break forth out of his holy Word. He took occasion also miserably to bewail the state and condition of the Reformed churches, who were come to a period in religion, and would go no further than the instruments of their reformation. As, for example, the Lutherans: they could not be drawn to go beyond what Luther saw; for whatever part of God's will he had further imparted and revealed to Calvin, they will rather die than embrace it. And so also (saith he) you see the Calvinists: they stick where he left them; a misery much to be lamented, for though they were precious shining lights in their times, God had not revealed his whole will to them, and were they now living (saith he), they would be as ready and willing to embrace further light as that they had received.

"Here also he put us in mind of our church covenant, or at least that part of it whereby we promise and covenant with God, and one with another, to receive whatever light or truth shall be made known to us from his written Word. But withal he exhorted us to take heed what we received for truth, and well to examine and compare it, and weigh it with other Scripture of truth before we received it.   For (saith he) it is not possible the Christian world should come so lately out of such thick antichristian darkness, and full perfection of knowledge break forth at once.

" Another thing he commended to us was that we should use all means to avoid and shake off the name of Brownist, that being a mere nickname and brand to make religion and the professors of it odious to the Christian world.   And to that end (said he), I should be glad if some godly minister would go over with you before my coming ; for there will be no difference between the unconformable ministers and you, when they come to the practice of the ordinances out of the kingdom.   And so he advised us to close with the godly party of the kingdom of England, and rather to study union than division, viz., how near we might possibly without sin close with them, rather than in the least measure to affect division or separation from them.   And be not loath to take another pastor or teacher (saith he), for that flock that hath two shepherds is not endangered but secured by it."

These retrospective details have arrested the progress of our story ; but they help us to realize what was going on while the *Speedwell* and the *Mayflower*, at Southampton, were receiving their freight and passengers for a transatlantic voyage.   A few Christian people, earnest in their faith, self-sacrificing in their zeal, long trained under the discipline of hardships and of suffering for Christ, taught by a devoted pastor who had brought them out of " the bitterness of separation " into more catholic sympathies, and bound by covenant to receive whatever new light might shine upon them from the Word of God, were going forth to develop, in a new world beyond the ocean, that conception of organized Christianity which had been given to them, but for which there was not room enough in the old world of Europe.   They were not, consciously, political reformers, going to organize civil government on a new theory; nor does it appear that they had formed a definite judgment on the question whether the government which had protected them in Holland was theoretically better than that which had driven them out of England. Far less were they dreaming of a reconstructed civilization which should abolish the distinction of rich and poor, and all the ills that flesh is heir to; their industrious spirit abhorred even the temporary and limited communism into which they were forced by the mercantile spirit of their partners. Nor had they a new scheme of Christian doctrine to provide for. They held in all sincerity what was then the common Protestant orthodoxy. What had been given to them, as that for which they were to testify and to suffer in behalf of coming ages, was an idea new to that age, and rejected by the wise and the mighty—the recovered idea of the Christian church in the primitive purity of its separation from the world, and in the primitive simplicity of its government. What would be the consequences of their attempt to realize that idea in the colonization of America, they could not be expected to know. But we, who live at this day, can see that their theory of the church necessitated a new theory of the relations between the church and the state. In their theory, beginning at the postulate of " reformation without tarrying for any," the church is nothing else than the spontaneous association of " the Lord's free people " for spiritual fellowship; and neither king nor Parliament can put a man into a church or put him out of it. Let that theory be recognized in the beginning of a commonwealth, and, unless the opposite theory come in afterward with prevailing force, all churches in that commonwealth, whatever their pretensions, will be simply voluntary churches, dependent on the state for nothing but protection against violence. The outcome of that theory, when political organisms shall have been moulded by its influence, will be a new era of religious liberty.

CHAPTER XV.

THE VOYAGE OF THE "MAYFLOWER," EXPLORATION, AND THE LANDING OF THE PILGRIMS.

A VOYAGE across the Atlantic, two hundred and fifty years ago, might be accomplished, perhaps, in thirty days.   When those two little vessels—the *Mayflower* and the *Speedwell*— sailed from Southampton (1620, Aug. 5 = 15), with a hundred and twenty passengers, and all the material provided for founding a colony in the wilderness, there was time to complete the voyage, if prosperous, before the autumnal equinox. After such a voyage, there would still be time, in the early days of autumn, to make the needful preparation for safety and comfort through the winter.   But hardly were they at sea when the *Speedwell* was reported so leaky that both ships put back to the port of Dartmouth for repairs.   Two weeks of fine weather and prosperous winds had been lost when they sailed again (Aug. 23 = Sept. 2).   A hundred leagues from Land's End, the master of their misnamed *Speedwell* declared that he must return or sink; and so, once more, they turned back.   This time they put in at Plymouth.   There the *Speedwell* was discharged, as unfit for such a voyage; and there was no time, if there had been means, to provide a substitute.   Some of the company were so far discouraged by these disasters that they were, at least, willing to wait for another opportunity.   Chief among these was Cushman, exhausted by so many months of incessant labor, enfeebled by illness, and depressed under the feeling that what he had done in the matter of the contract with the Adventurers was disapproved by his brethren.   Others, in consideration of their weakness, or of the young children in their care, were selected as those who could best be spared, or who were least fitted "to bear the brunt of this hard adventure." Twenty of the passengers, willingly or reluctantly, were left behind, with whatever freight could not be crowded into the other vessel; and at last, another fortnight having been lost since the departure from Dartmouth, the *Mayflower*, deeply laden with one hundred and two passengers and all the outfit of the colony they were to plant, sailed once more (Sept. 6 = 16), alone, to struggle with the storms of the equinox.

Could we forget for a moment this nineteenth century, and all that God has wrought since that sad, but resolute company of Pilgrims sailed from the old port of Plymouth, we might realize, as we can not now, the uncertainties of the adventure. Our thoughts follow the lonely *Mayflower* on the broad ocean, with her freight of human life—of brave and loving hearts, of undaunted courage and unswerving faith — making her way slowly against adverse winds, tossed by the waves, yet struggling toward the west. What if she should founder? A few loving friends in Leyden, and a few more in England, will wait for tidings; their trembling hopes for loved ones on the sea will change to fears—their anxious fears will sadden into despair; the London merchants who have risked a little money on the enterprise will charge their investment to the account of profit and loss; and the great world will never miss the *Mayflower*. May she not go down —as many a better ship goes down—in mid-ocean? The probabilities are against her, but God is with her. She carries in her freight the future of the world's history. He whom the winds and seas obey is in her, and his angels that excel in strength—those ministers of his that do his pleasure—are guarding her. He brings her to her predestined haven, and a new chapter opens in the history of the Universal Church and of humanity.

Some particular incidents of the voyage were thought worthy to be put on record : the death of one passenger, a servant to one of the Pilgrims; the birth of another, whom his parents, in commemoration of his birthplace, named Oceanus; the "serious consultation" which some of the chief of the company held with "the master and other officers of the ship," when, having sailed half way across the Atlantic, she was in danger of going to pieces in the "fierce storms;" and how, in that imminent peril, the "bowed and cracked" main-beam in the ship's frame was forced back to its place and made fast by "a great iron screw" which one of the passengers had brought from Holland, with no thought of its being put to that use. After sixty-four days of tossing on the sea, they saw land (Nov. 9=19), which proved to be Cape Cod; "and the appearance of it"—so they wrote not long afterward—"much comforted us, especially seeing so goodly a land, and wooded to the brink of the sea. It caused us to rejoice together and praise God that had given us once again to see land." Two days later (Nov. 11=21) the *Mayflower* dropped her anchor in the still water of what is now Provincetown Harbor.[1]

There they were to find "a place for their habitation." But where was the government that could protect them? "Some of the strangers among them" had given out "discontented and mutinous" intimations, to the effect that "when they came ashore they would use their own liberty, for none had power to command them." Their patent conceded to them certain rights in Virginia; but over the territory where they were now to establish their colony the Virginia Company had no jurisdiction. Either they must institute a government for themselves, or they would be at the mercy of unreasonable men. They were not at a loss what to do in that emergency; for, evidently, they had already considered the question, and had concluded that their own combination to institute a government "might be as firm as any patent, and in some respects more sure." A colony already planted in the New England wilderness, and having a government of its own, might negotiate with the "honor-

---

[1] Note at the end of the chapter.

CAPE COD. (FROM YOUNG.)

able lords" of the Plymouth Council for recognition and a concession of territory, and might obtain a more liberal patent than would have been granted to a company of Separatists negotiating before their migration.

It must not be supposed that those men in the cabin of the *Mayflower* had formed a system of political philosophy, still less that they had adopted the theory which deduces all social rights and duties from an imaginary social compact. They were practical men, not theorists; their minds had been enlightened and invigorated by the study of the Bible; as Englishmen, they were familiar with the idea of municipal self-government; and their political knowledge had been enlarged by a long residence in republican Holland. It was only necessary for them to use their common-sense in dealing with a practical question. As they formed a church, sixteen years before, by the simple method of a covenant, it was natural for them to use the same method in forming a state. The form of their "combination" was marvelously simple. Prefixing devoutly the words which were customarily regarded as giving sacredness to a compact or a testament, they first professed their loyalty as English subjects—and with good reason, for they were founding an English colony on soil belonging by the common consent of nations to the King of England, and they desired and expected that their native country would protect them against foreign aggression. They referred to the significant fact that they were planting "the first colony in the northern parts of Virginia." With no other profession or apology—with no recognition of any possible doubt whether they had a right to do what they were doing—they recorded and subscribed their compact. "We whose names are underwritten . . . do by these presents solemnly and mutually, in the presence of God and one of another, covenant and combine ourselves together into a civil body politic, for our better ordering and preservation and furtherance of the end aforesaid," namely, "the glory of God and advancement of the Christian faith, and the honor of our king and country." "By virtue hereof," they said— that is, by the powers inherent in the civil body politic which we now constitute—we are "to enact, constitute, and frame such just and equal laws, ordinances, acts, constitutions, and offices, from time to time, as shall be thought most meet and convenient for the general good of the colony— unto which we promise all due submission and obedience."

The compact was subscribed not only by members of the Pilgrim church and friends who had been associated with them in Holland or had joined them in England, but also by some who were "strangers among them," employed, perhaps, by the Adventurers. At the same time, it may be noted that some of the men who came in the *Mayflower*, and were counted among the earliest settlers in the colony—on whom therefore the laws that might be enacted under the compact would be binding—are not found among those who are reported to us as subscribers to that memorable instrument.

Having subscribed their agreement, the Pilgrims seem not to have thought it necessary, at that time, to make any laws, or to define the powers of any magistrate. "They chose, or rather confirmed, Mr. John Carver—a man godly and well approved among them—their governor for that year;" and that was enough. A governor and two or three assistants had been chosen at Southampton for each ship;[1] and Carver, it seems, had been governor of the *Mayflower* on the voyage. His administration had been satisfactory while they were at sea; and at the end of the voyage he was "confirmed" in the same office.

"Being thus arrived in a good harbor and brought safe to land, they fell upon their knees and blessed the God of heaven, who had brought them over the vast and furious ocean, and delivered them from all the perils and miseries thereof, again to set their feet on the firm and stable earth, their proper element." But they had not yet found a place

---

[1] *Ante*, p. 288.

of habitation.   Late as the season was, and weary as they were of their life on shipboard, they must cautiously explore the coast, and must use their best discretion in selecting a site for their colony, before they could venture to disembark. They had now become "a civil body politic," with an organization adequate to their present need.   Their governor had already an armed force at his command, and that same day a pioneer party, with "fifteen or sixteen men well armed," was sent on shore to renew the exhausted supply of fuel, as well as to make a beginning of exploration.   At night the pioneers returned in safety, having found the neighborhood a perfect solitude, and with a boat-load of red cedar, which they called juniper.   Welcome was the supply of fuel in that chill November air; and in later years some of those passengers remembered how sweet was the odor of it after their nine weeks' experience of bilge-water smells, and all the similar annoyances in their overcrowded vessel.

The next day was the Christian day of weekly rest; and in their unswerving deference to God's commandments, they remembered the Sabbath-day to keep it holy.   On Monday (Nov. 13 = 23), they hurried forward their preparation for determining where their new home should be.   They had brought with them, among all the miscellanies of their cargo, a shallop for use in exploring the coast, and as part of the necessary furniture of their colony.   When the shallop, having been partly taken to pieces, and otherwise needing repairs, had been unshipped and drawn on land for the carpenter (which was the first work of that Monday morning), the people went ashore to refresh themselves; and there the women, with housewifely zeal, improved the opportunity to do the homely Monday work of washing clothes, "as they had great need."   Joyful was that washing-day—odors of pine and sassafras in the air, and "coals of juniper" under their kettles—not less joyful than toilsome; for their feet were at last on the soil of New England.

X

We need not rehearse in detail the story of their three expeditions in search of a place for settlement.   The briefest summary will serve our purpose.   First, while the carpenter was proceeding with the "slow work" of repairing the shallop, sixteen volunteers obtained leave to travel by land, and set out, on Wednesday, "with every man his musket, sword, and corslet, under the conduct of Captain Miles Standish." They saw Indians, who fled from them in terror and could not be overtaken.   After twenty-four hours of thirst (for they carried "neither beer nor water" with them, and their food was "only biscuit and Holland cheese"), they found fresh springs in one of the sandy valleys of Cape Cod; and delightful was their first draught of New England water. They found old Indian corn-fields, Indian graves, a ship's kettle—with other obscure signs that shipwrecked mariners had been there, and perhaps had perished there.   They found, also, deposits of Indian corn, from which they took what they could carry, but no Indian habitation.   Near the deserted corn-fields, they found what seemed a convenient harbor; but they were constrained to "leave the further discovery of it to the shallop."   When their two days' leave of absence had expired, they returned, "like the men from Eshcol, carrying with them of the fruits of the land;" and thus, said they, "we came both weary and welcome home, and delivered in our corn into the store to be kept for seed, for we knew not how to come by any, and therefore were very glad, purposing so soon as we could meet with any of the inhabitants of that place to make them large satisfaction."

Their second expedition, much more considerable than the first, was when the shallop had been at last made ready. Twenty-four men were selected and armed (Nov. 27 = Dec. 7), to "make a more full discovery" of the supposed harbor and its environs.   Jones, the master of the *Mayflower*, and ten of his men, with his long-boat, accompanied them.   Hardly had they parted from the ship, when "rough weather and cross winds" compelled them to row to the nearest land the

wind would permit them to reach; then, wading to the
shore, they marched several miles in a driving and freezing
snow-storm before encamping for the night.   The next day,
when their boats, not long before noon, had come to the rendezvous (Nov. 28=Dec. 8), they found that the creek which
had seemed to invite their settlement, though a harbor for
boats, was not deep enough for ships.   Then visiting the
place where the former expedition had found deposits of Indian corn, and finding larger supplies, they brought away
"in all about ten bushels" for the next spring's planting.
At this point Jones left them, and with him they sent back
to the *Mayflower* those of their company whose strength
seemed inadequate to the hardships they were enduring.
Eighteen of the thirty-four remained "to make further discovery, and to find out the Indians' habitations;" for they
desired to meet their wild neighbors, to open a friendly intercourse with them, and "to make them large satisfaction"
for the seed-corn.   They found at last two wigwams "which
had been lately dwelt in, but the people were gone;" and
with that unsatisfactory discovery they returned to their
friends after an absence of three days (Nov. 30=Dec. 10).

A debate followed in the little commonwealth on the report of that second exploring party.   "The heart of winter
and unseasonable weather was come upon us" (such was the
most urgent argument against continued exploration), "so
that we could not go upon coasting and discovery without
danger of losing men and boat, upon which would follow the
overthrow of all."   On the other hand, Robert Coppin,
second mate of the *Mayflower*, who served as pilot, told them
of a place which he had visited in some former voyage—a
"navigable river and good harbor" near the opposite head-
land of Cape Cod Bay, about twenty-four miles in a straight
line from where their weather-beaten vessel was then anchored.   In the end it was resolved to make one more attempt.
Ten men, some of them the most distinguished in the company, offered themselves for the perilous service, and were

appointed by common consent. To these were added two of the seamen who had been employed to remain in the colony, and six of the *Mayflower's* officers and crew. Eighteen in all—ten of them, at least, heavily armed—embarked in the frail shallop, laden with as much provision as could be afforded for their voyage, to encounter the perils of that last and most unseasonable exploration. Should they be lost, all would be lost.[1]

Wednesday of another week—the fourth since the arrival at Cape Cod—had come (Dec. 6 = 16), before the final expedition could be sent forth, the weather on Tuesday having been " too foul." In their shallop, and under that " very cold and hard weather," they could not venture to sail directly across the bay toward the " navigable river and good harbor," which their pilot had undertaken to find, and beyond which their instructions forbade them to go. After clearing, with much difficulty, the sandy point behind which their ship was anchored, they sailed southward along the eastern shore of the bay, where they had smoother water. But so severe was the cold that their clothes, wet with the spray, were frozen, and became " like coats of iron." As night came on, they went on shore, built a slight defense, gathered firewood, posted their sentinels, and took what rest was possible under such conditions. The next day (Dec. 7 = 17) they divided their force, eight of them marching through the woods, while the shallop with the rest was creeping along the coast; and at night they encamped again as before. Long before dawn they " began to be stirring;" and, though they had been roused in the night by what they supposed to be a pack of wolves howling around their camp, and repulsed by firing a couple of muskets, they suspected no danger. " After prayer," while they were preparing, in the twilight, for breakfast and for their journey, they were alarmed by " a great and strange cry," and a shower of Indian arrows. A

---

[1] The story of these expeditions is given by Bradford, p. 80–88, and by Bradford and Winslow. in Young, p. 117–162.

short engagement followed—the shooting of arrows on one side and of bullets on the other; but the Indians fled as soon as one of them, who seemed to be their leader, had been wounded. The victors, after pursuing the enemy far enough to show that they were "not afraid nor any way discouraged, gave solemn thanks to God for their deliverance," and gathered up a bundle of arrows that might help to show in England what manner of entering in they had among the wild natives.

Such was the beginning of their third day on this expedition. It was almost the shortest day of the year (Dec. 8 = 18), and the hours of light were precious. With a wind which favored them at first, they ran westward along the curving shore, then turning northward, and finding no place that seemed to invite their attention, they hastened toward the harbor of which Coppin had told them. After an hour or two of sailing, that northeast wind brought rain and snow, and later in the day it grew violent. The shore, trending northward, had become a lee shore, and "the seas began to be very rough." In that storm their rudder broke, and two men with oars were hardly able to steer the crippled boat. "Be of good cheer," said the pilot, "I see the harbor." The storm was increasing; night was coming on; they raised all the sail they could carry, rowing at the same time for their lives, "to get in while they could see." Just then, the darkness every moment thickening, their mast was splintered in the gale, and the sail fell overboard. "Yet, by God's mercy, they recovered themselves;" and the flood-tide, coming in from the east, carried them into the harbor. But they were not yet safe. "The Lord be merciful to us!" cried the pilot, Coppin; "my eyes never saw this place before." They had doubled the point now called Gurnet Head, and were in a cove full of breakers, the white foam just visible in that fading light. Coppin and Clark (the two master's mates of the *Mayflower*) would have run the boat ashore, when a stout sailor, one of the steersmen, shouted to the rowers, "About with her! or we are cast away," and she was saved from the breakers. Peering through the darkness, "he bade them be of good cheer and row lustily, for there was a fair sound before them, and he doubted not they would find a place where they might ride in safety." He was right. The rowers did their part, and, in the darkness and the pouring rain, they found themselves "under the lee of a small island," in smooth water, where there was "sandy ground." There they waited for the morning. Some of them, remembering how that day begun, would have remained in the boat, deeming it better to brave the elements than to stumble upon a nest of savages. Others were so exhausted with fatigue and cold that they ventured ashore, and having succeeded in kindling a fire, they were followed by the rest; "for after midnight the wind shifted to the northwest, and it froze hard."

A day full of labor and peril had ended in a night without rest. "Yet God gave them a morning of comfort and refreshing; . . . for the next day [Dec. 9 = 19] was a fair sunshining day, and they found themselves to be on an island secure from the Indians, where they might dry their stuff, fix their pieces, and rest themselves; and [they] gave God thanks for his mercies in their manifold deliverances." That was the last day of the week, and by recruiting their strength, drying their clothes and equipments, and refitting their firearms, "they prepared there to keep the Sabbath." Precious as time was to them and to their companions at Cape Cod, they were sure that no time would be gained, even in that emergency, by not keeping religiously the day of holy rest. (Dec. 10 = 20).

On Monday, they first sounded the harbor, and were satisfied with its capabilities (Dec. 11 = 21). Then they "marched also into the land, and found divers corn-fields, a place very good for situation." At least, it was the best they could find; and the season, and their present necessity, made them glad to accept it. So they returned to their ship again

PLYMOUTH. (FROM YOUNG.)

with this news to the rest of their people, which " did much comfort their hearts."[1]

On Friday of the same week (Dec. 15 = 25), the *Mayflower* weighed anchor for the harbor where her passengers and cargo were to be landed ; but, the wind being adverse, she did not arrive till the next day.   Just five weeks from the day of her arrival at Cape Cod she " furled her tattered sails " in the harbor which Captain John Smith, six years before, had named Plymouth.   The Pilgrims, remembering their relation to the Plymouth Council, as well as the kindness of friends at the port from which they last sailed, had no occasion to inquire what the name of their colony should be. After their long voyage from Plymouth, in England, they found themselves at another Plymouth in New England.

Again the church, which through four months had floated in the *Mayflower*, kept its Sabbath on shipboard (Dec. 17 = 27), worshiping under the presidency of its ruling elder, and taught by him and by each other, according to their gifts of wisdom and of utterance, in the exercise of prophesying.   On Monday the Pilgrims entered on a more careful examination of the environs of their harbor.   They found traces of former inhabitants, and where they had planted corn, but not even a ruined wigwam to indicate that the place had been recently occupied.   While they saw much that seemed inviting, they were not ready, at first view, to fix upon a site for building.   Another day was devoted to similar inquiries, and was closed with a resolution that, after another night's repose, they would determine at which of several places their settlement should begin.   Accordingly, the next morning, after calling on God for direction, they eliminated from the problem all but two of the places they had thought of, and then went ashore to take a better view of those two before deciding between them.   By a majority of voices they determined

[1] Bradford, returning with the other explorers, met the news of his wife's death.   She fell overboard, and was drowned (Dec. 7 = 17), the day after his leaving her.

to begin their settlement "on a high ground" which offered them many advantages.   Their own description tells what the place was as they then saw it.   "There is a great deal of land cleared, and hath been planted with corn three or four years ago; and there is a very sweet brook runs under the hillside, and many delicate springs of as good water as can be drunk, and where we may harbor our shallops and boats exceeding well; and in this brook much good fish in their seasons; on the farther side of the river also much corn-ground cleared.   In one field is a great hill, on which we point [propose] to make a platform and .plant our ord-nance, which will command all round about.   From thence we may see into the bay, and far into the sea; and we may see thence Cape Cod.[1]   Our greatest labor will be fetching of our wood, which is half a quarter of an English mile; but there is enough so far off."

That day they made a beginning there; and at night, re-solving that in the morning they would come ashore in full force to build houses, they left a few men encamped on the spot.   Two days of tempest followed, in which it was im-possible for those on shipboard to communicate with those on shore.   But on Saturday they began, with all their avail-able strength, to provide material for building, cutting down trees for timber and dragging them to the place.   Some re-mained through the next day to keep guard on shore while keeping the Sabbath; but the public worship was where the church was, on the *Mayflower*.

---

[1] The "great hill" is "Burial Hill, rising one hundred and sixty-five feet above the level of the sea, and covering about eight acres.   The view from this eminence — embracing the harbor, the beach, the Gurnet, Manomet Point, Clark's Island, Saquish, Captain's Hill in Duxbury, and the shores of the bay for miles around—is unrivaled by any sea-view in the country."— Young, p. 167, 168.   So says Pierpont:

> "The earliest ray of the golden day
>   On that hallowed spot is cast;
> And the evening sun, as he leaves the world,
>   Looks kindly on that spot last."

PLYMOUTH. BURIAL HILL.

Monday was the great ecclesiastical festival of Christmas —a day which neither Christ nor his apostles had made holy —a holiday which, in the view of the Pilgrims, was more nearly related to the pagan Saturnalia than to any due commemoration of the world's Redeemer, and against which they had testified even in Holland. It was with a not unpleasant consciousness of being in a new world that they returned to their work. "We went on shore," they say, "some to fell timber, some to saw, some to rive, and some to carry; *so no man rested all that day.*" On that day they "began to erect the first house for common use, to receive them and their goods." Another circumstance made it a memorable Christmas to them. The supply of beer with which they had left England was beginning to fail. On that day, they say, "we began to drink water aboard. But at night the master caused us to have some beer; and so on board we had, divers times, now and then, some beer, but on shore none at all." They had something to learn about the virtues of water as a drink.

With frequent interruptions by "foul weather, that they could not go ashore," they pursued their work. Three days after the Christmas when "no man rested," they began to build their fortification on Burial Hill. On the same day they laid out a street now known as Leyden Street, and made arrangements for building a common house, and private houses for the nineteen families into which they divided their company. Under their busy hands, the street soon began to show the beginning of a civilized settlement. Now and then "great smokes of fire," miles away, reminded them that, while they trusted in God, they must be ready to defend themselves. Some of them attempted to find the Indians, in hope of establishing friendly relations with them; but they could find only deserted wigwams. No Indian showed himself near them; but they never knew how many savages might be lurking and watching in the woods around them. When the common house—only about twenty feet square—

was so nearly completed that it needed only the thatched roof that was to cover it (Jan. 9 = 19), they distributed by lot, according to Bible precedents, "the meersteads and garden-plots" of their little town, and agreed that every man should build his own house, thinking that "by that cause men would make more haste than working in common."

The day came when they had purposed, as a church, to keep the Sabbath on shore (Jan. 14 = 24), the majority of the congregation being there.   But that morning, about six o'clock, in a high wind, the thatch of their "great new rendezvous" took fire from a spark, and went off in a blaze.   The house was full of beds laid side by side; loaded muskets were hanging on the walls or standing in corners; powder was under the beds in canisters or powder-horns; Carver and Bradford, lying sick, were in imminent danger of being "blown up with powder."   But they "rose with good speed," and the building and all the lives were saved, though the chief loss came on those two.   The people on shipboard, more than a mile from the shore, saw the fire, and naturally supposed that the Indians were there; but they could do nothing, for the tide was out.   When the coming in of the tide, an hour later, permitted them to land and to see how little harm the fire had done, we may be sure the worship of the assembled church, under that wintry sky, though it may have deviated in some points from their ordinary public worship, was fervent with the thankfulness of joy.   For the next Sunday (Jan. 21 = 31) their simple record is, "We kept our meeting on land."

The church that embarked at Delft-Haven, and re-embarked at Southampton — the organized church that has floated in the *Mayflower* so many weeks and weary months, keeping its holy Sabbaths, mingling its prayers and psalms with the voices of the wind and the sea—is landed at last "on the wild New England shore."   From the day when it begins to hold its worshiping assembly on Burial Hill, organized Christianity—Christ's catholic Church in its simplest and most prim-

SABBATH IN THE COMMON HOUSE AT PLYMOUTH

SABBATH IN THE COMMON HOUSE AT PLYMOUTH.

itive organization—is planted here.   The Christian church
has brought with it the Christian state, organized for the
time under the form of a pure democracy.   But in these arrangements there is no identification of the church with the
state—no subjection of either in its own sphere to the dictation of the other.   In the Separatist colony of Plymouth there
is a free church, dependent on the state for nothing but protection; and a free state, in which the church has no control otherwise than by quickening and enlightening the moral sense of the people.   That which will be the American
system of the relations between the church and the state has
come into being in the cabin of the *Mayflower ;* and a church
history distinctively American has begun when the Pilgrims
transfer the government of their little commonwealth, and
the Sabbath assemblies of their church, from the ship which
has brought them across the ocean to the shore which their
footsteps consecrate to liberty and to God.

Note referred to on page 308 :
" After some deliberation had among themselves and with the master
of the ship, they tacked about and resolved to stand for the southward, . . . to
find some place about Hudson's River for their habitation.   But after they
had sailed that course about half the day, they fell among dangerous shoals
and roaring breakers ; and they were so far entangled therewith as they conceived themselves in great danger ; and, the wind shrinking upon them withal, they resolved to bear up again for the cape."—Bradford, p. 77.
It has been assumed that the intention of the Pilgrims, when they sailed
from England, was to settle in the territory for which they had a patent
from the Virginia Company— in other words, south of the Hudson.   But
had not their plan been gradually modified ever since the beginning of their
intercourse with Weston ?— *Ante*, p. 276, 278 ; Bradford, p. 43, 44.   Did
they not, when they sailed, regard themselves as " having undertaken, for
the glory of God and advancement of the Christian faith, and honor of our
king and country, a voyage to plant the first colony in the *northern parts*
of Virginia," where the Virginia Company had no jurisdiction or possession ?   That voyage was undertaken at the very time when the disorganized
Plymouth Council for colonizing "the north parts of Virginia" were urging
their petition to be reincorporated, and "that their territory may be called
—as by the Prince, his Highness, it hath been named—New England."   The

Y

arrival of the Pilgrims at Southampton (from Leyden) was ten days before the date of the king's warrant to his solicitor (July 21, O. S.), "to prepare a new patent for the Adventurers to the northern colony of Virginia." Six days before the *Mayflower* came in sight of Cape Cod, the new patent incorporating the Plymouth Council, "for the planting, ruling, ordering, and governing of New England," received the royal signature.—Prince, p. 160. "Some place about Hudson's River" might be found on either side of the 40th degree of N. latitude, the boundary between Virginia proper and those "northern parts of Virginia hich were the domain of the Plymouth Council.

THE " MAYFLOWER."

CHAPTER XVI.

THE FIRST YEAR AT PLYMOUTH.

WHEN the Pilgrim Church had planted itself on American soil, there was no certainty that it could live through the remainder of that winter. The question whether they could keep together under the distress that was coming upon them might have been considered doubtful. What was to hinder them from quarreling, as hungry men are prone to do? If they were the unintelligent fanatics which they are sometimes supposed to have been, what was to hinder them from falling into anarchy? What reason was there to hope that the slight bond which held their body politic together would not break at the first trial of its strength? The character of the men gives the answer to such questions. "After they had provided a place for their goods or common store, and begun some small cottages for their habitation as time would admit, they met and consulted of laws and orders both for their civil and military government as the necessity of their condition did require." The members of the nascent commonwealth were not all from Leyden, nor all of one mind and temper. "In those hard and difficult beginnings," there were "discontents and murmurings among some, and mutinous speeches and carriage in others; but they were soon quelled and overcome by the wisdom, patience, and just and equal carriage of things by the governor and better part." Gradually the simple democracy, the earliest instance of New England town-meeting government, was proving itself equal to the need of the little republic.

There was another way in which the colony might be annihilated. After so long a voyage in a crowded vessel, with insufficient accommodations at the best, and such food as sea-farers in those days were compelled to live on, and after their great exposures to cold and rain, many of them could have only a feeble hold on life ; and it is difficult to conceive how there could be one in whom there was not some lurking disease.   Six of the passengers died while the ship was lying at Cape Cod.[1]   Almost from the date of their arrival in Plymouth harbor they were wasting away.   Bradford tells the sad story with characteristic simplicity : "In two or three months' time half of their company died, . . . being infected with the scurvy and other diseases which this long voyage and their inaccommodate condition had brought upon them."   "There died, sometimes, two or three of a day."   When the spring opened upon them, "of one hundred persons, scarce fifty remained."[2]   "In the time of most distress, there were but six or seven sound persons, who (to their great commendation be it spoken) spared no pains night or day ; but, with abundance of toil and hazard of their own health, fetched them wood, made them fires, dressed them meat, made their beds, washed their loathsome clothes, clothed and unclothed them ; in a word, did all the homely and necessary offices for them which dainty and queasy stomachs can not endure to hear named ; and all this willingly and cheerfully, without any grudging in the least, showing herein their true love to their friends and brethren. . . . Two of these seven were Mr. William Brewster, their reverend elder, and Miles Standish, their captain and military commander ; to whom myself and many others were much beholden in our low and sick condition. . . . What I have said of these, I may say of many others who died in

---

[1] One of the six, Mrs. Bradford, was drowned.   The others may be regarded as having died of the privations, hardships, and exposures which they had suffered.

[2] More exactly, the deaths were : in December, six ; in January, eight ; in February, seventeen ; in March, thirteen—forty-four in four months.   Before the arrival of the first reinforcement the number of the dead was just fifty.

this general visitation, and others yet living, that while they had health—yea, or any strength continuing—they were not wanting to any that had need of them."

Details like these, illustrative of character and of the Christian spirit, are always pertinent in church history. For the same reason we must not omit from our story those incidents which show how wide a difference in moral character and human sympathy there was between the Pilgrims and the rough sailors of the *Mayflower*. Bradford tells us that at first " the calamity fell among the passengers that were to be left here to plant. They were hastened ashore and made to drink water that the seamen might have the more beer."[1] When Bradford himself, " in his sickness, desired but a small can of beer," he was harshly denied. But soon the hardier and more favored seamen began to succumb; and before April nearly half of their company had died. Master Jones was "something strucken" when his own men began to be sick and to die. He thought more kindly of "the sick ashore," and told the governor to "send for beer for them that had need of it," professing himself willing to "drink water homeward bound" rather than that they should suffer. "But among his company there was far another kind of carriage in this misery than among the passengers. They that before had been boon companions in drinking and jollity, began now to desert one another, saying they would not hazard their lives for them—they should be infected by coming to help them in their cabins; and so, after they began to die, would do little or nothing for them. Such of the passengers as were yet aboard showed them what mercy they could, which made some of their hearts relent." The boatswain, in particular, "a proud young man," had often cursed the passengers, and had scoffed at them (foolish Brownists, pretending to be saints); "but when he grew

---

[1] A more tonic and nutritious drink than water seemed necessary as a preventive of scurvy and similar diseases resulting from low diet and the loss of vital force.

weak, they had compassion on him and helped him.   Then he confessed he had not deserved it at their hands, and had abused them in word and deed.   'Oh!' saith he, 'you, I now see, show your love like Christians indeed one to another; but we let one another lie and die like dogs.'"   Other instances there were of savage selfishness, which not even the sight nor yet the experience of Christian kindness could overcome.

Along with the epidemic, which was sweeping so many into graves carefully concealed, there was the growing danger of an attack from the Indians—danger that the surviving Pilgrims might be cut off all at once, and the traces of their enterprise be obliterated.   It was almost six weeks after their arrival before a single Indian came in sight.   Then, in a cold and sleety morning (Jan. 31 = Feb. 10), "the master and others saw two savages" who had been on Clark's Island, but had paddled so far away before they were seen that they could not be spoken to.   A few days later one of the people, watching among tall reeds by a creek to shoot water-fowl, saw twelve Indians marching by him toward the village, and at the same time heard in the woods the noise of many more.   "He lay close till they were passed; and then, with what speed he could, he went home and gave the alarm."   The few who were dispersed at work in the woods, of whom Miles Standish was one, returned at the alarm and armed themselves; but nothing more was seen of the Indians, save that, just before sunset, they made a great fire near the place where they were discovered; and that some of them stole the tools which Captain Standish and another who was with him in the woods had left when they heard the call to arms.   "This coming of the savages," says the Pilgrim journal, "gave us occasion to keep more strict watch, and to make our pieces and furniture ready, which by the moisture and rain were out of temper."

The next morning they held a legislative meeting to put the colony into readiness for any martial enterprise.   Miles Standish—not a member of their church, but an experienced and valiant soldier—was chosen captain, and formally invested with "authority of command" in military affairs. But while the meeting was in deliberation about other arrangements for defense, the business was suddenly interrupted. Two savages presented themselves on the top of a neighboring hill, and made signs which were understood as an invitation to come to them. The Pilgrims, responding with a similar invitation, immediately armed themselves and stood ready. Standish, accompanied by Stephen Hopkins, who seems to have had some military experience, went over the brook to hold a parley with the strangers. One of the two carried a musket part of the way, and then laid it on the ground, to show that their intention was peaceable. But the Indians would not wait. They seemed to have come on a reconnoissance; for behind the hill there was a noise as if many more were there. It was evidently time to have their great guns in position; and that part of the work was hastened forward.[1]

Slowly the terrible winter passed away. Milder winds began to blow from the south. The streams were no longer bridged with ice; the snows were disappearing from the hills; "warm and fair weather" cheered the convalescent; "the birds sang in the woods most pleasantly." On "a fair, warm day," soon after the vernal equinox (March 16 = 26), the survivors were again assembled to complete the military arrangements which they had left unfinished, when they were again interrupted by an alarm. A savage came boldly along their little street, "straight to the rendezvous," where their town-meeting was deliberating on the means of defending the settlement against hostile visitors. At that point they came out to meet him, "not suffering him to go in;" for they were naturally unwilling to let him see how few and weak they were. To their surprise, he bade them "Welcome!"

---

[1] The authority for all the particulars of this chapter is Bradford's History, p. 91–116; and the documents in Young, p. 171–268.

saluting them in broken English.   They regarded him with close attention, for he was the first native with whom they had been able to have any communication.   "He was a tall, straight man, the hair of his head black, long behind, only short before, none on his face at all;" and his costume was very much as if he had just come out of the primeval para-dise[1]—"stark naked, only a leather about his waist, with a fringe about a span long or little more."   For arms, he had only a bow and two arrows, one of them headed.   They found him "free in speech, so far as he could express his mind, and of a seemly carriage."   Conversation with him could not be very free, for his acquaintance with their language was only such as he had gained by intercourse with fishing vessels on what is now the coast of Maine; but they "questioned him of many things," and "he discoursed of the whole country, and of every province, and of their saga-mores, and their number of men and strength," giving out, withal, that he was himself a sagamore, though he had been eight months absent from his dominions.   The chill March wind "beginning to rise a little," they had compassion on his shivering nakedness, and "cast a horseman's coat about him."   He had not learned to ask for whisky, but with an Indian's appetite for the white man's drinks he asked for beer; and as they had no beer, they gave him some of their precious "strong water, and biscuit and butter, and cheese, and pudding, and a piece of mallard, all which he liked well, and had been ac-quainted with such among the English."   From him they learned that the place where they were was called Patuxet; that, about four years before, it had been devastated by a dis-ease which had left "neither man, woman, nor child remain-ing," and that there was no Indian claim to the soil which they had begun to occupy.   They learned also that their next neighbors on the south were subject to a chief named Massasoit; and that another tribe near them were the Nau-

---

[1] Gen. iii., 21.

sites, who had attacked their exploring party, and who, being "much incensed and provoked against the English," had killed three Englishmen only a few months ago. They found that the Indians who had stolen their tools, and who had been lurking about them with various indications of hostility, were Nausites, whose grudge against the English was not without cause.[1]

After some hours of such conversation as they could hold with him, they "would gladly have been rid of him;" for not only were they unwilling to let him see how few and weak they were, but they knew not how far it might be safe to trust him. They were a little disconcerted by the discovery that he thought he was in a comfortable place, and intended not to go away that night. It was then proposed that he should pass the night on shipboard, and he consented; but the wind was high and the tide low, so that they could not send him to the ship. Finding that he was not to be got rid of, they "lodged him that night at Stephen Hopkins's house, and watched him."

In the morning (March $17 = 27$) they dismissed their guest, giving him a knife for use, and a bracelet and a ring for ornament. On his part, he promised that "within a night or two" he would come again, and bring to them some of their Indian neighbors, with such beaver skins as they had to sell. After long and anxious waiting, they had at last a hopeful prospect of amicable intercourse with the natives.

The next day was Sunday; and, true to his word, their

---

[1] "These people are ill affected toward the English by reason of one Hunt, a master of a ship, who deceived the people, and got them, under color of trucking with them, twenty out of this very place where we inhabit, and seven men from the Nausites, and carried them away, and sold them for slaves, like a wretched man that cares not what mischief he doth for his profit."—Mourt's [Bradford and Winslow's] "Relation," in Young, p. 186.

Many an Indian massacre on the frontier has been only a wild and blind vengeance on innocent settlers for the crimes of white men like that Hunt.

new friend Samoset (for that was his name) came again, and "brought with him five other tall, proper men." Such a visit on that day was hardly desired by them, for it was a serious interruption of their Sabbath. Certainly the visitors must have made a sensation in the little village. They were more elaborately dressed than Samoset was at his former visit. Every man of them wore a deer-skin for his outer garment; and the one who seemed to be the chief among them "had a wild-cat's skin, or such like, on one arm." Most of them wore leggins, or "long hosen," of leather, reaching to the body and fastened to a leathern girdle. Like Samoset, they wore their hair long, some of them having it "trussed up with a feather, broadwise, like a fan," while one head was adorned with the pendent tail of a fox. "Some of them had their faces painted black, from the forehead to the chin, four or five fingers broad; others, after other fashions, as they liked." Evidently they had got themselves up with their best apparel and in their most impressive style, as if they knew it was Sunday. In accordance with advice given to Samoset at his first visit, they had left their bows and arrows a quarter of a mile from the town, thus indicating the peaceableness of their intentions. They had a friendly and hospitable welcome, the more friendly because they brought back the tools that had been stolen. In the words of the Pilgrim narrative, "They did eat liberally of our English victuals. They made semblance to us of friendship and amity. They sang and danced after their manner, like antics." A strange Sabbath it was in the Pilgrim settlement, for the duty of hospitality and kindness to heathen neighbors was recognized as more important in that instance than Puritan strictness of Sabbath-keeping. But when the Indians produced their beaver skins and wanted to make a bargain, they were made to understand that among those new neighbors of theirs that day of the week was not a day for trade. They were not offended by the refusal to trade on that day, but promised to come again "within a night or two." So they were dismissed, each with some little present, as soon as they could be sent away without offense. They were accompanied by an armed escort to the place where they had deposited their own weapons; and thence, glad and with many thanks, they went their way, repeating their promise to come again.

But Samoset, as before, was not easily dismissed. Under pretense of sickness, or perhaps really ill, he remained at Plymouth till Wednesday morning; when the Englishmen, having fitted him out with "a hat, a pair of stockings, and shoes, a shirt, and a piece of cloth to tie about his waist," sent him as their messenger to ascertain why his friends had not come back according to their promise.

Meanwhile, in those bright, warm days of advancing spring, they were digging their grounds and planting the garden seeds they had brought from England; though they were not yet quite sure that their relations with their wild neighbors would be peaceful. On the very day on which they sent away the reluctant Samoset, they saw, on the hill-top over against them, two or three savages whose gestures seemed to intimate hostility and defiance, and who, when they were approached, betook themselves to flight. But on Thursday—"a very fair, warm day"—while they were again in deliberation on their public affairs (March 22 = April 1), Samoset came the third time, and four others with him. One of the four was Squanto, the sole survivor of the tribe that had lately inhabited Patuxet. He, too, could speak a little English, and could speak it better than Samoset, for he was one of twenty that were kidnapped by Hunt seven years before, and sold for slaves in Spain. In some way he had passed from Spain into England. There he had "dwelt in Cornhill with Master John Slainie," a London merchant, who, being interested in fishing voyages on the New England coast, had sent him over to be useful as an interpreter. But his knowledge of English, added to Samoset's, was not much. They succeeded, however, in communicating the information "that their great sagamore, Massasoit,[1] was hard by, with Quadequina, his brother, and all their men." About an hour later the royal personage thus heralded made his appearance, with sixty followers, on the hill-top beyond the brook. On each side there was something of suspicion: "We were not willing to send our governor to them, and they were unwilling to come to us." Squanto, the more intelligent of the two interpreters, was sent to make arrangements for an interview. He brought back a request from Massasoit for a parley with some authorized messenger. Winslow was therefore sent to negotiate with the savage chief, "to know his mind, and to signify the mind and will of the governor." He carried with him conciliatory presents from the white men—"to the king a pair of knives, and a copper chain with a jewel at it; to Quadequina a knife, and a jewel to hang in his ear;" also, "a pot of strong water, a good quantity of biscuit, and some butter." By those little gifts out of their poverty, the Pilgrims expressed their friendliness. "A man's gift maketh room for him, and bringeth him before great men."[2]

With no other attendance than the two interpreters, but not without his sword and his defensive armor, Winslow passed over the brook, went up the hill, and, the gifts making room for him, he stood before the great men in the crowd of their warriors. He saluted Massasoit, in the name of King James, "with words of love and peace," and informed him that Governor Carver "desired to see him and to truck with him, and to confirm a peace with him as his next neighbor." Before making any definite answer, the king refreshed himself from the biscuit and butter and the strong water, and gave to his followers what remained after he was satisfied. He intimated a desire to trade for Winslow's sword and armor, but was informed that those precious things were not

---

[1] This name is sometimes written by Bradford "Massasoyet;" and Prince says: "I find the ancient people from their fathers in Plymouth colony pronounce his name Ma-sas-so-it."—"Annals," p. 187.

[2] Prov. xviii., 16.

for sale. After a while, his confidence had been so far gained that he ventured over the brook with about twenty of his men, all leaving their bows and arrows behind them, while Winslow remained with Quadequina as a hostage. Some pomp was displayed in the reception of the king. Standish and Allerton met him at the brook, and with a guard of honor conducted him to an unfinished house, where a green rug had been spread, and a few cushions laid. Then came the governor, " with drum and trumpet after him, and some few musketeers." After ceremonious salutations, the governor kissing the king's hand, and receiving a kiss from royalty in return (neither of which could have been very agreeable), the two sat down together, as for business. It was a sight to be remembered, and vividly was it described by some who were there.

Massasoit was at that time in the prime of life, a stalwart man, " grave of countenance and spare of speech." A " chain of white bone beads about his neck " was the principal ornament that distinguished him from his followers, and from that necklace there was suspended a little pouch of tobacco. " His face was painted with a sad red," and head and face were oiled, " that he looked greasily." His followers, too— all strong, tall men — wore paint on their faces in similar style, " some black, some red, some yellow, and some white, some with crosses and other antic works." It was a picturesque congress in that rude council-house : on one side, Carver, Bradford, Standish, Allerton, and—gravest and stateliest among them—their revered elder, Brewster ; on the other side those painted wild men, some clad in skins of wild beasts and some naked.

The Pilgrims had not yet learned the fatal influence of strong drink over the Indians. It was natural, therefore, for Carver, in dealing with his royal visitor on so important an occasion, to perform, without scruple or reserve, the ritual of hospitality. He " called for some strong water, and drank to him ;" and the savage responded with " a great draught that made him sweat all the while after." He also "called for a little fresh meat"—a luxurious banquet in that first year of life at Plymouth—"which the king did eat willingly, and did give his followers." Eating and drinking together, especially as guest and host, is recognized as always a natural symbol of friendly relations; and with that symbol the great business of the day was begun. A treaty was then and there concluded, which remained unbroken for more than fifty years, and under which the intercourse between the two communities, the civilized and the savage, was entirely amicable.[1]   At the close, Massasoit lighted a pipe filled with tobacco from his pouch, and, after a solemn whiff or two, passed it to Carver and the other white chiefs, who accepted what they probably supposed to be nothing more than an act of courtesy on his part. They had never heard of the Indian's pipe of peace, and knew not that by those few whiffs of tobacco-smoke the treaty was ratified, and became to the king and his people a sacred compact.

---

[1] An abstract of that unwritten treaty was incorporated into the Journal of the Pilgrims, published in London the next year, and was copied almost without change into Bradford's History twenty-four years later :

"1. That neither he nor any of his should injure or do hurt to any of our people.

"2. And if any of his did hurt to any of ours, he should send the offender that we might punish him.

"3. That if any of our tools were taken away, when our people were at work [or if any thing were taken away from any of ours], he should cause it to be restored; and if ours did any harm to any of his, we should do the like to them.

"4. If any did unjustly war against him, we would aid him; if any did war against us, he should aid us.

"5. He should send to his neighbor confederates to certify them of this, that they might not wrong us, but might be likewise comprised in the conditions of peace.

"6. That when their men came to us, they should leave their bows and arrows behind them, as we should do our pieces when we came to them.

"Lastly, That doing thus, King James would esteem of him as his friend and ally."

When all was done the governor accompanied his visitor to the brook, where they parted, a few of the Indians being still detained as hostages for Winslow's safety. Then followed a visit from Quadequina, "and a troop with him," who had not yet seen the white men's village. The king's brother "was a very proper, tall young man, of a very modest and seemly countenance;" and though so much afraid of the fire-arms that, to relieve his mind, they were put out of sight, he was much pleased with his reception. When he went over the brook, there was the formal exchange of hostages. Two of his men proposed to remain through the night, but were not permitted; for the confidence of the Pilgrims in their new friends was not perfect. "That night," says their journal, "we kept good watch; but there was no appearance of danger."

Even the friendship of Indian neighbors is not in every respect desirable. The king and all his men, and their squaws with them, had encamped in the woods not more than half a mile off; and the next morning "divers of their people" were in Plymouth again, evidently "hoping to get some victuals." They said that the king would be pleased with a visit from some of the white men. Standish and Allerton "went venturously," and were hospitably entertained with "three or four ground-nuts and some tobacco." Meanwhile the Indian visitors at Plymouth were making themselves familiar, and "stayed till ten or eleven of the clock," but were at last got rid of by the governor's sending for the king's kettle and filling it with pease for them to carry home, "and so they went their way." On the whole, the Pilgrims, weak and impoverished as they were, could not have been very much gratified with the promise of their allies "that within eight or nine days they would come and set corn on the other side of the brook, and dwell there all summer." At the best, it was as if they were to have in their immediate neighborhood, through the summer, a great encampment of gypsies, trucking, begging, stealing, and committing all sorts of trespasses.   Happily for both parties, the promise was not kept.

The Pilgrims were beginning to understand their neighbors; but they were not on that account disposed to relax their preparations for self-defense.   As the new year (according to the ancient calendar) was about to open (March 23 = April 2), they completed their "military orders," and ordained some other laws which seemed necessary in their "present estate and condition."   At the same time they renewed their choice of Carver as governor of the colony — their sole magistrate, with indefinite powers, but continually responsible to "the whole company."   Within a week from that day there was occasion for them to demonstrate the fact that they had a government.   John Billington, a profane and worthless fellow, who came from London, and had been "shuffled into their company," perhaps by "friends" who thought that he might be made better by transportation, seems to have had a violent dislike of Captain Miles Standish, and to have uttered in "opprobious speeches" his "contempt of the captain's lawful commands."   Thereupon he was "convented before the whole company;" and for his offense he was sentenced "to have his neck and heels tied together." It was beginning to be manifest that the government must be respected, that the "military orders" were not to be trifled with, and that Captain Miles Standish was the lawful commander of a force sufficient for the punishment of evil-doers. John Billington, therefore, upon hearing the sentence, "humbled himself and craved pardon;" and, as this was the first offense since the arrival in New England, the penalty was remitted.

All this while the *Mayflower* had been lying in the harbor. Carver and the others had judged it unwise to send her away in midwinter, while the colony, daily growing weaker by sickness and death, might be destroyed any day by a sudden attack from the Indians.   Jones, too, the master of the ship, though at first impatient of delay, became afraid to encoun-

ter the perils of a winter voyage while the survivors of his crew were slowly recovering from the sickness of which so many had died.   But when the spring had come, when a treaty had been made with the neighboring Indians, and when all practicable arrangements for the defense and the continued life of the colony had been completed, "they began to dispatch the ship away which brought them over;" and about the middle of April, as we measure the months (April 5 = 15), she sailed for England.   It was a new trial to be left—only about fifty of them, men, women, and children—in that almost boundless solitude; and, doubtless, it was through their tears that they saw her sail lessening till it became a dim speck in the horizon.   But the thought of what they had suffered in their great undertaking, and of the graves which they had dug through the snow into the frozen earth —the thought of the love and hope that were lingering at Leyden, and of the prayers which brethren in England were offering for their success, would not permit them to retreat from the position they had gained at so great a cost.   Not one returned in the *Mayflower*—though why John Billington and some others of the same sort did not return has never been explained.

It was now time for planting.   All the force of the colony must be turned in that direction; for Plymouth was to be not merely a trading station (which might have been satisfactory to the Adventurers in London), but a permanent abode of civilization, a place attractive to Christian families, a refuge for the church of God.   Bradford and others of the company had practiced in their youth "the innocent trade of husbandry;" but during the twelve years of their pilgrimage in Holland they had been employed in the various industries of a manufacturing city.   What would their almost forgotten skill in husbandry be worth on a soil which, till then, had never been furrowed, and under a climate of which they knew indeed how cold it was in winter, but knew not as yet what might be the vicissitudes of the seed-time, the summer, and the harvest. "Some English seed they sowed, as wheat and pease, but it came not to good, either by the badness of the seed, or the lateness of the season, or both, or by some other defect." Fortunately—rather let us say, wisely—they sowed only six acres with the exotic "wheat and pease," while they planted twenty acres with the native grain, which they knew had flourished there through untold ages. In the planting of those twenty acres, they had Squanto's Indian lore to guide their English inexperience. He taught them how to plant the corn in hills, how to manure it with fish, and how to dress and tend it. At the same time, he initiated them into his ancestral methods of taking fish, for, strangely enough, their outfit at Southampton had not included a supply of "small hooks." He told them also how soon their brook would be alive with herring, and "where they might get other provisions necessary for them." Grievously as he had been wronged by Englishmen, he had learned to "discern between the righteous and the wicked." So long as he lived, he was to these Englishmen a faithful friend.

While they were thus busy with their planting, their governor, on one of those hot days which sometimes vary so suddenly the temperature of a New England spring, came in from the field, complaining as if he had suffered a sunstroke. He lay down, soon became unconscious and speechless, and in a few days he died. "This worthy gentleman," says the church record, in affectionate commemoration, "was one of singular piety, and rare for humility—which appeared, as otherwise, so by his great condescendency. When as this miserable people were in great sickness, he shunned not to do very mean services for them—yea, the meanest of them. He bare a share likewise of their labor in his own person, according as their great necessity required. Who being one also of a considerable estate, spent the main part of it in this enterprise, and from first to last approved himself not only as their agent in the first transacting of things, but also all

along to the period of his life, to be a pious, faithful, and
very beneficial instrument. He deceased in the month of
April, in the year 1621, and is now reaping the fruit of his
labor with the Lord."[1]   Little more is known of him than that,
after Robinson and Brewster, there was no man among the
Pilgrims so honored and beloved, or so much the author and
leader of their great enterprise, as he.   "Devout men carried him to his burial, and made great lamentation over him."
Feeble as they were, the funeral was not without some military pomp. "He was buried in the best manner they could,
with some volleys of shot by all that bore arms."   His wife,
"a weak woman," had lived through many hardships and
sufferings with him, but it soon appeared that she could not
live without him. In five or six weeks after his death her
weary pilgrimage was ended.

No arrangement had been made in anticipation of such an
event as the death of the governor.   The little commonwealth was left without a magistrate; but the vacancy was
soon filled. William Bradford was chosen governor, "and
being not yet recovered of his illness, in which he had been
near the point of death, Isaac Allerton was chosen to be an
assistant unto him."   On that occasion, the office of assistant — thenceforth a permanent office — had its beginning.
The organization of the state was slowly developed as new
arrangements became necessary; and already it was felt that
there was no one man on whose life the continued existence
of the colony depended.   But for the death of Carver, his
brethren might have thought that their colony could not
live without him for governor.

As yet there had never been a Christian wedding on the
soil of New England; and, but for the breaking up of families in the mortality of the first winter, there might have

---

[1] The quotation from the record of the church in Plymouth is found in
Young, p. 200.   It seems to imply that Carver's social position from his
birth was somewhat higher than that of the plain husbandmen who dwelt
near Scrooby, and that he had never been accustomed to any manual labor.

been none till some of the children brought over in the *May-flower* had become old enough to marry. Edward Winslow's wife, Elizabeth, died in that mortality, and his house was left to him desolate. William White, one of the chief men in the colony, had died before her; and his widow, Susanna, was left with two little boys to care for (one of them an infant, born while the *Mayflower* was lying at Cape Cod); and with neither man-servant nor maid-servant to help her, for they had died also. It can not be thought strange, when the circumstances of the case are considered, that, at an early day, Edward Winslow and Susanna White were married. At that time, and long afterward, there could be no lawful marriage in England without sacerdotal intervention and the use of ceremonies which Puritan scrupulousness denounced as superstitious. By the compromises of the Anglican Reformation, marriage had ceased to be in name a sacrament, without being distinctly recognized as any thing either less or greater than a sacrament. In Holland, the Pilgrims had seen what is now called civil marriage; and by that method they had themselves (many of them) been joined in holy wedlock. There the law was "that those of any religion, after lawful and open publication, coming before the magistrates in the town-house, or stadt-house, were to be by them orderly married, one to another." Accordingly, the first wedding in the Pilgrim colony was an open contempt of the canon law maintained in England; and, to that extent, it was an informal declaration of independence. In conformity with "the laudable custom of the Low Countries in which they had lived," marriage "was thought most requisite to be performed by the magistrate, as being a civil thing upon which many questions about inheritances do depend," and which for other reasons comes properly under the cognizance of the state—a thing, too, which is "nowhere found in the Gospel to be laid upon ministers as a part of their office." Therefore as Adam and Eve, in the beginning of the world, were married without any priestly intervention—as Boaz took Ruth, the Moabite widow, to be his wife, before the elders of Bethlehem—so Edward Winslow and Susanna White, before the magistrate, Governor Bradford, and with public solemnities, entered into the sacred covenant of marriage. Nor was theirs a godless wedding. Acknowledging God in all their ways, they acknowledged him especially in that momentous act. They married " in the Lord," [1] and the church, we need not doubt, invoked a blessing on their union. Thus, in the first New England wedding, a precedent was given which has never yet been set aside, and which marked clearly the distinction between the jurisdiction of the civil power in " causes matrimonial " and the legitimate jurisdiction of the church.

The first offense in the colony had been pardoned, after conviction and sentence, because it was the first, and because the culprit's acknowledgment of his fault and his submission to the authority which he had reviled were deemed sufficient for the ends of justice. But the next offense was of a more serious character. Stephen Hopkins had brought with him two servants—probably minors bound to service for a term of years. Between those two there was a quarrel, a challenge given and accepted, and a fight with swords and daggers—the first duel in New England. The wounds which they inflicted on each other were not thought to be an adequate punishment, and the parties were " adjudged by the whole company to have their head and feet tied together, and so to lie for twenty-four hours, without meat or drink." It seems that the judicial power, as well as the legislative, was exercised by " the whole company." The sentence was partly executed, but before one hour had passed the pain which the criminals were suffering was so great that they were released by the governor " at their own and their master's humble request, upon promise of better carriage."

Among the incidents of the year was the sending of an

---

[1] 1 Cor. vii., 39.

embassy from Plymouth to Pokanoket, "the habitation of the great king Massasoit." The friendly visits of hungry and curious natives had become so frequent as to be troublesome; and it was necessary to have some new regulations and a mutual understanding on that subject. It was important not only to make farther exploration of the country, but also to know where the Indians might be found in any emergency requiring communication with them. As Massasoit and his warriors, by their visit, had become acquainted with the weakness of the settlement as well as with its means of defense, it was thought that a deputation sent to return their visit would see the strength of those wild and uncertain allies. There was, at the same time, a desire to make satisfaction for some injuries which the Pilgrims thought they had done to Indians they knew not who. But the main and comprehensive purpose of the mission was "to continue the league of peace and friendship," which might at any moment be broken by misunderstanding or jealousy. Winslow and Hopkins were appointed by the governor to represent him at the court of Massasoit. Squanto went with them, dragoman to the legation. "That both they and their message might be more acceptable," they were to be the bearers of a present for the king—"a horseman's coat of red cotton, laced with a slight lace."

The message which they were to deliver from the governor at Plymouth to the king at Pokanoket was in these words: "That forasmuch as his subjects came often and without fear upon all occasions among us, so we were now come unto him, and, in witness of the love and good-will the English bear unto him, the governor hath sent him a coat, desiring that the peace and amity that was between them and us might be continued; not that we feared them, but because we intended not to injure any, desiring to live peaceably as with all men, so especially with them our nearest neighbors. But whereas his people came very often and very many together unto us, bringing for the most part their wives and children with them, they were welcome; yet, we being but strangers as yet at Patuxet, and not knowing how our corn might prosper, we could no longer give them such entertainment as we had done and as we desired still to do. Yet if he would be pleased to come himself, or if any special friend of his desired to see us, coming from him they should be welcome. And to the end we might know them from others, our governor had sent him a copper chain, desiring if any messenger should come from him to us we might know him by [his] bringing it with him, and hearken and give credit to his message accordingly. [Our governor] also requested him that such as have skins should bring them to us, and that he would hinder the multitude from oppressing us with them. And whereas, at our first arrival at Paomet, called by us Cape Cod, we found there corn buried in the ground, and finding no inhabitants, but some graves of dead new-buried, took the corn, resolving, if ever we could hear of any that had right thereto, to make satisfaction to the full for it; yet, since we understand the owners thereof were fled for fear of us, our desire was either to pay them with the like quantity of corn, English meal, or any other commodities we had to pleasure them withal; requesting him that some one of his men might signify so much unto them, and we would content him for his pains. And, last of all, our governor requested one favor of him, which was that he would exchange some of their corn for seed with us, that we might make trial which best agreed with the soil where we live."

With this message and the presents, Winslow and Hopkins, on one of the long days in the hottest part of a New England summer (July 2 = 12), set forth, the friendly Squanto guiding them through the wilderness. Leaving Plymouth Monday morning, and passing the first night "in the open fields," they arrived the next day (July 3 = 13), after various adventures, at the royal residence, about forty miles from Plymouth. The king, though not at home, was near enough to be sent for, and to come with no great loss of time on

their part.   At his return they gave him, as Squanto had requested, a military salute by discharging their pieces.   He,
after the Indian fashion, kindly welcomed them, took them
into his .house, and set them down by him.   Then, having
delivered their message and the presents, they put the red
cotton coat on his back and the copper chain about his neck,
and had the satisfaction of observing that " he was not a little proud to behold himself—and his men also to see their
king—so bravely attired."

The king's answer, on all points save one, was promptly
given.   " He told us we were welcome, and he would gladly
continue that peace and friendship which was between him
and us; and, for his men, they should no more pester us as
they had done; also, he would send to Paomet, and would
help us with corn for seed, according to our request."   But
in respect to the trade in beaver and other skins, he seemed
to feel that more formality was necessary to the validity of
the answer.   He made " a great speech " to his men who
gathered near him, " they sometimes interposing, and, as it
were, confirming and applauding him."   For each of thirty
places which he claimed, one after another, as his own, using
the same form of words, they responded in a similar formula.
It was his, and they would be at peace with the Englishmen,
and would bring their skins to Plymouth.   Satisfactory as
these affirmations were, the repetition of the same words
thirty times could not but seem tedious to the weary and
hungry embassadors.

They were hungry as well as weary, for, of the provision
for their journey, they had imparted freely to the Indians
near whose camp they passed the preceding night, not
doubting that they would have enough wherever they might
come; and though they " broke their fast " very well in the
morning, they had traveled all day without finding much to
eat.   The pipe of peace, which was solemnly circulated at
the close of the formal conference, was a very inadequate
substitute for food.   Massasoit, with the aid of Squanto, talk-

ed about England and King James, also about the Frenchmen, who, to his disgust, had intruded into Narraganset Bay, but he said nothing about supper. "Late it grew, but victuals he offered none; for indeed he had not any, being he came so newly home." So the embassadors sought such refuge from hunger as sleep might give them. "On hospitable thoughts intent," the king shared his own couch with them —he and his wife at one end of the long, low platform, they at the other. Then, as if that accommodation were not scanty enough, they found "two more of his chief men" crowding in with them for want of room elsewhere. They might well say, "We were worse weary of our lodging than of our journey."

Morning came at last (July 4 = 14), but no breakfast. There was a fresh throng of petty chiefs and other Indians, attracted to see the strangers, but using the opportunity to play "their manner of games"—whether of chance or of skill—"for skins and knives." So the long summer morning wore away, and about an hour after noon "Massasoit brought two fishes that he had shot" with arrows. The fish were large, and good for food; but what were they among so many? At least forty, when the fish were boiled, "looked for share in them," and few of the forty failed of getting something. "This meal only," said Winslow, "we had in two nights and a day; and had not one of us bought a partridge, we had taken our journey fasting." The king was "very importunate" to have them stay longer; and why they declined his urgent invitation, Winslow tells us: "We desired to keep the Sabbath at home, and feared we should be light-headed for want of sleep; for what with bad lodging, the savages' barbarous singing (for they use to sing themselves asleep), lice and fleas within doors, and mosquitoes without, we could hardly sleep all the time of our being there; we much feared that if we should stay any longer, we should not be able to recover home for want of strength. So, on the Friday morning (July 6 = 16), before sunrising, we took our leave and departed, Massasoit being both grieved and ashamed that he could no better entertain us." Through that day they suffered from want of food, being able to purchase from Indians on the way only " a little fish " and a handful of their parched corn, pulverized by pounding. But at night they obtained " good store of fish " —enough for supper and for their breakfast on Saturday. Drenched in rain, which began to come down like a deluge in the night and continued all the next day, they pressed forward, and " came safe home that [Saturday] night," thankful, " though wet and weary."

Their own report abounds in picturesque details both of their personal adventures and of their observations on the country through which they passed—at that time a pathless wilderness, almost emptied even of its wild inhabitants—now " a delightsome land," studded with towns and villages, hallowed with temples of intelligent and spiritual worship, adorned with homesteads perched on the hillsides or nestling in the valleys, and abounding in the wealth created by the industry of Christian civilization. But the historian of Plymouth colony gives the results of their embassy in a few words: "They found but short commons, and came both weary and hungry home. For the Indians used then to have nothing so much corn as they have since the English have stored them with their hoes, and seen their industry in breaking up new grounds therewith. They found Massasoit's place to be forty miles from hence, the soil good and the people not many, being dead and abundantly wasted in the late mortality which fell in all these parts, about three years before the coming of the English, and in which thousands of them died. They not being able to bury one another, their skulls and bones were found in many places, lying still above ground where their houses and dwellings had been—a very sad spectacle to behold. But they brought word that the Narragansets lived but on the other side of that great bay, and were a strong people and many in number, living compact together, and had not been at all touched with this wasting plague."

An intense feeling of loneliness must have been habitual with those surviving exiles—so few, and so cut off from communication with the civilized world.   Seven months since they sailed from the old English Plymouth—months how full of suffering and sorrow!—had passed when the *May-flower* left them in their solitude.   Month after month was passing, the year was completing its round; and all the while they had not one word from Leyden or from England. The summer gave them busy employment, not only with their corn-field and gardens, and with the building of their cottages in preparation for another winter, but also with various excursions for exploration and for opening trade with the natives.   An unlucky boy, one of the Billingtons (July), strayed into the woods, and wandered, famishing, till he came to a village of Indians, twenty miles away, who sent him to a still greater distance.   This gave occasion for an expedition of ten men in the shallop to the Nausites, the tribe who attacked the exploring party when the *Mayflower* was lying at Cape Cod.   Finding a harbor for the first night at Cummaquid (now Barnstable), they encountered there an aged woman, who came to see them because she had never seen an Englishman, yet, when she saw them, "broke forth into great passion, weeping and crying excessively."   Her story was "very grievous" to them.   Seven years before,[1] an Englishman seized and carried off in his vessel her three sons, "by which means she was deprived of the comfort of her children in her old age."   They assured her that all good Englishmen abhorred the man who robbed her of her sons; and, in token of their sympathy, they gave her some little presents to appease her grief.   Touching next at Nauset (now Eastham), they were in the midst of the savages whose arrows, flying around them, gave them so great an alarm a

---

[1] *Ante*, p. 329.

few months before.[1] Yet they succeeded, not only in recovering the boy, " behung with beads," [2] but also in gaining the confidence of that tribe.   Nor did they neglect the opportunity of making full satisfaction for the corn which, in their necessity, when the winter was upon them in the wilderness, they had taken from Indian granaries, and for the owners of which they had already made inquiry.   Of a military expedition, sent forth (Aug. 13 = 23) when a report came that Squanto had been killed because he was their friend; and of a more peaceful expedition (Sept. 18 = 28) which explored the harbor where Boston now is, and which resulted in opening commercial intercourse with the natives there, we need not tell the story.   While some were thus employed in affairs abroad, others were busy in fishing; and by that industry were endeavoring to provide for every family a supply against the winter.   Their own historian says, with unaffected acknowledgment of the divine Providence over them, " They found the Lord to be with them in all their ways, and to bless their outgoings and incomings; for which let his holy name have the praise forever."

" All summer there was no want."   In due time the harvest was gathered.   They had " a good increase of Indian corn;" their barley was " indifferent good;" but their pease, that came up well and blossomed hopefully, were " not worth the gathering."   Meanwhile their harbor was beginning to show how successful the wild ducks had been with their broods, " and now began to come in store of fowl" as the autumn advanced; and, besides water-fowl, there was " great store of wild turkeys " in the woods, as well as venison.   Then they had what they might have called, in Scriptural phrase, " the feast of ingathering."   Winslow, in a letter to a friend, tells how they kept it.   " Our governor sent four men on fowling, so that we might, after a special manner, rejoice to-

---

[1] *Ante*, p. 314, 315.

[2] Already the Nausites had begun to make an Indian of him.   Boys and men of the Billington sort are easily converted into savages.

gether after we had gathered the fruit of our labors. They four in one day killed as much fowl as, with a little help besides, served the company almost a week. At which time, among other recreations, we exercised our arms, many of the Indians coming among us, and among the rest Massasoit, with some ninety men, whom for three days we entertained and feasted." The Indian guests "went out and killed five deer, which they brought to the plantation, and bestowed on our governor and upon the captain and others." It is not altogether fanciful to call that three-days' feast "the first Thanksgiving." The New England autumnal feast, now kept with gladness in the homes and with worship in the churches, all the way from Plymouth to the Golden Gate, began spontaneously when the Pilgrim remnant had harvested their first crop of Indian corn.

Not many days later, the governor was startled by a message from the now friendly Nausites, that they had seen what they supposed to be a French ship (Nov. 9 = 19) putting in at the harbor where the *Mayflower* dropped her anchor just a year before. While he was wondering what such an arrival might portend, the unknown vessel was seen approaching. Instantly "he commanded a great piece to be shot off, to call home such as were abroad at work. Thereupon," as Winslow wrote to his friend, "every man, yea boy, that could handle a gun, was ready, with full resolution that, if she were an enemy, we would stand in our just defense, not fearing them." But as soon as she came near enough for them to see what flag she bore, there was no need of guns save for a joyful welcome. She was the *Fortune*, from London, a small vessel, sent out by the Adventurers, and bringing a reinforcement to the colony. Cushman came in her, and thirty-five others, including some at least of those who had been left behind when the *Speedwell* failed. But these new-comers were not all such as Bradford and Brewster would have chosen. "Many of them were wild enough"—unthinking young men—who had been picked up without carefulness, and persuaded to enlist in an enterprise which they could not appreciate, and who had been sent without any definite notion of whither they were going or wherefore. So little did the Adventurers in London realize what kind of a work it was which they had undertaken, or what was necessary to its success. The reinforcement had been sent without any reasonable outfit. Instead of bringing supplies of food that might help them to live through the winter, they were so many more mouths to be fed out of the scanty store of the colony till another harvest. Even the ship that brought them needed to be provisioned for her return voyage. Nor were the new emigrants well supplied with other necessaries.[1] "The plantation was glad of this addition of strength, but could have wished that many of them had been of better condition, and all of them better furnished with provisions."

The *Fortune* had not sailed from London till two months after the arrival of the *Mayflower* with intelligence of all that had befallen the Pilgrims on their long voyage and through the sorrowful winter. She brought letters from Leyden as well as from the mother country. A business letter from Weston to Governor Carver was " full of complaints and expostulations about former passages at Southampton, and the keeping the ship so long in the country, and returning her without lading." Some expressions in that letter were characteristic of the writer's unfeeling selfishness: "That you sent no lading in the ship is wonderful, and worthily distasted. I know your weakness was the cause of it, and, I believe, more weakness of judgment than weakness of hands. A quarter of the time you spent in discoursing, arguing, and

---

[1] " There was not so much as biscuit-cake or any other victuals for them ; neither had they any bedding but some sorry things they had in their cabins, nor pot nor pan to dress their meat in ; nor over-many clothes, for many of them had brushed away their coats and cloaks at Plymouth as they came. But there was sent over some Burchin-lane suits [cheap ready-made clothing], out of which they were supplied."—Bradford, p. 106.

consulting would have done much more; but that is past."
At the same time, he did not forget to make fresh promises,
conditioned upon early and profitable returns: "Consider
that the life of the business depends on the lading of this
ship, which if you do to any good purpose, that I may be
freed from the great sums I have disbursed for the former
and must do for the latter, I promise you I will never quit
the business though all the other Adventurers should." In
other words, the cry of their friend Thomas Weston from the
other side of the ocean was—Send fish, send beaver, send
something that I can turn into money at a good profit, and
I will stand by you; but unless you make my adventure a
gainful one, you are weak in judgment, and good for nothing
but to waste time in discoursing, arguing, and consulting.

Of other letters that came by the *Fortune*, only one has
been preserved, an official letter from Robinson to the church.
It was in these words:

"*To the Church of God at Plymouth, in New England:*

"MUCH BELOVED BRETHREN,—Neither the distance of
place nor distinction of body can at all either dissolve or
weaken that bond of true Christian affection in which the
Lord, by his Spirit, hath tied us together. My continual prayers are to the Lord for you; my most earnest desire is unto
you, from whom I will not longer keep (if God will) than [till]
means can be procured to bring with me the wives and children of divers of you, and the rest of your brethren, whom
I could not leave behind me without great injury both to you
and them, and offense to God and all men. The death of
so many, our dear friends and brethren, oh! how grievous
hath it been to you to bear, and to us to take knowledge of;
which, if it could be mended with lamenting, could not sufficiently be bewailed. But we must go unto them, and they
shall not return unto us. And how many even of us God
hath taken away, here and in England, since your departure,
you may elsewhere take knowledge. But the same God has

A a

tempered judgment with mercy—as otherwise, so in sparing the rest, especially those by whose godly and wise government you may be and (I know) are so much helped.[1]   In a battle, it is not looked for but that divers should die; it is thought well for a side if it get the victory, though with the loss of divers, if not too many or too great.   God, I hope, hath given you the victory, after many difficulties, for yourselves and others; though I doubt not but many do and will remain for you and us all to strive with.

"Brethren, I hope I need not exhort you to obedience unto those whom God hath set over you in church and commonwealth, and to the Lord in them.   It is a Christian's honor to give honor according to men's places; and his liberty to serve God in faith and his brethren in love, orderly, and with a willing and free heart.   God forbid I should need to exhort you to peace, which is the bond of perfection, and by which all good is tied together, and without which it is scattered.   Have peace with God first, by faith in his promises, good conscience kept in all things, and oft renewed by repentance; and so one with another for His sake who is though three one, and for Christ's sake who is one, and as you are called by one Spirit to one hope.   And the God of peace and grace and all goodness be with you, in all the fruits thereof, plenteously, upon your heads, now and forever.

"All your brethren here remember you with great love, a general token whereof they have sent you.

"Yours, ever in the Lord,   JOHN ROBINSON.

"LEYDEN, HOLLAND, June 30, anno 1621."

As a communication to the church from its pastor, the letter would naturally be read in the public assembly for worship.   Such assemblies the church had "every Sabbath," as those who came by the *Fortune* reported to their friends in

---

[1] Robinson, when he wrote this letter (preserved in Bradford's Letter-Book), did not know that Carver was among the dead.

England; and, though the pastor was still so far away, the congregation was not therefore without the preaching of the Word.[1] That "exercise of prophesying"' for which Robinson contended[2] against those who held that preaching is exclusively the function of men ordained to govern in the church, was kept up at Plymouth. A sermon that was delivered by Robert Cushman on one of the three or four Sabbaths that occurred while the *Fortune* was taking in her return cargo, was soon afterward printed in England, and it is the only extant specimen of the preaching which the Pilgrims listened to. If all the sermons which they heard in those early times were like Cushman's "On the sin and danger of self-love," from the text, "Let no man seek his own, but every man another's wealth," they had no lack of practical preaching.[3] Their church, in its Sabbath assemblies, was a school of mutual instruction and edification. However they might miss their pastor's discourses, so rich in doctrine, and so illustrated with various learning, they did not neglect the assembling of themselves together, nor cease to help each other in the application of Christian principles and motives to the exigencies of their condition.

The *Fortune* sailed homeward on or soon after the first anniversary of the landing at Plymouth (Dec. 11 = 21). Brief

---

[1] William Hilton, who, in 1623, became one of the first settlers of Dover, in New Hampshire, was a passenger by the *Fortune*. He, in a letter written soon after his arrival, described the moral and religious aspect of Plymouth in these words: "Our company are, for most part, very religious, honest people; the word of God [is] sincerely taught us every Sabbath."

[2] *Ante*, p. 239.

[3] The sermon—or so much of it as seemed to be of historic value—is found in Young, p. 256–258. Felt's "Ecclesiastical History of N. E." (i., 67) calls the author of it "Elder Cushman." Thomas Cushman, son of Robert, was chosen ruling elder after Brewster's death; but Robert seems never to have held any office in the church. It is worth remembering that the first printed American sermon was preached against selfishness, applying Christian principles and motives to stimulate public spirit; and that a non-professional preacher—an active business man—was the author of it.

as her stay had been, she sailed with a freight of lumber and of beaver and other peltry, valued at "near five hundred pounds sterling." Cushman, having come out as a special agent for the Adventurers, went back to make his report, carrying with him the manuscript of his sermon. At last, yielding to his persuasion and to advice from Leyden, the colonists had accepted the hard conditions which they would not accept while in England, and it was now expected that the enterprise in which they had invested their all would be carried forward with more effectual co-operation from the Adventurers, and especially from Weston, who had promised so much. If we had, to-day, the entire contents of the *Fortune's* letter-bag on her return voyage, they would be deemed worth more than their weight in gold. Governor Bradford's reply to Weston's harsh "complaints and expostulations" was among those letters, and is a beautiful example of Christian dignity in rebuke. "Your large letter written to Mr. Carver," said the Pilgrim governor, "I have received, . . . wherein (after the apology made for yourself) you lay many heavy imputations upon him and us all. Touching him, he is departed this life, and is now at rest in the Lord from all those troubles and incumbrances with which we are yet to strive. He needs not my apology; for his care and pains was so great for the common good, both ours and yours, as that therewith (it is thought) he oppressed himself and shortened his days. . . . At great charges in this adventure, I confess you have been, and many losses may sustain; but the loss of his and many other honest and industrious men's lives can not be valued at any price. Of the one, there may be hope of recovery; but the other no recompense can make good."

The letter adverted to the blame which Weston imputed to them "for keeping the ship so long in the country, and then sending her away empty." It described, in a few telling phrases, the events and circumstances which made the detention of the *Mayflower* inevitable: their "seeking out in

the foul winter a place of habitation," "with many a weary
step and the endurance of many a hard brunt;" their work
"in so tedious a time" to provide shelter for themselves
and their goods, a work so severe, and involving such exposures, that many of them were still bearing in their bodies
the marks of it; the visitation of God upon them "with
death daily, and with so general a disease that the living
were scarce able to bury the dead, and the well not in any
measure sufficient to tend the sick"—particulars which Weston already knew before he wrote his insulting complaints.
"And now," said the governor, "to be so greatly blamed for
not freighting the ship, doth indeed go near us, and much
discourage us.   But you say you know we will pretend weakness.   And do you think we had not cause?   Yes, you tell
us you believe it, but it was more weakness of judgment
than of hands.   Our weakness herein is great, we confess;
therefore we will bear this check patiently among the rest,
till God send us wiser men."   Then — touching upon the
cruel charge that they had wasted "in discoursing, arguing,
and consulting" the time in which they might have been at
work for their masters the Adventurers—the pen struck fire,
and the meek spirit of the Pilgrim blazed out in righteous
indignation.   Intimating that he knew or strongly suspected whence the slander came, he said, with evident allusion
to some of those who did not come from Leyden, but had
been shuffled into their company in England: "They who
told you, . . . their hearts can tell their tongues they lie.
They cared not, so they might salve their own sores, how
they wounded others.   Indeed, it is our calamity that we are
(beyond expectation) yoked with some ill-conditioned people, who will never do good, but corrupt and abuse others."

The remainder of the letter was occupied with matters of
business between the Adventurers and the colony.   Among
other things, it insisted on the necessity of sending a timely supply of provisions, because otherwise the reinforcement
"would bring famine on them unavoidably."   It closed with

the hope that, inasmuch as the controversy about the conditions of their partnership had been terminated by the submission of the Planters to the demands of the Adventurers, offenses would be forgotten, and Weston would remember his promise to stand by them.

As soon as the *Fortune* had been supplied with food for her voyage and dispatched homeward, the thirty-five " newcomers " were distributed into families, and a careful inventory was made of the provisions remaining for the sustenance of the colony. It was found that, with the increased number of consumers, there was only half a supply for six months. " So they were presently put to half allowance, one as well as another—which began to be hard; but they bore it patiently under hope of supply."

The winter solstice had passed; the days were beginning to lengthen; a year had been completed since they " began to erect the first house for common use " (Dec. 25 = Jan. 4). One incident of that anniversary is narrated by Bradford as "rather of mirth than of weight." The story, in his quaint words, is too picturesque, and too characteristic of the Pilgrims, their governor, and the "new-comers," to be lost : " On the day called Christmas-day, the governor called them out to work, as was used; but the most of this new company excused themselves, and said it went against their consciences to work on that day. So the governor told them that, if they made it matter of conscience, he would spare them till they were better informed. So he led away the rest and left them; but when they came home at noon from their work, he found them in the street at play, openly—some pitching the bar, and some at stool-ball, and such like sports. So he went to them and took away their implements, and told them that was against his conscience, that they should play and others work. If they made the keeping of it matter of devotion, let them keep their houses; but there should be no gaming or reveling in the streets. Since which time nothing hath been attempted that way, at least openly."

CHAPTER XVII.

ADVERSITY AND PROGRESS.—WESTON'S COLONY, AND WHAT CAME OF IT.

THE second year of the colony at Plymouth, and the third, brought no such sorrow as that of the first winter. Yet they were years of peril and of suffering.

While the Pilgrims were on good terms with their neighbor Massasoit, and with all the Indians under his authority, they had not been able to enter into similar relations with Canonicus, the sachem of a much more powerful nation. The Narragansets, inhabiting nearly all the territory now included in the State of Rhode Island, are supposed to have been at that time about thirty thousand, for they had been strangely spared by the pestilence which had wasted other tribes. It was natural for them to be jealous of the advantages which their neighbors under Massasoit were likely to gain from alliance and intercourse with the English; and it began to be reported that they were preparing for an attack on Plymouth. They knew, indeed, that the colony had been reinforced, but they knew also that the men who came by the *Fortune* had brought neither arms nor provisions.

After not many days, there came into the village a messenger from the Narragansets (Jan., 1622), whose message Governor Bradford and Assistant Allerton, in the absence of their interpreter, were able to understand only in part. He brought a bundle of new arrows tied up in a rattlesnake's skin, and, having intimated that the suspicious gift was for Squanto, he "desired to depart with all expedition." From a friendly and faithful Indian who was with him, they could learn no more than what they must have inferred without his aid, namely, that the symbol meant mischief. The messenger was committed to the custody of Captain Standish, to be detained till his message could be more distinctly understood and answered.   After a night's detention, he was set at liberty, as being under the protection of "the law of arms." He was charged "to certify his master that the governor had heard of his large and many threatenings, and was much offended;" to tell him that, "if he would not be reconciled to live peaceably," the governor "dared him to the utmost;" and to assure him that the Englishmen at Plymouth, though not at all afraid of him, were desirous of peace with him as with all men.   All this was while Squanto was absent.   On his return, he informed the governor "that to send the rattlesnake's skin in that manner imported enmity, and that it was no better than a challenge."   After some consultation with the assistant, the captain, and perhaps others, "the governor stuffed the skin with powder and shot, and sent it back, returning no less defiance to Canonicus, assuring him that if he had shipping now present, thereby to send his men to Narraganset, they would not need to come so far by land to us; yet withal showing that they should never come unwelcome or unlooked for."   An Indian was found who consented to be the bearer of the message with the stuffed snakeskin; and so well did he perform his task that the Narraganset king was not disposed to maintain his challenge.   "He would not once touch the powder and shot, nor suffer it to remain in his country."   The terrible symbol was sent from place to place, till it came back to Plymouth in good condition.

Meanwhile all hands were busy with preparations for defense.   Bradford and his associates, "notwithstanding [their] high words and lofty looks" toward those who threatened them, knew the weakness of the colony, and what skill they had in military engineering was put in requisition.   By thirty or forty days of united labor, the village was inclosed (Feb.) with a stockade, having "flankers in convenient places, with gates to shut, which were every night locked, and a watch kept, and, when need required, there was also warding in the daytime." Every man under the captain had his immediate commander, and knew the point to which he must instantly repair in case of an alarm. In such insecurity were they night and day. The entire force to defend that outpost of civilization against uncounted hordes of savages was, at the utmost, not more than fifty men and boys, including all who had lately come by the *Fortune*. Keeping watch by night and ward by day, on their half-rations, no man of them sleeping but with his weapons beside him ready for battle, theirs must have been a stalwart faith if they could sing, "The Lord is my Shepherd," unfalteringly in Ainsworth's uncouth verse :

> "Jehovah feedeth me, I shall not lack.
>   In grassy folds he down doth make me lie :
>   He gently leads me quiet waters by.
> He doth return my soul : For his name's sake,
>   In paths of justice leads me quietly.

> "Yea, though I walk in dale of deadly shade,
>   I'll fear none ill : For with me thou wilt be ;
>   Thy rod, thy staff eke, they shall comfort me.
> 'Fore me a table thou hast ready made
>   In their presènce that my distressers be."

Amid such anxieties, the question was raised whether it would be safe for them to weaken their power of self-defense by sending out a trading expedition which they had planned, and which the Indians around Boston harbor were expecting. Bradford, Allerton, and Standish (the governor, the assistant, and the captain), held a consultation (March) with other principal men, and their conclusion was that, " as hitherto, upon all occasions," they " had manifested undaunted courage and resolution," so in these circumstances no other policy would be safe. Their storehouse was almost empty, and unless they could obtain food by traffic they must soon perish ; nor could they shut themselves up in their fortification without exposing at once their weakness and their fear. " Therefore," said they, " we thought best to proceed in our trading voyage, making this use of that we heard" about hostile intentions on the part of the savages, "to go the better provided, and use the more carefulness both at home and abroad, leaving the event to the disposing of the Almighty.   As his providence had hitherto been over us for good, so we had now no cause (save our sins) to despair of his mercy in our preservation and continuance, while we desired rather to be instruments of good to the heathen about us than to give them the least measure of just offense."

Just at this time their confidence in Squanto was shaken; for the temptations incident to his position seemed to have overpowered him.   They found reason to believe that, among his fellow-savages, he was pretending to have unbounded influence over the English, and under that pretense was taking bribes (perhaps he would have preferred to say fees) to avert the hostility or to conciliate the favor of the growing power at Plymouth.   The exposure of his practices made him dependent on them for his personal safety; for it brought upon him the wrath and life-long hatred of Massasoit.   He dared not desert them, and they allowed him to remain among them.   But in the mean time they had already taken under their patronage another Indian, Hobbamoc, whom they found faithful in their service, and who was especially useful as a check upon Squanto.   If at any time they distrusted what one of them said, they could bear the testimony of the other, and could require that at the mouth of two witnesses every word should be established.   Poor Squanto lived only a few months after the exposure of his duplicity.   He died, "desiring the governor to pray for him that he might go to the Englishmen's God in heaven, and bequeathed sundry of his things to sundry of his English friends as remembrances of his love."   Hobbamoc lived several years among the Pilgrims, and seems to have received an allotment of land in their township.   After his death, he was held in affectionate remembrance.   When his memory had not yet passed into tradition, it was said of him : "As he increased in knowledge, so in affection and also in practice, reforming and conforming himself accordingly; and though he was much tempted by enticements, scoffs, and scorns from the Indians, yet could he never be gotten from the English, nor from seeking after their God, but died among them, leaving some good hopes in their hearts that his soul went to rest."

In the early summer, when the supply of provisions was failing, and stark famine was beginning to pinch the company at Plymouth, they were one day startled by the sight of a sail-boat coming into their harbor (June). The boat proved to be a shallop from the *Sparrow*, a vessel which Weston and another of the Adventurers had sent to the coast of Maine for a fishing voyage on their private account. Any hope of relief which the sight of an English sail might have awakened was soon dispelled, for " this boat," says Bradford, " brought seven passengers and some letters, but no victuals, nor any promise of any." The *Sparrow* had sailed from England before any intelligence of the *Fortune* had been received there, and the letters which she brought gave to the governor such views of what might be expected from Weston, and of discord and mutual antipathy among the Adventurers, that he dared not communicate the discouraging information save to the few in whom he could most safely confide. Weston was proposing to withdraw from the partnership; and though he reiterated his professions of friendship, he and his associate were intending to send out a colony which should be their own, and of which these seven passengers were to be the pioneers. He complained that " the parsimony of the Adventurers," overruling his generous intentions, was the reason why the emigrants by the *Fortune* were so ill provided with necessaries, and that the same parsimony was keeping back the " supply of men and provisions " which, without waiting for her return, he had been soliciting for the colony. He, therefore, and those who were of his faction among the Adventurers, invited the Planters to unite with them in demanding that the partnership should be dissolved immediate-

ly by general consent, and its assets divided among the share-
holders.   Bradford and the friends whom he consulted were
alarmed at these schemes of Weston's.   They thought they
saw the reason why the men whom he sent by the *Fortune*
were what they were, and that some of them had been sent
in the expectation of their deserting Plymouth when the time
should come for beginning his intended plantation.   Once
they had trusted that man, believing in their simplicity that
he had some sympathy with their enterprise; but now it was
plain to them that, all the while, he had only been using them
for his own advantage, and that he intended so to use them
still, whatever the cost might be to them.   "Well might it
make them remember what the Psalmist saith: 'It is better
to trust in the Lord than to have confidence in man;' and
'Put not your trust in princes'—much less in the merchants
—'nor in the son of man, for there is no help in them;'
'Blessed is he that hath the God of Jacob for his help, whose
hope is in the Lord his God.'"[1]
     What were they to do?   Should they shut their doors
against the seven men who had been kept fishing in Weston's service "till planting-time was over," and had now come
to demand their hospitality?   They took in the strangers,
who "might have starved if the plantation had not succored
them;" and, day by day till the harvest came, those seven,
who had never done or suffered any thing for the colony,
shared equally with the best and most honored in the distribution of food from the common stock.   Winslow, under
orders from the governor, and in a boat belonging to the
colony, accompanied the shallop on its return to the eastern
fishing-grounds, where the *Sparrow* was only one of about
thirty vessels employed in the same business.   He found a
kind reception among his countrymen there, and came back
with a boat-load of provisions freely contributed by them for
the suffering colony.   With this new supply, the daily allow-

---

[1] Psa. cxviii., 8; cxlvi., 3, 5.—Geneva Version.

ance of bread was only a quarter of a pound to each person; but inadequate as the relief was, it enabled the colony to live till harvest. The colony storehouse seems to have been, while Winslow was absent, and we know not how long before, entirely destitute of bread and bread-stuffs. "I returned home," he says, "with all speed convenient, and found the state of the colony much weaker than when I left it; for till now we were never without some bread, the want whereof much abated the strength and flesh of some, and swelled others." "Had we not been in a place where divers sorts of shell-fish are that may be taken with the hand, we must have perished."[1]

It was evident that the Indians knew how weak the colony had become; and that the Narragansets, especially, were thinking how soon it would be easy to cut off the starving remnant. Massasoit himself seemed to be losing his respect for his English allies. "These things occasioned further thoughts of fortification." Part of "the Mount," now known as Burial Hill, was within the stockade which inclosed the village. On that height the Pilgrims, in their weakness, "built a fort with good timber both strong and comely, . . . made with a flat roof and battlements, on which their ordnance were mounted, and where they kept constant watch—especially in time of danger." "This work," says Winslow, "was begun with great eagerness and with the approbation of all men, hoping that this being once finished, and a continual guard there kept, it would utterly discourage the sav-

---

[1] Winslow gives this explanation. "It may be said, if the country abound with fish and fowl in such measure as is reported, how could men undergo such measure of hardness, except through their own negligence? I answer, every thing must be expected in its proper season. No man, as one saith, will go into an orchard in the winter to gather cherries; so he who looks for fowl there in the summer will be deceived in his expectation." . . . "I confess that as the fowl decrease, so fish increase;" . . . but, "though our bay and creeks were full of bass and other fish, yet for want of fit and strong seines and other netting, they for the most part broke through and carried all away before them."—Winslow's "Relation," in Young, p. 294.

ages from having any hopes or thoughts of rising against us."
Labor that could not well be spared from their fields of Indian corn was expended on this building. "It was a great
work for them in this weakness and time of wants," says
Bradford ; "but the danger of the time required it ;" and not
only the rumors of " insulting speeches " by the savages in the
surrounding regions, but " also the hearing of that great massacre in Virginia, made all hands willing to dispatch the
same." [1]   This fortress "served them also for a meeting-
house."   Their citadel was their temple.[2]

   While they were busy in this work—so great in comparison
with their strength—two more of Weston's vessels (the *Charity* and the *Swan*) arrived (July), but brought them no relief
nor any good news.   The *Fortune*, on her return voyage,
had been captured and plundered by Frenchmen, and that
was the end of the five hundred pounds' worth of beaver and
other merchandise with which she had been freighted by the
colony.   Fifty or sixty men, employed by Weston in his enterprise of making a new plantation, came in those vessels,
expecting to find hospitality in Plymouth.   The larger vessel, after landing those of her passengers whom he had sent
on his business, proceeded on her voyage to Virginia; the
other, of only sixty tons, was to remain for the service of his
plantation—as the *Speedwell*, two years before, would have
remained for the service of the Pilgrim colony, had she come
safely with the *Mayflower.*   How to deal with Weston's men

---

   [1] The "great massacre" which, in the night of March 22, 1622, struck terror through the Virginia colony, and in which about three hundred and fifty
English people were killed, had just been reported at Plymouth, and was
reason enough why the people there should strengthen their defenses, even
at the expense of their corn-fields.

   [2] The building is thus described by a Dutchman who visited Plymouth
from New Amsterdam in 1627 : " Upon the hill, they have a large square
house, with a flat roof, made of thick sawn planks, stayed with oak beams :
upon the top of which they have six cannons, which shoot iron balls of four
or five pounds, and command the surrounding country.   The lower part they
use for their church."

was a perplexing question. Letters that came with them gave new illustrations of his treachery, and of the quarrel between him and some of the other Adventurers. He was no longer connected with the enterprise, for the company had bought him out, and thought they were well rid of him; but, in his letter to Bradford, he was still intent on a dissolution of the partnership, repeating and urging his advice to that effect, with professions of disinterested friendship, and with malicious accusations against his late associates. On the other hand, a letter from two of the Adventurers, Pickering and Greene—a letter designed to be secret, but betrayed to Weston, and then forwarded by him with his commentary annexed—warned Bradford and Brewster against his designs. They alleged that he would permit no letters to be sent by his ships. He replied that he had invited them to send both letters and victuals. But why was there no communication from Cushman, their fellow-pilgrim? He had always been on good terms with Weston, and had trusted him. Why did he not himself report to them the ill success of his voyage in the *Fortune?* While they were wondering at this, a letter, addressed on the outside as from a wife in England to her husband in the colony, had been opened by the husband, and found to be a communication from Cushman to the governor. It was accordingly delivered to Bradford; and the fact of its having been sent under that disguise was proof that the writer agreed with Pickering and Greene in their opinion of Weston. After mentioning the capture of the *Fortune,* and that their friends did not seem to be discouraged, he said: "I purpose, by God's grace, to see you shortly, I hope in June next, or before. In the mean space know these things, and I pray you to be advertised a little. Mr. Weston hath quite broken off from our Company, through some discontents that arose betwixt him and some of our Adventurers, and hath sold all his adventures, and hath now sent three small ships for his particular plantation. . . . The people which they carry are no men for us, wherefore, I pray

you, entertain them not, neither exchange man for man with
them, except it be some of your worst. . . . If they offer to
buy any thing of you, let it be such as you can spare, and
let them give the worth of it. If they borrow any thing of
you, let them leave a good pawn. . . . I fear these people
will hardly deal so well with the savages as they should. I
pray you therefore signify to Squanto that they are a distinct body from us, and that we have nothing to do with
them, neither must be blamed for their faults, much less can
warrant their fidelity." Cushman was a sanguine hoper, or
he would not have added, so confidently, "We are about to
recover our losses in France"—a prediction which, like his
purpose to visit Plymouth that summer—does not seem to
have been fulfilled. In the same cheerful and hopeful spirit
he closed his letter. "Our friends at Leyden are well, and
will come to you as many as can this time. I hope all will
turn to the best; wherefore I pray you be not discouraged,
but gather up yourself to go through these difficulties cheerfully and with courage in that place wherein God hath set
you, until the day of refreshing come. And the Lord God
of sea and land bring us comfortably together again, if it
may stand with his glory."

The letter was indorsed with a few lines from John Pierce,
a friend of theirs, in whose name the patent obtained for the
colony from "the Governor and Council of New England"
had been taken out. "I desire you to take into consideration that which is written on the other side, and not in any
way to damnify your own colony, whose strength is but
weakness, and may thereby be more enfeebled. . . . As for
Mr. Weston's company, I think them so base in condition,
for the most part, as in all appearance not fit for an honest
man's company. I wish they may prove otherwise."

What the men were who swayed the little community at
Plymouth, and what their religion was, appears in the fact
that with so full a revelation of Weston's plans, and with
such warning against the men, concerning whom he had him-

self confessed that many of them were "rude fellows," they "concluded to give his men friendly entertainment." They were unwilling to forget what he had formerly done for them, and that some of them were under particular obligations of gratitude to him. At the same time they could not but pity "the people who were now come into a wilderness and were presently to be put ashore," altogether unacquainted with what was before them and ignorant what to do. Those "rude fellows" bore no such resemblance to Christ as would make them his "brethren," yet they were "strangers" thrown upon the hospitality of an impoverished but Christian community, and they were taken in. It was a generous magnanimity toward Weston, and a rare charity toward his worthless gang, when the Plymouth people, instead of bidding them shift for themselves, received them hospitably, gave them shelter for their persons and their goods, and succored the many of them who were sick with "the best means the place afforded." Fortunately these new guests were not destitute of food, as the seven were who came by the *Sparrow*, and whom the colony had received to share in its scanty supply. But of the provision brought by the *Charity* and the *Swan* for Weston's men, Plymouth received nothing. While some of the most capable were exploring to find a place for the intended plantation, the others waited for the result till the end of summer. They made some show of service in the corn-fields; but there they were more mischievous than vermin, stealing the unripe ears at night, and even in the daytime, and so destroying the harvest for which others had labored. After some exploration, a place called by the natives Wessagusset — now known as Weymouth, near Boston—was selected for Weston's plantation; and as many of his men as were deemed fit for service went to begin their work. The story of the hospitality shown by the Pilgrims to those disagreeable guests is not fairly told without adding that the invalids of Weston's company—the "sick and lame"—were left at Plymouth by permission from the gov-

B B

ernor, and received gratuitously the best medical treatment
the colony could give, till accommodations were provided
for them at Wessagusset.   Nothing was received in return
for all this hospitality.   Nothing was desired; for evidently
the strangers "were an unruly company, and had no good
government over them, and would soon fall into wants," and
it was wiser to treat them as beggars dependent on charity
than to deal with them as equals.

   The longed-for time of harvest was approaching.   Sixty
acres had been planted with Indian corn — the only grain
which the colony attempted to raise that year; and it had
been expected that the yield from that planting would be a
sufficient supply.   But so imperfect was the crop — partly
through the inexperience of the cultivators, partly by deficiency of strength for the necessary work in the fields, and
partly because thieves (not only Weston's men but some of
their own) had stolen the unripe ears—that the prospect of
food for another winter was discouraging.   "Markets there
were none to go to, but only Indians;" and the colony had
nothing to spare which the Indians would purchase with
corn.   At that crisis, the religious spirit of Bradford and his
brethren saw, in the relief that came to them, the providence
of God, who feeds the ravens and much more his own children.   Some English merchants had sent out a vessel—the
Discovery—to explore the New England coast and observe
its harbors; and it was a glad day at Plymouth (Aug.) when
she arrived there.   From her commander they obtained such
provisions as they most needed and he could best spare, and,
what was of more importance to them, a supply of commodities for their trade with the Indians; but he was careful to
have a good bargain.   "As he used us kindly," says Winslow, "so he made us pay largely."   They exchanged with
him "coat beaver" at the lowest price for cheap knives and
beads at the highest price; but "by this means they were
fitted again to trade for beaver and other things."   They
were well aware that savage industry produced little else

than peltry for any market; but they "intended to buy what corn they could."

The anticipations of the Plymouth governor in regard to Weston's men began to be realized very soon. "They had not been long from us," says Winslow, "ere the Indians filled our ears with clamors against them for stealing their corn and other abuses." Such clamors were the more ominous of evil because they came from Indians who had desired to have more intimate relations with the white men. Unfortunately for the complainants, Bradford had no jurisdiction over the men of Wessagusset. So long as they were at Plymouth, they were under his government; and the stripes inflicted on some of them for stealing corn from the field were a testimony to them that the Pilgrim magistrate did not bear the sword in vain. But after their removal to their own plantation, he could only remonstrate with them and advise them. The men whom Weston had thought fit for the work of planting a colony that should be more prosperous than Plymouth —men unaccustomed to regard the moral quality and the ulterior consequences of their actions—could not be restrained without something more potent than remonstrance and advice. Little thought would they give to the argument that their savage neighbors, if thus wronged, would soon become implacable and dangerous enemies.

After a little while the results of their recklessness began to appear in another direction. Instead of husbanding their supply of food, they had wasted it and were beginning to be in want. Richard Greene, Weston's brother-in-law, and in his behalf the overseer and governor of his plantation, having learned that the Plymouth people had obtained means for purchasing corn of the Indians, proposed to join them, and offered the *Sparrow* for that service (Oct.). Conditions of partnership were agreed upon; for it was obviously better to have even so slight a check on the proceedings of his people than to let them operate entirely at their own discretion. Two short voyages were made along the coast; one under the personal direction of Governor Bradford, the other commanded by Captain Standish, and supplies of Indian corn were obtained, to be divided between the two colonies. Bradford and Standish made also some journeys by land to purchase more corn for Plymouth.

But the winter had not gone by when there came to Plymouth a messenger with a letter from Sanders (March, 1623), who, by the death of Greene, had been left in command at Wessagusset. The plantation there being in want, Sanders had in vain attempted to borrow corn of his Indian neighbors, and he desired Bradford's advice whether he might not take from them by force enough to feed his people in his absence, for he was going eastward to procure supplies. Immediately the governor and his assistant held a consultation with the principal men of Plymouth. The result was a letter by Bradford, which they all subscribed, and of which Winslow gives a summary too characteristic of the men to be left out of our story. The contents were to this purpose :

" We altogether disliked their purpose as being against the law of God and nature. We showed them how it would cross the worthy ends and proceedings of the king's majesty and of his honorable council for this place, both in respect of the peaceable enlarging of his majesty's dominions, and also of the propagation of the knowledge and law of God and the glad tidings of salvation, which we and they were bound to seek. . . . We assured them their master would incur much blame hereby, neither could they answer the same. For our own parts, our case was almost the same with theirs. We had but a small quantity of corn left, and were enforced to live on ground-nuts, clams, muscles, and such other things as naturally the country afforded, and which would maintain strength and were easy to be gotten—all which things they had in great abundance ; yea, oysters also, which we wanted. Therefore necessity could not be said to constrain them. Moreover, they should consider that, if they proceeded therein, all they could so get would maintain them but a small time, and then they must perforce seek their food abroad, which would be very difficult for them, having made the Indians their enemies.　Therefore it would be much better to begin a little sooner, and so continue their peace — upon which course they might with good conscience desire and expect the blessing of God.

"Also (we told them) that they should consider their own weakness—the effect of disease—and that they should not expect help from us in that or any the like unlawful actions. Lastly, that however some of them might escape, yet the principal agents should expect no better than the gallows, whenever any special officer should be sent over by his majesty or his council for New England (which we expected), who would undoubtedly call them to account for the same."

This letter, subscribed by the leading men of Plymouth, was directed to the whole company at Wessagusset.　At the same time the governor addressed a special and personal letter to Sanders, advising him to desist from the proposed robbery, and warning him that it would be dangerous for him above the rest, inasmuch as he was their leader and commander.　With such replies the Indian messenger—probably as unconscious of his errand, either way, as the wires over which messages pass in these days—returned to those who had sent him.　The appeal to their fears was so far successful that they receded from their purpose, and concluded to live after the Plymouth fashion till Sanders should return from his eastward expedition.　But he could not fit out even a shallop for that voyage without first coming to Plymouth, where Bradford, from their scanty store, supplied him with corn to feed his boat's crew.

Such a company of runagates as Weston had sent over could not but breed, sooner or later, a conspiracy of the savages against the English.　The experience of two hundred and fifty years, since that time, has shown that on whatever frontier reckless and half-savage white men come into com-

munication with savage red men, whom they teach at once
to hate them and to despise them, "Indian hostilities" are
the consequence, and that the Indian in taking vengeance
rarely discriminates between one sort of white men and another.   Bradford tells how it was that Weston's people were
distressed so soon, though the ship had left them "competent-
ly provided," and though they had their half of the corn
purchased of the Indians, besides what they obtained of the
natives in their vicinity.   He says that they "spent excessively" whatever they had or could get.   He intimates that
they "wasted part among the Indians" in a way which he
suggests by declining to vouch for the story which some of
them told about what "he that was their chief" expended
in his relations with Indian women.   After they began to be
in want, many of them sold their garments and bedding;
others became servants to the Indians—hewers of wood and
bearers of water "for a cap-full of corn;" others "fell to
plain stealing" from their savage neighbors.   "In the end,
they came to that misery that some starved and died with
cold and hunger."   In that misery "most of them left their
dwellings and scattered up and down in the woods and by
the water-side, where they could find ground-nuts and clams."
All this while the Indians were learning to despise and scorn
them, even to the extent of insulting them, and now and then
robbing them of food or of "a sorry blanket" by main
strength.   Such was the distress which they proposed to relieve by plundering the corn-heaps of the more provident
savages around them; and that design of theirs, though they
were dissuaded from it, was by some of them betrayed to
those who were to have been the victims.   After all this,
what else than "a conspiracy against the English" could be
expected of the Indians?

Meanwhile the vigilance of Standish and other Plymouth
men had already discovered that some, at least, of the savages, at no great distance from them, were becoming hostile,
and were planning mischief.   Just then (March) the news

... die.
... was
... in

... was told that his friends the English
... He was sufficiently roused to ask who
told him "Winslow," and he desired to see his English friend. "When I came to him," says the narrator, "they told him of it, he put forth his hand to me, was he not so?" Then he said twice, though very inwardly, *Matta neen wonck.... Winsnow?* which is to say, "Am I then Winslow?" I answered, *Ahhe,* that is, "Yes." Then he cried out, these words, *Matta neen wonck Innet namen Winsnow?* that is to say, "Oh, Winslow, I shall never see thee again." ... With aid ... Hobbamock, Winslow told him that the governor, being unable to come in person, had sent him with such things as might do good to one in such extremity. What med...

...

... Master John H... a cordial gentleman of London ... for ... by some to be identified with ... ... to person, John Barn ... ... from the celebrity of the matter, this was not so ... ... of common ... ...
Indian life ... See Young, p. 314.

... Winslow, in Young, p. 315.

... was told that his friends ... him. ... he was sufficiently certain ... told him "Winslow," and ... his ... a ... first ... friend. "When I came to ... ... say to him or to ... put forth to ... ... to ... said ... Then he said twice, though very cowardly, ... *Winanow?* which is to say, "Art thou Winslow?" ... ... answered *MΙ,* that is, "Yes." Then he ... ... words, *Matta neen wonck nut nee, n.Wee* ... ... to say, "Oh, Winslow, I shall never see thee again" ... ... "Hobbamock," Winslow told him that if ... ... he, ... to come in person, had sent him with such things as might do good ... to one in such extremity. ... ...

* ... Master John Hampden, a gentleman of London," ... by some ... ... well you ... will be ... as the Narrat— ... from ... city in the matter, ... a person to ... "... respect of ... to the European ... makes ... Father Winslow. See Young, p. ...

... ... and ... ... Aunt and ... ... Winslow. See Young, p. ...

ser Francesco lub 6 17 9bre oli
1639

came that their friend Massasoit was sick and likely to die. Winslow was sent by the governor to visit him, for it was " a commendable manner of the Indians " to visit a friend in that extremity. Accompanied by a friend from London,[1] who had wintered in the colony, and was desirous of seeing more of the country, and with Hobbamoc for guide and interpreter, he undertook the journey. On their way, they were told once and again that their friend was dead. But when they arrived at Pokanoket, they found him still alive, though his sight had failed, and he seemed very near to death. The house was full of Indians in the midst of their incantations for him, " making," says Winslow, " such a hellish noise as distempered us that were well, and was therefore unlikely to ease him that was sick." Six or eight women were chafing the patient's limbs " to keep heat in him." When an interval of comparative silence had been obtained, he was told that his friends the English had come to see him. He was sufficiently conscious to ask, " Who ?" They told him " Winsnow ;"[2] and he desired to speak with his English friend. " When I came to him," says that friend, " and they told him of it, he put forth his hand to me, which I took. Then he said twice, though very inwardly, ' *Keen Winsnow ?*' which is to say, ' Art thou Winslow ?' I answered, ' *Ahhe*,' that is, ' Yes.' Then he doubled these words, ' *Matta neen wonckanet namen, Winsnow !*' that is to say, ' Oh, Winslow, I shall never see thee again.' " With the aid of Hobbamoc, Winslow told him that the governor, being unable to come in person, had sent him with such things as might do good to one in such extremity. What medical

---

[1] " One Master John Hamden, a gentleman of London," has been thought by some to be identical with the illustrious patriot, John Hampden. But, aside from the similarity of the names, there is no reason to believe that the " gentleman of London " was the Hampden who makes so great a figure in English history. See Young, p. 314, 315.

[2] " For they can not pronounce the letter *l*, but ordinarily *n* in the place thereof."—Winslow, in Young, p. 318.

virtue there was in the "confection of many comfortable conserves" which he had brought, we know not; but with some difficulty he succeeded in administering a little of it, and soon he had the satisfaction of seeing his patient somewhat relieved. By his assiduous and ingenious nursing, added to the efficacy of the "confection," the recovery was in a few hours decided, though not yet complete. "With admiration," Winslow and his English friend "blessed God for giving his blessing to such raw and ignorant means," the sachem and all his Indian friends "acknowledging them as the instruments of his preservation."

Something of nobleness in the nature of the savage showed itself when he began to know that he was recovering. His first thought was of others needing similar relief, and he desired the kind friend, who had saved his life, to go from one to another of the sick throughout the village, and to give them the benefit of his healing skill; for, he said, "they were good folk," and worth caring for. At the same time he was profuse in the expression of his gratitude. He had been told the day before Winslow came, "You see how hollow-hearted your English friends are; had they been what they pretend to be, they would have visited you in your sickness." Remembering this, he said, repeating it often, "Now I see the English are my friends, and love me. . . . While I live, I will never forget this kindness." When his visitors, after two days, were ready to depart, he revealed to Hobbamoc, in the presence of only two or three trusty counselors, the whole story of a plot to destroy the English—how it began with the Massachusetts near Weston's colony—how the people of Nauset, Paomet, and other places had joined in the conspiracy—how he himself had been solicited and argued with—how the Massachusetts, having determined to exterminate Weston's colony, and not doubting their ability to do so, had considered that the men of Plymouth would be likely to take vengeance on them, and were postponing the execution of their purpose only till the conspiracy should be wide enough to annihilate Plymouth also.   He therefore charged Hobbomoc not only to make his English friends acquainted with these facts, but also to advise them, as from him, that if they regarded the lives of their countrymen or their own safety, they must act promptly, and must prevent the intended massacre by putting the chief conspirators to death.   Hobbamoc communicated all this to Winslow as they were returning to Plymouth, and to Bradford immediately after their arrival.   Information of the conspiracy came at the same time from another source.   What was to be done?

It was the time for the annual town-meeting or legislative assembly.   To that assembly (March 23 = April 2) the governor, "having a double testimony and many circumstances agreeing with the truth thereof," communicated the alarming intelligence.   "This business was no less troublesome than grievous" (such is Winslow's account of the meeting), "especially for that we knew no means to deliver our countrymen and preserve ourselves save by returning the malicious and cruel purposes" of the conspirators "upon their own heads, and causing them to fall into the same pit they had digged for others; though it much grieved us to shed the blood of those whose good we ever intended and aimed at, as a principal [object] in all our proceedings."   The conclusion was that, inasmuch as prompt action was required, and the measures to be taken for the salvation of the colony must by no means be divulged among the Indians who were daily coming and going, the governor, the assistant, and the captain, consulting with others at their discretion, were authorized to take care that the commonwealth should receive no detriment.

By that triumvirate it was determined that Standish should take "so many men as he thought sufficient" for the occasion, and, going to Wessagusset as if on a trading expedition, should first communicate with Weston's men and ascertain what they knew concerning the conspiracy, so that "he might the better judge the certainty of it," and might be ready for any opportunity of punishing the authors of it. It was well known that one chief instigator of the plot was Wituwamat, of the Massachuset tribe, "a notable insulting villain, who had formerly imbrued his hands in the blood of English and French, and had oft boasted of his own valor and derided their weakness, especially because, as he said, they died crying, making sour faces, more like children than men." It was therefore determined that the captain, after ascertaining by inquiry at Wessagusset the inevitableness of a conflict, "should forbear, if it were possible, till he could make sure of that bloody and bold villain—whose head he had order to bring with him, that he might be a warning and terror to all of that disposition."

Standish, without delay, made ready for the expedition, selecting eight men, who, he thought, would be a sufficient force. But the next day, before they could sail, a fugitive, who had found his way through the woods from Wessagusset, arrived with a sad story of the condition into which that colony had fallen, and with confirmation of what had been learned from other sources about the impending danger. Evidently the exigency required haste; and the nine chosen men went on their errand with a clear conviction that, under God, all the future of New England was depending on their valor.

The captain and his little force—more like a squad of armed policemen than like a military expedition—sailed along the coast (March 25 = April 4) and entered what was then called the Massachuset Bay, but is now the "broad-armed" port of Boston. As the *Sparrow* was lying in that smooth water, they went first to her, "but found neither man nor so much as a dog therein"—so entirely was she at the mercy of the Indians, who, as the truth afterward came to light, were only waiting for some of Weston's unsuspecting men to make them two more canoes before taking possession of her. The discharge of a gun served as a signal, and brought into sight a few of the wretched settlers, "who were on the shore gathering ground-nuts, and getting other food." After a little talk with them, the captain went to their village, where he conferred with such of the people as seemed most capable, telling them what their peril was, and offering, in the governor's name, a refuge for their whole company at Plymouth, if they were afraid to remain where they were. At the same time, he assured them that, if they thought they could provide for their safety in some other way, he would help them to the utmost of his power. His revelation of the plan which the Indians were just ready to execute was confirmed by circumstances which those incompetent men had observed but had not understood; and his offer of relief and protection was eagerly accepted. The stragglers from the village were immediately called home, and were kept from starving by a daily though scanty allowance of Indian corn from the captain's military stores. Wet and stormy weather prevailed for a few days; but through the wet and storm there came an Indian, ostensibly for trade, though it was evident enough that what he wanted was information as to why those men from Plymouth were there. He found more reserve than he had been used to in his intercourse with the white men of Wessagusset; and his report at his return was, "I saw by the captain's eyes that he was angry in his heart." The savages began to know that their plot had been unveiled.

Yet they did not accept the discovery as a defeat. They thought themselves strong enough for open war. "One Pecksuot," who was what would now be called "a brave," came to Hobbamoc with a message of defiance: "Tell the captain we know why he has come, but we fear him not, nor will we shun him; but let him begin when he dare, he shall not take us at unawares." In various forms and by various messengers the defiance was repeated with insulting threats — all which "the captain observed, yet bare with patience for the present." But when his time for action had come, he began by putting to death Pecksuot, Wituwamat, and two others; the first two and another in a hand-to-hand fight, the fourth by hanging.   Three more Indians were killed, two of them by some of Weston's people, and the war which was to have annihilated both settlements was ended.   Three of Weston's men, being, as they thought, on good terms with the savages because of services rendered, had gone, in contempt of strict orders, to the Massachuset sachem with offers of more service for more victuals.   One of these was prudent enough to escape.   The others were killed before they could be rescued.

Weston's men had seen all they desired to see of life in New England.   They were resolved to forsake their plantation; though "the captain told them that, for his own part, he durst there live with fewer men than they were."   A few accepted his offer, and embarked with him and his eight in the shallop for Plymouth.   The others set sail in the *Sparrow* for the fishing-grounds, hoping to find passage thence for England.   Standish, having supplied them with food for their voyage, saw them "clear of the Massachuset Bay;" and then returned to Plymouth, bringing, according to instructions from the council of war, the head of Wituwamat.

Such was the end of Weston's attempt to colonize New England by dealing exclusively with the selfish element in human nature.   His men, on their arrival at Plymouth nine months before, had " boasted of their strength (being all able, lusty men), and of what they would do and bring to pass, in comparison of the people there, who had many women and children and weak ones among them."   When they saw how impoverished the little colony was which Bradford governed, they promised themselves " that they would take another course, and not fall into such a condition as this simple people were come to."   No thought had they of self-sacrifice for Christ's sake—no dream of a refuge which they, in that wilderness, were to make for truth and purity, persecuted in the old world—no inspiration even from household affections and anxieties. They—practical men, amply provided for and unincumbered—were sure to prosper. ". But," said Bradford, making the record of their failure, " a man's way is not in his own power: God can make the weak to stand; let him also that standeth take heed lest he fall."

The sequel of Weston's story may be given in a few words. Not long after the breaking up at Wessagusset, he arrived on the coast of Maine, a passenger in one of the fishing vessels. For some reason, he had come disguised and under a fictitious name. At his arrival, he learned " the ruin and dissolution of his colony." He obtained a boat, and, with a man or two, set forth for Wessagusset to see if any thing remained. Overtaken by a storm, he was cast away somewhere on what is now the coast of New Hampshire, hardly escaping with his life. Falling among Indians, he was robbed of what he had saved from the sea, and was stripped to his shirt. In that forlorn condition he found his way to the settlement just begun on the Piscataqua River. There he succeeded in borrowing clothes for his most urgent need, and in obtaining means for proceeding to Plymouth. At that place, those who had known him in his better days, and whom he had wronged and insulted in their distresses, had compassion on him. He wanted to borrow of them the beaver which they had collected, and which was their only dependence for the purchase of supplies from England, and he made them large promises. They distrusted his promises; but they " remembered former courtesies," and in pity they loaned him a hundred beaver-skins. With this new capital he went eastward, took possession of the *Sparrow*, and, having rallied some of his men who had fled from Wessagusset, resumed business, endeavoring to retrieve his fortune. Yet, like the ungrateful knave that he was, he never repaid the loan, nor requited the kindness otherwise than by persistent enmity. Afterward, when he was in trouble with the representative of the great " Council for New England," Governor Bradford kindly interceded for him. But to the last he

was the enemy of the Pilgrims.   Thus he disappears from
our history, though he lived a few years longer.

The third season for planting Indian corn had come (April).
So largely had the colony divided its supplies of corn with
strangers, that none remained save what had been reserved
for seed.   For more than two years all labor in the settlement had been exacted and performed in the communistic
method on which the Adventurers had so unwisely insisted
—no man had labored for himself and his own family; but
every man had been required to labor, as under a task-mas-
ter, for the community.   Bradford and the others had maintained in good faith the contract against which their good
sense protested.   But now, there being no supply of food in
the public store, it had become impossible to enforce the
preposterous engagement.   "It was therefore thought best,"
and in a general meeting of the company it was agreed,
"that every man should use the best diligence he could for
his own preservation, both in respect of the time present, and
to prepare his own corn for the year following."   At the same
time it was ordered that "a competent portion" of every
man's crop should belong to the colony for the maintenance
of those who, being constantly employed in the public service, could not be expected to raise corn for themselves.   As
yet the relation of the Planters to the Adventurers would not
permit a permanent division of the soil, so that each family
should have its own freehold and inheritance; but, for that
year, there was assigned by lot to each individual a certain
quantity of land which he was to cultivate at his own discretion and according to his own ability.   The beneficial effects of the new arrangement were immediately manifest.
"It made all hands very industrious, so as much more corn
was planted than otherwise would have been by any means
the governor could use."   The forces of human nature, made
for free industry, began to have fair play.   Even "the women
now went willingly into the field, and took their little ones
with them to set corn, . . . whom to have compelled would
have been thought tyranny and oppression."

That third summer was, not less than the first and second, a time of pinching want. Bradford tells us that when their corn had been planted, they had nothing in store for their subsistence. "They were only to rest on God's providence, many times not knowing at night where to have a bit of any thing the next day. And so, as one well observed, they had need to pray that God would give them their "daily bread above all people in the world." "When they had Indian corn, they thought it as good as a feast; but sometimes, for two or three months together, they had neither bread nor any kind of corn." Their boat (for at this time they had only one) was constantly employed in fishing, the men taking their turns in that service; and when the boat was long gone or returned unsuccessful, all were busy in digging clams from the sand at low water. Hunters also, one or two, were continually ranging the woods, and sometimes a deer was brought home and divided. "Yet they bore these wants with great patience and alacrity of spirit;" and, when they had nothing to eat but clams, they gave thanks to God who had given them "of the abundance of the seas and of treasures hid in the sand." [1]

In that time of want they had other discouragements. For about six weeks after the planting of their corn there was no refreshing rain. The crop on which they had bestowed so much labor seemed likely to perish. While they were thus anxious, they received discouraging intelligence from England. A ship, the *Paragon*, with supplies for the colony and with passengers, among whom were many of their old friends, had been driven back by tempests. After being repaired at great cost and with long delay, she had sailed again, had been spoken with three hundred leagues at sea, had been lost sight of in a storm, and had not since been heard of. Every day the thought that she might have foundered was growing more painful—especially as signs of a

---

[1] Deut. xxxiii., 19.

C c

wreck were seen on the coast.   It seemed to them as if God had forsaken them.

In these circumstances they remembered with what prayer and fasting they had sought God's favor on their enterprise when they were yet at Leyden.   Had he indeed forsaken them?   Had they forsaken him?   They felt themselves called, as individuals and as a community, to humiliation before God, whom in other days they had sought with fasting and prayer.   "To that end," Winslow tells us, "a day was appointed (July) by public authority, and set apart from all other employments, in hope that the same God who had stirred us up hereunto would be moved hereby in mercy to look down upon us and grant us the request of our dejected souls, if our continuance there might any way stand with his glory and our good."   It was not reserved for the philosophy of the nineteenth century to deny, for the first time, that prayer has any place among the forces of the universe. Undevout speculation, before science or history began to be, could ask as flippantly as now, "What is the Almighty, that we should serve him; and what profit shall we have if we pray to him?"   But the faith which, learning by spiritual intuitions, recognizes an infinite will creating and sustaining all things, an infinite wisdom ruling the worlds, and an infinite love accessible to human supplication, has a deeper insight and a wider outlook than mole-eyed science, groping among material atoms, can attain to while refusing to acknowledge that there are more things in heaven and earth than microscope or telescope reveals.   Till faith shall fail from the earth, and the intuitions and yearnings which generate faith shall have been eliminated from the human soul, there will be prayer—as there is to-day and ever has been. Bradford and Winslow knew, as well as any modern scientist, that the vapors, rising from sea and land, are condensed into clouds and come down again in rain; but they did not think it reasonable to infer from the laws of nature the uselessness of prayer.   They did not expect the rain they prayed for

would come without clouds, nor that clouds would come out
of the clear northwest; yet they prayed. We have no right
to suppose that they hazarded their confidence in the utility
of prayer on the uncertainty of what a day might bring forth ;
or that, should their fields have yielded no food, they would
have lost their faith in God.   Had their soil become powder
and dust for lack of rain, they would nevertheless have acknowledged, even in the ruin of their hopes, the will and the
wisdom of Him to whom they prayed.   Why, then, might
they not acknowledge the Providence that relieved them,
and accept the relief as God's answer to their prayer?   It is
folly and not wisdom that sneers or smiles at their simplicity when they say, " Oh, the mercy of our God ! who was as
ready to hear as we to ask."   The morning of their fast-day
was clear and sultry, with no sign of rain.   According to the
Puritan custom—and they, as Separatists, were not behind
the Puritans in that respect—the observance of such a day
was very unlike any thing that now takes place on fast-day
in the Puritan metropolis of New England.   That morning
the Pilgrims assembled as early, probably, as nine o'clock;
and their " exercise " of prayer and appropriate exhortation
or preaching was continued, with little or no intermission,
" eight or nine hours."   While they were thus assembled, a
change came over the face of the sky ; and, when they departed, the clouds had gathered which, the next morning,
" distilled soft, sweet, and moderate showers of rain, continuing," with some intervals of fair weather, " fourteen days."
Their gratitude recorded itself in the phrase, " It was hard to
say whether our withered corn or our drooping affections were
most revived, such was the bounty and goodness of our God."

    While the timely rain was cheering them, Captain Standish,
who had been sent eastward by the governor to purchase
food, returned with enough for a temporary relief, so that,
for a few days, they had bread of some sort with their clams
and bass.   Then, too, came letters from the Adventurers, announcing that the *Paragon*, instead of foundering in the

storm, had been driven back, and had arrived at Portsmouth, in England, with their friends all safe; and also that, about three weeks after the date of those letters, another vessel, the *Anne*, chartered by the Adventurers, was to sail with sixty passengers and sixty tons of goods for the colony.   In every direction the prospect was brightening. "We thought" —such is their testimony—"it would be great ingratitude if . . . we should content ourselves with private thanksgiving. . . . Therefore another solemn day was set apart and appointed for that end, wherein we returned glory, honor, and praise, with all thankfulness, to our good God who dealt so graciously with us—whose name, for these and all other his mercies toward his church and chosen ones, by them be blessed and praised, now and evermore."

About two weeks intervened between their reception of the intelligence which revived their hopes and the expected arrival of the *Anne*, followed a few days later by the *Little James*, "a fine new vessel of about forty-four tons," built for the colony, and to remain in its service.   The two had sailed together, but had been separated by foul weather.   It was a joyful meeting when the passengers by those two vessels arrived, all in health save one (who soon recovered), and found, notwithstanding the wants and hardships which the colony was enduring, not one sick person in Plymouth. Greetings full of tender memory were exchanged among friends who had parted, three years before, at Delft-Haven or at Leyden.   Husbands received their wives, parents their children; brothers and sisters looked each other in the face again through tears of mingling joy and sadness.[1]   But in

---

[1] Two of the newly arrived were daughters of Elder Brewster.   Another was the wife of Deacon Fuller, the physician.   Six were wives of men who came in the *Fortune* or the *Mayflower*.   George Morton, who brought with him his family of five children, was also accompanied by his wife's sister, Alice, the widow of Edward Southworth.   A few days after her arrival she was married to Governor Bradford.   Her maiden name was Carpenter. Her two Southworth sons, honorably represented by the Southworths of to-

company with those old friends from Leyden, were others from England who were not all of the same sort. The Adventurers, in their greed for early profits, and in their ignorance of the work they had undertaken, were always ready to accept as competent recruits for the colony men whom the Pilgrims would have rejected as deficient in moral character. Some of that sort came in the *Fortune.* Some had been even crowded into the *Mayflower.* So, of this third company, " some were so bad " that the government of the colony was " fain to be at charge to send them home again next year." Cushman, who was still in England, busy as ever in the great enterprise, had made earnest but ineffectual protest against the heedlessness of the Adventurers in this respect. It was much easier, he said, to enlist recruits for the colony than to raise supplies. " People come flying in upon us; but moneys come creeping in to us. Some few of your old friends are come, . . . and, by degrees, I hope ere long you shall enjoy them all. And because people press so hard upon us to go, I pray you write earnestly to the treasurer and direct what persons should be sent. It grieveth me to see so weak a company sent you, and yet, had I not been here, they had been weaker. You must still call upon the Company here to see that honest men be sent you, and threaten to send them back if any other come. . . . We are not any way so much in danger as by corrupt and naughty persons." Bradford, transcribing the letter into his history, left unnamed the men of whom Cushman said, They " came without my consent, but the importunity of their friends got promise of our treasurer in my absence. Neither is there need

---

day, came over perhaps five years later. The family tradition is that between William Bradford and Alice Carpenter there had been in their early youth some disappointment of affection, and that their engagement to each other was made by correspondence across three thousand miles of ocean. Another of those passengers was Barbara (her maiden name not known), who soon became the wife of Captain Standish, whose first wife, Rose, " died in the first sickness."

we should take any lewd men, for we may have honest men enough."

The new colonists saw not much that was, at the first view, encouraging. "Some wished themselves in England again; some fell a-weeping, fancying their own misery in what they saw; some pitied the distress they saw their friends were under"—in a word, all were full of sadness. Yet some who, at Leyden, had been familiar with penury endured for Christ's sake, rejoiced not only to see their old friends, but also to hope with them that "better days" were coming. By a few homely details, Bradford makes us understand in what extremity of need those Pilgrims of the *Anne* found the survivors of the *Mayflower* and the *Fortune:* "They were in a very low condition. Many were ragged in apparel, and some little better than half-naked; though some," who had brought with them a full supply of clothing, "were well enough in this regard. But for food they were all alike, save some that had got a few pease of the ship that was last here. The best dish they could present their friends with was a lobster, or a piece of fish, without bread, or any thing else but a cup of fair spring water. The long continuance of this diet, and their labors abroad," in the summer sunshine of New England, "had somewhat abated the freshness of their former complexion. But God gave them health and strength in a good measure, and showed them by experience the truth of that word, ' Man liveth not by bread only, but by every word that proceedeth out of the mouth of the Lord doth man live.' "[1]

A letter from the Adventurers, subscribed by thirteen of their names, expressed an undiminished interest in the colony as a religious undertaking: "Loving friends, we most heartily salute you in all love and hearty affection; being yet in hope that the same God who hath hitherto preserved you in a marvelous manner, doth yet continue your lives and health

---

[1] Deut. viii., 3. The entire verse is to the point: "He humbled thee, and suffered thee to hunger, and fed thee with manna, which thou knewest not, neither did thy fathers know; that he might make thee know that," etc.

to his own praise and all our comforts. . . . We would not have you discontent, because we have not sent you more of your old friends, and, in special, him," Robinson, "on whom you most depend. Far be it from us to neglect you or contemn him. But as the intent was at first, so the event at last shall show, that we will deal fairly, and squarely answer your expectations to the full. . . . Although it seemeth you have discovered many more rivers and fertile grounds than that where you are, yet seeing by God's providence that place fell to your lot, let it be accounted as your portion; and rather fix your eyes upon that which may be done there, than languish in hopes after things elsewhere. . . . If the land afford you bread and the sea yield you fish, rest you a while contented; God will one day afford you better fare. And all men shall know that you are neither fugitives nor discontents, but can, if God so order it, take the worst to yourselves with content, and leave the best to your neighbors with cheerfulness. Let it not be grievous to you that you have been instruments to break the ice for others who come after with less difficulty. The honor will be yours to the world's end.

"We bear you always in our breasts; and our hearty affection is toward you all; as are the hearts of hundreds more who never saw your faces, who doubtless pray for your safety as their own—as we ourselves both do and ever shall—that the same God who hath so marvelously preserved you from seas, foes, and famine, will still preserve you from all future dangers, and make you honorable among men and glorious in bliss at the last day. And so the Lord be with you all, and send us joyful news from you, and enable us with one shoulder so to accomplish and perfect this work that much glory may come to Him that confoundeth the mighty by the weak, and maketh small things great—to whose greatness be all glory forever."

In a few days, the *Anne* sailed homeward (Sept. 10 = 20) with a cargo which was likely to encourage the Adventurers

in their part of the work.   Winslow was at the same time
sent as agent for the colony, to confer with its patrons, and to
procure either from them or by other means such things as
were indispensable to its progress.   "By this time harvest
was come," the yellow corn began to be gathered into the
granary ; "and instead of famine God now gave them plenty.
The face of things was changed, to the rejoicing of the hearts
of many, for which they blessed God."   The experiment on
which they had ventured contrary to the letter of their contract with their partners in London—the allotment of lands
for that year to families or to individuals, so that every man
might work for himself, instead of putting his labor into the
common stock—had been successful.   There were few, if any,
who had not enough, "one way and another, to bring the
year about, and some of the abler and more industrious had
to spare."   Thenceforth there was no more general want or
famine in Plymouth.   Instead of buying corn from the Indians, they had corn to sell for beaver and other peltry.

Once more the apocalyptic vision,[1] so often illustrated in
the progress of Messiah's kingdom, was translating itself into
history.   The woman, after her birth-pangs, had fled from
the dragon into the wilderness; and the earth had begun to
help the woman.   Manifestly, the Pilgrim colony, so devoutly
imagined and planned at Leyden, had become a fact.   Christianity had obtained in New England "a place prepared of
God."   The Church of Christ was here in the simplest possible organization, separating itself alike from the great apostasy ruled by the Roman pontiff, and from the anomalous institution set up in England by the imperious will of Elizabeth Tudor, and was building itself "on the foundation of
the apostles and prophets, Jesus Christ himself being the
chief corner-stone."[2]

It disowned the claim of the princes of this world to rule
in that kingdom which is not of this world.   It permitted

[1] Rev. xii.   [2] Eph. ii., 20.

no priestly intervention between the redeemed soul and its divine Redeemer. It was simply "the communion of the saints;" the free and loving fellowship of those whom Christ had made "kings and priests unto God;" the spontaneous association of believers for united worship, for mutual helpfulness in holy living, and for strength to labor or to suffer in the service of God.

CHAPTER XVIII.

ATTEMPTS OF NATIONALISM AGAINST THE PILGRIM CHURCH.

THE success of the few exiles who had migrated from Leyden to America was beginning to take effect in England. For a long time there had been in English minds the hope and the scheme of a colonial empire beyond the ocean. Capital and labor had been lavishly expended in Virginia; and the settlements there, after many disasters, were just beginning to have some appearance of prosperity. But the attempt, simultaneous with the founding of Jamestown (1607), to establish a colony in North Virginia, afterward named New England, had failed in less than a year, though magnificently patronized. Weston's more recent attempt had been more ignominiously unsuccessful. Such failures made the success of the settlement at Plymouth more conspicuous.[1]

Sir Ferdinand Gorges, who had always been the life of King James's "Council for New England," was encouraged to hope that the dominion which the royal charter had given to that council might soon become something more than a name. Hitherto the imperial powers of that august body had been chiefly productive of fruitless attempts to impose tribute on the fishing vessels which resorted to the coast; but while Plymouth was struggling through its third sum-

---

[1] Captain John Smith, in his "New England's Trials," 1622, had briefly described the beginning and already hopeful progress of the Plymouth colony. The same year there was published the invaluable document commonly cited as "Mourt's Relation," but identified and republished by Young ("Chronicles of the Pilgrims," p. 109, sq.) as "Bradford and Winslow's Journal," with a preface by George Morton. Cushman's "Sermon," with a glowing preface, descriptive of New England and inviting emigration, is of the same date. Winslow's "Good News from New England" was published in 1624.

mer (July, 1623), there came into its harbor a ship with a captain on board, " who had a commission to be Admiral of New England." About two months later, Captain Robert Gorges, son of Sir Ferdinand, came with a commission to be Governor-General of the country. Arriving " in the bay of the Massachusetts with sundry passengers and families," he attempted to make another beginning at the place which Weston's men had so recently forsaken (Sept., 1623). The plan for a general government over all the territory granted to the Council for New England acknowledged the existence and in some sort the autonomy of Plymouth, inasmuch as the governor of that colony for the time being was to be, by virtue of his office, one of the Governor-General's council. But, on the other hand, it seems to have assumed that the ecclesiastical authority which prescribed and controlled the religion of England was to have the same sway in New England. Accordingly, the great Council took care for the religious welfare of the expedition led forth by Governor-General Gorges. There was in his suite a chaplain, who was not only charged with the care of souls in the renewed plantation at Wessagusset, but was also expected to have some sort of superintendence over the Separatists of Plymouth. He found, however, no opportunity of asserting his jurisdiction; nor does he seem to have had any disposition to do so. Gorges, " not finding the state of things here to answer his quality and condition," returned to England (1624) after the experience of one winter in the country which he had undertaken to govern. Planting colonies in such a wilderness was not the agreeable employment which he, the son of Sir Ferdinand, " being newly come out of the Venetian war," had hoped for. His departure was, in effect, the breaking up of his attempted colony. Some of the people whom he had brought followed him to England; others went to Virginia; a few " remained and were helped with supplies " from Plymouth. Among the few was the chaplain, whose conduct in relation to the Plymouth people seems to have been such as

gave them no offense.   He was a man of culture and of po-
etic sensibility.   Enamored of the natural beauty which he
saw in New England, he recorded his observations on the
country in a Latin poem which, with a free translation of it
into less polished English verse, seems to have been his chief
employment here.[1]   After another year, he also returned to
England (1625), his office at Wessagusset having become a
sinecure.   Bradford says of him, as if with an unconscious
smile, "He had I know not what power and authority of su-
perintendency over other churches granted him, and sundry
instructions for that end; but he never showed" his commission "or made any use of it (it should seem he saw it
was in vain); he only spoke of it to some here at his going
away."

So ended that attempt to introduce Nationalism, or the
national-church theory of Christianity, into New England.
The Separatists of Scrooby, the exiles of Leyden, the Pilgrims of the *Mayflower*, had brought with them a theory
which permitted neither king nor parliament to rule in the
Church of Christ.   For them the wilderness and solitary
place were beginning to be glad, and it was not in the book
of God's decrees that the system which had driven them

---

[1] That bi-lingual poem was published after the author's return to England.
It may be found entire in the first series of the Mass. Historical Society's
Collections, i., 125–139.   He thus describes the "ground-nut," so often men-
tioned by Bradford and Winslow, the *Apios tuberosa* of the botanists:

> "Vimine gramineo nux subterranea suavis
> Serpit humi, tenui flavo sub cortice pingui
> Et placido nucleo nivei candoris ab intra
> Melliflua parcos hilarans dulcedine gustus
> Donec in æstivum Phœbus conscenderit axem."

In English:

> "A ground-nut there runs on a grassy thread
> Along the shallow earth as in a bed;
> Yellow without, thin-film'd, sweet, lily-white,
> Of strength to feed and cheer the appetite."

into banishment should follow them hither.   Apparitors and pursuivants, acts of uniformity and bishops' prisons, commissary courts and High Commission, found no entrance on this side of the ocean, though so gentle and genial a man as William Morrell had been sent to prepare the way for them.

Another attempt against Separatism in New England was already in progress from a very different quarter.   Before the coming over of Gorges with his planters of a new colony, and with his state-church chaplain, the Pilgrims were aware of disagreements and complaints among the Adventurers, though Weston was no longer a partner in the Company.   For that reason the friendly letter which came to them by the *Anne,* with thirteen names of the Adventurers subscribed, was the more welcome, especially because of the regard which it expressed for their "old friends" and their pastor still detained at Leyden.[1]   But the full significance of that letter became painfully apparent when Winslow returned from his mission in England (March, 1624).   He came in the ship *Charity,* which brought supplies for the colony,[2] together with some passengers whose names will appear in our story.   By the same vessel came letters which, even without his report of what he had himself observed, revealed the fact that among the Adventurers there was a strong and active party adverse to the Pilgrim church.

James Sherley, one of the Adventurers, and "a chief friend of the colony," wrote to his "most worthy and loving friends," and explained to them the difficulties which had embarrassed "the setting forth of this ship:"   "We have some among us who undoubtedly aim more at their own private ends, and at the thwarting and opposing of some here and other worthy instruments of God's glory elsewhere" (referring especially to Leyden and to Robinson), "than at the general good and the furtherance of this noble and laud-

---

[1] *Ante*, p. 386, 387.

[2] "He brought three heifers and a bull, the first beginning of any cattle of that kind in the land, with some clothing and other necessaries."

able action.   Yet again we have many other, and I hope the
greater part, very honest Christian men, whose ends and intents (I am persuaded) are wholly for the glory of our Lord
Jesus Christ in the propagation of his Gospel, and hope of
gaining those poor savages to the knowledge of God.   But...
these malcontented persons and turbulent spirits do what
in them lieth to withdraw men's hearts from you and your
friends, yea, even from the general business; and yet under
show and pretense of godliness and furtherance of the plantation."   After describing some of their contentions, the letter ended with a more cheerful view.   "On the 12th of January, . . . at night, when we met to read the general letter, we
had the lovingest and friendliest meeting that ever I knew.
. . . So I sent for a pottle of wine (I would you could do
the like[1]), which we drank friendly together.   Thus God can
turn the hearts of men when it pleaseth him."   Sherley did
not then know the reason why that meeting appeared to be
so "loving and friendly."   The faction opposed to Leyden
and to Robinson had taken measures which, they thought,
would guard the colony and New England against the
growth of Separatism.

Already the Adventurers had introduced into the colony
an element which could hardly fail to work disturbance.   Besides the sixty in the *Anne*, who were under the same engagement to the Adventurers with the original Planters,[2]
"there came a company that did not belong to the general
body, but came on their particular, and were to have lands
assigned them and be for themselves, yet subject to the gen-

---

[1] Bradford says in a note appended to his transcript of the letter: "It is
worthy to be observed how the Lord doth change times and things; for what
is now more plentiful than wine? and that of the best, coming from Malaga,
the Canaries, and other places, sundry ships lading in a year.   So as there
is now more cause to complain of the excess and the abuse of wine (through
men's corruption), even to drunkenness, than of any defect or want of the
same.   Witness this year 1646.   The good Lord lay not the sins and un-
thankfulness of men to their charge in this particular."

[2] *Ante*, p. 282, 283.

eral government." Those privileged planters were received
without remonstrance, two things having been stipulated
by the Adventurers in sending them : first, that the entire
trade in peltry should be retained "for the general" till the
dissolution of the partnership, and the final division of its
property ; and, secondly, that the assignment of lands to
those who "came on their particular" should be at such convenient distance from the town as would not interfere with
the laying out of lands to be cultivated by the community.
Some of those persons were disappointed, having "looked for
greater matters than they found or could attain to." Several of them took the first opportunity of returning to England—"some out of discontent and dislike of the country ;
others by reason of a fire that broke out and burned the
houses they lived in, and all their provisions, so as they were
necessitated thereunto."[1] Naturally they carried back an ill
report. Some, also, of the men whom Bradford had found
too lazy, or otherwise worthless, and had sent home for that
reason, gave out malicious stories in disparagement of Plymouth. Sherley's letter was accompanied with a summing up
of the things which were said against the colony. "These,"
said he, "are the chief objections which they that are now
returned make against you and the country. I pray you
consider them, and answer them by the first conveniency."
Bradford, in his "History," sets them down at full length,
with the answers which he sent by the return of the vessel.
Some of the objections to the country are absurd enough to
be amusing, and the answers are appreciative. One objection was, "The water is not wholesome." The reply was, "If
they mean, not so wholesome as the good beer and wine in
London, which they so dearly love, we will not dispute with
them ; but . . . for water, it is as good as any in the world

---

[1] "This fire was occasioned by some of the seamen [of Gorges's ship] that
were roistering in a house where it began, making a great fire in very cold
weather [Nov. 5 = 15], which broke out of the chimney into the thatch and
burned down three or four houses."

(for aught we know), and it is wholesome enough to us that can be content therewith." To another objection, "The ground is barren, and doth bear no grass," Bradford answered that woods, even in England, do not yield such grass as grows in fields and meadows; that the cattle imported by the *Charity* were already thriving on the native grass; and that, to all who had eyes to see, that objection, like some of the rest, was simply "ridiculous." Somebody had been foolish enough to say, "The fish" of New England "will not take salt to keep sweet," and others had been weak enough to think it might be true; to which Bradford replied, "They might as well say there can no ale or beer in London be kept from souring." A less absurd objection was that the country was "annoyed with foxes and wolves;" but this was disposed of by a simple reference to "other good countries" annoyed in the same way, and to the efficacy of "poisons, traps, and other such means" for the destruction of predatory animals. "The Dutch," too, were already "planted near Hudson's River,"[1] and (worse than foxes and wolves) might become rivals in trade. But Bradford had learned, at Leyden, to think kindly of the Dutch instead of fearing them, and his reply was, "They will come and plant in these parts also, if we and others do not, but go home and leave it to them. We rather commend them than condemn them for it." Of "objections against the country," the last, and not the least formidable, was, "The people are much annoyed with mosquitoes;" to which it was answered, "They are too delicate and unfit to begin new plantations and colonies who can not endure the biting of a mosquito. We would wish such to keep at home till they be at least mosquito-proof. Yet this place is as free as any; and experience teacheth that the more the land is tilled and the woods cut down, the fewer there will be." Such "objections against the country" were, how-

---

[1] "Hudson's *Bay*" in Bradford; but the reference is evidently to the Dutch attempts at settlement on the Hudson River.

ever, of small account when compared with objections which had been urged against the colony itself on the ground of its religious character, and which were therefore placed at the head of the catalogue: "Diversity about religion;" "Neglect of family duties on the Lord's day;" "Want of both the sacraments;" "Children not catechized nor taught to read."

Evidently these were Puritan objections against a colony characterized by Separatist principles and tendencies. One by one they were answered, curtly but explicitly. As for diversity about religion, "We know no such matter; for here was never any controversy or opposition, either public or private (to our knowledge), since we came." As for neglect of family duties on the Lord's day, "We allow no such thing, but blame it in ourselves and others; and they that thus report it would have showed their Christian love the more if they had in love told the offenders of it, rather than thus reproach them behind their backs. But (to say no more) we wish themselves had given better example." Admitting their want of both the sacraments, they took occasion to remonstrate against the wrong they were suffering in that respect: "The more is our grief that our pastor is kept from us, by whom we might enjoy them; for we used to have the Lord's Supper every Sabbath, and baptism as often as there was occasion of children to baptize." To the cruel charge that their children were not catechized nor taught to read, they answered, "Neither is true; for divers take pains with their own as they can. We have, indeed, no common school, for want of a fit person, or (hitherto) means to maintain one, though we desire now to begin." A "common school" — public as the highway — was in their plan and purpose, even when they were just emerging from their long conflict with starvation, and when their entire number —men, women, and children—did not exceed one hundred and eighty.

It was the religious condition of those Separatists at Plym-

D d

outh, waiting and longing for their Separatist pastor, that weighed so heavily on the minds of Puritans among the Adventurers.   But before that "lovingest and friendliest meeting" which so delighted Sherley, they had engaged a clergyman to go over among the passengers on the *Charity*, and they were trusting that his ministrations, if the Brownist Robinson could still be detained at Leyden, would supply the religious destitution of Plymouth, and contribute something to the ecclesiastical future of New England.   It must not be supposed that they knew the man whom they were sending on a mission so delicate and so important.   John Lyford had lately returned from Ireland.   In that country he had " wound himself into the esteem of sundry godly and zealous professors, . . . who, having been burdened with the ceremonies in England, found there some more liberty to their consciences."   The reasons, not yet divulged, which had constrained him to forego the liberty enjoyed by Puritans in Ireland, were such as might naturally induce him to accept an employment in some distant colony.   Having "wound himself into the esteem of sundry godly and zealous professors" in the company of Adventurers, it was thought by them that he might also wind himself into the esteem of the godly though wrongheaded people at Plymouth, and counteract the undesirable influence of John Robinson.   Cushman, who was still in England, at work with all his might for the colony, seems to have given a reluctant assent to the sending of Lyford.   He knew how the Pilgrims longed for a minister who would accept, as Brewster would not, the office of a teaching elder, and who might be associated with their pastor in the care of the church ; and, in his enthusiastic hopefulness, he might easily persuade himself that this preacher, at the worst, would do no harm.   In a letter to the governor, he said : "The preacher we have sent is, we hope, an honest, plain man, though none of the most eminent and rare. About choosing him into office, use your own liberty and discretion.   He knows he is no officer among you, though per-

haps custom and universality may make him forget himself.
Mr. Winslow and myself gave way to his going, to give content to some here; and we see no hurt in it, but only his
great charge of children." Evidently both Winslow, who
was to be a fellow-passenger with Lyford, and Cushman, who
was to remain in England, had some suspicion of a sinister
design, but were confident of the ability of the church to
hold fast its principle of congregational independence.

Two letters from the beloved pastor in Leyden came by
the *Charity*, one to Bradford, the other to Brewster. Robinson had his own means of information concerning the factions among the Adventurers; and his statements bring into
clear light the fact that it was Puritanism which was so cruelly pertinacious in keeping him away from the place where
all his hopes, this side of heaven, were centred. To Bradford he wrote (1623, Dec. 19 = 29):

"MY LOVING AND MUCH-BELOVED FRIEND, whom God
hath hitherto preserved, [may he] preserve and keep you still
to his glory and the good of many; that his blessing may
make your godly and wise endeavors answerable to the valuation which they there [in Plymouth] set upon the same.
Of your love to and care for us here we never doubted; so
are we glad to take knowledge of it in that fullness we do.
Our love and care to and for you is mutual; though our
hopes of coming unto you be small and weaker than ever.
But of this at large in Mr. Brewster's letter, with whom you
—and he with you mutually—I know, communicate your
letters, as I desire you may do these.

"Concerning the killing of those poor Indians,[1] of which
we heard at first by report, and since by more certain relation, oh! how happy a thing had it been if you had converted some before you had killed any! Besides, where blood
is once begun to be shed, it is seldom stanched of a long

---

[1] *Ante*, p. 378.

400 GENESIS OF THE NEW ENGLAND CHURCHES. [CH.XVIII.

time after. You will say they deserved it. I grant it; but upon what provocations and invitements by those heathenish Christians! Besides, you, being no magistrates over them, were to consider not what they deserved, but what you were by necessity constrained to inflict. Necessity of this, especially of killing so many (and many more, it seems, they would if they could), I see not. Methinks one or two principals should have been full enough, according to that approved rule, 'The punishment to the few, and the fear to the many.' Upon this occasion, let me be bold to exhort you seriously to consider the disposition of your captain, whom I love, and am persuaded the Lord in great mercy and for much good hath sent you him, if you use him aright. He is a man humble and meek among you, and toward all, in ordinary course. But now, if this be merely from a human spirit,[1] there is cause to fear that, by occasion especially of provocation, there may be wanting that tenderness of the life of man, made after God's image, which is meet. It is also a thing more glorious in men's eyes than pleasing in God's or convenient for Christians, to be a terror to poor barbarous people, and, indeed, I am afraid lest, by these occasions, others should be drawn to affect a kind of ruffling course in the world.

"I doubt not but you will take in good part these things which I write, and, as there is cause, make use of them. It were to us more comfortable and convenient that we communicated our mutual helps in presence, but seeing that can not be done, we shall always long after you, and love you, and wait God's appointed time. The Adventurers, it seems, have neither money nor any great mind of us, for the most part. They deny it to be any part of the covenants between

---

[1] What Robinson means is: "If the captain's humbleness and meekness, and the traits for which we love him, are not inspired and sanctified by the divine Spirit, there is cause to fear," etc. Standish, much as the Pilgrims loved and honored him, and devoted as he was to their heroic enterprise, was not a member of their church.

us that they should transport us; neither do I look for any further help from them, till means come from you. We here are strangers, in effect, to the whole course; and so both we and you (save as your own wisdom and worth have interested you further), [instead] of [being] principals, [as was] intended, in this business, are scarce accessories.

"My wife, with me, resalutes you and yours. Unto Him who is the same to his in all places, and near to them who are far from one another, I commend you and all with you."

While the almost despairing sadness of this letter touches our sympathy, its tenderly affectionate and Christian spirit, and its wise but gentle admonitions, show what the writer's influence would have been could he have had the privilege —for which his heart was ready to break—of living and dying among the friends who longed for his presence. His hopes of coming to New England are "small and weaker than ever." The majority of the Adventurers, "it seems," have no money to expend in reinforcing their colony with such people as those exiles left at Leyden, "nor any great mind" if they had the money. Nay, they deny that any obligation of that sort was implied in the contract between themselves and the Pilgrims. For explanation of these hints, the writer makes express reference to a letter of one day's later date, addressed to an older and more intimate friend, his co-presbyter Brewster:

"LOVING AND DEAR FRIEND AND BROTHER,—That which I most desired of God in regard of you, namely, the continuance of your life and health, and the safe coming of those sent unto you, I most gladly hear of, and praise God for the same. And I hope Mrs. Brewster's weak and decayed state of body will have some repairing by the coming of her daughters,[1] and the provision which, I hear, is made for you in this and

---

[1] *Ante.* p. 384.

former ships, which makes us with more patience bear our languishing state and the deferring of our desired transportation—desired rather than hoped for, whatsoever you are borne in hand by any others. For, first, there is no hope at all (that I know or can conceive of) of any new stock to be raised for that end, so that all must depend upon returns from you, in which are so many uncertainties that nothing with any certainty can thence be concluded. Besides, howsoever for the present the Adventurers allege nothing but want of money, which is an invincible difficulty, yet, if that be taken away by you, others without doubt will be found.

"For the better clearing of this, we must dispose the Adventurers into three parts. (1.) Some five or six, as I conceive, are absolutely bent for us above any others. (2.) Other five or six are our bitter, professed adversaries. (3.) The rest, being the body, I conceive to be honestly minded, and lovingly also, toward us, yet such as have others, namely, the forward preachers, nearer unto them than us [than we are], and whose course, so far as there is any difference, they would rather advance than ours. Now what a hank [hold] these men have over the professors, you know. And I persuade myself that for me, they of all others are unwilling I should be transported—especially such as have an eye that way themselves; as thinking, if I come there, their market will be marred in many regards. And for these adversaries, if they have but half the wit to their malice [i. e., half as much wit as malice], they will stop my course when they see it intended, for which this delaying serveth them very opportunely. And as one restie [restive] jade can hinder, by hanging back, more than two or three can (or will, at least, if they be not very free) draw forward, so will it be in this case. A notable experiment of this they gave in your messenger's presence, constraining the Company to promise that none of the money now gathered should be expended or employed to the help of any of us toward you.

"Now touching the question propounded by you : I judge

it not lawful for you—being a ruling elder (Rom. xii., 7, 8, and 1 Tim. v., 17), as opposed to the elders that teach and labor in word and doctrine—to which the sacraments are annexed—to administer them [the sacraments], nor convenient [expedient], if it were lawful. Whether any learned man will come unto you or not, I know not. If any do come, you must *consilium capere in arena.*[1]

"Be you most heartily saluted, and your wife with you, both from me and mine. Your God and ours, and the God of all his, bring us together if it be his will; and keep us, in the mean while and always, to his glory, and make us serviceable to his majesty and faithful to the end. Amen."

These being the latest letters now extant from the pen of Robinson, are, on that account, worthy of a place in this narrative, as well as on account of the light which they give concerning the purpose of Lyford's mission. The Adventurers were induced to send him by the influence of "the forward preachers" over "the professors." Giffard, the Puritan "minister of God's holy Word in Malden," who wrote against Barrowe and Greenwood, was in his day one of "the forward preachers." Bernard, the Puritan vicar of Worksop, whose "invective entituled 'The Separatists' Schisme,' " called forth from Robinson the "Justification of Separation from the Church of England," was a "forward preacher."[2] The "Pontificals" were never called "forward preachers" either by Puritans or by Separatists, nor were their admiring hearers known by any such name as "professors of godliness."

Those "forward preachers" whose influence over their friends among the Adventurers effected the sending of Lyford to Plymouth in the interest of Puritanism against Sep-

---

[1] By this phrase Robinson means: "If a minister come to you from England, you must 'take counsel in the field' "—decide the question for yourselves; or, as Cushman said, "use your own liberty and discretion about choosing him into office."

[2] *Ante*, p. 120–122, 244.

aratism, were sadly mistaken in the character of their missionary.   Probably they could see, as easily as Cushman saw,
that in his quality of preacher he was "none of the most
eminent and rare;" but they must have shared Cushman's
confidence in him as "an honest, plain man."   His gifts, we
must assume, were considered adequate to the work so long
as Robinson could be kept from going to baffle him.   On his
arrival at Plymouth, he made extraordinary professions of
"reverence and humility" toward the chief men of the
church.   "He wept and shed many tears, blessing God that
had brought him to see their faces, and admiring the things
they had done in their wants, as if he had been made all of
love, and were the humblest person in the world."   In their
simplicity they received him with hearty welcome.   "They
gave him the best entertainment they could, and a larger allowance of food out of the store"—for himself and his wife,
and "his great charge of children" that Cushman had mentioned—a larger allowance "than any other had."   Recognizing him as (in Robinson's phrase) "a learned man," they
desired the benefit of his intelligence in their deliberations
on the affairs of their commonwealth.   "As the governor
had used in all weighty affairs to consult with their elder,
Mr. Brewster, together with his assistants," elected for that
purpose,[1] "so now he called Mr. Lyford also to consult with
them in their weightiest businesses."   They were becoming
acquainted with him, and he with them.

   "After some short time, he desired to join himself, as a
member, to the church here"—the church which those forward preachers in London held to be schismatic, because it
had separated itself from that National Church which they
recognized and were striving to reform.   He "was accordingly received" in the way in which other members were
received.   "He made a large confession of his faith;" and
—what was deemed hardly less important than any profes-

---

[1] At the annual election in 1624, five assistants were chosen.

sion of dogmatic belief, however sound—he made "an acknowledgment of his former disorderly walking " in that he
had submitted to an ecclesiastical government which was
not according to the Word of God, and how he had been " entangled in many corruptions which had been a burden to his
conscience." With many expressions which in that time and
in that place had great significance, he " blessed God for the
opportunity of freedom to enjoy the ordinances of God in
purity among his people." While thus receiving him as a
member, on his personal profession of faith and his engagement to walk with them in the order of the Gospel, the
church did not forget the advice—" About choosing him into
office, use your own liberty and discretion." It was only
reasonable prudence to wait for a larger experience of his
gifts, and a better acquaintance with his Christian graces,
before calling him to the office of pastor or of teacher. He
preached among them, not in " the ministry of office," but in
" the exercise of prophesying."

At the same time, Mr. John Oldham, who, without being
a very zealous Puritan, had been known as opposing the Separatist principles professed and practiced by the Pilgrims,
became, suddenly, a professed friend of the church and of
the course of affairs in the commonwealth. He had been in
the colony since the arrival of the *Anne*, being one of those
who came " on their particular," or as adventurers on their
own account. With others of the particulars, " drawing to
their side some of the weaker sort of the company," he had
helped to form a party of malcontents in relations of mutual
intelligence with the anti-Separatist party among the Adventurers at London. " But now," since the arrival of the
Charity with supplies, and with passengers of whom Lyford
was one, " he took occasion to open his mind to some of the
chief" among the Pilgrims, " and confessed that he had done
them wrong both by word and deed, and by writing into
England." He told them that " he now saw the eminent
hand of God to be with them and his blessing upon them,

which made his heart smite him." In his professed repent-ance, he promised that their adversaries in England should never more use him as an instrument against them. "He also desired that former things might be forgotten, and that they would look upon him as one that desired to close with them in all things." It does not appear that he was re-ceived, nor that he desired to be received, as a member of the Pilgrim church, but "they showed all readiness to em-brace him in love;" and from that time, in consideration of his ability as a man of business and his position among those who "came on their particulars," he was invited to take part in the consultations on all important affairs.

Great joy was there in the hope that now things were to "go comfortably and smoothly." But ere long it was dis-covered that Lyford and Oldham were at work as the lead-ers of a party adverse to the church and to the influ-ence that was moulding the commonwealth. They were good friends with any body, "however vile or profane," that would speak against the church and its rigid principles of Separation; and they were "feeding themselves and others with what they should bring to pass in England by the faction of their friends there." Perhaps Lyford was dis-pleased to find that his reception into the church had not given him any authority in that body, and that he was not considered competent to administer sacraments in the church of Plymouth by virtue of his ordination in the National Church of England.

While these things were in progress, the *Charity* com-pleted the fishing voyage on which she had been sent by her owners, and she was now ready for her return to England (July). It was observed that Lyford had been very much occupied with writing, and that the letters which he had prepared in expectation of this opportunity were numer-ous. He was indiscreet enough to give out, among those who were of his party, some hints of the great effects which his letters would produce in England and of the revolution which would ensue in the colony. It seemed to the governor, and to his friends with whom he consulted, that the safety of their commonwealth required prompt and decisive measures. "Knowing how things stood in England, and what hurt these things might do, he took a shallop and went out with the ship a league or two to sea, and called for all Lyford's and Oldham's letters." The master of the ship was William Pierce,[1] a steadfast friend of the colony, who well knew what was going on both in England and here, and who " afforded him all the assistance he could." They found more than twenty of Lyford's letters—" many of them large, and full of slanders and false accusations tending not only to the prejudice " of the Pilgrim commonwealth, but its " ruin and utter subversion." Of those letters they made careful copies before permitting them to proceed. Some of the most important they retained for testimony, sending the copies instead of the originals. In a letter of his to a minister, who seems to have been one of those " forward preachers " referred to by Robinson, they found, inclosed, his copies of two letters which he had found lying sealed in the cabin of the *Charity*, and had ventured to open — one from a gentleman in England to Elder Brewster, the other from Winslow to Pastor Robinson in Holland. Those copies, with " many

---

[1] William Pierce was master of the *Paragon* (p. 383), and then of the *Anne* (p. 384). He had the best of opportunities for becoming acquainted with the Pilgrims, and with the adverse faction among the Adventurers and in the colony. Oldham and others of " the particulars " were passengers under him in their coming over. He had been a passenger with Lyford on the *Charity*, which he was to command on her home voyage. Several times afterward he visited Plymouth.

This Captain William Pierce is to be distinguished from John Pierce, who was one of the Adventurers. The patent of 1621 from the President and Council of New England was granted to " John Pierce and his associates " in trust for the benefit of the colony. He afterward obtained from the same council another patent which would have made him a lord proprietor, under whom all settlers were to hold their lands, but which, after some disasters, he sold to the company.

scurrilous and flouting annotations," he was now sending to his friend, the known adversary of Brewster and of Robinson.   It was toward evening when the ship went out of Plymouth harbor, and in the night the governor returned.

For a few days there was some appearance of consternation among the conspirators.   They seemed to fear that their plans had been discovered.   But as the governor said nothing, their anxiety began to be relieved, and, having concluded that he followed the ship that evening only to dispatch his own letters, they took courage.   After a while they "were as brisk as ever," not aware that the government was watching them, and was waiting "to let things ripen." That waiting was not without some foresight of what would be attempted; for among the letters which had been examined was one in which a partner in the conspiracy "had written that Mr. Oldham and Mr. Lyford intended a reformation in church and commonwealth, and that, as soon as the ship was gone, they intended to join together and have the sacraments."   "Reformation in the commonwealth" could mean nothing else than a violent subversion of the government which had grown out of the compact in the cabin of the *Mayflower*.   "Reformation in church," introducing the ministration of sacraments by Lyford, could mean nothing less than a suppression of the detested Separation, that the ideas and practices of ecclesiastical Nationalism might come in.   That Church of England for which reforming Puritans and Pontifical conservatives were equally vehement against the schismatic Brownists, Barrowists, Donatists, or by whatever other reproachful names they might be called, was to be set up in New England by the religious zeal of John Oldham and the purity of John Lyford.

With no great lapse of time things ripened.   The conspirators, "thinking they were now strong enough, began to pick quarrels at every thing.   It had not yet become safe, in Plymouth, to dispense with the nightly watch, and all able-bodied men were required to take their turns, under the command of Captain Standish, in guarding the repose of the village. Oldham, being called to that service in his turn, took the opportunity to raise a quarrel with the captain, calling him "rascal" and "beggarly rascal," and drawing his knife at him, with no other provocation than that of having been required to do his duty. So great and so noisy was the tumult that the governor, hearing it, "sent to quiet it." Oldham was not to be quieted by a word. "He ramped more like a furious beast than a man, called them all 'traitors' and 'rebels,'" and used other opprobrious language too foul to be recorded; "but, after he was clapt up a while, he came to himself, and, with some slight punishment, was let go upon his behavior, for further censure." In other words, Oldham's conduct in relation to the order and government of the colony was to be further investigated and judicially passed upon.

The crisis came. "Lyford and his accomplices, without even speaking one word to governor, church, or elder, withdrew themselves, and set up a public meeting apart, on the Lord's day, with sundry such insolent carriages, too long here to relate." They were "beginning now publicly to act what privately they had been long plotting." Let us not suppose that they were acting in the name or in the interest of religious liberty. Far from them was the thought of asserting the now universally acknowledged right of every man to worship God under such forms and in such associations as seem best to his conscience. That setting up of a public meeting on the Lord's day was the intrusion, not of liberty, but of the national-church theory; and it signified that the Pilgrims, after their twelve years of exile in Holland, and with three thousand miles of ocean between them and England, were still within the jurisdiction of the ecclesiastical Nationalism from which they fled so long ago.

Evidently the time had come for decisive measures. "The governor called a court, and summoned the whole company to appear." It was a General Court—a town-meeting. Lyford and Oldham were charged with having conspired to subvert the commonwealth. "But they were stiff, and stood resolutely upon the denial of most things, and required proof." Reserving to a later stage the most conclusive evidence in the case, the prosecution first produced the letters from England concerning the plans there formed against the colony, and argued from "the doings and practices here" of those two men that they were agents or partners of the faction there. How injurious and malicious their plot was against the peace of the colony, "both in respect of its civil and church state," they could not but know; "for they and all the world knew" that the people of Plymouth—the Pilgrims—"came hither to enjoy the liberty of their conscience and the free use of God's ordinances"—a liberty of which the conspirators were seeking to deprive them. For that end the men of Plymouth "had ventured their lives and passed through much hardship hitherto." For that end, "they and their friends had borne the charge of these beginnings, which was not small." Lyford was told that he had been sent over, with "his great family," at the expense of the colony, and was maintained out of their means; that he had, by his own choice and profession, become a covenanted member of their church, and was in all respects counted among them; and that "for him to plot against them and seek their ruin was most unjust and perfidious." Oldham and the others who like him had "come over at their own charge, and were on their particular," were reminded that they had been received in courtesy by the plantation when "they came to seek shelter and protection, . . . not being able to stand alone;" and they were likened to "the hedgehog in the fable, whom the cony in a stormy day received into her burrow." As the hedgehog "would not be content to take part, but in the end, with her sharp pricks, forced the poor cony to forsake her own burrow, so these men, with the like injustice, endeavored to do the same to those that entertained them."

No mention having been made of intercepted letters, Lyford ventured to deny that he had any thing to do with those in England who were adversaries of the colony, and affected much surprise at being charged with that and other things. "Then his letters were produced and some of them read, at which he was struck mute." Oldham's letters were few; indeed, "he was so bad a scribe" that what of his writing had been intercepted was hardly legible. But he was in a rage at the exposure, and "in very high language" threatened vengeance. Appealing to those whom he supposed to be of his party and to be ready for mutiny, he cried, "Now show your courage! You have often complained to me; now is the time, if you will do any thing; I will stand by you!" But there was no response; "not a man opened his mouth." In that silence, "the governor turned his speech to Mr. Lyford, and asked him if he thought they had done evil to open his letters; but he would not say a word, well knowing what they might reply." But not deeming himself sufficiently vindicated by Lyford's mute confession, the governor proceeded to tell the people why he had taken that extreme measure of searching the letters which the conspirators were sending to England. "He did it as a magistrate, and was bound to it by his place, to prevent the mischief and ruin that this conspiracy of theirs would bring on this poor colony." Then he informed them about the letters which Lyford stole from Winslow, and of which he was sending copies, "with disgraceful annotations," to some of those in England who were adversaries of the Pilgrim commonwealth. The exhibition of those copies, and of other letters in Lyford's own handwriting, was conclusive; and those whom he might have expected to befriend him in the assembly were silent and ashamed.

Some of the allegations against the Pilgrim colony, in the intercepted letters, are worth repeating for the sake of showing how they were answered, then and there, in a full assembly that knew what the facts were. Lyford had alleged

that "the church would have none to live here but themselves;" that "neither were any willing so to do if they had
company to live elsewhere," and that "if there come over
any honest men that are not of the Separation, they"—the
Pilgrim planters — "will quickly distaste them." All this,
with more of the same sort, was peremptorily contradicted.
"They were willing and desirous that any honest men may
live with them, that will carry themselves peaceably and
seek the common good, or at least do them no hurt." They
affirmed "there are many"—not members of the church—
"that will not live elsewhere so long as they may live with
us." As for the assertion that "honest men, not of the Separation," were "distasted" and unwelcome, they pronounced
it "a false calumniation," declaring that "they had many
[such] among them, whom they liked well of, and were glad
of their company," and that "any such like that should
come" would be welcome. Such evidence is there that they
neither intended nor expected to establish a religious or ecclesiastical uniformity. They would gladly receive into their
commonwealth "all honest men" of peaceable behavior, who
would "seek the common good, or at least do them no hurt."
All that they demanded was that "the hedgehog" of Nationalism should not "with her sharp pricks force the poor
cony to forsake her own burrow."

What Lyford was proposing that his friends should do in
order to his intended "reformation in church and commonwealth" was full of significance as to the nature and extent
of the changes that were to be effected. First of all, "the
Leyden company (Mr. Robinson and the rest) must still be
kept back, or else all will be spoiled; and, lest any of them
should be taken in privately somewhere on the coast of England, they must change the master of the ship (Mr. William
Pierce), and put another also in Winslow's stead for merchant." Next the anti-Separatist party must be strengthened by emigration and otherwise. Such a number must be
provided and sent as would be enough to take possession of

the colony, and "oversway them here;" the "particulars" must "have voices in all courts and elections, and be free to bear any office;" and certain other arrangements, more cunning than honest, were suggested which "would be a means to strengthen this side the more." Then a military man, who had been spoken of, should be sent over, and he would surely be chosen captain; "for this Captain Standish" (quoth Lyford) "looks like a silly boy, and is in utter contempt." If the attempt to capture Plymouth by that method should not succeed, a distinct settlement should be begun within three or four miles' distance. In other words, if the place could not be taken by stratagem, it must be besieged. Finally, by way of giving more urgency to all these counsels, the suggestion was made that unless the anti-Separatist party in the colony should be reinforced, there would be no great hope of its holding out much longer.

Lyford, "after the reading of his letters before the whole company," was called upon for such defense or explanation as he might offer. He put the blame of what he had done upon "Billington and some others," who, he said, had made complaints to him, and had given him the information on which he acted. Was that — said some one, in behalf of the court—a sufficient ground for you thus to accuse and traduce us by your letters, and never say a word to us—considering the many bonds between you and us? Those whom he had thus accused and traduced took up the several particulars of accusation, and told him, We desire you, or any of your friends and confederates, not to spare us in any thing. If you or they have any proof of any corrupt or evil doing of ours, the evidence must needs be here present; for here are the whole company and sundry strangers. All the answer they could get was that he had been abused, as he now saw, by the men who had given him information. Billington and any whom he named as having informed him, "protested that he wronged them;" and while they acknowledged that "they were sometimes drawn to his meetings," they insisted that they had not consented to his revolutionary proposals.

He was then "dealt with" in respect to "his dissembling with them about the church." He was reminded "what a large confession he made at his admittance;" how he professed "that he held not himself a minister till he had a new calling;" and how he was now, after so short a time, working in opposition to the church, setting up a hostile congregation, and proposing to administer sacraments by virtue of that episcopal ordination which he had so recently renounced, and all "without ever speaking a word to them either as magistrates or as brethren."

Thus baffled in every attempt at defense, deserted by those whom he had regarded as confederates, only his fellow-culprit Oldham on his side, shut up to the necessity of acknowledging his baseness, the unhappy man "burst out into tears" and made ample confession. "He feared he was a reprobate; his sins were so great that he doubted God would not pardon them; he was unsavory salt, fit only to be trodden under foot; he had so wronged them that he could never make amends; all he had written against them was false both for matter and manner." The show of humility and sorrow was "with as much fullness as words and tears could express."

The trial having resulted in so complete a conviction, there remained the question, What shall the sentence be? "The court censured them to be expelled the place, Oldham presently—though his wife and family had liberty to stay all winter, or longer, till he could make provision to remove them comfortably." On Lyford, notwithstanding the exposure of his hypocrisy, the sentence of expulsion was less peremptory. He was permitted to remain six months; and that delay "was indeed with some eye to his release, if he carried himself well in the mean time, and his repentance proved sound." He acknowledged that the sentence was less than he deserved, and "afterward he confessed his sin pub-

licly in the church, with tears, more largely than before." [1]
Such was the charitableness of the Pilgrims toward offenders, and their readiness to absolve from censure when they
found a plausible profession of repentance, that they, in consideration of his tears and his self-humiliation, " began again
to conceive good thoughts of him," and soon permitted him
again to exercise his gift of preaching in their assembly.
"Some tender-hearted men among them" (one of the tender-
hearted being Deacon Samuel Fuller, their beloved physician)
" were so taken with his signs of sorrow and repentance, that
they professed they would fall upon their knees " if so they
might obtain the remission of his sentence.

Their charitable trust in the sincerity of his professed repentance was disappointed. Not half of the six months allowed to him had passed, when another letter from him to the
Adventurers fell into the governor's hands (Aug. 22 = Sept.
1), exposing the extreme duplicity of the man. " I suppose,"
said he, " my letters, or at least the copies of them, are come
to your hands, for so they here report.   If it be so, I pray
you take notice of this, that I have written nothing but what
is certainly true." Knowing the Puritan zeal and anti-Separatist prejudices of the men to whom he was writing, he appealed to them in behalf of " divers poor souls here, destitute

---

[1] Bradford adds : " I shall here put it down, as I find it recorded by some
who took it from his own words as himself uttered them, acknowledging
' That he had done very evil and slanderously abused them ; and thinking
most of the people would take part with him, he thought to carry all by violence and strong hand against them.   And that God might justly lay innocent blood to his charge, for he knew not what hurt might have come of these
his writings ; and [he] blessed God they were stayed.   And that he spared
not to take knowledge from any of any evil that was spoken, but shut his
eyes and ears against all the good.   And if God should make him a vaga-
bond in the earth, as was Cain, it was but just, for he had sinned in envy and
malice against his brethren as he did.   And he confessed three things to be
the ground and causes of these his doings : pride, vainglory, and self-love.'
Amplifying these heads with many other sad expressions in the particulars
of them."

of the means of salvation," and added fresh calumnies against
the church.   Adopting a Puritan misrepresentation of Separatist principles, he alleged that the church, though only a
minority in the colony, " appropriated the ministry to themselves, holding this principle that the Lord hath not appointed any ordinary ministry for the conversion of those that
are without."   "Some of the poor souls," he said, " have
with tears complained of this to me, and I was taxed for
preaching to all in general."   At the same time he had his
fling at the lay preaching of Elder Brewster, and the prophe-
syings wherewith the brethren were wont to edify one another.   " In truth, they have no ministry here, since they
came, but such as may be performed by any of you, . . .
whatsoever great pretenses they make.   Herein they equivo-
cate, as in many other things they do."

Full of these and other calumnies, the letter went forward
to its destination; but with it Bradford sent an ample refutation.   On the last point, especially, the reply was pungent.
" He saith we have had no ministry since we came. . . . We
answer, The more is our wrong, that our pastor is kept from
us by these men's means, who then reproach us for it when
they have done.   Yet have we not been wholly destitute of
the means of salvation, as this man would make the world
believe; for our reverend elder hath labored diligently in
dispensing the Word of God to us before he [Lyford] came,
and since hath taken equal pains with him in preaching the
same; and (be it spoken without ostentation) he is not inferior to Mr. Lyford and some of his betters, either in gifts or
learning—though he would never be persuaded to take higher office upon him. . . . For 'equivocating,' he may take it
to himself.   What the church holds it has manifested to the
world in all plainness, both in open confession and doctrine
and in writing."

Notwithstanding this new provocation, the doubly convicted hypocrite was permitted to remain till the end of his
six months.   But meanwhile the church was strengthened.

Some who had stood aloof were brought to a decision by the exposure of Lyford's malignity, and asked for admission to the covenanted brotherhood, "professing that it was not out of the dislike of any thing that they had stood off so long, but only out of a desire to fit themselves better for such a state." They now chose to unite themselves with the church, because "they saw the Lord called for their help."

The six-months' postponement of Lyford's removal from the colony—a postponement which had been granted partly out of regard to his wife and children, that their flight might not be in the winter — was ending, when Oldham, without permission obtained or asked, returned to Plymouth (April, 1625), in company with some strangers. His behavior was so insolent and outrageous that his companions were ashamed of him, and rebuked him. But rebuke, even from them, inflamed his rage, and the governor found it necessary to "commit him till he should be tamer." For his punishment, afterward, "a guard of musketeers was drawn up, through which he was to pass, receiving from every one a parting thump with a musket on his rear as he went by." He was then "conveyed to the water-side, where a boat was ready to carry him away." So they dismissed him with a word of exhortation—"Go, and mend your manners."

It was a singular coincidence that Winslow and William Pierce arrived, just then, on their return from England, and landed at Plymouth while the whole village was occupied with the ceremonies of Oldham's dismissal. They brought with them new and abundant proof both of Oldham's machinations against the colony and of Lyford's extreme depravity. In England they had encountered the accusations which went over in Lyford's letters, and which were urged by the anti-Separatists among the Adventurers. Much bickering had they there with the men of that party. Those whose pity for the spiritual needs of the colony had moved them to send Lyford on his unsuccessful mission were clamorous. They could not endure to see "a minister, a man so godly," ac-

cused of falsehood.   They deemed it a great scandal, and
threatened a prosecution in the courts.   A full meeting of
the Adventurers was called to hear the whole case, and to
decide all questions concerning it; and for that meeting two
moderators were agreed upon beforehand.   The moderators
were "Mr. White, a counselor at law," chosen by Lyford's
party, and "the Reverend Mr. Hooker" (Thomas Hooker, afterward of New England), chosen by the other party.   At
the appointed time, "many friends on both sides were brought
in, so as there was a great assembly."   The result was a
complete discomfiture of the anti-Separatist party by an exposure of shameful facts in the life of the man with whom
their cause had been unhappily identified.   For that result,
and the facts which produced it, some at Plymouth were already prepared by certain confidential disclosures which Lyford's wife, in "her grief and sorrow of mind," had made to
them.

When Lyford, after his first exposure at Plymouth, and
the show of penitence which he then made, had been again
detected in his work of calumnious accusation, his wife, terrified by his wickedness, and apprehensive that God's providence in dealing with such wickedness might bring some
dire calamity on her and her children,[1] told the story of her
wrongs and of her husband's extreme baseness, " to one of the
deacons and some other of her friends."   She could no longer
endure, without some Christian sympathy, the agony of
knowing how vile he had been in his relations with other
women, both before her marriage to him and through all her
wedded life.   The friends in whom she confided kept her
secret.   But while Winslow and Pierce, in London, were
managing the cause of the colony against Lyford's employ-
ers, it came to pass that some of the other party in the Company of Adventurers had received information concerning

---

[1] The text 2 Sam. xii., 11, seemed to her like a divine threatening against
her person, which might be executed, if, in their removal from Plymouth,
they should fall into the hands of Indians.

"his evil carriage in Ireland," and had put Winslow into
communication with "two godly and grave witnesses who
would testify the same, if called thereunto, upon their oath."
The story in detail is too shameful to be narrated here. It
is enough to repeat what Bradford tells of the procedure in
that assembly of the Adventurers, "with many friends on
both sides," under the joint moderatorship of Mr. Counselor
White and Rev. Mr. Hooker. "In handling the former matters about the letters, Mr. Winslow, upon provocation, in
some heat of reply to some of Lyford's defenders, let fall
these words, 'That he had dealt knavishly.'" Thereupon
one of the adverse party bade the hearers take notice that
Winslow "had called a minister of the Gospel a knave," and
to be ready to testify that fact in a court of law. In the excitement which ensued, the reputation which that "minister
of the Gospel" had in Ireland was referred to; "and the
witnesses were produced, whose persons were so grave, the
evidence so plain, and the fact so foul (yet delivered in such
modest and chaste terms, and with such circumstances), as
struck all his friends mute, and made them all ashamed."
In conclusion, "the moderators with great gravity declared
that the former matters gave" the Plymouth people "cause
enough to refuse him, and to deal with him as they had
done; but that these matters made him unmeet forever to
bear ministry any more, what repentance soever he should
pretend." With that expression of their opinion, they advised "his friends to rest quiet. Thus was this matter ended." The attempt of Puritanism in the Company to overcome Separatism in the colony by sending out a minister
who should supplant Robinson in the affection and confidence of the Pilgrims, had come to naught.

Such were the tidings which Winslow and Pierce brought
to Plymouth at the moment when the colony was expelling
Oldham the second time. Lyford and his family settled
down, for a time, with Oldham and a few others, at Nantasket, the southern cape of Boston harbor. From that

place he and they soon removed to Cape Ann, as pioneers of a colony to be established on other than Separatist principles. Thence—probably not long after his character had begun to be more thoroughly understood in the new settlement and among its patrons—he removed to a greater distance. Bradford says: "Whether for hope of greater profit, or what ends else, I know not, he left his friends that followed him, and went to Virginia, where he shortly after died, and so I leave him to the Lord."

Oldham, about a year and a half from the date of that insolent behavior of his which was so promptly and fitly punished by the Plymouth government, had embarked with many other passengers for a voyage to Virginia. He found himself, with them, in great peril of shipwreck "on the shoals of Cape Cod." Despairing of life, some of them, and he among them, betook themselves to prayer, and to the mutual confession of "such sins as did most burden them." On that occasion, as was reported by "some of good credit who were themselves partners in the same dangers," he made "a free and large confession of the wrongs and hurt he had done to the people and church" in Plymouth. Delivered from that danger, "he afterward carried himself fairly toward them, and acknowledged the hand of God to be with them, and seemed to have an honorable respect of them." They, on their part, retained no grudge against him. He "so far made his peace with them that he had liberty to go and come," and to "converse" or transact business "with them at his pleasure." [1]

Thus the feeble church of Christ at Plymouth held its ground, and no weapon that was formed against it prospered.

---

[1] Oldham lived till 1636, and was then murdered by Indians, on his own vessel, near Block Island. His death was among the causes of the Pequot War.

CHAPTER XIX.

THE PILGRIM COLONY ABANDONED BY THE PURITAN ADVENT-
URERS.—PROSPERITY AT PLYMOUTH.—DEATH OF
ROBINSON.—THE LEYDEN REMNANT.

HAD the colony yielded speedy and large profits to the capital invested in it, the anti-Separatist Adventurers might, perhaps, have forgotten their scruples about the ecclesiastical unsoundness of the Pilgrims.   A brilliant prospect of commercial success might have tempted them to tamper with their convictions.   But, as things came to pass, no such temptation befell them.   From the purchase of the *Speedwell* onward, there had been a series of disasters.   Larger investments were continually demanded, but the returns in furs and fish had fallen short of expectations which seemed reasonable at the beginning.   A superstitious abhorrence of Brownism might lead some to believe that the providence of God was against an enterprise so tainted with the sin of schism.   Worldly wisdom might suggest that a colony of Separatists, who rejected not only "the ceremonies and the vestments" and the prelatical government, but the National Church itself, could not be made attractive to any large number of respectable Englishmen, and therefore could not flourish.   Such were the mingled motives which induced the sending of Lyford to Plymouth.   The ignominious failure of his mission was a discouragement to the zealous Puritans in the Company of Adventurers; but for all that their antipathy to Brownism was not overcome.

After the meeting in which Lyford's character was so fatally exposed, the majority of the Adventurers withdrew their patronage from the colony and their co-operation from the enterprise.   In effect the Company, though not yet formally dissolved, was broken to pieces.   The minority, who had

been, through all discouragements, steadfast friends of the
Pilgrim church and colony, did not forsake them in this
emergency.   Unwilling to make any additional investment
in a concern which two thirds of their partners had deserted,
they sent, nevertheless, a small supply of goods, which, instead of going into the common stock, were to be sold on
their private account.   The malcontent Adventurers, on the
other hand, sent out a vessel which was to co-operate with
Oldham and Lyford and their followers in the fishery at
Cape Ann.   Letters were sent in which the views and purposes of each of those parties were explained.

The malcontents, in a letter subscribed by some of them
professing to represent the rest, set forth " certain reasons of
their breaking off from the plantation," and offered " certain
conditions " on which they were willing to continue their
partnership.   The " reasons of their breaking off" were two.
First, they alleged that the Pilgrims had " dissembled with
his majesty in their petition, and with the Adventurers, about
the French discipline;" and, secondly, that they had "received
a man into their church who, in his confession, renounced all
universal, national, and diocesan churches;" it being understood that Lyford, their informant, was himself the man.
Therefore, inasmuch as the Pilgrims, while " denying the
name of Brownists," were evidently conducting their church
affairs according to the principles stigmatized by that name,
" we," said the malcontent Adventurers, " should sin against
God in building up such a people."   In brief, they would
not be partakers of other men's sins ; and, to Puritan thought,
the Brownist Separation from that National Church of England which all good men were laboring to reform, was the
very sin of schism.   If there were to be any more co-operation between them and the colony, certain concessions must
be made to their " dislikes."   " First, that as we are partners
in trade, so we may be in government there—as the patent
doth give us power.   Secondly, that the French discipline
may be practiced in the plantation, as well in the circum-

stances thereof as in the substance; whereby the scandalous name of the Brownists, and other church differences, may be taken away.   Lastly, that Mr. Robinson and his company may not go over to our plantation unless he and they will reconcile themselves to our church by a recantation under their hands."   In short, what those malcontents demanded was that the civil autonomy which the Pilgrims had maintained under their compact in the cabin of the *Mayflower* should be abolished to make room for the government of a commercial company; and that the ecclesiastical system of the colony should be Puritanism and not Separatism.

No such concessions would the men of Plymouth make. In what terms they expressed their rejection of the proposal we are not informed, for only that portion of their letter has been preserved which replies to the charge of dissimulation concerning their agreement with the French Protestant churches.[1]   On that point they said : "Whereas you tax us for dissembling with his majesty and the Adventurers about the French discipline, you do us wrong; for we both hold and practice the discipline of the French and other Reformed churches (as they have published the same in the 'Harmony of Confessions') according to our means, in effect and substance.   But whereas you would tie us to the French discipline in every circumstance, you derogate from the liberty we have in Christ Jesus.   The apostle Paul would have none to follow him in any thing but wherein he follows Christ; much less ought any Christian or church in the

---

[1] The charge of dissimulation was founded on the note of explanation which they sent from Leyden to Sir John Wolstenholme, for him to use at his discretion, and which he did not use "lest he should spoil all."   See *ante*, p. 267, 268.   The note was in these words: "Touching the ecclesiastical ministry, namely, of pastors for teaching, elders for ruling, and deacons for distributing the church's contribution; as also for the two sacraments—Baptism and the Lord's Supper—we do wholly and in all points agree with the French Reformed churches, according to their public confession of faith." In the alternative form of the note, they added a specification of "some small differences to be found in our practices."

world to do it.   The French may err, we may err, and other
churches may err, and doubtless do in many circumstances.
That honor, therefore, belongs only to the infallible Word of
God and pure Testament of Christ, to be propounded and
followed as the only rule and pattern for direction herein, to
all churches and Christians.   And it is too great arrogancy
for any man or any church to think that he or they have so
sounded the Word of God to the bottom as precisely to set
down the church's discipline without error in substance or
circumstance, so that no other without blame may digress
or differ in any thing from the same.   And it is not difficult
to show that the Reformed churches differ in many circumstances among themselves."   So steadfastly did that church
insist upon its liberty; and so resolutely did it refuse to be
measured by any standard other than the Scriptures.

From the friendly and faithful minority of Adventurers
there came a large epistle addressed " To our beloved friends,
Mr. William Bradford, Mr. Isaac Allerton, Mr. William Brewster, and the rest of the general society of Plymouth in New
England."   That letter, so full of Christian wisdom and of a
purely Christian spirit, while it shows what the men were
whose confidence and love the Pilgrims, " unknown by face,"
had gained, is a most honorable testimony to the character
of the men to whom it was addressed.   The history of the
church in Plymouth would be incomplete without it.

"Though the thing we feared be come upon us, and the
evils we strove against have overtaken us, we can not forget
you, nor our friendship and fellowship which together we
have had some years; wherein, though our expressions have
been small, yet our hearty affections toward you (unknown
by face) have been no less than to our nearest friends—yea,
even to ourselves.   And though your and our friend, Mr.
Winslow, can tell you the state of things here, and what hath
befallen us, yet—lest we should seem to neglect you to whom,
by a wonderful providence of God, we are so nearly united
—we have thought good once more to write unto you; first,

to show you what is here befallen; secondly, the reason and cause of it; thirdly, our purposes and desires toward you hereafter.

"The former course for the generality[1] here is wholly dissolved; and whereas you and we were formerly sharers and partners in all voyages and dealings, this way is now so no more, but you and we are left to bethink ourselves what course to take in the future that our lives and our moneys be not lost. . . .

"The reasons and causes of this alteration have been these: First and mainly, the many crosses and losses and abuses by sea and seamen, which have caused us to run into so much charge and debts and engagements, as we were not able to go on without impoverishing ourselves, and much hindering if not spoiling our trades and callings here—unless our estates had been greater, or our associates had cloven better to us. Secondly, as there hath been a faction and siding among us more than two years, so now there is an utter breach and sequestration among us, and in two parts of us[2] a full desertion and forsaking of you, without any intent or purpose of meddling more with you. And though we are persuaded the main cause of this their doing is want of money (for need whereof men use to make many excuses), yet other things are by many pretended, and not without some color urged—which are these: First, a distaste of you there, for that you are, as they affirm, Brownists, condemning all other persons and churches but those of your own way; that you are contentious and cruel toward such as in all points, both civil and religious, jump not with you; and that you are negligent, careless, wasteful, and spend your

---

[1] The words "general" and "generality" seem to have been used by the Pilgrims and their friends as meaning what we mean by such words as "partnership," "company," and "community." In this instance, "the generality" is the joint-stock company of Merchant Adventurers.

[2] Two thirds of the whole number.

time in idleness and talking and conferring;[1]—secondly, a distaste and personal contempt of us for taking your parts and striving to defend you and make the best of all matters touching you, insomuch as it is hard to say whether you or we are least loved of them.

"Now what use either you or we may make of these things remaineth to be considered; and the more for that we know the hand of God to be present in all these things; and he, no doubt, would admonish us of something which is not yet so looked to and taken to heart as it should be. And though it be now too late for us or you to prevent or stay these things, yet it is not too late to exercise patience, wisdom, and conscience in bearing them, and in carrying ourselves in and under them for time to come. And as we stand ready to embrace all occasions that may tend to the furtherance of so hopeful a work, rather admiring at what is than grudging at what is not, so it must rest in you to make all good again. And if in nothing else you can be approved, yet let your honesty and conscience be still approved, and lose not one jot of your innocence amid your many crosses and afflictions. Surely, if you upon this alteration behave yourselves wisely and go on fairly, as men whose hope is not in this life, you shall need no other weapon to wound your adversaries; for when your righteousness is revealed as the light, they shall cover their faces with shame that causelessly sought your overthrow.

"And although we hope you need not our counsel in these things, having learned of God how to behave yourselves in

---

[1] This, it will be remembered, was Weston's complaint after that first winter of struggle with disease and death. See *ante*, p. 350, 351, 355. It reminds us of Pharaoh's complaint against the Hebrews: " Ye are idle, ye are idle, therefore ye say, Let us go and do sacrifice to the Lord." Exod. v., 17. Notwithstanding the exposure of Lyford's character, his letters, with those from Oldham, and perhaps from other malcontents in the colony, seem to have left, even upon the authors of this letter, an impression that such accusations were " not without some color urged."

all states in this world, yet a word for your advice and direction, to spur those forward who, we hope, run well already :

"First, seeing our generality here is dissolved, let yours be the more firm. Do not you like carnal people who run into inconveniences and evils by examples, but rather be warned by your harms to cleave faster together hereafter. Take heed of long and sharp disputes and oppositions ; give no passage to the waters—no, not a tittle. Let not hatred or heart-burning be harbored in the heart of any of you one moment ; but forgive and forget all former failings and abuses, and renew your love and friendship together daily. There is often more sound friendship and sweeter fellowship in afflictions and crosses than in prosperity and favors ; and there is reason for it, because envy flieth away when there is nothing but necessities to be looked on, but it is always a bold guest where prosperity shows itself.

"Although we here, who are hedged about with so many favors and helps in worldly things and comforts, forget friendship and love, and fall out oftentimes for trifles—you must not do so, but must in these things turn a new leaf and be of another spirit. We here can fall out with a friend and lose him to-day, and find another to-morrow ; but you can not do so—you have no such choice—you must make much of them you have, and count him a very good friend who is not your professed enemy. We have a trade and custom of talebearing, whispering, and changing old friends for new, and these things with us are incurable ; but you who do, as it were, begin a new world, and lay the foundation of sound piety and humanity for others who are to follow, must suffer no such weeds in your garden, but nip them in the head and cast them out forever ; and must follow peace and study quietness, having fervent love among yourselves as a perfect and entire bond to uphold you when all else fails you. . . .

"If any among you have still a withdrawing heart, and will be all to himself and nothing to his neighbor, let him think of these things: the providence of God in bringing you there together; his marvelous preserving you from so many dangers; the hopes that yet are of effecting somewhat for yourselves, and more for your posterity, if hand join in hand; the woeful estate of him that is alone, especially in a wilderness; the succor and comfort which the generality can daily afford, ... pulling together with the varieties of trades and faculties employed by sea and land, the gain of every one stretching itself to all; but such as withdraw themselves, tempting God and despising their neighbors, must look for no share or part in any of these things — but alone they must work, and alone they must eat, and alone they must be sick and die; or else alone return to England, and there cry out of the country and the people, counting the one fruitless and the other merciless. Besides all these things, the conscience of making restitution, and paying those debts and charges which have befallen to bring you there and send those things to you which you have had, must hold you together. . . .

"In a word: we think it but reason that all such things as there are, appertaining to the general, be kept and preserved together, and rather increased daily than any way dispersed or embezzled away for any private ends or intents whatsoever. We advise that, after your necessities are served, you gather together such commodities as the country yields, and send them over, to pay debts and clear engagements here, which are not less than £1400—all which debts, besides adventures,[1] have been made about general commodities and implements—and for which divers of us stand more or less engaged. And we dare say of you that you will do the best you can to free and unburden us who for your sakes and help are so much hazarded in our estates and names. If there be any that will withdraw himself from the general, as he must not have nor use any of the general's goods, so it is but rea-

---

[1] Capital invested in the stock of the company.

son that he give sufficient security for payment of so much of the debts as his part cometh to.

"In a word: since it falleth out that all things between us are as you see, let us all endeavor to keep a fair and honest course, and see what time will bring forth, and how God in his providence will work for us. *We are still persuaded you are the people that must make a plantation and erect a city in those remote places, when all others fail and return;* and your experience of God's providence and preservation of you is such that we hope your hearts will not now fail you. Though your friends should forsake you (which we ourselves shall not do while we live, so long as your honesty so well appeareth), yet surely help would arise from some other place while you wait on God with uprightness.

"To conclude: as you are especially now to renew your love one to another, so we advise you, as your friends, to these particulars. First, let all sharpness, reprehensions, and corrections of opposite persons be still used sparingly, and take no advantage against any for any by-respects; but rather wait for their mending among you, than mend them yourselves by thrusting away any of whom there is hope of good to be had. Secondly, make your corporation as formal as you can, under the name of 'the Society of Plymouth in New England,' allowing some peculiar privileges to all the members thereof, according to the tenure of the patents. Thirdly, let your practices and course in religion, in the church, be made complete and full; let all that fear God among you join themselves thereunto without delay; and let all the ordinances of God be used completely in the church, without longer waiting upon uncertainties or keeping the gap open for opposites. Fourthly, let the worship and service of God be strictly kept on the Sabbath, and—both together and asunder—let the day be sanctified; and let your care be seen on the working days, every where and upon all occasions, to set forward the service of God. And, lastly, be you all entreated to walk so circumspectly and

F F

carry yourselves so uprightly in all your ways, as that no man may make any just exceptions against you, and, more especially, that the favor and countenance of God may be toward you, and you may say with David, 'Though my father and my mother should forsake me, yet the Lord will take me up.'

. . . "Good friends, have an eye rather on your ill-deservings at God's hand than on the failings of your friends toward you; and wait on him with patience and good conscience, rather admiring his mercies than repining at his crosses, with the assurance of faith that what is wanting here shall be made up in glory a thousandfold. Go on, good friends, comfortably; pluck up your hearts cheerfully, and quit yourselves like men in all your difficulties, that— notwithstanding all displeasure and threats of men — the work may go on which you are about, and which is so much for the glory of God and the furtherance of our countrymen, as that a man may with more comfort expend his life in it than live the life of a Methuselah in wasting the plenty of a tilled land or eating the fruit of a grown tree." [1]

---

[1] An abstract of this letter is given in Bradford's History. I have transcribed it almost entire from Bradford's "Letter-Book" (Mass. Historical Collections, iii., 29–34). While abridging it by the omission of here and there a sentence, and of some expressions that seemed tautological or redundant, I have also, in a very few instances, taken the liberty of changing the collocation of words in a sentence, and of substituting one word for another, where the reader might otherwise have been compelled to pause and inquire for the meaning.

The letter was subscribed by four—" James Sherley (sick)," being the first name. It was in the handwriting of Robert Cushman; and parts of it, at least, are in his style of composition. In a personal letter to Bradford, written four days later (Dec. 22, O. S.), Cushman says: " My friend and your friend, Mr. Sherley, who lieth even at the point of death; entreated me, even with tears, to write to excuse him, and to signify how it was with him. He remembers his hearty and (as he thinks) his last salutations to you, and to all the rest who love our common cause." " His unfeigned love toward us has been such as I can not indeed express. . . . He hath sometimes lent

The "cattle, cloth, hose, shoes, leather," and other commodities, sent by those friends, were to be paid for at prices "thought unreasonable by some;" but the new method of transacting the business seems to have been really much better than that which it superseded.   It was better to deal with individual merchants than with an ill-assorted company of Adventurers.   Goods sent by friends in London, on their private account, were purchased by "the generality," and were then disposed of to individuals by sale or otherwise. There being no longer any attempt to maintain a partnership "in all voyages and dealings" between "the generality" at Plymouth and the other "generality" in London, it only remained to dispose of outstanding engagements, and to wind up the concerns of that broken partnership at the earliest convenient day.   Before midsummer, the colony was able to send, in part payment for the goods which it had received from Sherley and the others, "as much beaver and other furs as would amount to upward of two hundred and seventy-seven pounds sterling," at the last year's prices." [1]

£800 at one time for other men to adventure in this business—all to draw them on.   He hath, indeed, by his free-heartedness been the only glue of the Company."

This proved to be Cushman's last letter.   " He wrote," said Bradford, "of the sickness and probability of the death of another, but knew not that his own was so near. . . . He purposed to be with us 'the next ships;' but the Lord did otherwise dispose, and had appointed him a greater journey to a better place."   Sherley recovered, and continued for many years a steadfast friend of Plymouth and its church.

[1] That precious freight of furs was sent in the *Little James*, the pinnace (*ante*, p. 384) which, after various disasters on this side of the Atlantic, having rendered little service to the colony, had become the property of Thomas Fletcher, one of those four Adventurers who were still pledged to the cause. In company with a larger vessel, she passed safely over the ocean; but in the English Channel, and almost within sight of old Plymouth—strange as the story seems at this day—she was "taken by a Turk's man-of-war and carried into Sallee, where the master and men were made slaves, and many of the beaver skins were sold for four pence a piece"—furs not being highly

"It pleased the Lord to give the plantation peace and health and contented minds;" and when their summer's work was ended, and their crops were gathered in, "they had corn sufficient and some to spare, with other food." After the Indian harvest, "when the time of the year begins to grow tempestuous," they loaded one of their two shallops with corn, and sent her, under the command of Winslow, with only landmen for sailors, "forty or fifty leagues to the eastward, up a river called Kennebec," to trade with the savages.   The loaded shallop, having "a little deck over her midships to keep the corn dry," went safely through the autumn storms (though "the men were fain to stand it out all weathers without shelter"), and "brought home seven hundred pounds of beaver besides some other furs."   Instead of buying corn from the Indians with "trucking stuff" imported from Europe (as they had been formerly compelled to do), they were exchanging the surplus product of their corn-fields for furs to be sold in England.   Under God they could now rely on their "innocent trade of husbandry," not only to yield them food, but to make them independent of the partners who had deserted them.

Meanwhile, there being more need than ever of some one to represent the colony in London, Captain Standish had been commissioned to perform that service.   He was to confer with such of the Adventurers as were still friendly to the Pilgrim church and commonwealth, and was also the bearer of a memorial to "the Right Honorable his Majesty's Council for New England."   The memorial, subscribed by the governor (June 28 = July 8), "with the knowledge, consent, and humble request of the whole plantation," represented, briefly and modestly, what they had done in less than five years, "having put some life into this then dreaded design;" and what hardships "incident to the raw and imma-

---

valued on the African coast.   How much of the loss was sustained by the colony does not appear; but to Fletcher that disaster was ruin.

ture beginning of such great exertions" they had undergone and were yet to undergo. It complained, "We are now left and forsaken of our Adventurers, who will neither supply us with necessaries for our subsistence, nor suffer others that would be willing ; neither can we be at liberty to deal with others or provide for ourselves, but they keep us tied to them and yet will be loose from us ; they have not only cast us off, but entered into particular course of trading, and have by violence and force taken at their pleasure our possession at Cape Ann ;[1] traducing us with unjust and dishonest clamors abroad, disturbing our peace at home, and some of them threatening that if ever we grow to any good estate they will then nip us in the head." The request of the memorial was that, by the intervention of the Council for New England, those Adventurers might be brought to a final settlement and division.

"Our people," said Bradford in a private letter (June 9 = 19), "will never agree any way again to unite with the Company who have cast them off with such reproach and contempt, and have also returned their bills and all debts upon their heads." "I think it best to press a clearance with the Company, either by coming to a dividend, or by some other indifferent course or composition. The longer we hang and continue in this confused and lingering condition, the worse it will be, for it takes away from men all heart and courage to do any thing. Notwithstanding any persuasion to the contrary, many protest they will never build houses, fence grounds, or plant fruits for those who not only forsake them, but use them as enemies. . . . Whereas if they knew what they should trust to, the place would quickly grow and flourish with plenty."

---

[1] A patent for Cape Ann had been taken out in the names of Robert Cushman and Edward Winslow for themselves and their associates in January, 1624. Under that patent the Plymouth people had established a fishing and trading station there, of which they were dispossessed by " some of Lyford and Oldham's friends and their adherents."

Captain Standish's mission was not in any considerable degree successful. He found that Cushman was dead, the "wise and faithful friend" with whom he was to consult, and on whose greater experience and skill in commercial affairs much was depending. "The state was full of trouble," for the disastrous reign of Charles I. had begun ; "the plague was very hot in London, so as no business could be done;" "all trade was dead and little money stirring."[1]   Yet Standish found opportunity of conferring with "some of the honored council," who promised their influence in aid of the plantation. Having obtained, at great cost, a very limited supply of "trading goods and other most needful commodities," he returned as a passenger in a fishing vessel. Yet, with so little present success, he had made a good beginning of the negotiations which were to result in a final settlement between the colony and the Adventurers.

Welcome as was his return after almost a year's absence (April, 1626), he brought with him a new and heavy sorrow. Robinson, the revered pastor, so "dearly beloved and longed for," had died in exile, not having seen the Pilgrims' land of promise. "His and their adversaries had been long and continually plotting how they might hinder his coming hither, but the Lord had appointed him a better place." Letters from Leyden, announcing his decease, expressed the grief of the waiting remnant there. Roger White, who called him "my brother Robinson," wrote such words as these: "He began to be sick on Saturday in the morning; yet the next day, being the Lord's day, he taught us twice. The week after, he grew weaker every day; yet he felt no pain all the time of his sickness. He fell sick the twenty-second of February, and departed this life the first of March. He had a continual inward ague, but free from infection, so that all his friends came freely to him.[2]   If either prayers and tears or

[1] The deaths by plague, in London and Westminster, from Dec. 22, 1624, to Dec. 23, 1625, were 41,313.

[2] Leyden, as well as London, suffered from a visitation of the plague that year.

means would have saved his life, he had not gone hence. But having faithfully finished his course, and performed the work which the Lord appointed him to perform here, he now rests with the Lord in eternal happiness.   Wanting him and all church governors (not having one at present that is a governing officer among us), we still, by the mercy of God, continue and hold close together in peace and quietness, and so I hope we shall do, though we be very weak—wishing (if such were the will of God) that you and we were again together."   In another letter, written by Thomas Blossom, there were similar expressions : " The Lord took him away, even as fruit falleth before it was ripe, when neither length of days nor infirmity of body did seem to call for his end."   " The loss of his ministry was very great unto me, for I ever counted myself happy in the enjoyment of it, notwithstanding all the crosses and losses otherwise which I sustained."   " We may take up that doleful complaint in the Psalm that there is no prophet left among us, nor any that knoweth how long. Alas ! you would fain have had him with you, and he would as fain have come to you."   " I know no man among us knew his mind better than I did about those things : he was loth to leave the church, yet I know he would have accepted the worst conditions which in the largest extent of a good conscience could be taken, to have come to you.   For myself and all such others as have formerly minded coming, it is much the same if the Lord afford means."   " If we come at all to you, the means to enable us so to do must come from you."[1]

John Robinson had lived only fifty years when he rested from his labors, leaving to the Church Universal a name worthy of everlasting remembrance.   In Leyden his death was lamented ·not only by the remnant of his congregation, but by others who had known his gifts, his learning, and his life of self-denying love to Christ.   Winslow affirms that

---

[1] Bradford's " Letter Book."

ministers of the city and learned men of the university accompanied his remains to their grave, "bewailing not only
the loss which one poor church sustained," but "some of
the chief of them sadly affirming that all the churches of
Christ sustained a loss by the death of that worthy instrument of the Gospel." The Pilgrim remnant, in their poverty, buried their pastor under the pavement of the old cathedral. Records at Leyden show that, on the fourth of
March, the "preacher of the English meeting by the Belfry" was "buried in the Peter's-church;" and that, on
the tenth, nine florins were paid for the "opening" and
"hire" of that English preacher's grave. A grave hired
at that price might be opened for another burial at the
end of fifteen years, but there would be no disinterment.
The "garnered dust" of Robinson is in the Leyden cathedral, though we may not know what stones in the pavement cover it.[1]

Though depressed by the unsuccessfulness of their latest
attempt to obtain supplies from England, and saddened by
the news from Leyden, the men of Plymouth were not wholly discouraged. "They gathered up their spirits, and the
Lord, whose work they had in hand, so helped them, that
now when they were at the lowest they began to rise again."
Having found by their last autumn's experience that their
surplus corn was "a commodity" of great value in their
trade with the Indians, "they used great diligence in planting the same." While every man planted for himself, and
all the products of his labor were to be his own, the trade of
the colony "was retained for the general good," and was conducted by the governor and other managers as trustees for
"the generality." Some unexpected opportunities for obtaining goods were so well improved by the managers, that
"they became well furnished for trade," and were able to pay

---

[1] Winslow, in Young, p. 392, 393 ; Dr. H. M. Dexter, in "Proceedings
of Massachusetts Historical Society," 1872, p. 184, 186.

their "engagements against the time," and to replenish their
store with clothing, which the people paid for with the products of their corn-fields. "Cast down, but not destroyed,"
the Pilgrim colony had begun to prosper.

To finish the negotiation, begun by Standish, for a final
settlement and division with the Adventurers, Allerton was
sent to England. He was to obtain from them the best proposals they could be persuaded to make ; but he had no power to conclude any contract till it should be considered and
ratified by the colony. He was also commissioned to borrow
a sum of money on the personal security of nine principal
men among the Planters (himself being one of them), and to
purchase goods for their trade. Returning "at the usual sea-·
son for the coming of ships " (April, 1627), he brought with
him the desired supply of goods "safe and well-conditioned,
which was much to the comfort and content of the plantation," and also the form of a contract which the Adventurers
had already subscribed, and which "was very well liked of
and approved by all the plantation." For the sum of eighteen hundred pounds, in nine annual payments of two hundred pounds each, the Adventurers surrendered all their property in the colony to their partners the Planters. Eight of
the chief men, in behalf of the colony, became personally responsible for the successive payments ; and "thus," Plymouth could exult, "all now is become our own, as we say in
the proverb, when our debts are paid."

Other arrangements, consequent upon this great change,
were made in a liberal and enterprising spirit. There remained in the colony "mingled among them " — notwithstanding removals to Virginia and "to other places," such
as Nantasket and Cape Ann — "some untoward persons,"
perhaps not equally untoward with Oldham, but such as Lyford and Oldham had attempted to organize into a faction.
They were men who had come "on their particular," or who
for other reasons had never been admitted to "the generality;" and therefore they had no shares in the stock of the

Company, nor in the new responsibilities which the colony was assuming.   What, then, was to be their place in the commonwealth?   What was to be their share in "the distribution of things both for the present and future?"   The governor and his assistants, " with other of their chief friends, had serious consideration how to settle things " in this respect; and they came to a wise conclusion.   "First, they considered that they had need of men and strength both for defense and carrying on of business."   Then they considered that these men, though untoward, "had borne their parts in former miseries and wants " with the rest; and that it was " therefore (in some sort) but equal that they should partake in a better condition, if the Lord be pleased to give it."   It was a still more urgent consideration that in no other way were those " untoward persons " so likely to be made peaceable and contented members of society, as by giving them an equal interest with others in the commonwealth.   The conclusion was that it would be best " to take into this partnership or purchase " all free men resident in the colony, whether heads of families or single, whose moral character and discretion were such as to authorize the expectation that they would be "helpful in the commonwealth."

That conclusion was, therefore, submitted to "the generality" in full assembly, and was approved.   In that meeting it was agreed, first, that the trade should continue, as before, a public concern in the hands of managers, all its profits pledged to the payments of the debts; next, that all free men of good character and discretion should be enrolled as purchasers of the property ceded by the late Adventurers, every such man having one share, and every father of a family being allowed to purchase an additional share for his wife and for each of his children, while servants (whose time was not their own) were to have only what their masters, out of their own shares, might allow them, or " what their deservings should obtain from the company afterwards;" and, thirdly, that if the profits of the trade should not be sufficient for the payment of the eighteen hundred pounds and other common debts, every man, according to the number of his shares, should pay his part of the deficiency. "This gave all good content." Well might they be content and joyful, for the enforced communism under which they had suffered was to cease, and all the impulses to industry and thrift which God has incorporated into the constitution of human nature were henceforth to have full play. Immediately measures were taken for an equitable division and allotment of what had been the common property of the Adventurers and the Planters. With as little delay as possible, lands, houses, and chattels were transferred to individual owners.[1]

Another step upward was soon taken. The governor and other leading men, aware that all the future of the colony depended on the discharge of "those great engagements," the nine annual payments, besides the sums which Standish and Allerton had been compelled to borrow for the colony at portentous rates of interest, were at the same time anxiously inquiring how to bring over some of the remnant at Leyden, who, in their deep depression, were so desirous of coming. Having well considered what was possible, "they resolved to run a high course and of great adventure." Their proposal was that if they could secure the co-operation of friends in England, they would "hire the trade" of the colony for six years, and in consideration of that exclusive privilege, together with the goods then in store, and the boats and implements belonging to the Company, and of three bushels of corn or six pounds of tobacco to be paid yearly by every partner in the recent purchase from the Adventurers, they

---

[1] There was an allotment of twenty acres of tillable land to every share. A cow and two goats, with swine in proportion, was set apart for every six shares, and distributed by lot to be disposed of among the owners as they might agree. "They gave the governor and four or five of the special men among them the houses they lived in; the rest were valued and equalized at an indifferent rate, and so every man kept his own, and he that had a better allowed something to him that had a worse, as the valuation went."

would undertake to pay all "the debts that then lay upon the plantation," amounting to twenty-four hundred pounds. "After some agitation of the thing" in a formal assembly (July, 1627), the proposal was accepted. Four tried friends in London were found to unite with the eight Undertakers at Plymouth, and the colony was relieved of the pecuniary obligations that lay so heavily upon it.

It was by Allerton's agency that this last arrangement was completed, for he was sent to England again "with the return of the ships,"[1] charged not only with the duty of consummating the contract with the Adventurers, but with other important trusts. The four London merchants whom he brought into partnership with the Undertakers of the trade, had been fast friends of the Plymouth church in all its trouble with the late Adventurers, and had been bitterly reproached for not siding with the Puritan majority against the Pilgrims and the going over of the Leyden remnant.[2] To them, therefore, he freely communicated the earnest desire of Bradford and the others, to "help over some of their friends from Leyden;" and he found them ready to co-operate in that part of the design. Returning in the spring (1628), he was able to report that the first payment of two hundred pounds to the late Adventurers had been punctually made; that the other debts assumed by the Undertakers for the colony had been reduced in the same amount, and that their London partners and some other friends were intending "to send over to Leyden for a competent number of them to be here the next year without fail, if the Lord pleased to bless their journey."

In one thing the agent had gone beyond his commission.

---

[1] Communication with England had begun to be in some sort regular. The fishing vessels ordinarily left England in the winter, arrived upon the eastern coast of New England in the spring, and returned in the latter part of summer or early in the autumn.

[2] Sherley to Bradford, in Bradford's "Letter-Book."—Mass. Historical Collections, iii., 49.

He was not the agent of the church, nor, properly, of the colony, but only of the commercial Undertakers.   Nor had he been in any way authorized or requested by the church to select and introduce a minister; "for they had been so bitten by Mr. Lyford that they desired to know the person well whom they should invite among them."   But, advised perhaps by some friend or friends in London, he assumed the responsibility of bringing with him a young man named Rogers, who, he thought, might be acceptable and useful in the ministry of the Word.   The young man was received by the church as kindly as Lyford was at his coming; for they could not refuse to try what he could do as a preacher. " But they perceived, upon some trial, that he was crazed in his brain; so they were fain to send him back again the next year, and lose all the charge that was expended in his hither-bringing."   Nothing more is known of the unfortunate young man, save that "after his return he grew quite distracted." It is not strange that "Mr. Allerton was much blamed" for imposing such a burden upon his brethren, "they having charge enough otherwise."

Notwithstanding this mistake, and some other things in which the proceedings of the agent were not satisfactory, his associates did not withdraw their confidence from him.   "Because love thinks no evil, nor is suspicious, they took his fair words for excuse, and resolved to send him again this year, . . . considering how well he had done the former business, and what good acceptation he had with their friends there; and also seeing sundry of their friends from Leyden were sent for who might be much furthered by his means."

The London partners were hearty in their co-operation; and before the end of another summer thirty-five of the Leyden remnant arrived at Plymouth.   A letter from Sherley to Bradford said of them, in a tone of exultation: "Here are now many of your and our friends from Leyden coming over [May 25 = June 4, 1629].   Though, for the most part, they be but a weak company, yet herein is obtained a good part of that end which was first aimed at, and which hath been so strongly opposed by some of our former Adventurers. But God hath his working, . . . which man can not frustrate." Another but less numerous company of the sojourners at Leyden came over early in the next year. At their departure from England, Sherley, knowing that the hope of effecting the transportation of those exiles was one reason why Bradford and the others had undertaken to pay the debts of the colony, expressed his hearty approval. "In the agreement you have made with the generality," said he, "you have done very well both for them and you, and also for your friends at Leyden. . . . We are willing to join with you, and, God directing and enabling us, will be assisting and helpful to you, the best we possibly can. Had you not taken this course, I see not how you could have accomplished the end which you first aimed at, and which some others endeavored these years past." As a partner with the Undertakers, he was aware that what they were then doing would not be commercially profitable; "for," said he, "most of those who came in May last unto you, as also of these now sent, though (I hope) honest and good people, are not like to be helpful to raise profit, but . . . must somewhile be chargeable to you and us." But "the burden," he intimated, would be not on the colony, but on the Undertakers, and "you," he added, "will so lovingly join together in affection and counsel that God, no doubt, will bless and prosper your honest endeavors."

It was, indeed, a "burden" on the Undertakers. The cost of transporting those two companies from Holland to England, and thence across the Atlantic, with other expenses incident, was more than five hundred and fifty pounds. Arriving at Plymouth after the planting-time, in two successive years, the first company in August and the second in May, their "corn and other provisions" must be supplied—in the first instance more than a year, in the other almost a year and a half—from harvests which they had not planted: a charge which was little less than the cost of their removal.

"All they could do in the mean time was to get them some housing, and to prepare them grounds to plant on against the season." What added to the burden, those who selected the second company "sent all the weakest and poorest," thinking that, "if these were got over, the rest might come when they would." "Yet," says Bradford, "they were such as feared God, and were to us both welcome and useful, for the most part."[1] So the migration of the exiles, by companies, from Leyden to Plymouth was ended.

Some of those at Plymouth who, though not of the Pilgrim Company, had become partners in "the generality," began to murmur at the great cost of bringing over that Leyden remnant; for, though they were told that "the burden lay on other men's shoulders," were they not bound to pay the stipulated "three bushels of corn or six pounds of tobacco" to the Undertakers? To remove their discontent, it was generously promised that, unless the six years' profits of the trade should prove insufficient for the payment of the debts, the tax should never be demanded, and that promise "gave them good content." It is no more than a modest appreciation of the truth, when Bradford, having told by what efforts and sacrifices the removal of those who had been so long detained in Holland was at last accomplished, asks that it may be noted as "a rare example of brotherly love and of Christian care" on the part of the Pilgrim Church "in performing their promises and covenants to their brethren." His devout spirit saw—and can not we see?—"that there was more than of man in these achievements." It was God's grace, he thought, that had "stirred up the hearts of such able friends to join with them in such a cause and to cleave so faithfully to them in so great adventures"—friends whose faces the most of them had never seen. Let God be praised!

---

[1] Bradford's "Letter-Book."—Mass. Historical Collections, iii., 65, 66, 68–70.

Plymouth was now passing through the tenth year of its struggle for existence; and in that conflict it had gained the victory.   Whether it should remain on the soil which the Pilgrims, by persistent labor, had conquered from the wilderness and were converting into fruitful fields, was no longer a doubtful question.   The body politic constituted by a few homeless Englishmen in the cabin of the *Mayflower*, and maintaining itself under the simplest form of democracy, was an established fact.   The Governor of Plymouth, deriving his authority from God through a yearly election by the people, was a functionary recognized by his Majesty's Council for New England.   The trade of the colony with the Indians, with English vessels resorting to the New England fisheries, and with merchants in London, was prospering, and was lifting it out of its pecuniary troubles.   The Hollanders who were trying to make a New Amsterdam at the mouth of the Hudson had sought the friendship of the Englishmen at New Plymouth, who had once lived in their country, and with whom they could hold communication in their own language; and the Leyden exiles, now fathers of a growing commonwealth, had enjoyed the opportunity of manifesting their grateful remembrance of the hospitality that sheltered them in Holland.   Plymouth, in its tenth year and with its growing prosperity, was still a Separatist colony, with only a voluntary church that acknowledged no jurisdiction of Cæsar or of Parliament over the things that are God's, and no dominion of either a priestly or a preaching clergy over the Lord's free people.   A bishop's commissary had been sent to New England, but did not venture to show his commission at Plymouth.   Puritanism had struggled pertinaciously to capture the obnoxious Brownist colony, and had given up the conflict.   Though Robinson had died in his exile—broken-hearted but for his trust in God—some of his children, and all but a remnant of his flock, had come at last into the New England which he so longed for; and the church which, with "hope deferred," waited in vain for his coming, had found a pastor to serve it in the ministry of word and doctrine, and to be associated with Brewster in its government.

To explain how the church found a minister whom it could venture to place in the pastoral office, we must go back to a date at which we may take up the story of what Puritanism attempted, with higher aims and on a grander scale, after its ignominious failure to circumvent the Separatism of Plymouth.

PILGRIM AUTOGRAPHS.

[The foregoing signatures (in *fac simile*) are not without value as an illustration of our story. "William Bradford," "Edw. Winslow," "Willm. Brewster," "Myles Standish," and "Isaac Allerton" are names with which the reader has become familiar. "John Bradford" was the son of William, left behind when the *Mayflower* sailed from England, but afterward brought over. "Tho. Prence" (or Prince), afterward a son-in-law of Brewster, and Governor of the colony, came in the *Fortune*, 1621. "Nathaniel Morton," afterward Secretary of the colony, and author of "New England's Memorial," came, at twelve years of age, with his father, George Morton, in the *Anne*, 1628. "Thomas Cushman" came, a boy of fourteen years, with his father in the *Fortune*; he was left under the care of Governor Bradford, and at the death of Brewster, twenty-eight years later, he became the Ruling Elder. "John Winslow," a brother of Edward, came in the *Fortune*. "Constant Southworth" and "Tho. Southworth" were the step-sons of Governor Bradford.]

G G

CHAPTER XX.

THE BEGINNING OF A PURITAN COLONY IN NEW ENGLAND, AND WHAT CAME OF IT.

IT is no part of the work now in hand to tell the story of the great Puritan Exodus, or to describe minutely its beginning. The present design will be completed when we shall have seen what Puritanism becomes as soon as it finds itself free in the American wilderness; and how, notwithstanding its zeal in England for ecclesiastical Nationalism, and the bitter feeling which it has cherished against the schism of Separatism, it finds, under its new conditions—in a new world, where the Church of Christ is to be formed, instead of being, as in the old world, reformed—no other way than that of calling out from among the ungodly and profane those " who desire to live godly in Christ Jesus," and binding them together " as the Lord's free people " in a voluntary covenant of allegiance to their Saviour and of brotherly helpfulness to each other.

In Dorchester, the shire town of Dorsetshire, about one hundred and fifty miles southeast from London, the Rev. John White had long been rector of Trinity Church. He was an earnest Puritan, venerated for his goodness and zealous for church reformation, though he was one of the many who, either because their scruples did not bring them under the penalties of the Act of Uniformity, or because they were winked at by the ecclesiastical authorities, retained their livings under the imperfectly reformed establishment, and were called " Conforming Puritans." Dorchester, though not a seaport, was a place of some trade; and young men from its families were going, year by year, on fishing voyages to the coast of New England. The good rector of

Trinity Church, having served in that place more than twenty years, had learned to care for his parishioners abroad as well as at home; and so forward was he in plans and efforts for the general interest of religion, that he was sometimes called "the patriarch of Dorchester." In his solicitude for his own parishioners long absent on voyages to the New England coast, and especially for their spiritual welfare, he thought how many others endured the same hardships on the sea, and were subjected to the same temptations of the wilderness. He conceived the plan of a settlement at some convenient point, where sailors and fishermen, going ashore, might find more comfortable shelter and better supplies than the mere wilderness could give them, and might have the benefit of religious ministrations. At his persuasion, a few merchants and gentlemen formed an association (1624) of "Dorchester Adventurers" for that purpose, and contributed a capital of three thousand pounds.[1]

The town of Gloucester, famous as a fishing town, received its name long afterward; but its place, on the northern cape of the great Massachusetts Bay, became important as early as the first resort of fishing vessels to the coast. A patent for Cape Ann and a not well-defined extent of adjoining territory, was taken out, in the names of Cushman and Winslow and their associates, for Plymouth colony. It was under that patent, and therefore (we must infer) by some arrangement with the London Adventurers for Plymouth colony,[2] that the Dorchester Adventurers began (1624) their

[1] The "Planter's Plea," in Young's "Chronicles of Massachusetts," p. 6; Hubbard's "History of New England," p. 106.

[2] See *ante*, p. 433. Captain John Smith, in his "General History," 1624, as quoted by Dr. Palfrey, i., 285, says: "By Cape Ann there is a plantation a-beginning by the Dorchester men, *which they hold of those of New Plymouth*, who also by them have set up a fishing work." The date of the patent is Jan. 1 = 10, 1624. It has been suggested that there was already some beginning of a settlement before the date of the patent. Very probably the needs of the fishing vessels had induced the building of a house or two.

plantation at Cape Ann.   White and his friends could hardly fail to be in communication and in sympathy with the
anti-Separatist or Puritan party among the Adventurers at
London.   Thus it naturally came about that when Oldham
and Lyford had been expelled from Plymouth, and when the
London partnership was breaking to pieces, the Dorchester
Adventurers, whose plantation had been far from prosperous,
were informed concerning "some religious and well-affected
persons that were lately removed out of New Plymouth out
of dislike of their principles of rigid separation."   One of
these, it is said, was Roger Conant, who seems to have been
not unfitly described as "a religious, sober, and prudent gentleman."[1]   Lyford and Oldham were also considered to be
religious persons "well affected" toward the Puritan idea of
a National Church and the Puritan method of church reformation.   On the invitation of the Dorchester Adventurers, Conant removed from Nantasket to Cape Ann (1625), and undertook, in their behalf, the government of the plantation
there.   Lyford, by the same invitation, went to exercise
there the ministry to which he had been ordained in the National Church, and which the incorrigible Separatists of Plymouth had refused to recognize.   Oldham was also invited,
and to him the superintendence of trade between the new
colony and the Indians was offered; but he preferred to remain at Nantasket, trading with the Indians on his own account.

The whole story implies that there was an intimate connection between the Dorchester men and those Puritan Adventurers in London, whose conscientious antipathies had convinced them that "they should sin against God by building
up such a people" as those Pilgrims were who "renounced

---

[1] No mention is made of him in Bradford's History, nor is any trace of
him discoverable at Plymouth.   Probably he was there only as a visitor.   It
may be that he came over in the *Charity* with Lyford and Oldham, and, instead of remaining in Plymouth with them, went eastward in the same
vessel.

all universal, national, and diocesan churches." When Cushman wrote, "We have taken a patent for Cape Ann," the men of Plymouth assumed that the patent was for them, or at least for the great partnership in which they were members; and with great alacrity they went into the enterprise of making an establishment at Cape Ann. Immediately, though the season was inconvenient, they sent some of their men to build stages for the fishery there, and the next year they transferred their salt manufacture from Plymouth to the new plantation, that it might be near the fishery. But as soon as the Puritan majority of Adventurers had resolved to do nothing more for Plymouth, and to break up the partnership between themselves and the Planters, they seem to have determined on seizing Cape Ann as their own. "Some of Lyford and Oldham's friends, and their adherents," says Bradford—"some of the west country merchants," says Hubbard, showing incidentally that those "adherents" of Oldham's friends were the Dorchester Adventurers—"set out a ship on fishing on their own account; and getting the start of the ships that came to the plantation, they took away their [the Plymouth people's] stage and other necessary provisions that they had made for fishing at Cape Ann the year before at their great charge, and would not restore the same except they would fight for it." Captain Standish was there to assert the right of the Plymouth Planters, and was ready to fight for it. But wiser counsels prevailed against the martial spirit of the captain, and the dispute about that fishing-stage was compromised. Nevertheless the Plymouth memorial, addressed immediately afterward to his Majesty's Council for New England, made complaint against those Adventurers who had broken their compact with the Planters: "They have not only cast us off, but entered into a particular course of trading, and have by violence and force taken at their pleasure our possession at Cape Ann." The Pilgrims at Plymouth knew the Dorchester or Western Adventurers only as allies or "adherents" of those London Adventurers whose Puritan scrupulousness would not permit them to co-operate in building up a schismatic colony. Puritanism, not schism, was to characterize the new plantation, and the expectation was that such an enterprise would be in favor with God and with godly men.[1]

Yet the fishing settlement under Puritan patronage had its disasters. At the end of its second year, the Dorchester Adventurers were discouraged. Their expectations of present advantage were not likely to be realized. A large part of their three thousand pounds had been lost in unsuccessful voyages. The men whom they employed in their plantation, though unsuspected of any Brownist opinions, were not the men for such a work. "Being ill-chosen and ill-commanded, they fell into many disorders, and did the company little service." The well-intending Adventurers had begun a great work, without knowing—what Plymouth might have taught them—that the successful founders of a colony, instead of hiring whom they can find to go and "bear the brunt," must go in person, full of the inspiring conception, and ready to suffer and to die for it. Unwilling to expend more money upon the unremunerative enterprise, they abandoned it; and we may suppose that they did so not without something of self-reproach that they had permitted their veneration for the patriarch of Dorchester to involve them in so great a loss. Ought they not to have remembered that the good man, being a Puritan minister, could not be expected to have much wisdom in secular affairs? They took order for the sale of their joint-stock property and the breaking up of their plantation. Yet they "were so civil to those that were employed under them as to pay them all their wages, and proffered to transport them back whence they came." The majority of "the land-men" at Cape Ann accepted the offer and went home. "But a few of the most honest and indus-

---

[1] Compare Bradford's account of the conflict at Cape Ann (p. 196, 197) with Hubbard's (p. 110, 111).

trious resolved to stay behind, and to take charge of the cattle sent over the year before; which they performed accordingly."

One of those few was Roger Conant, whom the Adventurers had appointed to govern their plantation, and who had seen at Plymouth what could be done by perseverance. Convinced that every attempt to make a fishing station the nucleus of a colony would end in failure, he had already selected a more hopeful place for a new beginning. Through a brother of his in England, he was in communication with the venerated Puritan minister at Dorchester; and to him as well as to other friends he intimated that a settlement might be more advantageously begun at a place "called Naumkeag, a little to the westward" from Cape Ann, and "might prove a receptacle for such as *upon the account of religion* would be willing to begin a foreign plantation in this part of the world." Already, with Charles on the throne, and Laud his chief counselor in ecclesiastical affairs, men's hearts were "failing them for fear and for looking after those things that were coming" upon England; and Puritans as well as Separatists were beginning to think of foreign plantations "on the account of religion." What Conant proposed was a distinctively Puritan colony, where Puritan principles, abhorrent alike of popery and prelacy on the one hand, and of schism on the other, should have free course and be glorified. White, grieved at the failure of his first attempt, but not disheartened, wrote to Conant, assuring him that if he and three others, known to be honest and prudent men, who had been employed by the Adventurers,[1] would remain at Naumkeag, they should not be forsaken. He undertook to provide a patent for them at their new settlement; and "would send them whatever they should write

---

[1] The three were John Woodbury, John Balch, and Peter Palfrey. The learned and honored historian of New England is descended from that Palfrey who was one of the four Puritan founders of Massachusetts.

for, either men or provision, or goods wherewith to trade with the Indians." They accepted the offer; and yet, before any return had come from England, Lyford, having received "a loving invitation" to Virginia, and being "thither bound," persuaded almost the entire company to "recoil from their engagement for fear of the Indians and other inconveniences." But Conant, "as one inspired by some superior instinct," was firm. He "peremptorily declared his mind to wait the providence of God in that place where they now were—yea, though all the rest should forsake him." The "superior instinct" prevailed. Lyford went where his character was less likely to become notorious; and we know not how many went with him. But the three designated associates of Conant, "observing his confident resolution, at last concurred with him." They knew the danger, but they had the inspiration of a purpose above and beyond themselves, and "stayed to the hazard of their lives." [1]

John White, the patriarch, had not overestimated his own influence with the "knights and gentlemen about Dorchester," and he kept his word with Conant. He made such arrangements that "the Council established at Plymouth for the planting, ruling, ordering, and governing of New England," by a patent under their common seal (March 19 = 29, 1628), "bargained and sold" to a company, not of merchants, but of two knights and four gentlemen in the west of England, "that part of New England which lies between Merrimack and Charles rivers in the bottom of the Massachusetts Bay." [2] Then he brought the six patentees into negotiation, and ultimately into partnership, "with several other religious

---

[1] Such is Conant's own statement—the last phrase being his language—in a petition to the General Court of Massachusetts, dated May, 1671.

[2] More exactly, the territory conveyed by the patent included the land within the space of three miles south from any part of Charles River and three miles north from any part of the Merrimack, and also three miles south of the southernmost part of what was then called Massachusetts Bay. All former patents for lands within those limits seem to have been considered as void.

persons of like quality in and about London," among whom
some merchants were included as well as "knights and gentlemen." [1]   Already there had been among Puritans in Lincolnshire discourse about New England and the planting of
the Gospel there; and from Lincolnshire there had been "letters and messages to some in London and the west country."
There were no newspapers through which the thoughts that
were moving simultaneously in so many minds could find
public expression; nor was it the custom of those times to
hold conventions for the discussion of such a scheme.   But
the scheme of a Puritan colony was agitated in the methods
which were then possible; and the Company of Massachusetts
Bay was organized to prosecute the work of planting and
governing the territory for which it had a patent from his
Majesty's Council for New England.   John White was performing his promise to Roger Conant.

The new Company was in earnest.   It was not a commercial company looking for dividends on the capital invested;
it had higher aspirations.   It was rather a society for Puritan colonization, and the end it aimed at was not gain to its
members, but achievement for the kingdom of God.   Having
obtained, by purchase from the Plymouth Council, the owner-
ship of an adequate territory, it was undertaking to plant in
that territory a Christian state after the Puritan theory.
Some men were "offering the help of their purses if fit men
might be procured to go over," and the question was, whether any such men—"fit" to be the founders of Puritan civil-

---

[1] The original patentees "about Dorchester" were "Sir Henry Boswell,
Sir John Young, *knights*, Thomas Southcoat, John Humphrey, John Endicott, and Simon Whetcomb, *gentlemen*."   Some of the "religious persons"
in and about London were such as Sir Richard Saltonstall, John Winthrop,
Isaac Johnson, Matthew Cradock, Increase Nowell, and (not to extend
the catalogue) Theophilus Eaton, afterward governor of a New England colony, and Thomas Goffe, who had been one of the Adventurers for the
Plymouth Pilgrims, and had found their Brownism too much for his Puritan
conscience.

ization in the New England wilderness—could be procured.
Captain John Endicott, one of the original patentees, " a man
well known to divers persons of good note," was judged
" fit ;" and being invited to lead and govern the proposed
plantation, he " manifested much willingness to accept the
offer." The pioneer expedition was soon fitted out ; and the
Abigail, freighted with forty-six and a half tons of goods,
and having for passengers Captain John Endicott and his
wife, with perhaps forty more, sailed from Weymouth (the
port of Dorchester) for Naumkeag (June 20=30, 1628).

Arriving at his destination, Endicott, in the name of the
new Company which had undertaken to " erect a new colony
on the old foundation," assumed the government. He found,
at first, some discontent on the part of the old planters, who
feared some encroachment on their rights ; but, " by the prudent moderation of Mr. Conant," the disagreement between
them and the new-comers was " quietly composed." In memory of that pacification, the plantation at Naumkeag received
not long afterward a Hebrew name from the Old Testament—
SALEM, signifying Peace. The leading men, both of the old
Planters and of those who came with the new governor,
were of one mind—religiously engaged in the great design
for which the Massachusetts Company was formed.

All the preparation which Conant and his few companions had been able to make for the reinforcement was inadequate. The population to be provided for was increased by
a body of " servants " who came over, either in the *Abigail*
or in some other vessel, to work for the Company. Important
as their labor was to the colony, it could not feed them with
food convenient for them after the privations of their voyage,
nor shelter them as their condition required. " Arriving
there in an uncultivated desert, many of them, for want of
wholesome diet and convenient lodgings, were seized with
the scurvy and other distempers, which shortened many of
their days, and prevented many of the rest from performing
any great matter of labor that year for advancing the work

Jo Endicott

of the plantation." [1]   While the colony was in that distress, its governor, understanding that at Plymouth there was a physician "that had some skill that way, and had cured divers of the scurvy and others of other diseases," wrote to the older colony for help.   Deacon Samuel Fuller had long been the beloved physician of the Pilgrim church.   Certainly he was experienced in the practice of his art; perhaps he had acquired at Leyden the medical science of that age.   He was sent to the relief of the sufferers at Naumkeag; and his service there was the beginning of affectionate intercourse between the two colonies, the liberalized Separatists of the one and the godly Puritans of the other having learned that the differences which so alienated each party from the other in their native country were comparatively unimportant in New England.   The frank and generous letter which Governor Endicott wrote to Governor Bradford after Fuller's visit is a significant fact in our story; for a letter is sometimes as much of a fact in history as a coronation or a battle.   A transcript of the letter (May 11 = 21, 1629) will be more to our purpose than any description of it could be:

"*To the Worshipful and my right worthy Friend,* WILLIAM BRADFORD, Esq., *Governor of New Plymouth, these:*

"RIGHT WORTHY SIR, — It is a thing not usual that servants to one Master and of the same household should be strangers; I assure you I desire it not—nay, to speak more plainly, I can not be so to you.   God's people are marked with one and the same mark, and sealed with one and the same seal, and have, for the main, one and the same heart guided by one and the same Spirit of truth; and where this is there can be no discord—nay, here must needs be sweet harmony. The same request with you I make unto the Lord, that we may, as Christian brethren, be united by a heavenly and unfeigned love, bending all our hearts and forces in furthering

---

[1] Hubbard, p. 110.

a work beyond our strength, with reverence and fear fastening our eyes always on Him that only is able to direct and prosper all our ways.

"I acknowledge myself much bound to you for your kind love and care in sending Mr. Fuller among us; and I rejoice much that I am by him satisfied touching your judgments of the outward form of God's worship. It is, as far as I can yet gather, no other than is warranted by the evidence of truth, and the same which I have professed and maintained ever since the Lord in mercy revealed himself to me; being very far different from the common report that hath been spread of you touching that particular. But God's children must not look for less here below, and it is the great mercy of God that he strengthens them to go through with it.

"I shall not need at this time to be tedious unto you; for, God willing, I purpose to see your face shortly. In the mean time, I humbly take my leave of you, committing you to the Lord's blessed protection, and rest.

"Your assured loving friend and servant,

"JOHN ENDICOTT."

It appears, then, that no sooner had Endicott and the Puritans who came with him begun to breathe the air of the free wilderness, than they began to lose the antipathy of their party against Separatism, and to see that the theory of the Pilgrims concerning "the outward form of God's worship"[1] was "warranted by the evidence of truth." But, meanwhile, the Massachusetts Company in England was watchfully

---

[1] In the language of those times, and especially of those parties, "the outward form of God's worship" included much more than the particular disputes about a certain book of printed prayers imposed on all worshipers by the state. It was the more comprehensive question concerning "the outward form"—the constitution and order—of the worshiping assembly or society, or, in other words, the nature and organization of the visible church. Such, evidently, was the meaning of the phrase in Endicott's letter, and in the talk between him and Deacon Fuller.

guarding itself against complicity with Separatism.   Its
members were loyal to the Church of England, praying and
(as they had opportunity) working for its welfare; though
they were constrained to bear witness, in one way or another, against the superstitious ceremonies, the popish vestments,
the stinted and ill-reformed liturgy, the prelatical government, and the canon law.   To them no less than to the Archbishop of Canterbury a renunciation of membership in the
National Church was schism, and schism was sin.   It was,
therefore, without any disingenuousness or self-deception that
they protested against the "suspicious and scandalous reports raised" in disparagement of their undertaking, "as if,
under the color of planting a colony, they intended to raise
and erect a seminary of faction and separation."   It was in
all honesty that they imputed such reports to "the jealousy
of some distempered mind"—or to "a malicious plot of men
ill-affected to religion, endeavoring, by casting the undertakers into the jealousy of state, to shut them out of those
advantages which otherwise they might expect from the continuance of authority." [1]

Doubtless, then, it was with a hearty dislike of Separatism,
and with an unfeigned adherence to the principle of ecclesiastical Nationalism, that the associated Puritans who were
attempting to found a colony in New England asked and
obtained from Charles I., in the fourth year of his reign
(March 4=14, 1629), a confirmation of their patent, and a
royal charter of incorporation, with ample powers for the colonization and government of their territory.   What had been
only a partnership or voluntary society became a body politic, entitled "The Governor and Company of Massachusetts
Bay in New England."   It proceeded under its charter without any change in its organization or its plans.   Its records
show that, before the date of the charter, large preparations
for another expedition were in progress; and in a catalogue

---

[1] The "Planter's Plea," in Young's "Chron. of Massachusetts," p. 15.

of necessaries which the Company was "to provide to send for New England," the first and most conspicuous item is "MINISTERS."

A letter, written twelve days before the date of the charter, by Matthew Cradock, Governor of the Company, informed Endicott that the Company had been greatly enlarged since he left England, and that three vessels, and perhaps another, were to sail in a few days with supplies and reinforcements for the colony. To us who read it to-day, some parts of that letter seem almost like a letter from the executive of a missionary society to a distant missionary. After some business details, the Governor of the Company said to the Governor of the Colony: "We are very confident of your best endeavors for the general good, and we doubt not that God will in mercy give a blessing upon our labors. We trust you will not be unmindful of the main end of our plantation, . . . to bring the Indians to the knowledge of the Gospel; which that it may be the speedier and better effected, the earnest desire of our whole Company is that you have a diligent and watchful eye over our own people, that they live unblamable and without reproof, and demean themselves justly and courteously toward the Indians, thereby to draw them to affect our persons and thereby our religion; as also" that you "endeavor to get some of their children to train up to reading, and consequently to religion, while they are young; and herein, to young or old, to omit no good opportunity that may tend to bring them out of that woeful state they are now in—in which case our predecessors in this land sometime were. . . . But God, who out of the boundless ocean of his mercy hath showed pity and compassion to our land, is all-sufficient, and can bring this to pass which we now desire in that country likewise. Only let us not be wanting on our parts, now we are called to this work of the Lord's; neither, having put our hands to the plow, let us look back, but let us go on cheerfully, and depend upon God for a blessing upon our labors."

In that connection, the letter announces the Company's resolution "to send over two ministers at the least" in the expedition which was so nearly ready; and it adds, for the satisfaction of Endicott, "Those we send you shall be by the approbation of Mr. White, of Dorchester, and Mr. Davenport."[1] It was in accordance with the Puritan ideas which were the bond of union to the Company, that the supply of ministers to its colony should be provided and controlled by the corporation.

A resolution had been taken by the Company to send "two ministers at the least;" but whom should they send? Whom could they find that would be at once fit for so important a mission, and willing to go? They must take care not to send another Lyford. Five weeks after Governor Cradock's letter to Endicott, "intimation was given" at a meeting of the Company, "by letters from Mr. Isaac Johnson," the largest contributor to the common stock, and one of the most efficient promoters of the design, "that one Mr. Higginson, of Leicester, an able minister," was willing to go on that mission.[2] The minister thus nominated was not unknown to members of the Company; for he was a brother-in-law of Theophilus Eaton, and Increase Nowell (present at the meeting) was his cousin. He, then, "being approved," says the record, " for a reverend, grave minister, fit for our present oc-

---

[1] The entire letter is in Young's " Chron. of Massachusetts," p. 131–137.

[2] Isaac Johnson's seat was at Clipsham, in the county of Rutland, and it may be assumed that, living so near to Leicester, he knew Higginson personally as well as by reputation.   Johnson's standing in England appears from the fact that his wife, the Lady Arbella, was a daughter of the Earl of Lincoln.   His commendation, even if Higginson had been unknown to the rest of the Company, was enough.   About eighteen months later, he and his wife found their graves in Massachusetts, the Lady Arbella at Salem, the honored and lamented Isaac Johnson, "a holy man and wise," at Boston.   His grave, on the lot which he had chosen for his dwelling-place, gave, as tradition tells us, a sort of consecration to what became the first burial-ground in that town, the one now known as "the King's Chapel Burial-ground.—"Chron. of Massachusetts," p. 317, 318.

casions," Mr. John Humphrey, one of the most eminent members of the Company, active from the first conception of the enterprise at Dorchester, was requested " to ride presently to Leicester, and, if Mr. Higginson may conveniently be had to go this present voyage," to deal with him.   The first of the conditions proposed by the Company as a basis for negotiation with Higginson was that his removal should be " without scandal to that people;" for though he had once been the incumbent of one of the parish churches in Leicester, his Puritanism had advanced to the stage of nonconformity, and he was at that time a lecturer, supported by voluntary contributions from former parishioners and other friends. Those friends, therefore, were to be consulted; and his removal must be with their approbation.   Mr. Hildersham was also to be consulted—the venerable arch-Puritan of Ashby-de-la-Zouch, who had been more than once silenced for nonconformity, and then restored—who had for the same cause been imprisoned by the High Commission, fined two thousand pounds, degraded from the ministry, excommunicated, and then again restored because the Earl of Huntington was his kinsman.   His approbation must be had before making the contract.   So thoroughly did the Company of Massachusetts Bay, even from its beginning, identify itself with the Puritan party in the Church of England, and with the most advanced and obnoxious leaders of that party.

How Mr. Humphrey's ride to Leicester prospered appears from the result.   The message which he bore seems to have been enforced by some communication from the patriarchal White; and Higginson, who had reason, perhaps, to expect a visit from officers of the High Commission rather than so friendly an invitation, " looked at it as a call from God, and (as Peter looked at the message from Cornelius) a motion which he could not withstand."[1]   Other ministers were found willing to go over with him; and when the expedition, after

---

[1] Acts xi., 17; Hubbard, p. 112.

many delays, set forth, the official letter from the Company to Governor Endicott introduced them to him and to the colony. After announcing the confirmation of title to the territory, and the extension of power to govern all its inhabitants which had been obtained from his Majesty " under the broad seal of England," and before touching upon any other matter, the Company proceeded to instruct the governor of its colony concerning those missionaries : " For that the propagating of the Gospel is the thing we do profess above all to be our aim in settling this plantation, we have been careful to make plentiful provision of godly ministers; by whose faithful preaching, godly conversation, and exemplary life we trust not only those of our own nation will be built up in the knowledge of God, but also the Indians may, in God's appointed time, be reduced to the obedience of the Gospel of Christ. One of them is well known to yourself, namely, Mr. Skelton, whom we have the rather desired to bear a part in this work, for that we are informed yourself have formerly received much good by his ministry. . . . Another is Mr. Higginson, a grave man, and of worthy commendations. . . . The third is Mr. Bright, sometime trained up under Mr. Davenport. . . . We pray you, accommodate them all with necessaries as well as you may; and in convenient time let there be houses built them, according to the agreement we have made with them. We doubt not but these gentlemen, your ministers, will agree lovingly together; and for cherishing of love betwixt them, we pray you carry yourself impartially to all. For the manner of their exercising their ministry, and teaching both our own people and the Indians, we leave that to themselves, hoping they will make God's Word the rule of their actions, and mutually agree in the discharge of their duties. And because their doctrine will hardly be well esteemed whose persons are not reverenced, we desire that both by your own example, and by commanding all others to do the like, our ministers may receive due honor."

Those three gentlemen, then, were to be the established

clergy of the colony—" our ministers," as employed by us and responsible to us—" your ministers," as you are to have the benefit of their ministry.   After instructing the colonial governor on many other subjects, the Company has more to say about its clergymen, and his duty as governor over them: " We have, in the former part of our letter, certified you of the good hopes we have of the love and unanimous agreement of our ministers, they having declared themselves to us to be of one judgment, and to be fully agreed on the manner how to exercise their ministry, which we hope will be by them accordingly performed.   Yet because it is often found that some busy persons, led more by their will than any good warrant out of God's Word, take opportunities by needless questions to stir up strife, and by that means to beget a question and bring men to declare some difference in judgment — most commonly in things indifferent, from which small beginnings great mischiefs have followed — we pray you and the rest of the council, if any such disputes shall happen among you, that you suppress them, and be careful to maintain peace and unity."

Religious uniformity, then, was to be maintained in the Puritan colony by its governor and council, under the authority of the Company.   No theory of religious liberty found entertainment in the minds of those earnest and godly men when they planned their heroic enterprise.   In their Utopia there was no room for the propagation or assertion of erroneous opinions, even about " things indifferent."   Therefore, in the Utopian commonwealth which they were calling into existence, " needless questions that stir up strife" were not to be permitted ; and a godly magistracy, abhorrent alike of superstition and of schismatic reformation, was to judge as to the needfulness or needlessness of any question on which there might be a strife of opinions.   In the plantation of the Massachusetts Bay, " such disputes" were to be suppressed ; and Governor Endicott, with the council which the Company in this letter assigned to him, must " be careful

to maintain peace and unity." The voice of one crying in
the wilderness to proclaim a theory of "soul-liberty"—if
such a voice should utter itself within the Company's domain
—must be stifled.

The letter gives yet another glimpse of the views which
the Company held about ministers in its colony. An unfortunate Separatist—one "Mr. Ralph Smith, a minister"—had
desired passage in one of the Company's ships, hoping, perhaps, to escape, by fleeing into New England, the penalties
from which the Pilgrims fled into Holland, and which the
laws of England provided against such crimes as they were
guilty of. His desire "was granted him," said the Company,
"before we understood of his difference in judgment in some
things from our ministers." What could they do? The permission might have been revoked; but, alas! his goods were
already on shipboard before they knew what he was. Such
being the case, they were too magnanimous to refuse him a
passage—perhaps they were also in too much of a hurry.
Yet the governor must be instructed to be on his guard
against that anomalous minister. "Forasmuch as from
hence it is feared there may grow some distraction among
you if there should be any siding (though we have a very
good opinion of his honesty), we shall not, we hope, offend
in charity to fear"—and to provide against—"the worst that
may grow from their different judgments." As if they said,
We can not but anticipate the conflict that may arise between our ministers and this interloper who disowns and de-
nounces all national churches. "We have therefore thought
fit to give you this order, that unless he will be conformable
to our government, you suffer him not to remain within the
limits of our grant." What they were endeavoring was to
open a safe refuge for clergy and laity who could not in conscience conform to the ecclesiastical regulations in England;
but the minister who would dwell within the limits of their
territory must "be conformable to their government." No
doubt, much may be said to justify their fears and to excuse

their precautions; but the fact is nevertheless important to our story.[1]

At last, after the many delays incident to the fitting out of such an expedition, three vessels, strongly manned and heavily armed, set sail, with one hundred and ninety-two passengers, and "all manner of munition and provision for the plantation."[2]   Among the passengers on one of those

---

[1] The letter, preserved in the archives of Massachusetts, was printed by Dr. Young in his "Chron. of Massachusetts," p. 141–171. An earnest care for the moral and religious welfare of the colony, and especially of those who were employed in the service of the Company, is manifest in many passages besides those relating to the ministers.   The servants of the Company were to be distributed into families, each with its chief, who was to maintain "morning and evening family duties," and to hold a watchful eye over his household, "that disorders may be prevented and ill weeds nipped before they take too great a head."   All those servants must "be kept to labor, as the only means to reduce them to civil, yea, a godly life, and to keep youth from falling into many enormities."   All inhabitants, as well as the Company's servants, were enjoined to "surcease their labor every Saturday throughout the year at three of the clock in the afternoon," and to "spend the rest of that day in catechising and preparation for the Sabbath, as the ministers should direct." The old Planters, before Endicott's arrival, had engaged in the planting of tobacco, and were still desiring to pursue that business.   On that point the Puritan feeling in London was strong.   The letter spoke of tobacco-planting as "a trade by this whole Company generally disavowed, and utterly disclaimed by some of the greatest Adventurers among us, who absolutely declared themselves unwilling to have any hand in this plantation if we intended to cherish or permit the planting thereof, in any other kind than for a man's private use for mere necessity."   Endicott and his council were therefore instructed that though they might tolerate for a time the planting of that weed by the old Planters (but by nobody else) under proper restrictions, they must have "an especial care, with as much conveniency as may be, utterly to suppress the planting of it except for mere necessity."   At the same time there was a touch of moral suasion in the statement that the price of tobacco in the London market was not much more than enough to pay the freight and duty, and that, "there being such great quantities made in other places," there was little hope of its becoming more profitable to New England producers.

[2] The three ships were "the *Talbot*, a good and strong ship of 300 tons and nineteen pieces of ordnance, and served with thirty mariners;" the

three vessels were several families of the Pilgrim Church, who had come from Leyden, and whose destination was to Plymouth.   The three ministers employed by the Company were assigned one to each vessel.   By their contract with the Company, they were under obligation "to do their endeavor in their places of the ministry, as well in preaching and catechising, as also in teaching or causing to be taught the Company's servants and their children, as also the savages and their children, whereby to their uttermost to further the main end of this plantation," which was declared to be, " by the assistance of Almighty God, the conversion of the savages."   On the other side, the Company contracted to pay each of the three an outfit of twenty pounds—wherewith to purchase "apparel and other necessities for the voyage"—ten pounds for the purchase of books, which should remain for the use of his successor, and a salary of twenty pounds annually for three years.   In addition to the little stipend, each of them was to have, for himself and his family, " necessaries of diet, housing, and firewood," as well as transportation to New England, and a free passage homeward if at the end of three years he should not desire to remain.   A parsonage house was to be built, "and certain lands allotted thereunto," for each minister and his successors.   At the end of three years, each was to receive a hundred acres of land as his own; and at the end of seven years, should he remain so long, another hundred.   Each of them had also an assurance that, if he should die in New England, the Company would provide for his wife and children during her widowhood and the continuance of her abode in their colony.   Higginson, in consideration of his eight children, was to have

George, of the same tonnage and an equal number of seamen, with an armament of twenty guns : and the _Lion's Whelp_ (or _Lion_), " a neat and nimble ship" of only 120 tons, but carrying eight guns and " many mariners."   England being then at war with Spain, merchants' vessels were necessarily armed vessels.   The thirty-five Plymouth people seem to have been passengers in the _Lion_, which was commanded by their tried friend William Pierce.

thirty pounds instead of twenty for his outfit, and an addition of ten pounds annually to his stipend.[1]

The incidents of the *Talbot's* voyage were carefully recorded by Higginson, who was assigned to that vessel, as Skelton was to the *George*, and Bright to the *Lion*. On a Saturday (April 25 = May 5, 1629), she dropped down the Thames from Gravesend with only a faint breeze; and near the mouth of the river they rested that night, and "kept Sabbath the next day." At the end of another week, the ship, after sundry adversities, and "with much tacking and turning," had not yet entered the Strait of Dover, but had been lying three days where a strong southwest wind, "causing her to dance," gave her passengers their first experience of sea-sickness, and there her passengers again "kept Sabbath" (May 3 = 13). The progress of two days more brought her "over against Yarmouth about eight of the clock at night." At that port some final arrangements were to be made for the long voyage, and the passengers had the opportunity of going ashore. Saturday saw them again on shipboard, and there, on the next day, they kept their third Sabbath, under the ministration of Higginson. He, after the morning service with his fellow-passengers, went ashore by invitation to preach at Yarmouth, where Captain Burleigh—"Captain of Yarmouth Castle, a grave, comely gentleman, and of great age," who had been a sea-captain in Queen Elizabeth's time, and had been "prisoner in Spain three years"[2]—expressed, with hospitable kindness, his interest in the voyage, and "earnestly desired to be certified of their

---

[1] Young, "Chron. of Massachusetts," p. 207–212.

[2] He was thus described by Winthrop, i., 4, who adds the information that twenty years before, that old man and three of his sons were captains in an expedition sent by Prince Henry (then Prince of Wales) to explore the coast of Guiana. Men who had fought the Spaniards in the time of Queen Bess, and whose notions of the difference between Romanism and Protestantism had been made more definite by an experience of captivity in Spain, were likely to share in the antipathies and aspirations of the Puritans.

safe arrival in New England, and of the state of the country." On Monday, "the *Lion* having taken in all her provision for passengers," they' sailed with a favoring wind;
but it was not till two days later that the record could be
made, "We left our dear native soil of England (May 13 =
23) behind us, . . . and launched the same day a great way
into the main ocean."

One author tells us : "When they came to the Land's End,
Mr. Higginson, calling up his children and other passengers
unto the stern of the ship to take their last sight of England,
said, 'We will not say, as the Separatists were wont to say
at their leaving of England, Farewell, Babylon! farewell,
Rome! but we will say, Farewell, dear England, farewell the
church of God in England and all the Christian friends there.
We do not go to New England as Separatists from the Church
of England, though we can not but separate from the corruptions in it; but we go to practice the positive part of
church reformation, and propagate the Gospel in America.'"
We may not affirm, without better authority, that there was
just that scene enacted on the deck of the *Talbot;* but we
know that the words thus ascribed to Higginson might have
been spoken by him, then and there, with perfect sincerity.
The Separatist minister, Ralph Smith, was among the passengers, and for that reason those words were more likely to
be spoken. They express the spirit and intention both of
the corporation which was planting the colony of Massachusetts Bay, and of the nonconforming ministers whom it was
sending forth to make that a Christian and a Puritan colony.
Those ministers, and the Company that employed them, were
not Ritualists—they had small reverence for any imposed
forms of prayer; they were not Episcopalians; but they
were loyal to "the church of God in England" as a Nation-

---

¹ The *Talbot*, commanded by Master Beecher, and the *Lion*, commanded
by Master William Pierce, sailed together. . . . The *George* had been dispatched some ten days earlier, "having some special and urgent cause of
hastening her passage."

al Church.   They were going to plant the church of God in
another country where they could "practice the positive part
of church reformation" without making a schism, where the
Act of Uniformity would have no force, and where bishops
and High Commission could not oppress them.

Their first Lord's day at sea was four weeks after their embarkation.   On that day (May 17=27) it was discovered that
two of Higginson's children were ill with small-pox, that terrible contagion having been "brought into the ship by one
Mr. Browne," who had the disease when he embarked with the
rest at Gravesend.   One of the two children, Mary, about five
years of age, died the next Tuesday; the other, Samuel, at
last recovered.   Afflicted by sickness and death, and at the
same time encountering adverse winds, the passengers agreed
to "keep a solemn day of fasting and prayer."   In the services of that day, Smith, the Separatist minister, was permitted to assist.   Higginson's record of that day is characteristic not only of himself but of his fellow-voyagers.   "There
being two ministers in the ship, Mr. Smith and myself, we
endeavored, together with others, to consecrate the day, as
a solemn fasting and humiliation to Almighty God, as a
furtherance of our present work.   And it pleased God the
ship was becalmed all day, so that we were freed from any
encumbrance.   And as soon as we had done prayers (behold
the goodness of God!), about seven o'clock at night, the wind
turned to northeast, and we had a fair gale that night as a
manifest evidence of the Lord's hearing our prayers.   I heard
some of the mariners say they thought this was the first sea-
fast that ever was kept."   Another fast-day they had before
the voyage ended.   While keeping their six Sabbaths on
the Atlantic, they found the Sunday weather, in almost every
instance, favorable to their religious services—as if the sea
itself, and the winds, were resting with them.   Their seventh Sabbath was in the harbor of Cape Ann.   The next day
(June 29=July 9, 1629), they were piloted through "the curious and difficult entrance into the spacious harbor of Naum-

keag," wondering, as they passed along, "to behold so many
islands replenished with thick wood and high trees, and
many fair green pastures." The *George* was already there,
having arrived seven days earlier.

At the end of the journal, Higginson recorded, with thankful mind, a summary of "divers things" which, in his review of the voyage, seemed to demand a devout acknowledgment of God's providence over him and his companions:

"First, through God's blessing, our passage was short and
speedy; for whereas we had a thousand leagues ... to sail from
Old to New England, we performed the same in six weeks
and three days" from Yarmouth to Naumkeag. "Secondly,
our passage was comfortable and easy for the most part,
having ordinarily fair and moderate wind." . . . "Thirdly,
our passage was also healthful to our passengers," for, notwithstanding the small-pox, and though "we were, in all
reason, in wonderful danger all the way, our ship being
greatly crowded with passengers," there were only three
deaths on the voyage.

"Fourthly, our passage was both pleasant and profitable.
For we received instruction and delight in beholding the
wonders of the Lord in the deep waters—sometimes seeing
the sea around us appearing with a terrible countenance, and,
as it were, full of high hills and deep valleys, and sometimes
it appeared as a plain and even meadow. And ever and
anon we saw divers kinds of fishes sporting in the great
waters, great grampuses and huge whales, going by companies and spouting up water streams. Those that love their
own chimney-corner, and dare not go beyond their own
town's end, shall never have the honor to see these wonderful works of Almighty God.

"Fifthly, we had a pious and Christian-like passage; for I
suppose passengers shall seldom find a company of more religious, honest, and kind seamen than we had. We constantly served God morning and evening by reading and expounding a chapter, singing, and prayer; and the Sabbath was

solemnly kept, by adding to the former, preaching twice and catechising.   And in our great need we kept two solemn fasts, and found a gracious effect.   Let all that love and use fasting and praying take notice that it is as prevailable by sea as by land, wheresoever it is faithfully performed.   Besides, the shipmaster and his company used every night to set their eight and twelve o'clock watches with singing and a psalm, and prayer that was not read out of a book."

It was for the privilege of such prayer—"prayer not read out of a book"—that Puritans were crossing the Atlantic. When out of England, whether on the ocean or in the wilderness, they felt themselves beyond the jurisdiction of the laws and the hierarchy that were oppressing the Church of England.   The "plentiful provision of godly ministers" consigned to Governor Endicott was distributed—Skelton and Higginson to care for the moral and spiritual welfare of the settlement at Naumkeag, and Bright to another plantation which was to be immediately begun.

The superfluous and undesired Ralph Smith, regarded as dangerous to the Puritan colony because of his Separatism, had been required to promise "under his hand, that he would not exercise his ministry within the limits of the patent without the express leave of the governor on the spot."[1] Whether he obtained from Endicott a license to preach is not known, but, with or without such license, he went to Nantasket, where Oldham had his trading station, and where a few other "straggling people" lived, who were perhaps thought to be in no great danger of being perverted from right ways by his preaching.   He found there no considerable opening for the exercise of his ministry; but, being there, he was soon found by some of the Plymouth people whose business had brought them thither in a boat, and who were not afraid of him.   He could not but be glad to become acquainted with men who knew, in their own experience, what it was to bear

[1] Hutchinson, i., 10.

the reproach and suspicions that rested on him.   "Weary of
being in that uncouth place, and in a poor house that would
neither keep him nor his goods dry," he begged of them a
passage to Plymouth.   "They had no order for any such
thing;" and they might have remembered how Allerton was
blamed for bringing poor Rogers over from England.   But
"seeing him to be a grave man, and understanding that he
had been a minister," they "presumed and brought him,"
and with him "such things as they could well carry" of his
goods.   At Plymouth "he was kindly entertained and housed,"
and "the rest of his goods and servants were sent for."   Immediately he became a helper to Brewster, preaching in the
exercise of prophesying.   When the church had become acquainted with his character and his gifts, and he had become
a member of their brotherhood, he was "chosen into the
ministry."   Thus, at last, the Pilgrim Church had its pastor—
the humble yet not unworthy successor of its lamented Robinson.   He was not distinguished by eminent gifts; he was
not regarded as equal to his colleague Brewster, either in
wisdom for government or in discourse for edification; but
he continued in office five or six years, and then resigned it,
"partly by his own willingness, as thinking it too heavy a
burden, and partly by the persuasion of others."

While Smith, under the reproach of Separatism, was finding his way to the Separatist colony, Skelton and Higginson,
as Puritans, were beginning to "practice the positive part of
church reformation" at Salem.   Having no occasion to inquire how the endowments which the National Church in
their native country had inherited from the ages before the
Reformation were to be preserved and made available for the
evangelization of the whole people, they arrived, before they
were aware, at new conclusions.   Governor Endicott, as we
have seen, had entered upon a fraternal correspondence with
the Governor of Plymouth, and, in his Christian intercourse
with Deacon Fuller, he had learned that the Plymouth Separatists were not so far out of the right way as he had once

thought. Probably the studies of the two clergymen were aided by conference with the governor, and with other intelligent and earnest men among the planters. The result was a conviction on their part that their appointment by the Company in London, though it might give them authority as chaplains to the Company's servants, did not place them in exactly right relations to the church of God in Salem, and that something must be done to supply that defect.

Accordingly it was concluded that the ministers must be elected and introduced into office by the Christian people among whom they were to be overseers. The positive part of church reformation was to begin at that point. In strict conformity with Puritan ideas, the governor took the lead. "It pleased God," says a contemporaneous letter, "to move the heart of our governor to set apart a solemn day of humiliation for the choice of a pastor and teacher;" and that was a great day in Salem—no buying and selling, no servile labor nor vain recreation, was permitted on that day. "The former part of the day being spent in prayer and teaching," the afternoon was given to the solemnities of the election. In the letter just mentioned, the whole transaction is described. "The persons thought on"—Skelton and Higginson—"who had been ministers in England," and who had been in some way named as candidates, were requested to give their views concerning the way in which God calls men to an official ministry of the Word. "They acknowledged there was a twofold calling: the one an inward calling, when the Lord moved the heart of a man to take that calling upon him and fitted him with gifts for the same; the second (the outward calling) was from the people, when a company of believers are joined together in covenant to walk together in all the ways of God." The people, thus convened by their governor, knew that the two men before them had the qualifications prescribed by the apostle Paul as necessary to a bishop.[1] They approved the answers which had shown that

---

[1] 1 Tim. iii., 1–7.

those two men expected to derive their right as official ministers of Christ in the church, not from a prelatical or hierarchical vocation, but only from an inward call from God's
Spirit together with an outward call from the church itself.
So they were ready to give their voices in the election of
their pastor and teacher.

"Their choice was after this manner: Every fit member
wrote, in a note, his name whom the Lord moved him to
think was fit for a pastor, and so, likewise, whom they would
have for teacher." When the votes were counted, it appeared (what was doubtless arranged and understood beforehand)
that the majority of voices " was for Mr. Skelton to be pastor,
and Mr. Higginson to be teacher." But a mere declaration
of the choice was not regarded as introducing the chosen
into their offices. An apostolic ordination must follow, for
it was not to be admitted that the "holy orders" which
these men had received in the National Church of Old England could invest them with any ecclesiastical power or office in free New England. Not much of ritual pomp was
there in the ordination of the chosen pastor and teacher.
"They accepting the choice, Mr. Higginson, and three or four
more of the gravest members of the church, laid their hands
on Mr. Skelton, using prayers therewith. This being done,
then there was imposition of hands on Mr. Higginson"
in like manner. Such was the first New England ordination.[1]

A first step had been taken in the positive part of church
reformation. It seems a long stride, but we must not regard
it as an intentional or conscious departure from the Puritan
theory. The right of the godly people in every parish to
choose their own minister—especially if it be done under the
supervision of a godly magistracy—might well be recognized

---

[1] Letter from Charles Gott to Governor Bradford, dated "Salem, July 30,
anno 1629," in Bradford's "Letter-Book" (Mass. Historical Collections, iii.,
67, 68).

and established in founding a Puritan commonwealth, for it was one of those rights which hierarchical usurpation had taken away, and which the unfinished English Reformation had not restored.   It was evident, also, to many a Puritan mind, that ordination ought to follow, and not precede, that outward calling by the people which was to recognize the inward calling by the Spirit of God.   The Salem Puritans, then, in formally electing their own ministers, and in their solemn ordination of the ministers whom they had chosen, were not conscious of separating themselves from the Puritan party in the church of their native country.   They were only doing what the principle of thorough church reformation seemed to require of them in their circumstances.   But their ecclesiastical organization was not completed by what they had done in that assembly.   An election of elders and deacons was proposed, and candidates were named; but, on a suggestion then made, it was judged best to wait for the arrival of another company from England, and so that day's transactions were ended.

On further consideration, it seems to have been thought that the proposed delay was, for some reason, inexpedient; and soon "another day of humiliation" was appointed for the election of elders and deacons.   But, in the mean time, such questions as whether there were a church in Salem— and, if so, who its members were, and how they were to be distinguished and identified—must be disposed of.   Were all the nominally Christian people—the christened people— who dwelt in Salem, the church of Salem?   If only the godly were the church, and were to participate in church affairs, who was to divide between the godly and the worldly; and how were the ungodly to be hindered from taking every thing into their own hands?   The necessity of constituting a church, more distinctly and formally than had yet been done, became apparent.   Neither the ministers nor the governor "had as yet waded so far into the controversy of church discipline as to be very positive in any of those points " on which the dispute between Puritans and Separatists turned. Yet, taking such hints as they found in the New Testament, they deemed it "necessary for those who intended to be of the church solemnly to enter into a covenant engagement one with another, in the presence of God, to walk together before him according to his Word." Of course they were not ignorant that Separatists in England formed their schismatic churches in that way—but what then? They were not in England, but in the promised land of Massachusetts Bay, and were already separated from the National Church of their native country, not by schism, but by a thousand leagues of ocean; and in what other way could the Church of Christ in Salem come into a definite form and organization? After they had come to such a conclusion concerning the church, another conclusion was inevitable, namely, that, in the right order, the church must be constituted before and not after the election and ordination of its officers.

In accordance with these conclusions, Higginson, at the desire of others, drew up a form in which the thirty persons selected to be the first members of a church might with one voice make profession of their faith and engage to walk together in obedience to Christ. Thirty copies of the form were written out, that each of the thirty whose faith and mutual covenant were to be publicly expressed might consider it well. Then, on the appointed day of humiliation, they, in those words, declared to each other and before all their Christian faith and hope, and their engagements to each other and to Christ as members of one church; and thereupon the pastor and the teacher were, by the constituted church, called and "ordained to their several offices" as before. The former ordination had made them the ministers of a parish; this made them the presbyter-bishops of a New Testament church.[1]

---

[1] The account of that second ordination is given both by Hubbard (p. 118, 119) and by Morton. It is difficult to think that either of them could have

I i

.

It had been arranged that the transactions of that day should be consummated by a formal recognition of fraternity and mutual confidence between the church that was coming into form and organization in the Puritan colony and the Separatist church at Plymouth.   Among the leading members of the Massachusetts corporation in London, were some who had withdrawn their patronage from the old colony lest " they should sin against God in building up such a people " stained with the guilt of renouncing all national churches ; and they had undertaken to have a colony in which there should be no place for Separatism.   But no sooner was their plantation begun than the leading men among their Planters learned to honor the saintly and heroic qualities, and all that was essential in the church polity, of those Pilgrim pioneers who had borne so long the odious name of Brownists.   A delegation from Plymouth was expected that day at Salem. Adverse winds hindered the voyage of the delegates across the great bay ; and the business of the day went forward without " their direction and assistance," which had been desired because Plymouth was supposed to have the wisdom of experience in the conduct of a self-governed church.   But later in the day, before the solemnities of ordination were concluded, the " messengers of Plymouth church," Governor Bradford himself being one of them, " came into the assem-

---

been mistaken.   After the sacerdotal idea (that ordination is almost a sacrament, and, like baptism, must not be repeated) had begun to be entertained in New England, the double ordination in Salem became a stumbling-block to some historians.   Cotton Mather is silent about it.   Prince (p. 262, 263) is perplexed over it.   Felt (i., 113–116) shares in the perplexity.   The fact is that Higginson, Skelton, and all the first fathers of the New England churches, repudiated the sacerdotal idea entirely.   They acknowledged no ordination at large.   They admitted no such distinction as is now made between ordination and installation.   If a man had been ordained by bishops in England, that was, to them, no reason why he should not be ordained again and again, with imposition of hands, so often as he was to be inducted into office in any church.   They were right, unless sacerdotalism is the right theory of Christianity.

bly." They saw what was going on, they heard the statement of what had been done—the mutual and public profession, the holy covenant, the free election by the church of its own officers; and then, in behalf of their own church, they declared "their approbation and concurrence." By them that elder church, cradled at Scrooby, nurtured and schooled at Leyden, and now at last victorious over the sufferings and temptations of the wilderness, greeted its younger sister, in apostolic fashion, with "the right hands of fellowship." The church that had been brought over the ocean now saw another church, the first-born in America, holding the same faith in the same simplicity of self-government under Christ alone. It had become manifest that, in the freedom of this great wilderness, there was no reason why the Separatist should separate from the Puritan, nor why the Puritan, who came "to practice the positive part of church reformation," should purge himself from Separatism. The first church formed in America was formed by a voluntary separation from the world and a voluntary gathering into Christian fellowship. Its charter was the New Testament, and from that charter it deduced its right to exist and to govern itself by officers of its own choice and ordination. It acknowledged no king in Christ's kingdom save Christ himself, and no priest in the spiritual temple save the one High-Priest within the veil. Robinson had not lived to see that day; but he had foreseen it, and his prophecy was fulfilled.[1]

Such was the beginning of a distinctively American church history. If we trace its progress, we shall find that it is essentially the history of voluntary churches—the history of tendencies and conflicts which have come to the result that now every American church forms itself by elective affinity, the principle of separation. We shall find that it is the his-

---

[1] "For, said he, there will be no difference between the conformable ministers and you, when they come to the practice of the ordinances out of the kingdom" of England.—Winslow, in Young, p. 398.

tory of Christianity working toward its own emancipation from secular power; and that it is at the same time the history of the state learning slowly, but at last effectually, that it has no jurisdiction in the sphere of religion, and that its equal duty to all churches is the duty, not of enforcing their censures, but only of protecting their peaceable worship and their liberty of prophesying.

INDEX.

THE END.

POETS OF THE NINETEENTH CENTURY. The Poets of the Nineteenth Century. Selected and Edited by the Rev. ROBERT ARIS WILLMOTT. With English and American Additions, arranged by EVERT A. DUYCKINCK, Editor of "Cyclopædia of American Literature." Comprising Selections from the Greatest Authors of the Age. Superbly Illustrated with 141 Engravings from Designs by the most Eminent Artists. In elegant small 4to form, printed on Superfine Tinted Paper, richly bound in extra Cloth, Beveled, Gilt Edges, $5 00; Half Calf, $5 50; Full Turkey Morocco, $9 00.

THE REVISION OF THE ENGLISH VERSION OF THE NEW TESTAMENT. With an Introduction by the Rev. P. SCHAFF, D.D. 618 pp., Crown 8vo, Cloth, $3 00.

This work embraces in one volume:

I. ON A FRESH REVISION OF THE ENGLISH NEW TESTAMENT. By J. B. LIGHTFOOT, D.D., Canon of St. Paul's, and Hulsean Professor of Divinity, Cambridge. Second Edition, Revised. 196 pp.

II. ON THE AUTHORIZED VERSION OF THE NEW TESTAMENT in Connection with some Recent Proposals for its Revision. By RICHARD CHENEVIX TRENCH, D.D., Archbishop of Dublin. 194 pp.

III. CONSIDERATIONS ON THE REVISION OF THE ENGLISH VERSION OF THE NEW TESTAMENT. By J. C. ELLICOTT, D.D., Bishop of Gloucester and Bristol. 178 pp.

NORDHOFF'S CALIFORNIA. California: For Health, Pleasure, and Residence. A Book for Travelers and Settlers. Illustrated. 8vo, Paper, $2 00; Cloth, $2 50.

MOTLEY'S DUTCH REPUBLIC. The Rise of the Dutch Republic. By JOHN LOTHROP MOTLEY, LL.D., D.C.L. With a Portrait of William of Orange. 3 vols., 8vo, Cloth, $10 50.

MOTLEY'S UNITED NETHERLAND'S. History of the United Netherlands: from the Death of William the Silent to the Twelve Years' Truce—1609. With a full View of the English-Dutch Struggle against Spain, and of the Origin and Destruction of the Spanish Armada. By JOHN LOTHROP MOTLEY, LL.D., D.C.L. Portraits. 4 vols., 8vo, Cloth, $14 00.

MOTLEY'S LIFE AND DEATH OF JOHN OF BARNEVELD. Life and Death of John of Barneveld, Advocate of Holland. With a View of the Primary Causes and Movements of "The Thirty Years' War." By JOHN LOTHROP MOTLEY, D.C.L. With Illustrations. In Two Volumes. 8vo, Cloth, $7 00.

HAYDN'S DICTIONARY OF DATES, relating to all Ages and Nations. For Universal Reference. Edited by BENJAMIN VINCENT, Assistant Secretary and Keeper of the Library of the Royal Institution of Great Britain; and Revised for the Use of American Readers. 8vo, Cloth, $5 00; Sheep, $6 00.

MACGREGOR'S ROB ROY ON THE JORDAN. The Rob Roy on the Jordan, Nile, Red Sea, and Gennesareth, &c. A Canoe Cruise in Palestine and Egypt, and the Waters of Damascus. By J. MACGREGOR, M.A. With Maps and Illustrations. Crown 8vo, Cloth, $2 50.

WALLACE'S MALAY ARCHIPELAGO. The Malay Archipelago: the Land of the Orang-Utan and the Bird of Paradise. A Narrative of Travel, 1854–1862. With Studies of Man and Nature. By ALFRED RUSSEL WALLACE. With Ten Maps and Fifty-one Elegant Illustrations. Crown 8vo, Cloth, $2 50.

WHYMPER'S ALASKA. Travel and Adventure in the Territory of Alaska, formerly Russian America—now Ceded to the United States—and in various other parts of the North Pacific. By FREDERICK WHYMPER. With Map and Illustrations. Crown 8vo, Cloth, $2 50.

ORTON'S ANDES AND THE AMAZON. The Andes and the Amazon; or, Across the Continent of South America. By JAMES ORTON, M.A., Professor of Natural History in Vassar College, Poughkeepsie, N. Y., and Corresponding Member of the Academy of Natural Sciences, Philadelphia. With a New Map of Equatorial America and numerous Illustrations. Crown 8vo, Cloth, $2 00.

WINCHELL'S SKETCHES OF CREATION. Sketches of Creation: a Popular View of some of the Grand Conclusions of the Sciences in reference to the History of Matter and of Life. Together with a Statement of the Intimations of Science respecting the Primordial Condition and the Ultimate Destiny of the Earth and the Solar System. By ALEXANDER WINCHELL, LL.D., Professor of Geology, Zoology, and Botany in the University of Michigan, and Director of the State Geological Survey. With Illustrations. 12mo, Cloth, $2 00.

WHITE'S MASSACRE OF ST. BARTHOLOMEW. The Massacre of St. Bartholomew: Preceded by a History of the Religious Wars in the Reign of Charles IX. By HENRY WHITE, M.A. With Illustrations. 8vo, Cloth, $1 75.

LOSSING'S FIELD-BOOK OF THE REVOLUTION. Pictorial Field-Book of the Revolution; or, Illustrations, by Pen and Pencil, of the History, Biography, Scenery, Relics, and Traditions of the War for Independence. By BENSON J. LOSSING. 2 vols., 8vo, Cloth, $14 00; Sheep, $15 00; Half Calf, $18 00; Full Turkey Morocco, $22 00.

LOSSING'S FIELD-BOOK OF THE WAR OF 1812. Pictorial Field-Book of the War of 1812; or, Illustrations, by Pen and Pencil, of the History, Biography, Scenery, Relics, and Traditions of the Last War for American Independence. By BENSON J. LOSSING. With several hundred Engravings on Wood, by Lossing and Barritt, chiefly from Original Sketches by the Author. 1088 pages, 8vo, Cloth, $7 00; Sheep, $8 50; Half Calf, $10 00.

ALFORD'S GREEK TESTAMENT. The Greek Testament: with a critically revised Text; a Digest of Various Readings; Marginal References to Verbal and Idiomatic Usage; Prolegomena; and a Critical and Exegetical Commentary. For the Use of Theological Students and Ministers. By HENRY ALFORD, D.D., Dean of Canterbury. Vol. I., containing the Four Gospels. 944 pages, 8vo, Cloth, $6 00; Sheep, $6 50.

ABBOTT'S FREDERICK THE GREAT. The History of Frederick the Second, called Frederick the Great. By JOHN S. C. ABBOTT. Elegantly Illustrated. 8vo, Cloth, $5 00.

ABBOTT'S HISTORY OF THE FRENCH REVOLUTION. The French Revolution of 1789, as viewed in the Light of Republican Institutions. By JOHN S. C. ABBOTT. With 100 Engravings. 8vo, Cloth, $5 00.

ABBOTT'S NAPOLEON BONAPARTE. The History of Napoleon Bonaparte. By JOHN S. C. ABBOTT. With Maps, Woodcuts, and Portraits on Steel. 2 vols., 8vo, Cloth, $10 00.

ABBOTT'S NAPOLEON AT ST. HELENA; or, Interesting Anecdotes and Remarkable Conversations of the Emperor during the Five and a Half Years of his Captivity. Collected from the Memorials of Las Casas, O'Meara, Montholon, Antommarchi, and others. By JOHN S. C. ABBOTT. With Illustrations. 8vo, Cloth, $5 00.

ADDISON'S COMPLETE WORKS. The Works of Joseph Addison, embracing the whole of the "Spectator." Complete in 3 vols., 8vo, Cloth, $6 00.

ALCOCK'S JAPAN. The Capital of the Tycoon: a Narrative of a Three Years' Residence in Japan. By Sir RUTHERFORD ALCOCK, K.C.B., Her Majesty's Envoy Extraordinary and Minister Plenipotentiary in Japan. With Maps and Engravings. 2 vols., 12mo, Cloth, $3 50.

ALISON'S HISTORY OF EUROPE. FIRST SERIES: From the Commencement of the French Revolution, in 1789, to the Restoration of the Bourbons, in 1815. [In addition to the Notes on Chapter LXXVI., which correct the errors of the original work concerning the United States, a copious Analytical Index has been appended to this American edition.] SECOND SERIES: From the Fall of Napoleon, in 1815, to the Accession of Louis Napoleon, in 1852. 8 vols., 8vo, Cloth, $16 00.

BALDWIN'S PRE-HISTORIC NATIONS. Pre-Historic Nations; or, Inquiries concerning some of the Great Peoples and Civilizations of Antiquity, and their Probable Relation to a still Older Civilization of the Ethiopians or Cushites of Arabia. By JOHN D. BALDWIN, Member of the American Oriental Society. 12mo, Cloth, $1 75.

BARTH'S NORTH AND CENTRAL AFRICA. Travels and Discoveries in North and Central Africa: being a Journal of an Expedition undertaken under the Auspices of H. B. M.'s Government, in the Years 1849-1855. By HENRY BARTH, Ph.D., D.C.L. Illustrated. 3 vols., 8vo, Cloth, $12 00.

HENRY WARD BEECHER'S SERMONS. Sermons by HENRY WARD BEECHER, Plymouth Church, Brooklyn. Selected from Published and Unpublished Discourses, and Revised by their Author. With Steel Portrait. Complete in 2 vols., 8vo, Cloth, $5 00.

LYMAN BEECHER'S AUTOBIOGRAPHY, &c. Autobiography, Correspondence, &c., of Lyman Beecher, D.D. Edited by his Son, CHARLES BEECHER. With Three Steel Portraits, and Engravings on Wood. In 2 vols., 12mo, Cloth, $5 00.

BOSWELL'S JOHNSON. The Life of Samuel Johnson, LL.D. Including a Journey to the Hebrides. By JAMES BOSWELL, Esq. A New Edition, with numerous Additions and Notes. By JOHN WILSON CROKER, LL.D., F.R.S. Portrait of Boswell. 2 vols., 8vo, Cloth, $4 00.

DRAPER'S CIVIL WAR. History of the American Civil War. By John W. Draper, M.D., LL.D., Professor of Chemistry and Physiology in the University of New York. In Three Vols. 8vo, Cloth, $3 50 per vol.

DRAPER'S INTELLECTUAL DEVELOPMENT OF EUROPE. A History of the Intellectual Development of Europe. By John W. Draper, M.D., LL.D., Professor of Chemistry and Physiology in the University of New York. 8vo, Cloth, $5 00

DRAPER'S AMERICAN CIVIL POLICY. Thoughts on the Future Civil Policy of America. By John W. Draper, M.D., LL.D., Professor of Chemistry and Physiology in the University of New York. Crown 8vo, Cloth, $2 50.

DU CHAILLU'S AFRICA. Explorations and Adventures in Equatorial Africa with Accounts of the Manners and Customs of the People, and of the Chase of the Gorilla, the Crocodile, Leopard, Elephant, Hippopotamus, and other Animals. By Paul B. Du Chaillu. Numerous Illustrations. 8vo, Cloth, $5 00.

BELLOWS'S OLD WORLD. The Old World in its New Face: Impressions of Europe in 1867–1868. By Henry W. Bellows. 2 vols., 12mo, Cloth, $3 50.

BRODHEAD'S HISTORY OF NEW YORK. History of the State of New York. By John Romeyn Brodhead. 1609–1691. 2 vols. 8vo, Cloth, $3 00 per vol.

BROUGHAM'S AUTOBIOGRAPHY. Life and Times of Henry, Lord Brougham. Written by Himself. In Three Volumes. 12mo, Cloth, $2 00 per vol.

BULWER'S PROSE WORKS. Miscellaneous Prose Works of Edward Bulwer, Lord Lytton. 2 vols., 12mo, Cloth, $3 50.

BULWER'S HORACE. The Odes and Epodes of Horace. A Metrical Translation into English. With Introduction and Commentaries. By Lord Lytton. With Latin Text from the Editions of Orelli, Macleane, and Yonge. 12mo, Cloth, $1 75.

BULWER'S KING ARTHUR. A Poem. By Earl Lytton. New Edition. 12mo, Cloth, $1 75.

BURNS'S LIFE AND WORKS. The Life and Works of Robert Burns. Edited by Robert Chambers. 4 vols., 12mo, Cloth, $6 00.

REINDEER, DOGS, AND SNOW-SHOES. A Journal of Siberian Travel and Explorations made in the Years 1865–'67. By Richard J. Bush, late of the Russo-American Telegraph Expedition. Illustrated. Crown 8vo, Cloth, $3 00.

CARLYLE'S FREDERICK THE GREAT. History of Friedrich II., called Frederick the Great. By Thomas Carlyle. Portraits, Maps, Plans, &c. 6 vols., 12mo, Cloth, $12 00.

CARLYLE'S FRENCH REVOLUTION. History of the French Revolution. Newly Revised by the Author, with Index, &c. 2 vols., 12mo, Cloth, $3 50.

CARLYLE'S OLIVER CROMWELL. Letters and Speeches of Oliver Cromwell. With Elucidations and Connecting Narrative. 2 vols., 12mo, Cloth, $3 50.

CHALMERS'S POSTHUMOUS WORKS. The Posthumous Works of Dr. Chalmers. Edited by his Son-in-Law, Rev. William Hanna, LL.D. Complete in 9 vols., 12mo, Cloth, $13 50.

COLERIDGE'S COMPLETE WORKS. The Complete Works of Samuel Taylor Coleridge. With an Introductory Essay upon his Philosophical and Theological Opinions. Edited by Professor Shedd. Complete in Seven Vols. With a fine Portrait. Small 8vo, Cloth, $10 50.

DOOLITTLE'S CHINA. Social Life of the Chinese: with some Account of their Religious, Governmental, Educational, and Business Customs and Opinions. With special but not exclusive Reference to Fuhchau. By Rev. Justus Doolittle, Fourteen Years Member of the Fuhchau Mission of the American Board. Illustrated with more than 150 characteristic Engravings on Wood. 2 vols., 12mo, Cloth, $5 00.

GIBBON'S ROME. History of the Decline and Fall of the Roman Empire. By Edward Gibbon. With Notes by Rev. H. H. Milman and M. Guizot. A new cheap Edition. To which is added a complete Index of the whole Work, and a Portrait of the Author. 6 vols., 12mo, Cloth, $9 00.

HAZEN'S SCHOOL AND ARMY IN GERMANY AND FRANCE. The School and the Army in Germany and France, with a Diary of Siege Life at Versailles. By Brevet Major-General W. B. Hazen, U.S.A., Colonel Sixth Infantry. Crown 8vo, Cloth, $2 50.

The borrower must return this item on or befc
the last date stamped below. If another us
places a recall for this item, the borrower w
be notified of the need for an earlier return.

*Non-receipt of overdue notices does **not** exem*
the borrower from overdue fines.

Please handle with care.
Thank you for helping to preserve
library collections at Harvard.

Check Out More Titles From HardPress Classics Series In this collection we are offering thousands of classic and hard to find books. This series spans a vast array of subjects – so you are bound to find something of interest to enjoy reading and learning about.

Subjects:
Architecture
Art
Biography & Autobiography
Body, Mind &Spirit
Children & Young Adult
Dramas
Education
Fiction
History
Language Arts & Disciplines
Law
Literary Collections
Music
Poetry
Psychology
Science
…and many more.

Visit us at www.hardpress.net

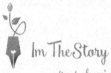

CPSIA information can be obtained
at www.ICGtesting.com
Printed in the USA
BVHW082339110819
555624BV00021B/3221/P